# ADVANCED MATHEMATICS
## ANSWERS AND HINTS
## FOR BOOKS 1 AND 2
## (METRIC)

# THE SCHOOL
# MATHEMATICS
# PROJECT

ADVANCED MATHEMATICS

ANSWERS AND HINTS
FOR BOOKS 1 AND 2

(METRIC)

CAMBRIDGE
AT THE UNIVERSITY PRESS
1971

Published by the Syndics of the Cambridge University Press
Bentley House, 200 Euston Road, London NW1 2DB
American Branch: 32 East 57th Street, New York, N.Y.10022

© Cambridge University Press 1968

This edition © Cambridge University Press 1969

Library of Congress Catalogue Card Number: 68-25087

ISBN: 0 521 07678 1

First published 1968
Metric edition 1969
Reprinted 1971

Printed in Great Britain
at the University Printing House, Cambridge
(Brooke Crutchley, University Printer)

# CONTENTS

# CONTENTS

This book is based on the
original contributions of

| | |
|---|---|
| P. G. BOWIE | A. G. GALLANT |
| H. M. CUNDY | C. C. GOLDSMITH |
| J. H. DURRAN | M. J. LEACH |
| L. E. ELLIS | D. A. QUADLING |

J. S. T. WOOLMER

and has been edited by

H. MARTYN CUNDY

.

## ACKNOWLEDGEMENTS

We are grateful to many who have assisted in
working out and checking the answers in this book.
We have appreciated the cheerful and painstaking
care exercised in its preparation by the staff of the
Cambridge University Press.

The Project owes much to its typists, and in
particular to Mrs E. Muir, Mrs H. Goggs, and
Mrs E. L. Humphreys for their work in preparing
the typescript of this book for the press.

# PREFACE

The Advanced Mathematics course of the School Mathematics Project is planned in a series of four books covering the A-Level syllabus. The treatment in these books is sufficiently full for them to be read without a teacher, but much of the subject-matter is new to a school course, and even the more familiar material is approached and expounded in new ways. Accordingly, while it was felt desirable to provide advanced students with answers to the exercises, the usual plan of including short answers at the end of the book appeared to be inadequate for teacher and pupils alike.

Accompanying texts to the advanced course have therefore been planned which will provide the reassurance that comes from printed answers, guidance in tackling the more difficult problems, and avenues to open up discussion and to lead to further study of interesting topics. There will be two such books, covering Books 1–2 and Books 3–4 of the advanced course, of which this is the first. In addition there will be a Companion to Advanced Mathematics, designed specifically for the teacher, which will seek to put the various topics into perspective as parts of a wider canvas, thereby giving them significance in the picture of mathematics as a whole.

It is at advanced level that the various lines of approach which have been taken by different reforming movements are seen to converge to a common apex. It is the hope, therefore, of the writers of the S.M.P. texts, both that their own advanced texts will prove useful and stimulating to those trained in other disciplines, and also that those using these texts for the S.M.P. A-Level examination will read and profit by the many other interesting books which are now being produced.

It would be rash to suppose that a book so full of factual detail is free from error; the Editor would be grateful to receive comments, criticisms and corrections arising in the course of its daily use.

# 1

# STRUCTURE

This chapter recapitulates previous work and draws out certain salient ideas from familiar material. Too much time should not be spent in discussing details arising from the exercises; many of the topics will come up for consideration at a later stage. Important, because fundamental for much that follows, are the ideas of relation, equivalence class, field, and isomorphism. Since such ideas do not flourish in a vacuum, it is useful to have examples ready to hand as a basis of discussion; these are provided in abundance in the chapter. The details of such examples are not important in themselves at this stage.

## 2. OPERATIONS

### Exercise A (p. 4)

1. Commutative: (i), (ii), (iv); in (iii) $a \circ b = c$, $b \circ a = a$.

2. Closed: (ii), (iii), (iv).

3. (1) Table (i) $b$,
   (ii) $b$,
   (iii) $b$,
   (iv) $a$.
   (2) Table (i) $a$,
   (ii) $a$,
   (iii) $d$,
   (iv) $a$.

   (3) Table (i) $b$ or $c$,
   (ii) $c$,
   (iii) $d$,
   (iv) $c$.

   There is not always a solution to this type of equation.

   There is a unique solution only if each row and column contains one and only one of each element.

   (i) The set is commutative under $\circ$;

   (ii) If the elements appear in the same order in the master row as they do in the master column, the table has reflection symmetry in the diagonal passing through the top left-hand corner.

**4.** Translations only.  **5.** Yes.

**6.**

| ○ | $p$ | $q$ | $r$ |
|---|---|---|---|
| $p$ | $q$ | $r$ | $p$ |
| $q$ | $r$ | $p$ | $q$ |
| $r$ | $p$ | $q$ | $r$ |

$x(yz) = (xy)z$.

The same statement can be made for (iv), but not (i); $b \circ (a \circ a)$ is not defined; $(b \circ a) \circ a = d$.

**7.**

| ○ | A | B | C | D |
|---|---|---|---|---|
| A | A | B | C | D |
| B | B | C | D | A |
| C | C | D | A | B |
| D | D | A | B | C |

A = identity,
B = $\frac{1}{4}$ turn,
C = $\frac{1}{2}$ turn,
D = $\frac{3}{4}$ turn

(*a*) Rotations about a fixed point are associative.

(*b*) Rotations about a fixed point of order $n$ are a closed set.

$e = f = $ A.

In (iv), $e = f = c$; in (iii) there is no $e$, but $f = d$.

**8.** (*a*) The zero translation.

(*b*) Enlargement of order 1.

(*c*) Rotation through $0°$, or any multiple of $360°$; the same as (*a*).

(*d*) No.

**9.** Yes; Yes; Yes.

**10.**

| ○ | I | H | X | Y |
|---|---|---|---|---|
| I | I | H | X | Y |
| H | H | I | Y | X |
| X | X | Y | I | H |
| Y | Y | X | H | I |

Closed. Yes; $a = $ I; Yes; Yes.

## 3. BINARY OPERATIONS

Associativity is often confused with commutativity; the point has to be made that associativity is not connected with *order*, but with the more subtle matter of closeness of bonding. If we have three books to transfer from one shelf to another in two hands, we may take

2

numbers 1 and 2 in the left-hand, and number 3 in the right, or number 1 in the left-hand and numbers 2 and 3 in the right. This does not affect the order, and in this case it does not affect the result; the operation is associative. On the other hand if the book(s) in the left-hand are those we are going to read today, and those in the right-hand those we shall read tomorrow, it will make a difference, and the difference is not in the order in which we read the books. Again, 'a fat-cattle merchant' and 'a fat cattle-merchant' do not mean the same thing, nor do 'half-cold chicken' and 'half cold-chicken'.

Where only one operation is concerned it is really immaterial whether we call it 'addition' and use 0 for the neutral element, or 'multiplication' and use 1; it has, however, become customary to use + only for commutative operations.

'Inverse' is sometimes confused with 'reciprocal'; stress needs to be laid on the possibility of additive inverses.

## Exercise B (p. 9)

**1.**

| | Closed? | Commutative? | Neutral element | Without inverse |
|---|---|---|---|---|
| (i) | Yes | No | $b$ | $a$ |
| (ii) | Yes | Yes | $d$ | None |
| (iii) | Yes | No | $d$ | None |
| (iv) | Yes | No | None | — |

**2.** (1) (i) $b$,    (2) (i) $b$,    (3) (i) –
       (ii) $d$,        (ii) $d$,        (ii) $d$,
       (iii) $d$,        (iii) $d$,        (iii) $f$,
       (iv) $d$.        (iv) $d$.        (iv) $a$.

**3.**

| $g$ | 1 | 2 | 3 | 4 | 5 | |
|---|---|---|---|---|---|---|
| 1 | 1 | 2 | 3 | 4 | 5 | Commutative. |
| 2 | 2 | 2 | 3 | 4 | 5 | 1 is neutral. |
| 3 | 3 | 3 | 3 | 4 | 5 | |
| 4 | 4 | 4 | 4 | 4 | 5 | |
| 5 | 5 | 5 | 5 | 5 | 5 | |

**4.**

| ○ | 1 | 2 | 3 | 4 | 5 | |
|---|---|---|---|---|---|---|
| 1 | 1 | 1 | 1 | 1 | 1 | Not commutative. |
| 2 | 2 | 2 | 2 | 2 | 2 | No neutral element. |
| 3 | 3 | 3 | 3 | 3 | 3 | Associative. |
| 4 | 4 | 4 | 4 | 4 | 4 | |
| 5 | 5 | 5 | 5 | 5 | 5 | |

3

**5.** (a)

| ∩ | ℰ | A | B | ∅ | |
|---|---|---|---|---|---|
| ℰ | ℰ | A | B | ∅ | Commutative. |
| A | A | A | ∅ | ∅ | ℰ neutral. |
| B | B | ∅ | B | ∅ | No inverses other than ℰ. |
| ∅ | ∅ | ∅ | ∅ | ∅ | |

(b)

| ∪ | ℰ | A | B | ∅ | |
|---|---|---|---|---|---|
| ℰ | ℰ | ℰ | ℰ | ℰ | Commutative. |
| A | ℰ | A | ℰ | A | ∅ neutral. |
| B | ℰ | ℰ | B | B | No inverses other than ∅. |
| ∅ | ℰ | A | B | ∅ | |

**6.** Commutative; not associative; 0 neutral; Yes, itself.

**7.** $\begin{pmatrix} a & -b \\ b & a \end{pmatrix} \begin{pmatrix} c & -d \\ d & c \end{pmatrix} = \begin{pmatrix} ac-bd & -(bc+ad) \\ bc+ad & ac-bd \end{pmatrix} = \begin{pmatrix} c & -d \\ d & c \end{pmatrix} \begin{pmatrix} a & -b \\ b & a \end{pmatrix}.$

Neutral element: $\begin{pmatrix} 1 & 0 \\ 0 & 1 \end{pmatrix}.$

**8.** (a) $\begin{pmatrix} a & b \\ c & d \end{pmatrix} \begin{pmatrix} e & f \\ g & h \end{pmatrix} = \begin{pmatrix} ae+bg & af+bh \\ ce+dg & cf+dh \end{pmatrix},$

$\begin{pmatrix} e & f \\ g & h \end{pmatrix} \begin{pmatrix} a & b \\ c & d \end{pmatrix} = \begin{pmatrix} ae+cf & be+df \\ ag+ch & bg+dh \end{pmatrix}.$

In general these two results are not the same. But it is sufficient and *far better* to show a single simple *counter-example*. For example,

$\begin{pmatrix} 1 & 0 \\ 1 & 0 \end{pmatrix} \begin{pmatrix} 1 & 1 \\ 0 & 0 \end{pmatrix} = \begin{pmatrix} 1 & 1 \\ 1 & 1 \end{pmatrix}$ but $\begin{pmatrix} 1 & 1 \\ 0 & 0 \end{pmatrix} \begin{pmatrix} 1 & 0 \\ 1 & 0 \end{pmatrix} = \begin{pmatrix} 2 & 0 \\ 0 & 0 \end{pmatrix}.$

(b) To prove it associative, show that

$\begin{pmatrix} a & b \\ c & d \end{pmatrix} \left[ \begin{pmatrix} e & f \\ g & h \end{pmatrix} \begin{pmatrix} i & j \\ k & l \end{pmatrix} \right] = \left[ \begin{pmatrix} a & b \\ c & d \end{pmatrix} \begin{pmatrix} e & f \\ g & h \end{pmatrix} \right] \begin{pmatrix} i & j \\ k & l \end{pmatrix}.$

**9.** (a) Closed, commutative, associative, no neutral element or inverses.

(b) Closed, commutative, not associative, no neutral element or inverses.

## 4. BINARY RELATIONS
### Exercise C (p. 15)

Note that, as defined, all transitive and symmetric relations must be reflexive for all elements related to others:

$$(x \, R \, y \quad \text{and} \quad y \, R \, x) \Rightarrow x \, R \, x.$$

**1.**

|   | a | b | c | d | e | f | g | h | i | j | k | l |
|---|---|---|---|---|---|---|---|---|---|---|---|---|
| R | × | × | × | √ | √ | × | × | √ | √ | × | × | √ |
| S | √ | × | √ | √ | √ | √ | √ | √ | √ | √ | × | √ |
| T | × | × | × | √ | √ | × | × | √ | √ | × | √ | √ |

**2.**

|   | a | b | c | d | e | f |
|---|---|---|---|---|---|---|
| R | √ | × | √ | √ | × | × |
| S | × | × | × | √ | × | × |
| T | √ | √ | √ | √ | × | × |

**3.** Friend: *S*
Mother: —
Aunt: —
Sister: —
'is a sister of' would be symmetric.

Some of these answers hinge on the meaning of the words used.

**5.**

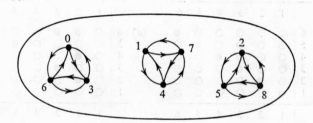

**6.**

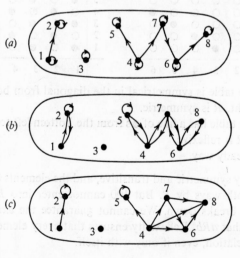

(a)

(b)

(c)

5

**7.**

| | P | J | N | D | C | M |
|---|---|---|---|---|---|---|
| M | ● | ○ | ● | ● | ● | ● |
| C | ● | ○ | ● | ● | ● | ● |
| D | ● | ○ | ● | ● | ● | ● |
| N | ● | ○ | ● | ● | ● | ● |
| J | ○ | ● | ○ | ○ | ○ | ○ |
| P | ● | ○ | ● | ● | ● | ● |

Reflexive; symmetric; transitive.

**8.**

(a)

| | 1 | 2 | 3 | 4 | 5 | 6 |
|---|---|---|---|---|---|---|
| 6 | ● | ● | ● | ○ | ○ | ● |
| 5 | ● | ○ | ○ | ○ | ● | ○ |
| 4 | ● | ● | ○ | ● | ○ | ○ |
| 3 | ● | ○ | ● | ○ | ○ | ○ |
| 2 | ● | ● | ○ | ○ | ○ | ○ |
| 1 | ● | ○ | ○ | ○ | ○ | ○ |

(b)

| | 1 | 2 | 3 | 4 | 5 | 6 |
|---|---|---|---|---|---|---|
| 6 | ● | ● | ● | ● | ● | ○ |
| 5 | ● | ● | ● | ● | ○ | ○ |
| 4 | ● | ● | ● | ○ | ○ | ○ |
| 3 | ● | ● | ○ | ○ | ○ | ○ |
| 2 | ● | ○ | ○ | ○ | ○ | ○ |
| 1 | ○ | ○ | ○ | ○ | ○ | ○ |

(c)

| | 1 | 2 | 3 | 4 | 5 | 6 |
|---|---|---|---|---|---|---|
| 6 | ○ | ○ | ○ | ○ | ○ | ● |
| 5 | ○ | ○ | ○ | ○ | ● | ○ |
| 4 | ○ | ○ | ○ | ● | ○ | ○ |
| 3 | ○ | ○ | ● | ○ | ○ | ○ |
| 2 | ○ | ● | ○ | ○ | ○ | ○ |
| 1 | ● | ○ | ○ | ○ | ○ | ○ |

(d)

| | 1 | 2 | 3 | 4 | 5 | 6 |
|---|---|---|---|---|---|---|
| 6 | ○ | ● | ● | ○ | ○ | ○ |
| 5 | ○ | ○ | ○ | ○ | ● | ○ |
| 4 | ○ | ● | ○ | ○ | ○ | ○ |
| 3 | ○ | ○ | ● | ○ | ○ | ○ |
| 2 | ○ | ● | ○ | ○ | ○ | ○ |
| 1 | ○ | ○ | ○ | ○ | ○ | ○ |

(e)

| | 1 | 2 | 3 | 4 | 5 | 6 |
|---|---|---|---|---|---|---|
| 6 | ○ | ○ | ○ | ○ | ○ | ○ |
| 5 | ○ | ○ | ○ | ○ | ○ | ○ |
| 4 | ○ | ○ | ○ | ○ | ○ | ● |
| 3 | ○ | ○ | ○ | ○ | ● | ○ |
| 2 | ○ | ○ | ○ | ● | ○ | ○ |
| 1 | ○ | ○ | ● | ○ | ○ | ○ |

(f)

| | 1 | 2 | 3 | 4 | 5 | 6 |
|---|---|---|---|---|---|---|
| 6 | ○ | ● | ○ | ● | ○ | ● |
| 5 | ● | ○ | ● | ○ | ● | ○ |
| 4 | ○ | ● | ○ | ● | ○ | ● |
| 3 | ● | ○ | ● | ○ | ● | ○ |
| 2 | ○ | ● | ○ | ● | ○ | ● |
| 1 | ● | ○ | ● | ○ | ● | ○ |

(i) If the table is symmetrical in the diagonal from bottom left to top right, $R$ is symmetric.

(ii) If the table has a line of ●s from the bottom left to top right corners, $R$ is reflexive.

(iii) No ready way.

**9.** $R$ is clearly symmetric and transitive, and the elements 2, 3, 4 are related both ways by $R$. But 100 cannot enter into $R$ and the argument breaks down. We cannot guarantee the *existence* of $a, b$ such that $aRb$. Reflexivity ensures that every element enters into the relation, even if only with itself.

## 5. EQUIVALENCE RELATIONS

These are of great importance, since such common objects as integers, rational numbers, vectors, can all be defined as equivalence classes. This idea—sets of things which are in some way alike—pervades all mathematics; indeed it underlies every generality in everyday life. Whenever we classify anything we are setting up equivalence classes.

Residue classes are often called 'congruence classes', and the relation $R$ of Example 11 is called 'congruent to, mod 3'. This again is a familiar feature of life; the date-numbers of each weekday in a monthly calendar are congruent mod 7; the times of departure of a train are congruent mod 24 hours. 'Mod' (short for *modulo*) here means 'in the measure of', and must not be confused with 'the modulus of' (meaning absolute value) which is written $|\ \ |$.

The ideas of this section are very useful in the theory of the integers (usually called, rather misleadingly, *theory of numbers*). Here we are particularly concerned with the fact that the residue classes to a *prime* modulus form a *field*. For an interesting treatment, see E. A. Maxwell, *A Gateway to Abstract Mathematics* (Cambridge).

### Exercise D (p. 17)

1.

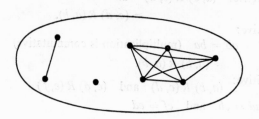

### Exercise E (p. 18)

1. *d, e, h, i, l.*

   *d*: Sheaves of parallel lines.

   *e*: People with birthdays in a given month.

   *h*: Sets of similar triangles.

   *i*: Odd numbers, even numbers.

   *l*: Sets with the same number of elements.

7

2. $0 = \{..., -10, -5, 0, 5, 10, ...\}$,
   $1 = \{..., -9, -4, 1, 6, 11, ...\}$,
   $2 = \{..., -8, -3, 2, 7, 12, ...\}$,
   $3 = \{..., -7, -2, 3, 8, 13, ...\}$,
   $4 = \{..., -6, -1, 4, 9, 14, ...\}$.

3. Symmetric:

   $(m, n) R (r, s) \Leftrightarrow m+s = n+r$
   $\Leftrightarrow r+n = s+m$ (addition is commutative)
   $\Leftrightarrow (r, s) R (m, n)$.

   Reflexive: $m+n = n+m \Rightarrow (m, n) R (m, n)$.

   Transitive: $(m, n) R (r, s)$ and $(r, s) R (p, q)$
   $\Rightarrow m+s = n+r$ and $r+q = s+p$
   $\Rightarrow m+s+r+q = n+r+s+p$ (adding)
   $\Rightarrow m+q = n+p$ (subtracting $r+s$)
   $\Rightarrow (m, n) R (p, q)$.

   An equivalence class consists of all ordered pairs $(m, n)$ for which $m-n$ is a fixed integer. This indicates the way in which the integers may be defined as equivalence classes of the natural numbers. (See Chapter 3, Miscellaneous Exercise, Question 15.)

4. Symmetric: $(a, b) R (c, d) \Leftrightarrow ad = cb$
   $\Leftrightarrow (c, d) R (a, b)$.

   Reflexive: $ab = ba$ (multiplication is commutative)
   $\Rightarrow (a, b) R (a, b)$.

   Transitive: $(a, b) R (c, d)$ and $(c, d) R (e, f)$
   $\Rightarrow ad = cb$ and $cf = ed$
   $\Rightarrow adcf = cbed$
   $\Rightarrow af = eb$ (unless $c = 0$, in which case $a = e = 0$ and $af = eb = 0$)
   $\Rightarrow (a, b) R (e, f)$.

   An equivalence class consists of all ordered pairs $(a, b)$ for which $a/b$ is a fixed rational number. This indicates the way in which the rationals may be defined as equivalence classes of the integers. (See Section 8 of Chapter 3.)

8

**6.**

| + | Even | Odd |
|---|------|-----|
| Even | Even | Odd |
| Odd | Odd | Even |

| × | Even | Odd |
|---|------|-----|
| Even | Even | Even |
| Odd | Even | Odd |

If 0 is substituted for even, 1 for odd, where 0 and 1 are the units bits in binary numbers, the same pattern will emerge.

## 6. ALGEBRA OF RESIDUE CLASSES

### *Exercise F (p. 20)*

**1.**

| + | 0 | 1 | 2 | 3 | 4 |
|---|---|---|---|---|---|
| 0 | 0 | 1 | 2 | 3 | 4 |
| 1 | 1 | 2 | 3 | 4 | 0 |
| 2 | 2 | 3 | 4 | 0 | 1 |
| 3 | 3 | 4 | 0 | 1 | 2 |
| 4 | 4 | 0 | 1 | 2 | 3 |

0 is neutral.
Every element has an inverse.
Closed.
Commutative.

**2.**

| + | 0 | 1 | 2 | 3 |
|---|---|---|---|---|
| 0 | 0 | 1 | 2 | 3 |
| 1 | 1 | 2 | 3 | 0 |
| 2 | 2 | 3 | 0 | 1 |
| 3 | 3 | 0 | 1 | 2 |

### *Exercise G (p. 21)*

**1.** *(a)*

| × | 0 | 1 | 2 | 3 | 4 |
|---|---|---|---|---|---|
| 0 | 0 | 0 | 0 | 0 | 0 |
| 1 | 0 | 1 | 2 | 3 | 4 |
| 2 | 0 | 2 | 4 | 1 | 3 |
| 3 | 0 | 3 | 1 | 4 | 2 |
| 4 | 0 | 4 | 3 | 2 | 1 |

1 is neutral.

0 has no inverse.

Commutative.
Closed.
Symmetry in top left - bottom right diagonal.

*(b)*

| × | 1 | 2 | 3 | 4 |
|---|---|---|---|---|
| 1 | 1 | 2 | 3 | 4 |
| 2 | 2 | 4 | 1 | 3 |
| 3 | 3 | 1 | 4 | 2 |
| 4 | 4 | 3 | 2 | 1 |

1 is neutral.

All elements have inverse.
Commutative.
Closed.
Symmetry in both diagonals, and hence point symmetry.

Associative; this follows from the associativity of multiplication of integers.

9

**2.** (a) **0, 1, 2.**  (b) **0, 1, 2, 3, 4, 5.**

$(Z_3, +)$:

| + | 0 | 1 | 2 |
|---|---|---|---|
| 0 | 0 | 1 | 2 |
| 1 | 1 | 2 | 0 |
| 2 | 2 | 0 | 1 |

$(Z_6, +)$:

| + | 0 | 1 | 2 | 3 | 4 | 5 |
|---|---|---|---|---|---|---|
| 0 | 0 | 1 | 2 | 3 | 4 | 5 |
| 1 | 1 | 2 | 3 | 4 | 5 | 0 |
| 2 | 2 | 3 | 4 | 5 | 0 | 1 |
| 3 | 3 | 4 | 5 | 0 | 1 | 2 |
| 4 | 4 | 5 | 0 | 1 | 2 | 3 |
| 5 | 5 | 0 | 1 | 2 | 3 | 4 |

| × | 1 | 2 |
|---|---|---|
| 1 | 1 | 2 |
| 2 | 2 | 1 |

| × | 1 | 2 | 3 | 4 | 5 |
|---|---|---|---|---|---|
| 1 | 1 | 2 | 3 | 4 | 5 |
| 2 | 2 | 4 | 0 | 2 | 4 |
| 3 | 3 | 0 | 3 | 0 | 3 |
| 4 | 4 | 2 | 0 | 4 | 2 |
| 5 | 5 | 4 | 3 | 2 | 1 |

**3.** (a) $x$ is a member of **4**;   (b) $x \in \mathbf{2} \pmod 5$.

**4.** (a) $x \in \mathbf{0} \pmod 5$;   (b) $x \in \mathbf{1} \pmod 5$.

**5.** $m$ has one of the forms $2n$, $2n+1$, where $n$ is an integer
$\Rightarrow m^2$ has one of the forms $4n^2$, $(2n+1)^2 = 4n^2+4n+1$,
which belong to **0, 1** respectively.

$$m^2 \in \mathbf{1} \Rightarrow m \in \mathbf{1} \quad \text{or} \quad \mathbf{3}.$$

**6.** $(Z_4^*, \times)$:    $(Z_7^*, \times)$:

| × | 1 | 2 | 3 |
|---|---|---|---|
| 1 | 1 | 2 | 3 |
| 2 | 2 | 0 | 2 |
| 3 | 3 | 2 | 1 |

| × | 1 | 2 | 3 | 4 | 5 | 6 |
|---|---|---|---|---|---|---|
| 1 | 1 | 2 | 3 | 4 | 5 | 6 |
| 2 | 2 | 4 | 6 | 1 | 3 | 5 |
| 3 | 3 | 6 | 2 | 5 | 1 | 4 |
| 4 | 4 | 1 | 5 | 2 | 6 | 3 |
| 5 | 5 | 3 | 1 | 6 | 4 | 2 |
| 6 | 6 | 5 | 4 | 3 | 2 | 1 |

The table for $Z_4^*$ is not closed, and **2** has no inverse. $Z_7^*$ is closed under multiplication and every element has an inverse.

(a) $\mathbf{x = 2}$;    (b) $\mathbf{x = 4}$;    (c) $\mathbf{x = 6}$;

(d) $\mathbf{y = 5}$;    (e) $\mathbf{y = 4}$;    (f) $\mathbf{y = 6}$;

(g) $\mathbf{y = 2}$.

**7.** (a) 7 o'clock in the afternoon (i.e. 1900 h G.M.T.);
6 o'clock (i.e. either 0600 h or 1800 h G.M.T.).
(b) Thursday.

10

**8.** 25. Each operation must leave the number of mangoes in the same congruence class mod 3. $\frac{2}{3}(x-1) = x \Rightarrow x = -2$, so that if we began with $-2$ mangoes there would always be $-2$. Since ultimately we have to divide by 27, we begin with

$$27 - 2 = 25 \text{ mangoes.}$$

## 7. ISOMORPHISM

This is an idea of crucial importance in modern algebra. Structures which are isomorphic are, from an abstract point of view, the same. Theorems which depend only on the structure which are proved for any particular structured set are true for all isomorphic sets. This idea, and the saving of labour implied by it, lies at the base of much of modern mathematics, and its influence will be felt throughout the Advanced Course.

The student should be warned that isomorphism (or the lack of it) is not always immediately apparent from the operation tables for finite sets; it is only when the tables are arranged in the same order, as dictated by the one-one correspondence, that their form is identical. In the case of infinite sets isomorphism cannot be shown in this way, and for finite sets of large order there may be better ways of showing isomorphism than by display of the whole table. Questions 5 and 6 provide two very simple examples of isomorphisms between infinite sets.

### Exercise H (p. 25)

**1.** Both are isomorphic to the group of rotational symmetries of the square $\{I, R, R^2, R^3\}$ under combination.

(a) $I \leftrightarrow 1$, $R \leftrightarrow 2$ or $3$, $R^2 \leftrightarrow 4$, $R^3 \leftrightarrow 3$ or $2$; and for (b), $I \leftrightarrow 6$, $R \leftrightarrow 2$ or $8$, $R^2 \leftrightarrow 4$, $R^3 \leftrightarrow 8$ or $2$. The alternatives show that this group has an *automorphism* in which $R$ and $R^3$ are interchanged.

**2.** (a)

| $\times$ | $-1$ | $1$ |
|---|---|---|
| $-1$ | $1$ | $-1$ |
| $1$ | $-1$ | $1$ |

(b)

| $\times$ | $1$ | $0$ |
|---|---|---|
| $1$ | $1$ | $0$ |
| $0$ | $0$ | $0$ |

(c)

| $\times$ | $O$ | $E$ |
|---|---|---|
| $O$ | $O$ | $E$ |
| $E$ | $E$ | $E$ |

(d)

| $+$ | $O$ | $E$ |
|---|---|---|
| $O$ | $E$ | $O$ |
| $E$ | $O$ | $E$ |

(e)

| $\cap$ | $A$ | $\emptyset$ |
|---|---|---|
| $A$ | $A$ | $\emptyset$ |
| $\emptyset$ | $\emptyset$ | $\emptyset$ |

(f)

| $\cup$ | $\emptyset$ | $A$ |
|---|---|---|
| $\emptyset$ | $\emptyset$ | $A$ |
| $A$ | $A$ | $A$ |

(g)

| | $H$ | $W$ |
|---|---|---|
| $H$ | $W$ | $H$ |
| $W$ | $H$ | $W$ |

(h)

| $\circ$ | $C$ | $N$ |
|---|---|---|
| $C$ | $N$ | $C$ |
| $N$ | $C$ | $N$ |

11

|     (i)     |      (j)     |      (k)     |
| --- | --- | --- |
| $\wedge$ \| 1  0 | $\vee$ \| 0  1 | \| O  D |
| 1 \| 1  0 | 0 \| 0  1 | O \| D  O |
| 0 \| 0  0 | 1 \| 1  1 | D \| O  D |

(a), (d), (g), (h) and (k) are isomorphic. (b), (c), (e), (f), (i), (j) are isomorphic.

**3.** Yes.

**4.** Yes: $a \leftrightarrow x$, $b \leftrightarrow y$, $c \leftrightarrow z$.
   Yes: $a \leftrightarrow y$, $b \leftrightarrow x$, $c \leftrightarrow z$.

**5.** The law $2^m \times 2^n = 2^{m+n}$ means that the mapping $n \leftrightarrow 2^n$ preserves the operation. This isomorphism is discussed fully in Chapter 6.

**6.** $(\frac{1}{2})^m \times (\frac{1}{2})^n = (\frac{1}{2})^{m+n}$.

## 8. SETS WITH TWO BINARY OPERATIONS

Only two familiar examples of structures with two operations are discussed here: the Algebra of Sets, where the elements are sets and the operations are $\cap$ and $\cup$, which has the structure known as *Boolean Algebra*; and the algebra of rational numbers where the operations are $+$ and $\times$, which has the structure known as a *field*. Formal treatment of such structures is deferred to the Further Mathematics course; here it is sufficient to point out that a field is a structure in which addition, subtraction, multiplication, and division (except by 0) can be carried out as in ordinary arithmetic. Fields which will become familiar include the rational field, the real field, the fields of residue classes to a prime modulus, and the field of complex numbers.

The section is starred, but some discussion of its contents is advisable with reference to the familiar examples.

### Exercise I (p. 27)

**1.** No additive or multiplicative inverses.

**2.** No multiplicative inverses.

**3.** No inverses.    **4.** Yes.

12

**5.** (a) Yes. (b) Yes.

Consider the set of prime factors of each number; distinguish repeated factors by a suffix. Thus $2^3 = 2_1 \times 2_2 \times 2_3$.

Then the prime factors of the HCF and LCM are the intersection and union of these sets.

Distributivity follows from that of $\cap$ and $\cup$.

**6.** $(p * q) \circ r = r \circ (p * q)$      ($\circ$ commutative)

          $= (r \circ p) * (r \circ q)$    (distributive from left)

          $= (p \circ r) * (q \circ r)$    ($\circ$ commutative)

Hence also distributive from the right.

**7.** Yes.

**8.** No, since **1** is neutral for multiplication, but $3x = 1$ has no solution, so that **3** has no inverse.

**1, 2, 4, 5** satisfy $x^2 + 3x + 2 = 0$.

This leaves only **0** and **3** as possible solutions of $x^2 + 3x + 3 = 0$, neither of which is.

### *Miscellaneous Exercise (p. 28)*

**1.** $m$ odd $\Rightarrow m = 2n + 1$

          $\Rightarrow m^2 = 4n^2 + 4n + 1$

          $= 4(n^2 + n) + 1$

$n^2$ and $n$ are either both odd or both even. It follows that $(n^2 + n)$ is even for all $n \Rightarrow m^2 \in \mathbf{1}$ (mod 8).

(Note: or see the diagonal entries in the first table of Question 2.)

**2.**

| $\times$ | 1 | 3 | 5 | 7 |
|---|---|---|---|---|
| **1** | 1 | 3 | 5 | 7 |
| **3** | 3 | 1 | 7 | 5 |
| **5** | 5 | 7 | 1 | 3 |
| **7** | 7 | 5 | 3 | 1 |

| | $I$ | $H$ | $X$ | $Y$ |
|---|---|---|---|---|
| $I$ | $I$ | $H$ | $X$ | $Y$ |
| $H$ | $H$ | $I$ | $Y$ | $X$ |
| $X$ | $X$ | $Y$ | $I$ | $H$ |
| $Y$ | $Y$ | $X$ | $H$ | $I$ |

These have all the properties listed. Isomorphism by the correspondence of order in which elements are written in the tables.

**3.**

|   | 0 | 1 | 2 | 3 | 4 |
|---|---|---|---|---|---|
| 0 | 0 | 1 | 2 | 3 | 4 |
| 1 | 1 | 2 | 3 | 4 | 0 |
| 2 | 2 | 3 | 4 | 0 | 1 |
| 3 | 3 | 4 | 0 | 1 | 2 |
| 4 | 4 | 0 | 1 | 2 | 3 |

The table for the rotational symmetries of the regular pentagon may be obtained from this by the isomorphism

$0 \leftrightarrow I, \quad 1 \leftrightarrow R, \quad 2 \leftrightarrow R^2, \quad 3 \leftrightarrow R^3, \quad 4 \leftrightarrow R^4.$

All properties listed hold.

**4.**

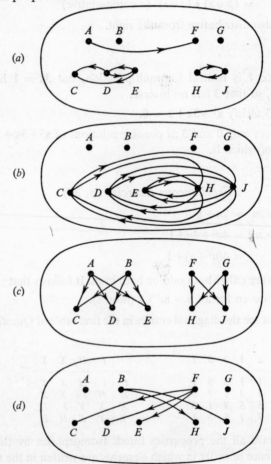

14

(e) Arrows from every point to every other point (if relations by marriage are allowed).

|  | (a) | (b) | (c) | (d) | (e) |
|---|---|---|---|---|---|
| Symmetric | × | √ | × | × | √ |
| Reflexive | × | × | × | × | √ |
| Transitive | × | × |  |  | √ |

We could say that (c) and (d) are transitive since '$x\,R\,y$ and $y\,R\,z$' never occurs. (e) is an equivalence relation.

**5.** Yes; $x\,R\,y$ means '$x$ is in same subset as $y$'.

**6.** (a) Reflexive and transitive; (b) reflexive and symmetric.

**7.** $x^2 \in 35 \pmod{100} \Rightarrow x^2 \in 5 \pmod{10} \Rightarrow x \in 5 \pmod{10}$. But

$$x \in 5 \pmod{10} \Rightarrow x = 10n+5$$
$$\Rightarrow x^2 = 100n^2+100n+25$$
$$\Rightarrow x^2 \in 25 \pmod{100}.$$

**8.** When expressed in prime factors $m$ must contain no repeated factor, i.e. $m$ is *square-free*.

**9.** Isomorphism: $a \leftrightarrow s \leftrightarrow R^2$.    The elements of the last two rows
$\qquad\qquad\quad b \leftrightarrow r \leftrightarrow I$    are interchangeable; e.g. we may
$\qquad\qquad\quad c \leftrightarrow p \leftrightarrow R$    have $c \leftrightarrow q \leftrightarrow R$ and $d \leftrightarrow p \leftrightarrow R^3$.
$\qquad\qquad\quad d \leftrightarrow q \leftrightarrow R^3$

**10.** $a = 7n+1, b = 7m+4 \Rightarrow a+b = 7(n+m)+5$   and
$$ab = 49nm+7(m=4n)+4;$$
(b) is isomorphic with the rotations of the regular hexagon under combination.

**11.** (a)                              (b)

| × | 1 | 3 | 5 | 7 |
|---|---|---|---|---|
| **1** | 1 | 3 | 5 | 7 |
| **3** | 3 | 1 | 7 | 5 |
| **5** | 5 | 7 | 1 | 3 |
| **7** | 7 | 5 | 3 | 1 |

| × | 1 | 5 | 7 | 11 |
|---|---|---|---|---|
| **1** | 1 | 5 | 7 | 11 |
| **5** | 5 | 1 | 11 | 7 |
| **7** | 7 | 11 | 1 | 5 |
| **11** | 11 | 7 | 5 | 1 |

(a) (b)
$1 \leftrightarrow 1$
$3 \leftrightarrow 5$
$5 \leftrightarrow 7$
$7 \leftrightarrow 11$

There are other isomorphisms. In each **1** is the neutral element, so they must correspond, but we may rearrange the correspondence of the other elements. Isomorphic to the symmetries of a rectangle or rhombus.

15

**12.**

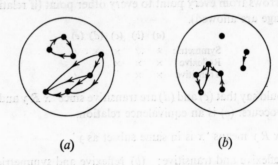

(a)                              (b)

**13.**

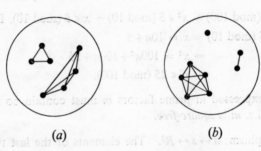

(a)                              (b)

(lines joining points replace two way arrows).

**14.** (a) All;                    (b) $Z_5, Z_7$.

*Note.* All the $4 \times 4$ tables in this exercise are examples of *groups*. We shall see in Chapter 10 that there are only two essentially different groups of order 4—the *cyclic* group and the *Klein* group. All groups of order 4 must be isomorphic to one or other of these two. The rotations of the swastika form a cyclic group and the symmetries of the rectangle form a Klein group.

16

# 2

# FLOW DIAGRAMS, NATURAL
# NUMBERS AND INDUCTION

The underlying mathematical ideas in this chapter are the properties of the system of natural numbers and the central role of the principle of induction amongst them. In order to make these essentially abstract concepts more accessible to the pupil, they have been hung on the peg of simple computer programming; for any program† which incorporates a loop operates essentially by a progression through the natural numbers, and any function developed in this way is generated inductively. It should be emphasized, however, that the primary objective in this chapter is not to teach programming (later, in *Advanced Mathematics*, Book 3, Chapter 28, programming techniques are described in greater detail), but to use the insights which come from thinking in computer terms to deepen understanding of mathematical concepts.

It has been found that confidence comes more quickly if we introduce an elementary notation for the writing of flow diagrams. It is not essential for the pupils to adhere slavishly to the practice described here; for example, there is little harm if instructions are used combining more than one operation at a time, such as

$$A: = A \times B \div 2,$$

although this has been avoided in the chapter. The individual teacher may use his discretion about this. (One advantage of the restriction to single binary operations is that the pupil can then work through his program step-by-step on a hand-calculating machine.)

There are, of course, many 'correct' programs for carrying out any particular computation; comparison of programs produced by different members of a class can provoke interesting discussion. Pupils should be encouraged to test the correctness of their programs by carrying out a 'dry run' with simple numbers through the first two or three stages of a computation.

† *Program*, in this technical sense, is usually so spelt.

Precisely what constitutes a 'natural number' is a matter of definition. Some writers include zero amongst the natural numbers; in this way the empty set is associated with a natural number, which is convenient, but historical precedent is against its inclusion. If the question arises in discussion it provides an opportunity, not for dogmatic assertion, but for pointing to the freedom of the mathematician to formulate his own axioms and definitions.

There are, of course, many ways of setting out proofs by induction. The method adopted in this chapter, using the truth set $T$, is followed throughout the S.M.P. Advanced Mathematics course. Pupils should be sufficiently familiar by this stage with the language of sets and with the use of the implication sign that the statement

$$k \in T \Rightarrow k+1 \in T$$

should not convey any suggestion of 'assuming the answer'. The approach outlined on p. 49, in which the pupil is encouraged first to set down the two propositions separated by blank lines, for example

$$16 \text{ divides } 5^k - 4k - 1$$
$$\Rightarrow \dots$$
$$\Rightarrow \dots$$
$$\Rightarrow 16 \text{ divides } 5^{k+1} - 4(k+1) - 1,$$

and then to fill in the argument by standard processes of deductive reasoning, can be a help in clarifying the logical structure of this method of proof.

## 2. COMPUTER STORES AND INSTRUCTIONS

### Exercise A (p. 37)

1.    (a)           (b)          (c)          (d)

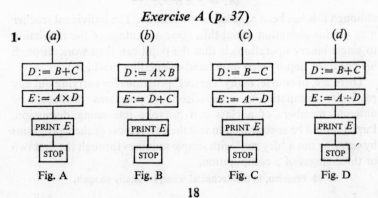

Fig. A        Fig. B        Fig. C        Fig. D

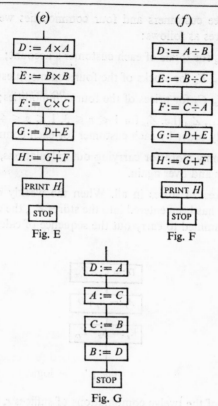

(e) Fig. E

$D := A \times A$
$E := B \times B$
$F := C \times C$
$G := D+E$
$H := G+F$
PRINT $H$
STOP

(f) Fig. F

$D := A \div B$
$E := B \div C$
$F := C \div A$
$G := D+E$
$H := G+F$
PRINT $H$
STOP

**2.**

$D := A$
$A := C$
$C := B$
$B := D$
STOP

Fig. G

**3.** A check on the stock of coffee can be kept by recording the amount of coffee in the shop in another store $K$, and giving the instruction $K: = K-1$ when the customer buys a tin of coffee.

If several tins are bought at a time, let the number bought be recorded in a separate store $Z$. Then the sequence

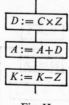

$D := C \times Z$
$A := A+D$
$K := K-Z$

Fig. H

keeps the customer's account and the stock of coffee up to date.

19

With three customers and four commodities we require computer stores as follows:

$A_1, A_2, A_3$ for totals of each customer's account;

$K_1, K_2, K_3, K_4$ for stocks of the four commodities;

$C_1, C_2, C_3, C_4$ for prices of the four commodities;

$Z_{11}, Z_{12}, ..., Z_{34}$ (i.e. $Z_{rs}$ for $1 \leqslant r \leqslant 3, 1 \leqslant s \leqslant 4$) for recording the weekly order by each customer for each commodity;

$D$, a dummy store for carrying out calculations, which can be used over and over again.

This makes 24 stores in all. When the weekly order for each customer has been entered into the stores $Z_{rs}$, the computer must be programmed to carry out the sequence of calculations:

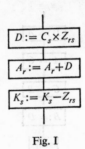

Fig. I

for each of the twelve combinations of suffices $r, s$.

**4.** As Figure 3 (p. 34) except that the third instruction is

$$R: = R \times 3;$$

or, in the general case,

$$R: = R \times A.$$

**5.**

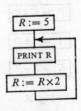

Fig. J

20

**6.** The *n*th number of the sequence is the sum of the first *n* natural numbers.

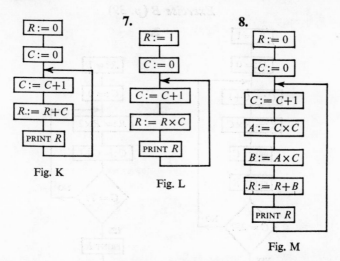

Fig. K

**7.**

Fig. L

**8.**

Fig. M

We observe that the successive values are the squares of the terms of the sequence in Question 6; that is,

$$1^3 + 2^3 + \ldots + n^3 = (1 + 2 + \ldots + n)^2.$$

**9.**

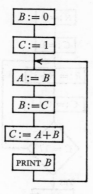

Fig. N

21

# 3. DECISION BOXES

## Exercise B (p. 39)

**1.**

R := 1

C := 0

C := C+1

R := R×C

PRINT C

PRINT R

C = 25? — NO

YES

STOP

Fig. O

**2.**

R := 1

C := 0

R := R×2

C := C+1

C = 7? — NO

YES

PRINT R

STOP

Fig. P

**3.** (a) $\frac{1}{100}+\frac{1}{99}+\frac{1}{98}+\ldots+\frac{1}{1}$.

(b) Print out the largest of the numbers $x$, $y$, $z$.

**4.**

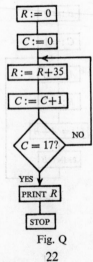

R := 0

C := 0

R := R+35

C := C+1

C = 17? — NO

YES

PRINT R

STOP

Fig. Q

Notice that it is quicker to find 17 times 35 (17 loops) than 35 times 17 (35 loops).

22

**5.**

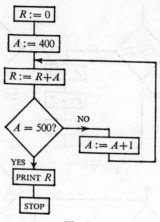

Fig. R

**6.** Two alternatives:

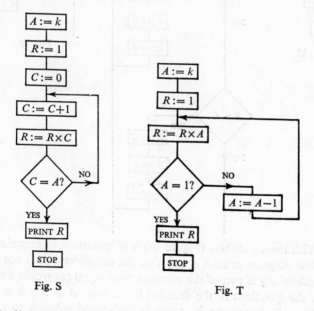

Fig. S

Fig. T

By 'counting down', as in Figure T, the store $A$ itself can hold the counter.

23

**7.**

**8.**

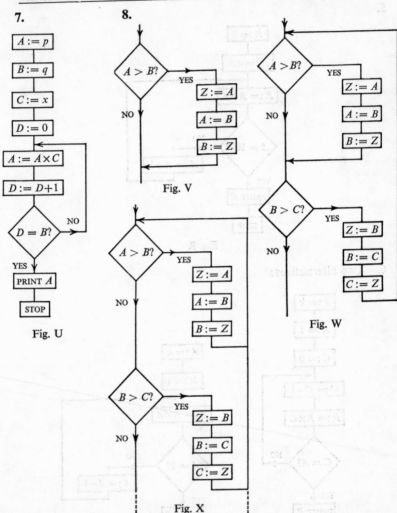

Fig. V

Fig. W

Fig. U

Fig. X

With three numbers (Figure W) it is important to organize the flow diagram in such a way that the computer would not loop indefinitely if two of the numbers were equal (as would happen if the questions in the decision boxes were $A \geqslant B$?, $B \geqslant C$?). A small change can be made in the second solution to give a pattern which generalizes easily to more than three numbers (see Figure X).

24

**9.**

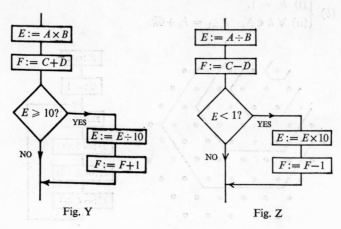

Fig. Y

Fig. Z

## 5. INDUCTIVE DEFINITION
### *Exercise C (p. 43)*

**1.** $\begin{cases} \text{(i)} & 1! = 1, \\ \text{(ii)} & \forall\, k \in N, \quad (k+1)! = (k+1).k!. \end{cases}$

**2.** *(a)* $\begin{cases} \text{(i)} & s_1 = 1, \\ \text{(ii)} & \forall\, k \in N, \quad s_{k+1} = s_k + (2k+1). \end{cases}$

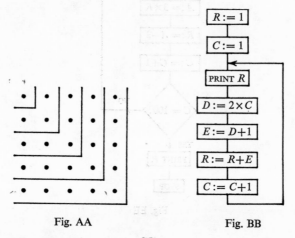

Fig. AA

Fig. BB

25

(b) $\begin{cases} \text{(i)} \quad h_1 = 1, \\ \text{(ii)} \quad \forall\, k \in N, \quad h_{k+1} = h_k + 6k. \end{cases}$

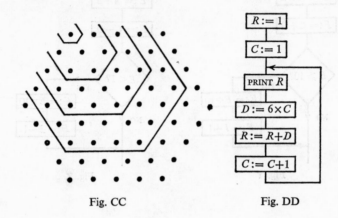

Fig. CC                    Fig. DD

3.  2, 4, 10, 28, 82, 244 (see Figure EE).

$u_n = 3^{n-1} + 1.$

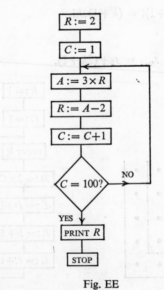

Fig. EE

**4.** (a) $u_7 = 257$, $u_8 = 513$.

(b) $\begin{cases} \text{(i)} \ u_1 = 5, \\ \text{(ii)} \ \forall\, k \in N, \ u_{k+1} = 2u_k - 1. \end{cases}$

(c) See Figure FF.

$u_n = 2^{n+1} + 1$.

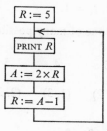

Fig. FF

**5.** $s_k = (1 - x^k)/(1 - x)$. This is a result which the pupils should commit to memory at some stage, but for the present it may be treated merely as an exercise. See Chapter 11, Section 2.3.

**6.** For example, if we interpret $t_0$ so that the rule

$$t_{k+1} = t_k + (k+1)$$

remains true when $k = 0$, then

$$t_1 = t_0 + 1,$$

so that $t_0 = 0$. In a similar way we derive the interpretations

$$2^0 = 1, \ 0! = 1, \ s_0 = 0, \ h_0 = 1.$$

**7.** $\begin{cases} \text{(i)} \ f_1 = 1, \ f_2 = 2; \\ \text{(ii)} \ \forall\, k \in N, f_{k+2} = f_k + f_{k+1}. \end{cases}$

**8.** $p_{k+1} = p_k + t_{k+1}$. In the flow diagram (Figure GG) successive values of $k$, $t_k$, $p_k$ are recorded in stores $C$, $Q$, $R$ respectively.

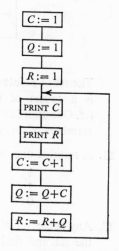

Fig. GG

27

**9.** $s_{k+1} = s_k + r_k.$

| $n$ | 1 | 2 | 3 | 4 | 5 | 6 | 7 | 8 | 9 | 10 |
|-----|---|---|---|---|---|---|---|---|---|----|
| $r_n$ | 2 | 4 | 7 | 11 | 16 | 22 | 29 | 37 | 46 | 56 |
| $s_n$ | 2 | 4 | 8 | 15 | 26 | 42 | 64 | 93 | 130 | 176 |

Notice that the inductive formula for $r_n$ has the same form as that for the triangular numbers $t_n$; but the sequences are not the same because $r_1 = 2$, $t_1 = 1$.

**10.** Figure HH suggests one of many possible methods of enumeration:

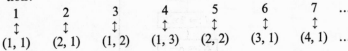

The set of points $(x, y)$ in which $x$ and $y$ have no common factor is a subset of the original set, and is therefore countable (cf. Question 12); and there is a one-one correspondence between members of this subset and positive rational numbers $y/x$.

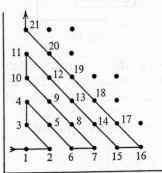

Fig. HH

**11.** A suitable one-one correspondence would be

$$
\begin{array}{cccccccc}
1 & 2 & 3 & 4 & 5 & 6 & 7 & \cdots \\
\updownarrow & \updownarrow & \updownarrow & \updownarrow & \updownarrow & \updownarrow & \updownarrow & \\
0 & 1 & -1 & 2 & -2 & 3 & -3 & \cdots
\end{array}
$$

**12.** Any subset of $N$ has a least member $u_1$, say. Remove this from the set and find the new least member $u_2$ of the subset that remains; and so on. The correspondence $n \leftrightarrow u_n$ proves that the subset is countable.

28

## 6. PROOF BY INDUCTION

### *Exercise D (p. 45)*

1. $T = \{1, 3, 6, 9, 21, 24, ...\}$. There is no regular pattern, and it is not known whether the set is finite or infinite. Every member except 1 must be a multiple of three, since $2(3m \pm 1)^2 + 1$ is always divisible by 3.

2. $T = N$.

3. $T$ contains 1 and all natural numbers from 10 on.

4. $T$ contains all natural numbers except 1.

5. $T = N$.

6. $T$ contains all natural numbers except 1.

7. $T = \{1, 2, 3\}$.

8. $T$ contains all natural numbers up to 40, also 43, 44, ... but not 41, 42, 45, .... There is no regular pattern, and it is not known whether the set is finite or infinite.

9. $T = \{1, 2, 3, 4, 5\}$.

10. The sum of the first $n$ odd numbers is $n^2$.

11. $t_{n-1} + t_n = n^2$. It is amusing to show this by deploying the patterns of dots in Figure 9 (p. 43) suitably; and also to show geometrically the connection with the result of Question 10.

12. $\dfrac{1}{1.2} + \dfrac{1}{2.3} + \dfrac{1}{3.4} + ... + \dfrac{1}{n(n+1)} = \dfrac{n}{n+1}$.

13. The $n$th term of the sequence is $2^{n-2}$ except when $n = 1$.

14. $\forall\, n \in N$, $3^n + 2n - 1$ is divisible by 4.

15. $1^3 + 2^3 + 3^3 + ... + n^3 = t_n^2 = \frac{1}{4}n^2(n+1)^2$.

16. The sum of the first $n$ Fibonacci numbers is one less than the $(n+2)$th Fibonacci number.

29

## Exercise E (p. 49)

**3.** Note that $2^k > k \Rightarrow 2^{k+1} > 2k \geqslant k+1$ if $k \in N$, since $k \geqslant 1$.

**4.** Note that
$$3|2 \times 4^k + 1 \Rightarrow 3|2 \times 4^{k+1} + 4 \Rightarrow 3|2 \times 4^{k+1} + 1.$$

**5.** Note that
$$4|3^k + 2k - 1 \Rightarrow 4|3^{k+1} + 6k - 3 \Rightarrow 4|3^{k+1} + 2(k+1) - 1.$$

**11.** Proof by multiplying both sides by $(1+x)$ (only valid if $1+x \geqslant 0$) and observing that $(1+kx)(1+x) > 1+(k+1)x$.

**13.** $T$ contains all natural numbers from 5 on.
$$k! < k^{k-2} \Rightarrow (k+1)! < k^{k-2}(k+1) < (k+1)^{k-2}(k+1)$$
$$= (k+1)^{(k+1)-2}.$$

**14.** $(n^n)^{(n^n)} = n^{n \cdot n^n} = n^{(n^{n+1})} < n^{(n^{n^2})} = n^{\{(n^n)^n\}}$.

**15.** The implication is valid for $k > 3$, but $3 \notin T$. We note that $5 \in T$, so that $2^n > n^2$ if $n \in \{5, 6, 7, \ldots\}$.

# 7. PROGRAMMES AND DATA

## Exercise F (p. 51)

**1.**

| $A$ | $C$ | $B$ |
|---|---|---|
| 0 | 4 | 4·67 |
| 4·67 | 3 | 1·85 |
| 6·52 | 2 | 3·27 |
| 9·79 | 1 | 5·93 |
| 15·72 | 0 | PRINT 15·72 |

**2.**

In Questions 3, 4 and 5 the data is supposed to be laid out as described in Section 7, Example 5: that is, the figures to be processed are preceded by the number of these figures.

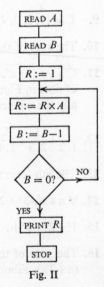

Fig. II

30

**3.**

**4.**

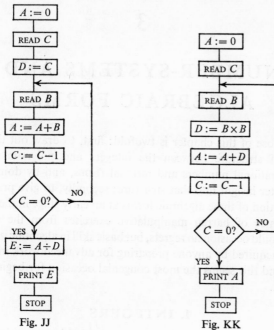

Fig. JJ

Fig. KK

**5.**

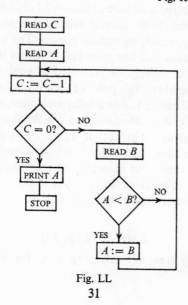

Fig. LL

31

# 3

# NUMBER-SYSTEMS AND ALGEBRAIC FORMS

The purpose of this chapter is twofold: first, to draw out the similarities of structure between the integers and polynomials, and between rational numbers and rational forms, and by doing so to gain greater insight into that structure; secondly, to give practice in manipulation of these algebraic forms at an early stage in the course. The absence of barren manipulative exercises from the O-Level course should occasion no regrets, but basic skill in algebraic processes must be acquired by anyone preparing for advanced work in mathematics, and this seems the most congenial occasion for beginning to acquire it.

## 1. INTEGERS

The integers are introduced here as undefined objects associated with the natural numbers: to the natural number $p$ there corresponds two integers $^+p$ and $^-p$, satisfying certain axioms. The wealth of illustration and preparation that has gone before makes this an easy step. Integers could alternatively be presented as equivalence classes of pairs of natural numbers; this point of view is outlined in Question 3 of Exercise E of Chapter 1. For a fuller treatment, see, for example, Irving Adler, *The New Mathematics*; W. W. Sawyer, *A Concrete Approach to Abstract Algebra*; or H. A. Thurston, *The Number System*. There are advantages in the notation $^-p$, which has been used in the O-Level course; for example, we may write $2^-p$ and $^-q.^-p$ without recourse to brackets. But $(-p)$ is so thoroughly established that the student must become familiar with it.

### Exercise A (p. 54)

1. (a) True; (b) true; (c) false; $^+p > {^-q}$ for all natural numbers $p, q$.

**2.** $^+p-^+q$ is the integer $x$ for which $x+^+q = {}^+p$. Hence

$$x = x+^+q+^-q = {}^+p+^-q = \begin{cases} ^+(p-q) & (p > q), \\ 0 & (p = q), \\ ^-(q-p) & (p < q). \end{cases}$$

In the same way $^+p-^-q = y$, where $y+^-q = {}^+p$. Hence

$$y = y+^-q+^+q = {}^+p+^+q = {}^+(p+q).$$

$$^-p-^+q = {}^-(p+q); \quad ^-p-^-q = {}^+q+^-p = \begin{cases} ^-(p-q) & (p > q), \\ 0 & (p = q), \\ ^+(q-p) & (p < q). \end{cases}$$

**3.** In $^+p$, etc., the upper symbol $+$ marks the integer as positive. In $p+q$, the symbol $+$ denotes addition of natural numbers. In $^+p+^+q$, the central symbol $+$ denotes addition of integers.

**4.** (*a*) Yes, $^-p \leftrightarrow p$;  (*b*) no.

The negative integers have a similar order structure to the natural numbers if $>$ is replaced by $<$.

**5.** (*a*) Yes, $^+2p \leftrightarrow p$;  (*b*) no. The order structure is the same.

**6.** We need the axioms for integers before we can say, for example, that $^+(a-c)$ is the same as $^+a+^-c$, and before we can establish the truth of the distributive law for integers

$$(^+a+^-c).^+p = {}^+a.^+p+^-c.^+p.$$

## 2. POLYNOMIALS

We are concerned here solely with polynomials as algebraic forms; they could have been called *polynomial forms* throughout. We are not concerned with polynomial *functions* of $x$ which have values when values are given to $x$. The distinction is important and occasionally it is necessary to draw attention to it. Thus $x+1$ and $(x^2-1)/(x-1)$ are formally equivalent, but they represent different functions, the second being undefined when $x = 1$. In the field of integers modulo 5 ($Z_5$) the polynomial forms $x^5+x^2$ and $x+x^2$ are different, but they represent the same function, since $x^5 = x$ for all $x$ in this field. For further comments, see the Appendix to the M.A. Report on *The Teaching of Algebra in Sixth Forms*.

It is worth pointing out that when we write numbers in the ordinary way in the scale of ten (or, for that matter, in any other scale) we are expressing them in polynomial forms; the number 1234 represents $1 \times 10^3 + 2 \times 10^2 + 3 \times 10 + 4$, and the operations of ordinary arithmetic are really polynomial operations of the type discussed here. This point is touched upon in the next section, but time can usefully be spent in following it through.

Pupils should be encouraged to work with polynomials in either ascending or descending order, and should not feel that they must use descending order every time.

### Exercise B (p. 57)

1. (a) $-1 + 5x - 4x^2 + 2x^3$;  (b) $2x^3 - 4x^2 + 5x - 1$.
   Degree 3. $(-1, 5, -4, 2)$.

2. (a) $3x + x^2 - 5x^3 - 7x^4$;  (b) $-7x^4 - 5x^3 + x^2 + 3x$.
   Degree 4. $(0, 3, 1, -5, -7)$.

3. (a) $4 - 2x^2 - x^3 + x^5$;  (b) $x^5 - x^3 - 2x^2 + 4$.
   Degree 5. $(4, 0, -2, -1, 0, 1)$.

4. (a) $3 + x + x^2$;  (b) $1 - 9x + 5x^2$;  (c) $2 + 6x - 21x^2 + 23x^3 - 6x^4$.

5. (a) $3x^3 - 2x^2 + x + 1$;  (b) $-x^3 - 2x^2 - x + 7$;
   (c) $2x^6 - 4x^5 + x^4 + 3x^3 + 6x^2 + 4x - 12$.

6. (a) $x^2 + 2x + 2$;  (b) $-8x^3 + x^2 + 8x - 2$;
   (c) $-16x^6 + 4x^5 + 32x^4 - 11x^3 - 13x^2 + 10x$.

7. $x^4 + 4x^3 - 8x + 4$.  8. $9 + 6x + x^2 - 12x^3 - 4x^4 + 4x^6$.

9. $11x^2$, $-6x^3$.  10. $0x$, $-4x^2$.

11. $12 + 5x - 2x^2$.  12. $x^3 + 2x^2 - 5x - 10$.

13. $x^4 - 16$.  14. $x^4 - 4x^2 + 12x - 9$.

15. $1 + 2x + x^2$,  $1 + 3x + 3x^2 + x^3$,  $1 + 4x + 6x^2 + 4x^3 + x^4$,
    $1 + 5x + 10x^2 + 10x^3 + 5x^4 + x^5$,
    $1 + 6x + 15x^2 + 20x^3 + 15x^4 + 6x^5 + x^6$.

16. Sum: $(5, -9, 1, 2)$.  Product: $(6, -23, 22, -1, -10)$.

17. Sum: $(4, 6, 2, -4)$.  Product: $(3, 6, 8, 6, -27, 4)$.

**18.** Sum: $(a_0 + b_0, \; a_1 + b_1, \; a_2 + b_2, \; b_3)$. Product: $(a_0 b_0, \; a_0 b_1 + a_1 b_0,$
$a_0 b_2 + a_1 b_1 + a_2 b_0, \; a_0 b_3 + a_1 b_2 + a_2 b_1, \; a_1 b_3 + a_2 b_2, \; a_2 b_3)$.

**19.** Deg $(A + B)$ and deg $(A - B)$ are both equal to max $(m, n)$ if
$m \neq n$, and must be $\leqslant m$ if $m = n$.
Deg $(A . B) = m + n$.

**20.** $\left. \begin{aligned} A &= a_0 + a_1 x + a_2 x^2 + \dots + a_m x^m \\ B &= b_0 + b_1 x + b_2 x^2 + \dots + b_n x^n \end{aligned} \right\} \Rightarrow$

$\quad rA + sB = (ra_0 + sb_0) + (ra_1 + sb_1)x + \dots$   which is a polynomial.

$rA + sB$ might be the zero polynomial, but this is not really an
exception.

$r = \frac{23}{14}, \quad s = -\frac{29}{14}.$

This result shows that polynomials form a vector space, of
infinite dimension. See, for example, W. W. Sawyer, *A Concrete
Approach to Abstract Algebra*.

## 3. POLYNOMIALS AND INTEGERS

The sets $Y$ and $Z$ defined here have much in common, but it should
be clearly appreciated why they are not isomorphic under addition or
multiplication. The set $Y$ can be put in one-one correspondence with
the set $Z$—in mathematical jargon it is a *countable* set—but this
cannot be done in any way which preserves the structure. That is, if
polynomial $A$ corresponds to the integer $a$, and polynomial $B$ to the
integer $b$, we cannot ensure that $A + B$ will correspond to $a + b$. We
cannot even do this if we restrict ourselves to polynomials with
integer coefficients. We could make $2x + 7$ correspond to 27, $2x + 8$
to 28, but their sum is $4x + 15$; if this corresponds to 55, then so does
$5x + 5$, and the correspondence is not one-one. Discussion will soon
show that we cannot avoid this, however we choose the correspondence.

## 4. DIVISION

The word 'division' is used in at least two different senses in elementary arithmetic. When we say $20 \div 5 = 4$, we are using 'division'
as 'the inverse process to multiplication', and this is its proper use.
This process can only be completely carried out in the field of

rational numbers, and there division by 5 is equivalent to multiplication by $\frac{1}{5}$, the multiplicative inverse of 5. The corresponding operation can be carried out with rational forms, as discussed in Sections 8 and 9. But we are also accustomed to saying '20 divided by 3 is 6 with remainder 2' and this is not the same process at all. We are here concerned essentially with integers; the process is not inverse to multiplication; it arises from the practical operation of partition—'distribute 20 sweets fairly among 3 children'—and should really have another name. The connection between the two processes is of course that if we carry out the second and the remainder turns out to be zero we have in fact achieved a solution of a problem involving the first process. It is the second process which is properly described as 'repeated subtraction' and which is effected by the 'long division' algorithm discussed here. Both processes are mathematically significant, but in different contexts. In dealing with integral domains, as here, the second process leads to important consequences; in dealing with groups it is the first process that we need and it is best thought of as multiplication by the (multiplicative) inverse. Mathematically, to solve $3x = 20$ implies that we are in the rational field, and the best solution is to multiply each side by $\frac{1}{3}$, leading to $x = \frac{20}{3}$. In certain practical applications the further step to $x = 6\frac{2}{3}$ may have significance, and the same is true of polynomials—for example, when we wish to integrate a rational function.

In the pupil's text we have not drawn attention to this ambiguity, but have been content to put the phrases involving 'divide' in quotation marks. With more sophisticated pupils a discussion of the reason for this might be helpful.

### Exercise C (p. 61)

1. (a) 18, 1; (b) $^-$19, 13; (c) $^-$4, 3; (d) $^-$1, 2.

2. $x^2 - 2x + 3$, $-5$.    3. $x^2 - 4x + 11$, $-27$.

4. $2x^2 + 2x - 3$, 0.    5. $\frac{3}{2}$, $\frac{11}{2}$.

6. $2x^2 - \frac{1}{2}x + \frac{1}{4}$, $-\frac{5}{4}$.    7. $x + 4$, $4x - 8$.

8. $x^2 + 2x - 3$, $-2$.    9. $x - 2$, $5x - 5$.

**10.** (a) No; $a-b$ not always in set; (b) yes.

(c) No; zero is $\begin{pmatrix} 0 & 0 \\ 0 & 0 \end{pmatrix}$ and there are zero-divisors, for example

$$\begin{pmatrix} 1 & 0 \\ 2 & 0 \end{pmatrix} \begin{pmatrix} 0 & 0 \\ 3 & 4 \end{pmatrix} = \begin{pmatrix} 0 & 0 \\ 0 & 0 \end{pmatrix}.$$

(d) Yes; (e) no; $a.b$ not always in set.

**11.** (a) 13; (b) no; (c) the remainder on division of 450 by 13; yes. This emphasizes that 'division by 13' is repeated subtraction of 13 until the remainder is in the interval $0 \leqslant x \leqslant 12$.

**12.** This is the same as Question 11 for polynomials instead of integers. $P$ must be $(x+2)$, the quotient, and the member of the set required is the remainder $-3x-4$, which is unique.

## 5. FACTORS

The two theorems in this section are often tacitly assumed; here we make the assumption explicit, though the proofs are not particularly trivial. The first corresponds to the so-called fundamental theorem of arithmetic, which states that the expression of a natural number as a product of prime factors is unique. Experience shows that students often have no experimental faith in this result: that is to say, while they admit that the search for prime factors is categorical and can only lead to one result, they cannot see at once that such a statement as $37 \times 79 = 61 \times 53$ is bound to be false. Appeal to experience at this stage is probably more convincing than the rather difficult formal proof. This, both for integers and for polynomials—indeed, for any integral domain—rests on the theorem that if $p$ has no factor in common with $a$ and $p$ divides $ab$, then $p$ divides $b$. This in turn rests on the H.C.F. theorem, that

If $h$ is the highest common factor of $a$ and $b$, then there exist elements $x$ and $y$ of the integral domain so that

$$ax+by = h.$$

A proof can be found in any text-book on polynomial theory. We can then argue as follows:

If $p$ divides $ab$, write $ab = pq$. If also $p$ has no factor in common with $a$, then there exist $x, y$ such that

$$ax+py = 1.$$

37

Hence $$abx + pby = b,$$

or $$pqx + pby = b,$$

so that $b = p(qx + by)$ and $p$ divides $b$.

Repeated use of this theorem shows that if

$$q_1 q_2 q_3 q_4 q_5 q_6 \cdots = p_1 p_2 p_3 p_4 p_5 \cdots,$$

where the $p$'s and $q$'s are primes, then each $p$ must divide and therefore be identical with at least one $q$, so that ultimately all the $p$'s are equal to $q$'s and all the $q$'s to $p$'s; that is, the prime factorization is unique except for the order of the factors.

To prove the second theorem, it is sufficient to establish that if the polynomial $$P = a_0 x^n + a_1 x^{n-1} + \ldots + a_n$$

with $a_0, a_1, a_2, \ldots$ integers is divisible by $x - p/q$, where $p/q$ is a rational number in its lowest terms, then $P = (qx - p)Q$, where $Q$ is another polynomial with integral coefficients.

Now $P$ is divisible by $(x - p/q)$

$$\Leftrightarrow P(p/q) = 0$$

$$\Rightarrow a_0(p/q)^n + a_1(p/q)^{n-1} + \ldots + a_n = 0$$

$$\Rightarrow a_0 p^n/q = -a_n q^{n-1} - a_{n-1} q^{n-2} p - \ldots - a_1 p^{n-1}$$

$$= \text{an integer.}$$

Hence $q$ must divide $a_0$. From this it follows that

$$P - (qx - p) \cdot [(a_0/q) x^{n-1}]$$

is another polynomial with integral coefficients which is zero when $x = p/q$, but this time of degree $n-1$. By repeating the argument we obtain in turn that all the coefficients of $Q$ are integral.

Too much fuss should not be made at this stage about factorizing quadratics; it can always be done by completing the square. The following is an interesting approach.

$$(ax + by)(cx + dy) = (x \quad y) \begin{pmatrix} a \\ b \end{pmatrix} (c \quad d) \begin{pmatrix} x \\ y \end{pmatrix}$$

$$= (x \quad y) \begin{pmatrix} ac & ad \\ bc & bd \end{pmatrix} \begin{pmatrix} x \\ y \end{pmatrix},$$

where the determinant of the square matrix is clearly zero. Hence to factorize, for example, $$36x^2 - 23xy - 70y^2,$$

we write it as

$$(x\ y) \begin{pmatrix} 36 & p \\ q & -70 \end{pmatrix} \begin{pmatrix} x \\ y \end{pmatrix},$$

where $p+q = -23$, and (from the determinant) $pq = -36 \times 70$. Therefore one of $p, q$ is positive and one negative; search beginning with $1, -24; 2, -25; \dots$ leads rapidly to $40, -63$ as the pair whose product is $-36 \times 70$. Solution is now immediate:

$$(x\ y) \begin{pmatrix} 36 & 40 \\ -63 & -70 \end{pmatrix} \begin{pmatrix} x \\ y \end{pmatrix} = (x\ y) \begin{pmatrix} 4 \\ -7 \end{pmatrix} (9\ 10) \begin{pmatrix} x \\ y \end{pmatrix}$$

$$= (4x-7y)(9x+10y).$$

## Exercise D (p. 65)

**1.** Yes. **2.** Yes. **3.** Yes. **4.** No.

**5.** Yes. **6.** No. **7.** No. **8.** Yes.

**9.** Yes. Treat this as a polynomial in $x$.

$$x^3 - 3x.yz + (y^3 + z^3) = [x+(y+z)].[x^2 - x(y+z) - yz + y^2 + z^2],$$

since $\quad\quad y^3 + z^3 = (y+z).(y^2 - yz + z^2).$

Hence, writing the result symmetrically

$$x^3 + y^3 + z^3 - 3xyz = (x+y+z).(x^2 + y^2 + z^2 - yz - zx - xy).$$

**10.** $(2x+1).(x-2)$.      **11.** $(x+5).(x-2)$.

**12.** Irreducible.      **13.** Irreducible (apart from trivial factor 2).

**14.** $(3-2x).(2+3x)$.      **15.** $(1+x)^2.(1-3x)$.

**16.** $(x-2).(x^2+2x+4)$.      **17.** Irreducible.

**18.** $(3+2x).(1-2x-x^2)$.      **19.** Irreducible.

**20.** $(x-2y).(x^2+xy-y^2)$.

**21.** $x^k - a^k - a(x^{k-1} - a^{k-1}) = x^k - ax^{k-1} = x^{k-1}.(x-a)$. Hence, if $x^{k-1} - a^{k-1}$ is divisible by $x-a$, we may write

$$x^{k-1} - a^{k-1} = (x-a).P,$$

39

where $P$ is some polynomial. Then
$$x^k - a^k = a(x-a).P + x^{k-1}.(x-a)$$
$$= (x-a).[aP + x^{k-1}].$$

so that $x^k - a^k$ is also divisible by $(x-a)$. Hence, by induction, $x^n - a^n$ is divisible by $x - a$ for all natural number $n$.

**22.** $(A+B).(2A-3B) = \begin{pmatrix} 3 & 0 \\ -1 & 5 \end{pmatrix} \begin{pmatrix} 1 & 5 \\ 3 & 0 \end{pmatrix} = \begin{pmatrix} 3 & 15 \\ 14 & -5 \end{pmatrix}.$

$2A.A = \begin{pmatrix} 8 & 10 \\ 0 & 18 \end{pmatrix}, \quad 2B.A = \begin{pmatrix} 4 & -4 \\ -4 & 10 \end{pmatrix},$

$-3A.B = \begin{pmatrix} -3 & 0 \\ 9 & -18 \end{pmatrix}, \quad -3B.B = \begin{pmatrix} -6 & 9 \\ 9 & -15 \end{pmatrix}.$

Addition verifies the equation

$2B.A - 3A.B = \begin{pmatrix} 1 & -4 \\ 5 & -8 \end{pmatrix} \neq -A.B = \begin{pmatrix} -1 & 0 \\ 3 & -6 \end{pmatrix}.$

**23.** $A - I = \begin{pmatrix} 1 & 1 \\ 0 & 2 \end{pmatrix}; \quad A - 3I = \begin{pmatrix} -1 & 1 \\ 0 & 0 \end{pmatrix}.$

Hence

$(A-I).(A-3I) = \begin{pmatrix} -1 & 1 \\ 0 & 0 \end{pmatrix}, \quad \text{while} \quad A.A = \begin{pmatrix} 4 & 5 \\ 0 & 9 \end{pmatrix};$

so that

$A.A - 4A + 3I = \begin{pmatrix} 4-8+3 & 5-4+0 \\ 0-0+0 & 9-12+3 \end{pmatrix} = \begin{pmatrix} -1 & 1 \\ 0 & 0 \end{pmatrix}.$

**24.** $A^2 - I = (A-I).(A+I) \Leftrightarrow \begin{pmatrix} 3 & 5 \\ 0 & 8 \end{pmatrix} = \begin{pmatrix} 1 & 1 \\ 0 & 2 \end{pmatrix} \begin{pmatrix} 3 & 1 \\ 0 & 4 \end{pmatrix}.$

**25.** $(M-I).(M^2+M-I) = M^3 - 2M + I.$

$M - I = \begin{pmatrix} 0 & -1 \\ 2 & -1 \end{pmatrix}; \quad M^2 = \begin{pmatrix} -1 & -1 \\ 2 & -2 \end{pmatrix};$

$M^2 + M - I = \begin{pmatrix} -1 & -2 \\ 4 & -3 \end{pmatrix}.$

$M^3 = \begin{pmatrix} -3 & 1 \\ -2 & -2 \end{pmatrix}; \quad M^3 - 2M + I = \begin{pmatrix} -4 & 3 \\ -6 & -1 \end{pmatrix}.$

$\begin{pmatrix} 0 & -1 \\ 2 & -1 \end{pmatrix} \begin{pmatrix} -1 & -2 \\ 4 & -3 \end{pmatrix} = \begin{pmatrix} -4 & 3 \\ -6 & -1 \end{pmatrix}.$

## 6. THE VALUE OF A POLYNOMIAL

The Factor Theorem may also be proved using the method outlined in Exercise D, Question 21 and Exercise E, Question 10. The presence of an inductive argument renders this proof slightly more sophisticated, but it avoids the division algorithm and leads to the conclusion stated in the form

$$P(x) - P(a) \text{ is divisible by } (x - a)$$

from which the Factor Theorem and the Remainder Theorem follow with equal ease. We have treated $x$ as a number in this section, but the Factor Theorem remains true for polynomials in any *field*; it is not true, however, for a *corpus* or *skew field* in which the commutative law of multiplication does not hold. In a corpus,

$$x^2 - a^2 = a(x - a) + (x - a)x,$$

but this expression is not now 'divisible' by $(x - a)$; that is to say, it cannot be expressed either as $(x - a).Q$ or as $Q.(x - a)$. The exercises also include examples of polynomials in $2 \times 2$ non-singular matrices; it should be clearly understood in this case where the proof of the Factor Theorem breaks down. Another case is that of polynomials in the differential operator $D = d/dx$ which arise in linear differential equations. The commutative law holds, and the Factor Theorem (in the form stated here), provided that the coefficients are constants; thus $D^2 - 3D + 2$ can be factorized as $(D - 1)(D - 2)$, but $D^2 - 3xD + 2x^2$ cannot be factorized as $(D - x)(D - 2x)$, since $xD$ and $Dx$ are different.

The 'nesting' process of Section 6.1 for evaluating a polynomial is not known as well as it might be; on a desk machine with transfer it can be carried out very quickly, and no intermediate results need be written down.

### Exercise E (p. 69)

3. (a) Yes; (b) never; (c) when $n$ is even; (d) when $n$ is odd.
 Quotients:

$$\text{(a) } x^{n-1} + ax^{n-2} + a^2x^{n-3} + \ldots + a^{n-1};$$
$$\text{(c) } x^{n-1} - ax^{n-2} + a^2x^{n-3} - \ldots - a^{n-1};$$
$$\text{(d) } x^{n-1} - ax^{n-2} + a^2x^{n-3} - \ldots + a^{n-1}.$$

4. $187, -1823, 51\frac{1}{4}, -769\frac{1}{4}.$    7.    $-5 \cdot 952.$

**8.** (a) (i) $2, -1$; (ii) $2, -1, -1\frac{1}{2}$; (iii) as (ii).

    (b) (i) none; (ii) $-\frac{1}{3}$; (iii) as (ii).

    Polynomial $= (1+3x).(2-2x+x^2)$.

    (c) (i) $-3$; (ii) $\frac{1}{2}, -3$; (iii) $\frac{1}{2}, -3, \pm\sqrt{3}$.

    Polynomial $= (x^2-3).(x+3).(2x-1)$.

**9.** Consider the polynomial $Q = P - P(b/a)$. Then $Q(b/a) = 0$ and by the Factor Theorem $(ax-b)$ divides $Q$. Hence
$$P - P(b/a) = (ax-b).R$$
for some polynomial $R$. That is,
$$P = (ax-b).R + P(b/a),$$
as required.

**10.** $P - P(a) = p(x^3-a^3) + q(x^2-a^2) + r(x-a)$; every bracket has $x-a$ as a factor.

**11.** (a) (i) $(2+x).(4-2x+x^2)$; (ii) as (i).

    (b) (i) $(3x-1).(x^2+2x-1)$;

       (ii) $(3x-1).(x+1+\sqrt{2}).(x+1-\sqrt{2})$.

    (c) (i) $(x+2).(x-2).(x^2-2)$;

       (ii) $(x+2).(x-2).(x+\sqrt{2}).(x-\sqrt{2})$.

**12.** The exception in parentheses in this question is strictly unnecessary, since the zero polynomial does not have a 'degree'. If we wish to have always that the product of a polynomial of degree $n$ and a polynomial of degree $m$ is a polynomial of degree $mn$, then we must attribute to the zero polynomial a 'degree' of $-\infty$.

If a polynomial has $m$ zeros, by the factor theorem it has $m$ linear factors, and must be of degree $\geqslant m$. If $m > n$, $d > n$. If $m = n-1$ and $d = n$, then, on dividing the polynomial by the $(n-1)$ linear factors, the last quotient is linear, and there is an $n$th zero (which may of course be the same as one of the others). There can therefore be exactly $(n-1)$ zeros only if one is repeated.

**13.** $A = \begin{pmatrix} 2 & 1 \\ 0 & 3 \end{pmatrix} \Rightarrow A^2 = \begin{pmatrix} 4 & 5 \\ 0 & 9 \end{pmatrix}$.

$$A^2 - 5A + 6I = \begin{pmatrix} 4-10+6 & 5-5+0 \\ 0-0+0 & 9-15+6 \end{pmatrix} = \begin{pmatrix} 0 & 0 \\ 0 & 0 \end{pmatrix}.$$

$$A - 3I = \begin{pmatrix} -1 & 1 \\ 0 & 0 \end{pmatrix} \quad \text{and} \quad A - 2I = \begin{pmatrix} 0 & 1 \\ 0 & 1 \end{pmatrix}.$$

Their product is
$$\begin{pmatrix} 0 & 0 \\ 0 & 0 \end{pmatrix}.$$

$2 \times 2$ matrices do not form an integral domain; we cannot conclude from $(\mathbf{A}-2\mathbf{I}).(\mathbf{A}-3\mathbf{I}) = 0$ that

$$\mathbf{A}-2\mathbf{I} = 0 \quad \text{or} \quad \mathbf{A}-3\mathbf{I} = 0.$$

$x^2-5x+6 = 0$ is called the *characteristic equation* of the matrix $\begin{pmatrix} 2 & 1 \\ 0 & 3 \end{pmatrix}$. The characteristic equation of the matrix $\begin{pmatrix} a & b \\ c & d \end{pmatrix}$ is

$$x^2-(a+d)x+ad-bc = 0 \quad \text{or} \quad \begin{vmatrix} a-x & b \\ c & d-x \end{vmatrix} = 0.$$

It can be proved (the Cayley–Hamilton Theorem) that all square matrices satisfy their characteristic equations.

**14.** (a) Yes; $\mathbf{IX} = \mathbf{XI}$ and the distributive law holds.

(b) No. $\mathbf{YX}$ is not necessarily the same as $\mathbf{XY}$.

## 7. POLYNOMIALS IN FINITE ARITHMETIC

There are two advantages to be gained from a study of this section. (1) It lights up the distinction between form and function, as already hinted. In a finite field there are polynomials of different form which represent the same function, that is, which map the various elements of the field onto the same images. This is because there are polynomials which map every element of the field onto zero. The factor theorem holds in any field, so that such polynomials must be of the form $Q.x.(x+1).(x+2)...$, where $Q$ is any polynomial and there is a factor $(x+m)$ for any element $m$ of the field. See Exercise F, Question 2. (2) It shows less artificially the point made in Section 5 about the trivial equivalence of factors such as $2x+3$ and $\frac{1}{2}x+\frac{1}{2}$. In a finite field there is no subclass of integers distinguished from fractions, no prime numbers and no Fundamental Theorem of Arithmetic. The second theorem of Section 5 is therefore meaningless, but Question 4(c) of Exercise F shows how dissimilar essentially identical factors may be.

Polynomials over a finite field are still ordered by degree, there is a division algorithm and factorization of polynomials is unique (apart from constant multipliers, as explained). But the absence of prime factors may make the actual factorization quite difficult, as will be discovered by trying to factorize the quadratic $13x^2+16x+9$ in $Z_{17}$.

(*Hint*: it is always possible to arrange that one factor is of the form $(x+a)$.)

The key theorem is Fermat's theorem which states that, regarded as functions, the polynomials $x^p$ and $x$ have identical values for every element of $Z_p$: that is

$$x^p = x \pmod p.$$

This theorem is an immediate deduction from Lagrange's Theorem (p. 286 of *Advanced Mathematics, Book* 1 (pupil's text)). For the non-zero elements of $Z_p$ form a group under multiplication, of order $p-1$. The powers of any element of this group, namely $x$, $x^2$, $x^3$, ... form a cyclic subgroup of the group, so that for some $n$, $x^n = 1$, and by Lagrange's Theorem, $n$ must be a factor of $p-1$. It follows at once that for non-zero $x$, $x^{p-1} = 1$ and $x^p = x$. For $x = 0$ the statement is obvious, so that $x^p = x$ for all $x$ in $Z_p$.

Fermat's Theorem assures us that we need not consider polynomial *functions* of degree higher than $p-1$. There are just $p^p$ polynomials up to this degree, which is just equal to the total number of *functions*, mapping $p$ elements into $p$ elements. In fact, each function has one polynomial representation (with degree $\leqslant p-1$), as is shown for example in *Some Lessons in Mathematics* (C.U.P.), pp. 78ff. (The reader is warned that this section speaks loosely of 'polynomials' when 'polynomial functions' are intended. There are of course infinitely many polynomials (forms) in $Z_p$.)

As an interesting example, consider the 27 polynomial functions in $Z_3$. They are:

| 0 | 1 | 2 |
|---|---|---|
| $x$ | $x+1$ | $x+2$ |
| $2x$ | $2x+1$ | $2x+2$ |
| $x^2$ | $x^2+1$ | $x^2+2$ |
| $x^2+x$ | $x^2+x+1$ | $x^2+x+2$ |
| $x^2+2x$ | $x^2+2x+1$ | $x^2+2x+2$ |
| $2x^2$ | $2x^2+1$ | $2x^2+2$ |
| $2x^2+x$ | $2x^2+x+1$ | $2x^2+x+2$ |
| $2x^2+2x$ | $2x^2+2x+1$ | $2x^2+2x+2$ |

Of these, the first row gives the three-one functions, the constants. The next two rows contain all the one-one functions, the linear functions; the second row giving the cyclic permutations, and the third row the 'reflections', in which two elements are interchanged and the third is unchanged. These six functions have inverses and form a group. The remaining 18 quadratic functions all map two elements onto one element, and the third onto itself or a different element. Thus $x^2+x+1$ maps 0 and 2 onto 1, and 1 onto 0, while $x^2+2x$ leaves 0 and 2 unchanged, and maps 1 onto 0.

Polynomial functions can thus be tailor-made to suit requirements. In the real field this can be done only for a finite number of elements, the appropriate formula being

$$f(x) = \Sigma \frac{(x-b)(x-c)...}{(a-b)(a-c)...} f(a),$$

which is Lagrange's Interpolation Formula for a polynomial function with prescribed values at $x = a, b, c, ...$.

Since in a finite field there are strictly no 'negative' integers, the factor theorem, though true, looks a little different. We now have that

$$P(a) = 0 \Leftrightarrow P \text{ has a factor } (x+{}^-a),$$

where $^-a$ is the additive inverse of $a$ ($= p-a$ in the field $Z_p$).

In the exercises we make frequent use of the fact that

$$(x+a).(x+{}^-a) = x^2+{}^-(a^2),$$

which corresponds to the 'difference of two squares' factors in the real field. To test for reducibility by completing the square, it is necessary to know which elements of the field are squares, and to note their additive inverses. Thus in $Z_5$, 1 and 4 are squares and

$$x^2+4 (= x^2+{}^-1) \quad \text{and} \quad x^2+1 (= x^2+{}^-4)$$

are reducible; but in $Z_7$ 1, 2 and 4 are squares and $x^2+6$, $x^2+5$, and $x^2+3$ are reducible. For $p > 2$, any non-zero element $a$ and its additive inverse $^-a$ are different (since $p$ is odd) but have the same square. Thus there are $\frac{1}{2}(p-1)$ squares (apart from 0) and $\frac{1}{2}(p-1)$ non-squares.

### Exercise F (p. 71)

1.  $x^2$, $x^2+1$, $x^2+2$, $x^2+x$, $x^2+x+1$, $x^2+x+2$, $x^2+2x$, $x^2+2x+1$, $x^2+2x+2$.

   $x^2 = x.x$, $\quad x^2+2 = (x+1).(x+2)$, $\quad x^2+x = x.(x+1)$,
   $x^2+x+1 = (x+2).(x+2)$, $\quad x^2+2x = x.(x+2)$,
   $x^2+2x+1 = (x+1).(x+1)$.

**2.**
$$x = 0 \quad 1 \quad 2,$$
$$x^4+x+1 = 1 \quad 0 \quad 1,$$
$$x^2+x+1 = 1 \quad 0 \quad 1,$$
$$x^4+x+1 = (x+2).(x^3+x^2+x+2),$$
$$x^2+x+1 = (x+2).(x+2).$$

In ordinary arithmetic—that is, in an infinite field—two *different* polynomials cannot have the same values for all $x$. If they did, their difference would not be the zero polynomial but would be zero for all $x$. In a finite field, however, there are non-zero polynomials that are zero for all $x$. In this case

$$x^4+x+1-(x^2+x+1) = x^4-x^2 = x^4+2x^2 = x^2.(x+1).(x+2).$$

Any polynomial of the form $P.x.(x+1).(x+2)$ is zero for all $x$ in this field.

**3.** $x.(x+1).(x+2)$.

**4.** (a) Sum $3x^2+2x+2$; product $2x^4+2x+1$.

(b) Quotient $2x^2+x+2$, remainder 1.

(c) Both are $3x^3+2x+2$. $x^2+2x+3$ is irreducible. (This is most quickly seen by writing it as $x^2+2x+1+2 = (x+1)^2+{}^-3$; 3 is not a square in this field.) Since the factor theorem holds, $3x+4$ and $x+3$ must be the same except for a numerical factor, and indeed $3(x+3) = 3x+4$. Equally

$$2(x+3) = 2x+1, \quad 4(x+3) = 4x+2,$$

so that we may write

$$3x^3+2x+2 = (x+3).(3x^2+x+4)$$
$$= (2x+1).(4x^2+3x+2)$$
$$= (3x+4).(x^2+2x+3)$$
$$= (4x+2).(2x^2+4x+1),$$

but these are not essentially different factorizations, any more than $(x+3).(2x+1)$ and $(2x+6).(x+\frac{1}{2})$ are essentially different in the rational field.

(d) $x^2+1 = (x+{}^-2).(x+2)$;

$2x^2+4x+1 = 2(x^2+2x+3) = 2[(x+1)^2+{}^-3]$ which is irreducible;

$x^2+x+4 = (x+3).(x+3)$;

$2x^3+3x^2+2 = 2, 2, 0, 3, 3$ when $x = 0, 1, 2, 3, 4$;

$x+{}^-2$ is thus a factor (that is, $x+3$) and we find

$$2x^3+3x^2+2 = (x+3).(2x^2+2x+4),$$

the second factor being irreducible.

$x^4+4 = (x^2+1).(x^2+4)$

$\quad\quad = (x+1).(x+4).(x+2).(x+3).$

(e) Yes, as in any field. $P(x) = Q(x) \Rightarrow P(a) = Q(a)$, for all $a$, although the converse is false for finite fields. Hence the proof of the factor theorem is unchanged.

(f) 25, since $a$ and $b$ can each be 0, 1, 2, 3, or 4. There are 5 squares and 10 pairs of different linear factors $(x+a).(x+b)$, so there are 15 pairs of linear factors in all. There must therefore be 10 irreducible quadratics of the form $x^2+ax+b$. We find:

$\quad\quad x^2 = x.x;$

$\quad\quad x^2+1 = x^2+{}^-4 = (x+2).(x+3);$

$\quad\quad x^2+2 =$ irreducible, since 3 is not a square;

$\quad\quad x^2+3 =$ irreducible, since 2 is not a square;

$\quad\quad x^2+4 = x^2+{}^-1 = (x+1).(x+4);$

$\quad\quad x^2+x = x.(x+1);$

$\quad x^2+x+1 = (x+3)^2+2$, irreducible;

$\quad x^2+x+2 = (x+3)^2+3$, irreducible;

$\quad x^2+x+3 = (x+3)^2+4 = (x+2).(x+4);$

$\quad x^2+x+4 = (x+3)^2;$

$\quad\quad x^2+2x = x.(x+2);$

$\quad x^2+2x+1 = (x+1).(x+1);$

$\quad x^2+2x+2 = (x+1)^2+1 = (x+3).(x+4);$

$\quad x^2+2x+3 = (x+1)^2+2$, irreducible;

$\quad x^2+2x+4 = (x+1)^2+3$, irreducible;

$\quad\quad x^2+3x = x.(x+3);$

$\quad x^2+3x+1 = (x+4)^2;$

$\quad x^2+3x+2 = (x+4)^2+1 = (x+1).(x+2);$

$\quad x^2+3x+3 = (x+4)^2+2$, irreducible;

$\quad x^2+3x+4 = (x+4)^2+3$, irreducible;

$$x^2+4x = x.(x+4);$$
$$x^2+4x+1 = (x+2)^2+2, \text{ irreducible};$$
$$x^2+4x+2 = (x+2)^2+3, \text{ irreducible};$$
$$x^2+4x+3 = (x+2)^2+4 = (x+1).(x+3);$$
$$x^2+4x+4 = (x+2)^2.$$

(g) The integers modulo 5 form a *field*; the natural integers only a *ring with unity* (integral domain).

5.  (a) 4 polynomials:

$$x^2; \quad x^2+1 = (x+1).(x+1); \quad x^2+x = x.(x+1);$$

$$x^2+x+1 \text{ irreducible}.$$

(b) 8 polynomials:

$x^3;$                              $\quad x^3+x^2 = x^2.(x+1);$

$x^3+x = x.(x+1).(x+1);$       $\quad x^3+x^2+x = x.(x^2+x+1);$

$x^3+1 = (x+1).(x^2+x+1);$     $\quad x^3+x^2+1 \text{ irreducible};$

$x^3+x+1 \text{ irreducible};$    $\quad x^3+x^2+x+1 = (x+1)^3.$

# 8. RATIONAL NUMBERS

The definition of a rational number as an equivalence class of ordered pairs of natural numbers may seem somewhat sophisticated, but is really implicit when we agree that $\frac{2}{3}, \frac{4}{6}, \frac{6}{9}, \ldots$ are 'different names for the same number'. This is in line with the modern mathematical habit of defining everything in terms of sets: naming classes of objects rather than abstracting properties of those objects. This obviates endless argument as to what a ratio is; to a mathematician it is simply an equivalence class of pairs of natural numbers.

Some teachers may prefer to omit this rather full discussion, but it is essential for what follows to insist on the basic, but sometimes surprisingly unfamiliar, fact, that any expression of a rational number (a 'fraction') can have its numerator and denominator multiplied by the same number and still represent the same rational number (have its 'value' unchanged). The form of words in parentheses is the traditional one, but one may well ask how a number can have a mysterious property called its 'value' which is different, apparently, from the number itself. It seems simpler and more logical to say that the same number can have a large number of different, but equivalent expressions.

The text studiously avoids the language and the practice of 'cancelling' which has almost nothing to be said in its favour. The word is ambiguous, the idea clouds understanding, and the practice is untidy and generates errors. It is better to rewrite than to slaughter what one has written. Those fortunate enough to possess a copy should read Hope-Jones's classic: 'Simplicity and Truthfulness in Arithmetic' in the *Mathematical Gazette* for February 1939; they will never be the same again.

## 9. RATIONAL FORMS

Careful teaching of Section 8 pays dividends in this section. Note once again that the expressions

$$\frac{x-(1/x)}{1-(1/x)}, \quad \frac{x^2-1}{x-1}, \quad \frac{x+1}{1},$$

are different ways of writing the same rational form, but represent different functions of $x$, the first being undefined for $x = 0$ and 1, and the second being undefined for $x = 1$. Formally (that is, when operating on algebraic fractions according to the rules) there is no question of multiplying or dividing by zero; $x-1$ is a polynomial, to be manipulated according to the formal rules; that it has values when $x$ is a real number is (formally) an irrelevance.

Considerable practice may be needed in manipulating rational forms; emphasis should be placed on understanding the principles, and extra examples, if needed, should not be too complicated. If they are, they become a test of endurance in sustaining accuracy rather than of comprehension.

### Exercise G (p. 78)

1. $\dfrac{13x}{6}$.  2. $\dfrac{5x-1}{6}$.  3. $\frac{5}{3}$.  4. $\dfrac{x^2-15}{3x}$.

5. $\dfrac{x^2}{15}$.  6. $\dfrac{1}{8x}$.  7. $\dfrac{20-9x}{x^2}$.  8. 3.

The answers to Questions 9–14 are arranged as follows:

$$A+B \qquad\qquad A-B$$
$$A.B \qquad\qquad A\div B$$

**9.** $\dfrac{3x+5}{(x+2).(x+1)}$ $\qquad\qquad -\dfrac{x+3}{(x+2).(x+1)}$

$\dfrac{2}{(x+2).(x+1)}$ $\qquad\qquad \dfrac{x+1}{2(x+2)}.$

**10.** $\dfrac{2(x^2+4)}{x^2-4}$ $\qquad\qquad \dfrac{-8x}{x^2-4}$

$1$ $\qquad\qquad \dfrac{(x-2)^2}{(x+2)^2}.$

**11.** $\dfrac{1+2x-x^2}{(1+x).(1-x)^2}$ $\qquad\qquad -\dfrac{1+x^2}{(1+x).(1-x)^2}$

$\dfrac{x}{(1+x).(1-x)^3}$ $\qquad\qquad \dfrac{x.(1-x)}{1+x}.$

**12.** $\dfrac{x^2}{5(x-5)}$ $\qquad\qquad \dfrac{x^2-50}{5(x-5)}$

$\dfrac{x+5}{x-5}$ $\qquad\qquad \dfrac{x^2-25}{25}.$

**13.** $\dfrac{2x^2-2x+5}{(x-2).(x-1).(x+1)}$ $\qquad\qquad \dfrac{3(2x-1)}{(x-2).(x-1).(x+1)}$

$\dfrac{1}{(x-1)^2}$ $\qquad\qquad \dfrac{(x+1)^2}{(x-2)^2}.$

**14.** $\dfrac{5x+12}{x.(x+2).(x+3)}$ $\qquad\qquad \dfrac{-1}{(x+2).(x+3)}$

$\dfrac{6}{x^2.(x+2).(x+3)}$ $\qquad\qquad \dfrac{2(x+3)}{3(x+2)}.$

**15.** $\dfrac{x+1}{x},\ \dfrac{x}{x-1},\ \dfrac{-1}{x+1}.$ Sum $=\dfrac{2x^3+x^2-1}{x.(x^2-1)}.$

Product $=\dfrac{1}{1-x}.$

**16.** $x.$ The relation $xy=x+y$ is symmetrical in $x$ and $y.$

### Exercise H (p. 78)

*Miscellaneous*

1. $P = A(x-\alpha).(x-\beta)$ where $A$ is a number. $P(\gamma) = 0 \Rightarrow A = 0$ and $P$ is the zero polynomial.

   If a polynomial of degree $n$ is zero for $n$ different values

   $$\alpha_1, \alpha_2, ..., \alpha_n,$$

   then by the factor theorem

   $$(x-\alpha_1), (x-\alpha_2), ..., (x-\alpha_n)$$

   are factors, and

   $$P = A(x-\alpha_1).(x-\alpha_2).(x-\alpha_3), ..., (x-\alpha_n),$$

   where $A$ is a number. If, in addition, $P(\alpha_{n+1}) = 0$, where $\alpha_{n+1}$ is not equal to any other $\alpha$, then $P$ is the zero polynomial.

2. $P(\alpha) = A(\alpha-\beta)(\alpha-\gamma)$;  $P(\beta) = B(\beta-\alpha)(\beta-\gamma)$; $P(\gamma) = C(\gamma-\alpha)(\gamma-\beta)$.

   Write the quadratic polynomial $P$ as

   $$P = A(x-2).(x-1)+B(x+1).(x-2)+C(x-1).(x+1).$$

   Then
   $$2 = P(-1) = 6A, \quad \text{so that} \quad A = \tfrac{1}{3};$$
   $$3 = P(1) = -2B, \quad \text{so that} \quad B = -\tfrac{3}{2};$$
   and $\quad 1 = P(2) = 3C, \quad \text{so that} \quad C = \tfrac{1}{3}.$

   Hence
   $$P = \tfrac{1}{3}(x-2).(x-1)-\tfrac{3}{2}(x+1).(x-2)+\tfrac{1}{3}(x-1).(x+1)$$
   $$= (-5x^2+3x+20)/6.$$

   This question and the following one are cases of Lagranges's interpolation formula.

3. Let
   $$P = A(x-2).(x-3).(x-4)+B(x-1).(x-3).(x-4)$$
   $$+C(x-1).(x-2).(x-4)+D(x-1).(x-2).(x-3).$$

   Then
   $$3 = P(1) = -6A, \quad \text{so that} \quad A = -\tfrac{1}{2};$$
   $$-2 = P(2) = 2B, \quad \text{so that} \quad B = -1;$$
   $$-3 = P(3) = -2C, \quad \text{so that} \quad C = \tfrac{3}{2};$$
   $$1 = P(4) = 6D, \quad \text{so that} \quad D = \tfrac{1}{6}.$$

4-2

Hence
$$P = -\tfrac{1}{2}(x-2).(x-3).(x-4)-(x-1).(x-3).(x-4)$$
$$+\tfrac{3}{2}(x-1).(x-2).(x-4)+\tfrac{1}{6}(x-1).(x-2).(x-3)$$
$$= (x^3+6x^2-55x+66)/6.$$

4. $P-Q$ is zero for $x = \alpha_1, \alpha_2, \alpha_3, \alpha_4$. Hence, by the factor theorem, if $P$ and $Q$ were two cubics which took equal values for $x = 1, 2, 3, 4$, then $P-Q = (x-1).(x-2).(x-3).(x-4)R$, which is of degree $\geqslant 4$ unless $R$ is the zero polynomial.

Hence, if $P$ and $Q$ are both cubics, $R = 0$ and $P = Q$.

5. $P = 4x^4+2x^3-6x^2-3x+4 = (2x-3).(x+1)Q+rx+s.$

Then
$$P(-1) = 3 = -r+s$$
and
$$P(\tfrac{3}{2}) = 13 = \tfrac{3}{2}r+s$$
$$\Rightarrow r = 4, s = 7.$$

6. $P = (x-\alpha).(x-\beta)Q+rx+s$

$$\Rightarrow \begin{cases} P(\alpha) = r\alpha+s \\ P(\beta) = r\beta+s \end{cases} \Rightarrow r = \frac{P(\alpha)-P(\beta)}{\alpha-\beta}, \quad s = \frac{\beta P(\alpha)-\alpha P(\beta)}{\beta-\alpha}$$

and the remainder is
$$\frac{\{P(\alpha)-P(\beta)\}x+\{\alpha P(\beta)-\beta P(\alpha)\}}{\alpha-\beta},$$
or
$$\frac{P(\alpha).(x-\beta)-P(\beta).(x-\alpha)}{\alpha-\beta},$$

a result sometimes known as the *Chinese remainder theorem*.

7. Reflexivity and symmetry are immediate. To prove transitivity, note that

$P \sim Q \Leftrightarrow P-Q = (x^2+1).M$   for some polynomial $M$;

$Q \sim R \Leftrightarrow Q-R = (x^2+1).N$   for some polynomial $N$;

hence
$$P-R = (x^2+1).(M+N) \quad \text{from which } P \sim R.$$

That each class has only one polynomial of degree less than 2 follows from the process of division by $x^2+1$; or we may argue that if $P \sim Q$ and $P.Q$ have degree $< 2$, then
$$P-Q = (x^2+1).M$$

and the right-hand side has degree $< 2$, which is impossible unless $M$ is zero.

$$a+bj+c+dj = (a+c)+(b+d)j,$$

$$
\begin{aligned}
(a+bx).(c+dx) &= ac+bdx^2+(ad+bc)x \\
&= ac-bd+(ad+bc)x+bd(x^2+1) \\
&\sim ac-bd+(ad+bc)x.
\end{aligned}
$$

Hence

$$(a+bj).(c+dj) = ac-bd+(ad+bc)j;$$

$$(1+0j).(a+bj) = a+bj; \quad (0+0j)+(a+bj) = (a+bj).$$

*Division.*

$$(c+dj).(r+sj) = (a+bj)$$

$$\Rightarrow cr+(cs+dr)x+dsx^2 = a+bx+M.(x^2+1)$$

$$\Rightarrow (cr-ds-a)+(cs+dr-b)x = (M-ds).(x^2+1),$$

which is impossible unless

$$
\begin{cases}
cr-ds = a, \\
cs+dr = b, \\
M-ds \text{ is the zero polynomial.}
\end{cases}
$$

From this we obtain

$$r = \frac{ac+bd}{c^2+d^2}, \quad s = \frac{bc-ad}{c^2+d^2},$$

since $c^2+d^2 \neq 0$ for any rational $c, d$.
Hence $X$ is the class

$$\frac{ac+bd}{c^2+d^2}+\frac{(bc-ad)j}{c^2+d^2}.$$

Alternatively, we may use the facts that:

$$(c+dx).(c-dx)+d^2(1+x^2) = c^2+d^2,$$

$$(c+dx).(d+cx)-cd(1+x^2) = (c^2+d^2)x$$

to obtain, in succession,

$$(c+dx).(ac-adx) \sim a(c^2+d^2),$$

$$(c+dx).(bd+bcx) \sim bx(c^2+d^2),$$

$$(c+dx).\{(ac+bd)+(bc-ad)x\} \sim (a+bx).(c^2+d^2),$$

$$(c+dj).\frac{\{(ac+bd)+(bc-ad)j\}}{c^2+d^2} = a+bj.$$

This is a model of the (rational) complex numbers, which form a field ('behave just like the numbers of ordinary arithmetic') which is a quadratic extension of the rational field by adjoining $j$ as a root of $x^2+1 = 0$ ('$j^2 = -1$').

8. This is another quadratic extension of the rational field.

$$\omega^2 = -1-\omega \Leftrightarrow x^2 = -1-x+(x^2+x+1).$$

$$(a+bx).(c+dx) = ac+(ad+bc)x-bd(1+x)+bd(x^2+x+1)$$

$$= ac-bd+(ad+bc-bd)x+bd(x^2+x+1)$$

$$\Rightarrow (a+b\omega).(c+d\omega) = ac-bd+(ad+bc-bd)\omega.$$

$$\Rightarrow (0+1\omega).(0+1\omega) = -1-\omega.$$

For division, either solve for $r, s$ the equations obtained from $(a+b\omega).(r+s\omega) = c+d\omega$ by equating the coefficients, or use the identities:

$$(a+bx).(a-b-bx)+b^2(1+x+x^2) = a^2-ab+b^2,$$

$$(a+bx).(ax+b)-ab(1+x+x^2) = (a^2-ab+b^2)x.$$

$$\frac{c+d\omega}{a+b\omega} = \frac{ac-bc+bd+(ad-bc)\omega}{a^2-ab+b^2},$$

$$x^3-1 = (x-1).(x^2+x+1) \Rightarrow x^3 \sim 1 \Rightarrow \omega^3 = 1.$$

Any field can be extended in this way by adjoining to its elements a root of a quadratic irreducible in the field. Thus we may adjoin $\sqrt{2}$ to the rational field $Q$ and obtain the field of elements $a+b\sqrt{2}$, $a, b \in Q$. The complex number field $C$ includes all such extensions; no polynomial is irreducible in $C$.

9. Here we extend a finite field; the result is called a *Galois Field*. Such fields exist with $p^n$ elements, for all primes $p$ and all integers $n$; here $p = 2$ and $n = 2$.

There are only four linear polynomials over this field $\{0, 1\}$; they are $0, 1, x, x+1$ and these four possible remainders characterize the classes.

| + | 0 | 1 | $\omega$ | $\alpha$ |   | $\times$ | 1 | $\omega$ | $\alpha$ |
|---|---|---|---|---|---|---|---|---|---|
| 0 | 0 | 1 | $\omega$ | $\alpha$ |   | 1 | 1 | $\omega$ | $\alpha$ |
| 1 | 1 | 0 | $\alpha$ | $\omega$ |   | $\omega$ | $\omega$ | $\alpha$ | 1 |
| $\omega$ | $\omega$ | $\alpha$ | 0 | 1 |   | $\alpha$ | $\alpha$ | 1 | $\omega$ |
| $\alpha$ | $\alpha$ | $\omega$ | 1 | 0 |   |   |   |   |   |

Both these tables are tables of commutative groups; each element is its own additive inverse, and $\omega$ and $\alpha$ are multiplicative inverses (reciprocals) of each other.

10. If $AB = 0$ and $B$ is not the zero polynomial, then $B$ has value zero only for a finite number of values of $x$. For all but this finite set of values, $A(x)$ must be zero. But this is impossible (see Question 1) unless $A$ is the zero polynomial. (This proof is of course invalid for finite fields.) We may also prove it directly without using values. If

$$A = (a_0, a_1, a_2, ..., a_n) \quad \text{and} \quad B = (b_0, b_1, b_2, ..., b_m),$$

then

$$0 = A.B = (a_0 b_0, a_0 b_1 + a_1 b_0, a_0 b_2 + a_1 b_1 + a_2 b_0, ...).$$

Hence

$$a_0 b_0 = 0 \quad (0),$$
$$a_0 b_1 + a_1 b_0 = 0 \quad (1),$$
$$a_0 b_2 + a_1 b_1 + a_2 b_0 = 0 \quad (2),$$
................................

Suppose $B$ is not the zero polynomial, and let $b_r$ be its first non-zero coefficient.

Then
$$a_0 b_r = 0 \quad (r) \quad \Rightarrow a_0 = 0,$$
so that
$$a_0 b_{r+1} + a_1 b_r = 0 \quad (r+1) \Rightarrow a_1 = 0,$$
so that
$$a_0 b_{r+2} + a_1 b_{r+1} + a_2 b_r = 0 \quad (r+2) \Rightarrow a_2 = 0,$$

and so on, so that $A$ is the zero polynomial.

An indirect proof is even simpler; if neither $A$ nor $B$ is 0, let $A$ have its first non-zero term $a_r x^r$, and $B$ have its first non-zero term $b_s x^s$. Then $AB$ begins $a_r b_s x^{r+s} + ...$ and cannot be 0, since $a_r b_s \neq 0$.

$$A.P = B.P \Rightarrow (A-B).P = 0 \Rightarrow A-B = 0 \text{ if } P \neq 0 \Rightarrow A = B.$$

11. $(a_6 x^6 + a_5 x^5 + ...) = (x-k)(c_5 x^5 + c_4 x^4 + c_3 x^3 + c_2 x^2 + c_1 x + c_0) + r$

$$\Rightarrow a_6 = c_5, \qquad \Rightarrow \quad c_5 = a_6,$$
$$a_5 = c_4 - kc_5, \qquad c_4 = a_5 + kc_5,$$
$$a_4 = c_3 - kc_4, \qquad c_3 = a_4 + kc_4,$$
$$a_3 = c_2 - kc_3, \qquad c_2 = a_3 + kc_3,$$
$$a_2 = c_1 - kc_2, \qquad c_1 = a_2 + kc_2,$$
$$a_1 = c_0 - kc_1, \qquad c_0 = a_1 + kc_1,$$
$$a_0 = r - kc_0, \qquad r = a_0 + kc_0.$$

55

Write
$$2 \quad -3 \quad +0 \quad +1 \quad -4 \quad +0 \quad +5,$$
$$\underset{1}{+4} \diagup \underset{2}{+2} \diagup \underset{5}{+4} \diagup \underset{6}{+10} \diagup \underset{12}{+12} \diagup \underset{29}{+24}$$

giving quotient as $2x^5 + x^4 + 2x^3 + 5x^2 + 6x + 12$ and remainder 29. This is called *Horner's Synthetic Division*.

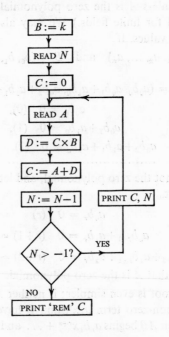

12. This is the nesting process of §6.1 applied to compute the remainder which is $P(k)$. This establishes the Remainder Theorem once again.

13. $A = B(x-k) + r_0 = (C(x-k) + r_1)(x-k) + r_0$
$$= C(x-k)^2 + r_1(x-k) + r_0 = \dots$$
$$= F(x-k)^5 + r_4(x-k)^4 + r_3(x-k)^3 + r_2(x-k)^2 + r_1(x-k) + r_0.$$

From coefficients of $x^5$, $F = a_5$.

We may also observe that if $A = f(x)$, then $r_0 = f(k)$, $r_1 = f'(k)$,

56

$r_2 = f''(k)/2!$, $r_3 = f'''(k)/3!$, and so on. This is in fact a special case of Taylor's Theorem.

$$
\begin{array}{rrrrrr}
3 & +\,2 & +\,4 & +\,0 & -\,1 & +\,5 \\
  & +\,6 & +\,16 & +\,40 & +\,80 & +158 \\
\hline
  & 8 & 20 & 40 & 79 & 163 = r_0 \\
  & +\,6 & +\,28 & +96 & +272 & \\
\hline
  & 14 & 48 & 136 & 351 = r_1 & \\
  & +\,6 & +\,40 & +176 & & \\
\hline
  & 20 & 88 & 312 = r_2 & & \\
  & +\,6 & +\,52 & & & \\
\hline
  & 26 & 140 = r_3 & & & \\
  & +\,6 & & & & \\
\hline
  & 32 = r_4 & & & & \\
3 = r_5 & & & & & \\
\hline
\end{array}
$$

$$A = 3(x-2)^5 + 32(x-2)^4 + 140(x-2)^3 + 312(x-2)^2 + 351(x-2) + 163.$$

This is the method used when a number is converted from one scale of notation to another.

For example, to express $43\,70182_9$ in scale 7, we divide successively (in scale 9) by 7. We obtain

$$
\begin{array}{r|l}
7 & 4370182 \\
7 & 561275+3 \\
7 & 72674+4 \\
7 & 10348+2 \\
7 & 1306+2 \\
7 & 164+5 \\
7 & 21+6 \\
  & 2+5 \\
\end{array}
$$

The number is therefore $256\,52243_7$. We have expressed

$$4 \times 9^6 + 3 \times 9^5 + 7 \times 9^4 + 1 \times 9^2 + 8 \times 9 + 2$$

as

$$2 \times 7^7 + 5 \times 7^6 + 6 \times 7^5 + 5 \times 7^4 + 2 \times 7^3 + 2 \times 7^2 + 4 \times 7 + 3.$$

**14.** (a) True: $(P+R)-(Q+R) = P-Q$.

(b) True: $(P-R) = (P-Q)+(Q-R)$, and the sum of two polynomials whose highest terms are positive must have its highest term positive. (Check when they have the same degree and when they have different degrees.)

(c) 'If' is clearly true, since $P.R-Q.R = (P-Q).R$, and the product of two upper grade polynomials is upper grade.

If $R$ is the zero polynomial or if $0 \Rightarrow R$ then $P.R \Rightarrow Q.R$ is false when $P \Rightarrow Q$; the $\Rightarrow$ is false, and 'only if' is proved.

$P \Rightarrow 0 \Rightarrow P(x) > 0$ for all *sufficiently large* $x$, but there is no $x$ for which $P(x) > 0$ for all polynomials $P$.

Every integer has an immediate successor under the order relation $>$; this is not true of polynomials under $\Rightarrow$ unless the coefficients are restricted to be integers. Furthermore, even in this last case, the polynomials are not 'well-ordered', that is, unlike the integers, they have subsets with no 'least' member. For example, there is no 'lowest grade' quadratic.

**15.** For this method of developing the integers see, for example, Irving Adler, *The New Mathematics*, or W. W. Sawyer, *A Concrete Approach to Abstract Algebra*.

# 4

# FUNCTION

In this chapter the idea of function as a mapping is introduced and applied to a wide variety of situations. Special attention to functions which can be represented by an $(x, y)$ graph (i.e. functions whose range and domain are subsets of the real numbers) is deferred until Chapter 5. It is hoped that in this way the pupils will appreciate the concept in greater generality, so that they recognize it when they meet (for example) the relation of a region of a plane to its area, an event to its probability, or an instant of time to the position vector of a particle, as well as in formulae expressed in the form $y = f(x)$. The work on geometrical transformations in the main school course, and the notation there developed, furnishes additional experience on which to build. This approach should make easier the transition at a more advanced level to functions of complex variables (mappings from $C \to C$), functions of several real variables (mappings from $R^n \to R$), and so on.

Properly a function is specified by a domain $D$, a codomain $\Delta$, and a relation between elements of $D$ and elements of $\Delta$; this relation can be delineated, as in Section 4.3 of Chapter 1, by a set of ordered pairs $(x, \xi)$ where $x \in D$ and $\xi \in \Delta$. If either $D$ or $\Delta$ is changed, we have a different function. Thus the function $f_1: x \to x+1$ mapping the integers into the integers is different from the function $f_2: x \to x+1$ mapping the integers into the real numbers, even though the pairs $(x, x+1)$ are precisely the same for the two functions. The purpose of the distinction may become clearer if we point out that $f_1$ defines an inverse function whereas $f_2$ does not (since there are elements of the codomain of $f_2$ which are not the images of any element of its domain). It would be inappropriate to stress these finer points of detail at this elementary level; but the teacher will find that, by keeping the distinction in his own mind, he will be able to expound the theory with greater clarity and precision.

59

## 1. THE CONCEPT OF FUNCTION
### *Exercise A (p. 87)*

Possible domains and codomains for those which define functions might be:

| | Domain | Codomain |
|---|---|---|
| **1.** | Points of space | Non-negative real numbers |
| **2.** | Words defined in the O.E.D. | Natural numbers |
| **4.** | Natural numbers $> 1$ | Sets of prime numbers |
| **5.** | Points of space | Points of space |
| **6.** | Pairs of real numbers | Real numbers |
| **7.** | *Non-negative* real numbers | *Non-negative* real numbers |
| **8.** | Points of the circle | Lines through $O$ |
| **10.** | Subsets of $\mathscr{E}$ | Subsets of $\mathscr{E}$ |
| **11.** | Natural numbers | Natural numbers |
| **12.** | *Non-zero* polynomials | Non-negative integers |
| **13.** | Real numbers | Real numbers |
| **14.** | Polynomials | Real numbers |
| **15.** | Real numbers *excluding* 1, 2 | Real numbers |
| **16.** | Real numbers *excluding* 1 | Real numbers |

Note the restrictions in Questions 7, 12, 15, 16 needed to define a function.

One could even devise a domain and codomain in which:

**3.** The point $A$ is one inch from the point $B$

defines a function: for example, they might both consist of just two points $P$, $Q$ an inch apart; the mapping would then be defined completely by $P \to Q$, $Q \to P$. But in ordinary space, for example, any point $A$ has a large number of points $B$ an inch away from it, so 'points of space' would not be suitable as domain and codomain.

60

In Question 9 there may be several boys in the class who take a particular size of shoe, and some shoe-sizes may not be represented at all, so that the conditions for a function are not satisfied. On the other hand,

boy in the class $\rightarrow$ size of shoe

does define a function with domain the set of boys in the class and codomain the set of shoe sizes.

## 2. SOME NOTATION AND TERMINOLOGY

### Exercise B (p. 93)

1. For example, $D = \Delta = R$.
   $f(-2) = -4$, $f(0) = 2$, $f(2) = 8$.
   Image of $\{x: 0 < x < 1\}$ is $\{\xi: 2 < \xi < 5\}$.
   $1 \rightarrow 5$, $-\frac{2}{3} \rightarrow 0$.

2. For example, $D = \{$real numbers excluding $-1\}$, $\Delta = \{$real numbers$\}$.
   $f(-2) = -1$, $f(0) = 1$, $f(2) = \frac{1}{3}$.
   Image of $\{x: 0 < x < 1\}$ is $\{\xi: \frac{1}{2} < \xi < 1\}$.
   $-0.8 \rightarrow 5$, no element of the domain has image 0.

3. $f(B) = \{\beta, \beta\gamma, \gamma\}$; $f(G) = \{\alpha, \beta\}$.

4. Powers of prime numbers.

5. (a) $f(D) = \{\xi: \xi \geqslant 0\}$, $f(X) = \{\xi: 0 \leqslant \xi < 4\}$;
   (b) $f(D) = \{\xi: \xi \geqslant 1\}$, $f(X) = \{\xi: 1 \leqslant \xi < 5\}$;
   (c) $f(D) = \{\xi: 0 < \xi \leqslant 1\}$, $f(X) = \{\xi: 0.2 < \xi \leqslant 1\}$.

6. $\{\xi: 0 < \xi \leqslant 1\}$.

7. $0, 0, 0$. (Note that $x^3 + 2x = x.(x+1).(x+2)$ and one of these factors must be zero.)
   (a) $x+1$; (b) $(x+1)^2 = x^2 + 2x + 1$; (c) $1$.
   For polynomials of degree greater than 2, add $(x^3 + 2x).Q$ to the above polynomials, where $Q$ is any non-zero polynomial whatever.

**8.**

| | | Number of mappings | |
|---|---|---|---|
| $n(D)$ | $n(\Delta)$ | $D$ into $\Delta$ | $D$ onto $\Delta$ |
| 3 | 4 | $4^3$ | 0 |
| 4 | 4 | $4^4$ | $4! = 24$ |
| 4 | 3 | $3^4$ | 36 |

Notice that if $n(D) = a$, $n(\Delta) = b$, then the number of distinct mappings of $D$ into $\Delta$ is $b^a$. Thus the meaning of exponentiation can be expressed in the language of sets—a point of view which comes to be of importance in the theory of 'transfinite numbers'. For example, the symbol $\aleph_0$ ('aleph zero') is used to denote the cardinal number of countable sets such as the natural numbers (see Chapter 2, Section 4.2). $2^{\aleph_0}$ would then be the number of distinct mappings of the natural numbers onto a set of two elements such as $\{0, 1\}$. Since any such function could be coded as a binary fraction (e.g. the function

$$1 \to 0, \quad 2 \to 1, \quad 3 \to 1, \quad 4 \to 1, \quad 5 \to 0, \quad 6 \to 1, \quad \ldots$$

could be coded as 0·011101...) we can set up a correspondence between the functions and all binary proper fractions; this shows that $2^{\aleph_0}$ is the cardinal number of the set of real numbers between 0 and 1. (We have ignored a minor complication about recurring binary fractions: some real numbers can be written in two forms —for example, 0·1011 can also be written 0·1010i̇ in binary notation.) For an account of transfinite arithmetic, see G. Birkhoff and S. MacLane, *A Survey of Modern Algebra* (Macmillan), Chapter XII; or, in lighter vein, E. P. Northrop, *Riddles in Mathematics* (English University Press), Chapter 7.

**10.** (*a*) Into; (*b*) into; (*c*) onto (unless $a = b = 0$, when the mapping is into).

**11.**

| $f(p$ and $q)$ | | | | $f(p$ or $q$ or both$)$ | | |
|---|---|---|---|---|---|---|
| | | $f(q)$ | | | | $f(q)$ |
| | | $T$ | $F$ | | $T$ | $F$ |
| $f(p)$ | $T$ | $T$ | $F$ | $f(p)$ $T$ | $T$ | $T$ |
| | $F$ | $F$ | $F$ | $F$ | $T$ | $F$ |

|          | $f$(not-$p$ or q or both) | | | $f$(neither $p$ nor $q$) | |
| --- | --- | --- | --- | --- | --- |
|          | $f(q)$ | | | $f(q)$ | |
|          | T | F | | T | F |
| $f(p)\begin{cases}T\\F\end{cases}$ | T | F | $f(p)\begin{cases}T\\F\end{cases}$ | F | F |
|          | T | T | | F | T |

# 4. FUNCTIONS WHICH PRESERVE STRUCTURE

## *Exercise C (p. 103)*

**1.** For example:

(*a*) $u_n = -n$.

(*b*) $0, 1, -1, 2, -2, ...$, that is,

$$u_n = \begin{cases} \tfrac{1}{2}-\tfrac{1}{2}n & \text{if } n \text{ is odd,} \\ \tfrac{1}{2}n & \text{if } n \text{ is even;} \end{cases}$$

or $\qquad u_n = \tfrac{1}{4}\{1+(-1)^n(2n-1)\}$.

(*c*) $2, 3, 5, 7, 11, ...$; that is, $u_n$ is the $n$th prime number, for which there is no algebraic formula. (We are using here the fact that there are infinitely many prime numbers, see S.M.P. *Book T*, Chapter 1, Section 1.2.)

(*d*) $u_n = (-1)^n$.

**2.** (*a*) $u_n = 3n-1$;     (*b*) $u_n = 3.2^{n-1}$.

**3.** (*a*)                       (*b*)

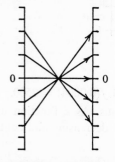 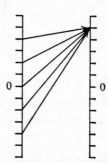

Fig. A. Reversal about $x = 0$.     Fig. B. Condensing to a single point.

*(c)*                                      *(d)*

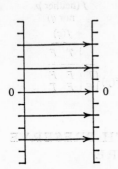 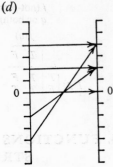

Fig. C. Stay-put.         Fig. D. Pinning down at $x = 0$ and reversing lower half.

4. (*a*) Translation of displacement $-4$;
   (*b*) reflection in $x = 2$;
   (*c*) enlargement from $x = 0$ of factor $\frac{1}{2}$;
   (*d*) enlargement from $x = 1$ of factor 3.

5. Take both domain and codomain as the non-negative real numbers. The relation defines a strictly increasing function.

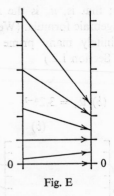

Fig. E

6. No, but it does map $R^* \to R^*$.
   Take, for example, $f(0 \cdot 001) = 1000$, $f(0 \cdot 0004) = 2500$.
   Not strictly increasing or continuous. As a function mapping $R^+ \to R^+$, or $R^- \to R^-$, it is strictly decreasing and continuous.

7. (*a*) $\{\xi : 1 < \xi < 4\}$.
   (*b*) $\{x : -\sqrt{2} < x < -1\} \cup \{x : 1 < x < \sqrt{2}\}$.

8. (a) Reflection in the $x_1$-axis;
   (b) reflection in $(0, 0)$ (enlargement of factor $-1$);
   (c) projection on the $x_1$-axis;
   (d) stretches of ratio $a, b$ parallel to $x_1$- and $x_2$-axes.

   Mappings (a) and (b) are 'onto', also (d) unless either $a$ or $b$ is zero; (c) is not. All are continuous, but they cannot be described as increasing since an order relation is not defined on $R^2$.

9. Many functions map $R^2$ onto $R$, such as $(x_1, x_2) \to x_1$, $(x_1, x_2) \to x_1^3 + x_2^3$.

   A function which maps $R$ onto $R^2$ can be constructed by the following arithmetical procedure. Write any element of $R$ in decimal form, and take alternate digits to form the $x_1$- and $x_2$-coordinates of an element of $R^2$, assigning the units digit to $x_2$; for example,

   $$37 \to (3, 7), \quad 842{\cdot}62 \to (4{\cdot}6, 82{\cdot}2), \quad 3{\cdot}14159 \to (0{\cdot}119, 3{\cdot}45),$$

   etc. Then a function is defined, since every real number can be processed in this way; and the mapping is 'onto', since from any member of $R^2$ one can construct a real number which gives rise to it—for example, $(1{\cdot}414, 2{\cdot}718)$ comes from the element $12{\cdot}471148$ of the domain. (There is a minor complication in that numerals such as $1{\cdot}0$ and $0{\cdot}\dot{9}$ are alternative decimal representations for the same number. Thus the rule would give

   $$0{\cdot}34\dot{9} \to (0{\cdot}3\dot{9}, 0{\cdot}4\dot{9}),$$

   which is the same as $(0{\cdot}4, 0{\cdot}5)$; but $0{\cdot}35 \to (0{\cdot}3, 0{\cdot}5)$. This can be overcome by adopting a suitable convention to handle such exceptions.)

11. $\forall\, a, b \in D, \quad a < b \Rightarrow f(a) > f(b)$.

12.

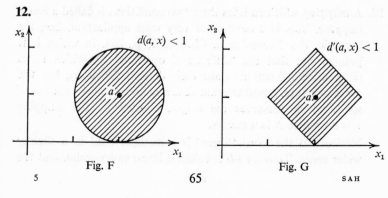

Fig. F          Fig. G

**14.** The domain is the set of pairs of points in the given domain; the codomain is the set of non-negative real numbers.

**15.** If the digits are separated as (3, 4, 1, 7), (2, 4, 1, 8), etc., then each telephone number can be regarded as a point of a lattice in four-dimensional space (in fact as a point of $T^4$, where

$$T = \{0, 1, 2, ..., 9\}).$$

The 'distance' described is precisely the same as the New York distance $d'$, defined in Section 4.3, extended into four dimensions. The possible values of $x$ such that $d'(x, 1903) = 1$ are 0903, 2903, 1803, 1913, 1902, 1904. If the numerals round the dial run consecutively from 0 to 9, these are all the wrong numbers that would be obtainable by dialling just one digit 'one hole off'.

**16.** Measures $(a)$, $(d)$, $(e)$, $(f)$ satisfy the conditions (provided that in $(e)$ we interpret $d(a, a)$ to be zero).

In $(b)$ the triangle law does not always hold. Thus to go $1\frac{1}{2}$ km it would pay to take two journeys of $\frac{3}{4}$ km each. With a different scale of charges (e.g. 10p, 15p, 20p, or a flat rate for any journey) the conditions could be fulfilled.

In $(c)$ it is probable that, between some pairs of points, $d(a, b) \neq d(b, a)$.

**17.** It may not be *strictly* increasing. For example, the function defined by

$$f(x) = \begin{cases} x & \text{if } x < 0, \\ 0 & \text{if } 0 \leqslant x \leqslant 1, \\ x-1 & \text{if } x > 1 \end{cases}$$

satisfies the conditions.

**18.** A mapping which satisfies these two conditions is called a *linear mapping*. This is a concept of very wide application. See, for example, the discussion in Chapter 7, p. 208, in which it is pointed out that the 'differential operator' $D$, which maps differentiable functions onto their derived functions, has the same structure. Another example is any linear transformation of space which preserves the origin, effected by the mapping $\mathbf{v} \to \mathbf{A}\mathbf{v}$ where $\mathbf{A}$ is a matrix.

Notice that the word 'linear' is sometimes used in a slightly wider sense. Thus $ax+b$ is called a linear polynomial, and the function $x \to ax+b$ from the real numbers to the real numbers is often called a linear function (because it possesses a straight line graph). Again, the more general transformation of space $\mathbf{v} \to A\mathbf{v}+\mathbf{b}$, in which the origin moves to the point with position vector $\mathbf{b}$, is still called a linear transformation (because it transforms straight lines into straight lines). But these functions do not possess the two attributes of linearity, viz.

$$kx \overset{f}{\to} kf(x) \quad \text{and} \quad x+y \overset{f}{\to} f(x)+f(y),$$

which constitute the conditions for a linear mapping (unless $b = 0$ in the first case, $\mathbf{b} = \mathbf{0}$ in the second). It is therefore important, when the word 'linear' is encountered, to make sure whether it is being used in the wide sense of a linear polynomial function or a linear transformation, or in the more restricted sense of a linear mapping as here described.

**19.** The measure $d'$ is invariant under translation, rotation through multiples of 90°, and reflection in lines parallel to the lines $x_1 = 0$, $x_2 = 0$, $x_1 = x_2$, $x_1 = -x_2$.

## 6. INVERSE IMAGES; PRINCIPAL VALUES
### *Exercise D (p. 110)*

**2.** $\{\frac{2}{3}\}$; $\{1, 2\}$; $\{-2, 1\}$.     **3.** $\{0, 2\}$; $\{1\}$; ∅.

**4.** $\{-2, 2\}$; $\{0\}$; ∅.

**5.** $3, 2, 5, 0, 2, -2, -3, -1$.

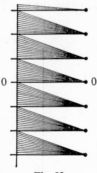

$\{x : 4 \leqslant x < 5\}$.

Fig. H

**6.** $2, 2\frac{1}{2}, \frac{1}{2}(3+\alpha)$.   $\xi \to \frac{1}{2}(3+\xi)$.

Where the inverse image of an element $\alpha$ is, as in Question 6, a single element $a$ of the domain, it is unimportant whether it is written $a$ or $\{a\}$. The most consistent way of presenting the work on inverse images is to use set notation throughout. For example, suppose that $f$ denotes the function from $R \to R$

$$f: x \to 2x - x^2$$

(cf. Question 3). Then we may write

$$f(0) = 0, \quad f(1) = 1, \quad f(2) = 0,$$

but $\qquad f(\{0, 1, 2\}) = \{0, 1\}, \quad f(\{0, 2\}) = \{0\}.$

One should perhaps, therefore, speak of the inverse image of $\{0\}$ (rather than of 0) as $\{0, 2\}$ and the inverse image of $\{1\}$ as $\{1\}$. But it would be pedantic to preserve the distinction.

7. $D =$ set of real numbers excluding $-1$, $\Delta =$ set of real numbers excluding 0.

The inverse image of $\alpha$ is $(1-\alpha)/\alpha$, so that the formula for the inverse function is $\xi \to (1-\xi)/\xi$.

8. The inverse image of $\alpha$ is the set of ordered pairs of real numbers whose sum is $\alpha$, represented by points of the line $x_1 + x_2 = \alpha$. No inverse function exists.

9. (a) $\{x: 1/\beta < x < 1/\alpha\};$ \qquad (b) $\{x: x > 1/\beta\} \cup \{x: x < 1/\alpha\}.$

Questions 10–14 are designed for the more able pupils. Their purpose is to lead the student towards an appreciation of the concept of continuity. The treatment of function in this chapter makes it possible to discuss continuity in greater generality than is usual at this level, and thus to pave the way for more advanced study later on.

10. (a) \qquad\qquad (b) \qquad\qquad (c)

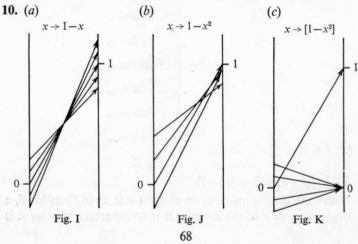

$x \to 1-x$ \qquad $x \to 1-x^2$ \qquad $x \to [1-x^2]$

Fig. I \qquad\qquad Fig. J \qquad\qquad Fig. K

(d)    (e)    (f)

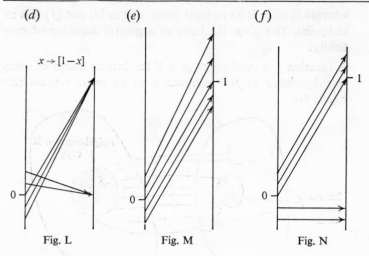

Fig. L                Fig. M                Fig. N

(a), (b), (e) are continuous at 0.

Inverse images are:

(a) $\{x: -0\cdot1 < x < 0\cdot1\}$;        (b) $\{x: -0\cdot32 < x < 0\cdot32\}$;

(c) $\{0\}$;        (d) $\{x: -1 < x \leqslant 0\}$;

(e) $\{x: -0\cdot1 < x < 0\cdot05\}$;        (f) $\{x: 0 \leqslant x < 0\cdot1\}$.

The designation of some of these inverse images may provoke dissent. In (b), for example, the image of $\{x: -0\cdot32 < x < 0\cdot32\}$ under the mapping $x \to 1-x^2$ is not $\{\xi: 0\cdot9 < \xi < 1\cdot1\}$ but $\{\xi: 0\cdot9 < \xi \leqslant 1\}$. In fact there are no real numbers $x$ whose image under the function is greater than 1. Can we therefore speak at all of the inverse image of $\{\xi: 0\cdot9 < \xi < 1\cdot1\}$?

This is a matter of definition. If $\Sigma$ is a subset of the codomain, then the inverse image of $\Sigma$ under $f$ is the set of elements $x$ of the domain such that $f(x) \in \Sigma$. The answers given above are based on this definition. It follows that, if the complete inverse image of $\Sigma$ is $S$, then

$$x \in S \Rightarrow f(x) \in \Sigma,$$

so that

$$f(S) \subset \Sigma;$$

but it may not be true that $f(S) = \Sigma$. (In fact, $f(S)$ is the intersection of $\Sigma$ and the range of the function.)

It will be noticed that in the three continuous cases (a), (b) and (e) the number 0 is an interior point of the inverse image;

69

whereas in (c) it is an isolated point, and in (d) and (f) it is an end-point. This gives the basis of a general definition of continuity:

A function f is continuous at a if the inverse image of every neighbourhood of f(a) contains a as an interior point (see Figure O).

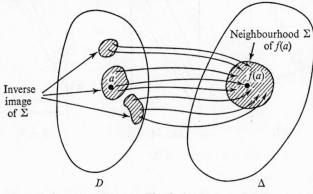

**Fig. O**

This definition is applicable not just to functions mapping $R \to R$, but to any function in whose domain and codomain a notion of distance obtains (that is, if these sets are 'metric spaces'); and it can be extended to even more general topological spaces.

Questions 11–14 develop this theme in further detail for functions mapping $R \to R$, $R^2 \to R^2$ and $R^2 \to R$. It is taken up again in Chapter 5, Section 9 (Book 1, pp. 155–9) and illustrated there with an $(x, y)$ graph.

**11.** 0·7, 0·7, 0·99, 0. Each interval $\{x: n \leqslant x < n+1\}$, where $n$ is an integer, is translated to the interval $\{\xi: 0 \leqslant \xi < 1\}$.

$$d(\xi, f(2\cdot 7)) < 0\cdot 01 \iff 0\cdot 69 < \xi < 0\cdot 71.$$

The inverse image under f is the union of an infinite set of intervals

$$\ldots \cup \{x: -0\cdot 31 < x < -0\cdot 29\} \cup \{x: 0\cdot 69 < x < 0\cdot 71\}$$
$$\cup \{x: 1\cdot 69 < x < 1\cdot 71\} \cup \{x: 2\cdot 69 < x < 2\cdot 71\} \cup \ldots.$$

The number 2·7 is an interior point of this inverse image (see Figure P).

On the other hand, $d(\xi, f(2)) < 0.01 \Leftrightarrow -0.01 < \xi < 0.01$. The inverse image is the union of intervals

$$\ldots \cup \{x: -1 \leqslant x < -0.99\} \cup \{x: 0 \leqslant x < 0.01\}$$
$$\cup \{x: 1 \leqslant x < 1.01\} \cup \{x: 2 \leqslant x < 2.01\} \cup \ldots.$$

The number 2 is an end-point of one of the constituent intervals, not an interior point (see Figure Q). The significance of this result is that the function $x \to x - [x]$ is continuous at 2·7 but not at 2.

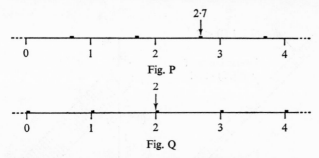

Fig. P

Fig. Q

**12.** $d(\xi, f(2)) < 0.1 \Leftrightarrow 0.15 < \xi < 0.35$. The inverse image is the union of two intervals

$$\{x: -2.58 < x < -1.69\} \cup \{x: 1.69 < x < 2.58\},$$

which contains 2 as an interior point (see Figure R). $\delta = 0.31$ satisfies the conditions, or any smaller positive number.

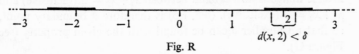

Fig. R

**13.** Stretches of factors 2, 3 parallel to the $x_1$- and $x_2$-axes respectively. The inverse image is the interior of an ellipse. Choose $\delta$ less than 0·06 (see Figure S).

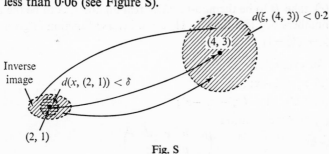

Fig. S

**14.** For $(x_1, x_2) \to x_1 + x_2$ the inverse image is a band between lines $x_1 + x_2 = 1\cdot9$ and $x_1 + x_2 = 2\cdot1$. The region $d(x, (0\cdot5, 1\cdot5)) < \delta$ lies within this provided that $\delta$ is not greater than $0\cdot1/\sqrt2$, or about $0\cdot07$. This demonstrates that $(0\cdot5, 1\cdot5)$ is an interior point of the inverse image, so that the function is continuous at $(0\cdot5, 1\cdot5)$ (see Figure T).

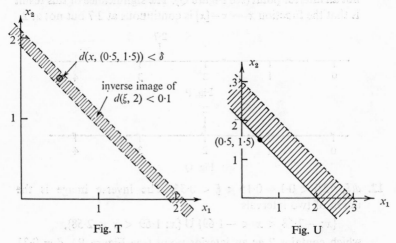

Fig. T  Fig. U

For $(x_1, x_2) \to [x_1 + x_2]$ the image of $(0\cdot5, 1\cdot5)$ is again 2, but the inverse image is now a band between $x_1 + x_2 = 2$ (inclusive) and $x_1 + x_2 = 3$ (exclusive). $(0\cdot5, 1\cdot5)$ is therefore a boundary point, so that no number $\delta$ can be found with the given property (see Figure U).

**15.** (a) $\xi \to \xi - 5$;

(b) $(\xi_1, \xi_2) \to (-\tfrac13\xi_2, \tfrac13\xi_1)$;

(c) take $D$ to be the non-negative real numbers, $\Delta$ to be the real numbers not less than 1. Then the inverse function is given by $\xi \to \sqrt{(\xi - 1)}$.

**16.** For example:

(a) $x \to k - x$;

(b) $(x, y, z) \to (x, -y, -z)$;

(c) the permutation
$$\begin{pmatrix} a & b & c & d & e \\ b & a & e & d & c \end{pmatrix}.$$

**17.** For a permutation there must be just one 1 in each row, and just one 1 in each column.

For a general function there must be just one 1 in each row.

**18.** $5! = 120.$        **19.** $-90°, 120°, 0°, 0°.$

**20.** The domain might be $\{x: 0 \leqslant x \leqslant 1\}$ and the codomain $\{\xi: 0 \leqslant \xi \leqslant 1\}$ (see Figure V). Then $f^{-1}(0{\cdot}3) = 0{\cdot}3$. With 'odd' for 'even' we might take the same domain and codomain, but $f^{-1}(0{\cdot}3) = 0{\cdot}7$ (see Figure W).

(The functions are periodic. The slight resemblance to the sine and cosine functions helps to suggest the restrictions to be imposed.)

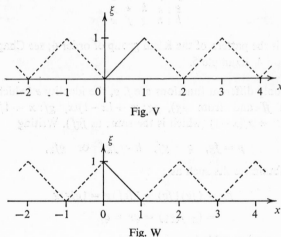

Fig. V

Fig. W

# 8. INVERSES OF COMPOSITE FUNCTIONS

### *Exercise E (p. 116)*

**1.** Exclude 0 from the domain of $f$, $-1$ from the domain of $g$.

$\tfrac{1}{2}, 3, 1\tfrac{1}{2}, \tfrac{1}{3}, 2, 4;$    $1/a, 1+a, (a+1)/a, 1/(1+a), a, 2+a.$

$$gf: x \to \frac{x+1}{x}, \quad fg: x \to \frac{1}{1+x}, \quad ff: x \to x, \quad gg: x \to 2+x.$$

**2.** Reflections in 0, 1.

$gf: x \to 2+x$, demonstrating that successive reflections in two parallel mirrors effects a translation through twice the distance between them.

**4.** $fg: \begin{pmatrix} x \\ y \end{pmatrix} \to \begin{pmatrix} a & b \\ c & d \end{pmatrix} \begin{pmatrix} p & q \\ r & s \end{pmatrix} \begin{pmatrix} x \\ y \end{pmatrix} = \begin{pmatrix} ap+br & aq+bs \\ cp+dr & cq+ds \end{pmatrix} \begin{pmatrix} x \\ y \end{pmatrix}.$

**5.** (a) $qs$;   (b) $sq$;   (c) $sqs$;   (d) $qq$;   (e) $sqq$;   (f) $ss$.

**6.**

|   | e | f | g | h |
|---|---|---|---|---|
| e | e | f | g | h |
| f | f | e | h | g |
| g | g | h | e | f |
| h | h | g | f | e |

This is the pattern of the Klein group of order 4; see Chapter 10, Section 4, Example 5.

**7.** The only different functions are $f$, $g$, the identity $e$ (which arises from $ff$ and from $gg$), $fg: x \to (x-1)/x$, $gf: x \to 1/(1-x)$, $gfg: x \to x/(x-1)$ (which is the same as $fgf$). Writing

$$p = fg, \quad q = gf, \quad h = fgf \text{ or } gfg,$$

we obtain results such as

$$pp = (fg)(fg) = (fgf)g = (gfg)g$$
$$= (gf)(gg) = qe = q.$$

The complete table is:

|   | e | p | q | f | g | h |
|---|---|---|---|---|---|---|
| e | e | p | q | f | g | h |
| p | p | q | e | h | f | g |
| q | q | e | p | g | h | f |
| f | f | g | h | e | p | q |
| g | g | h | f | q | e | p |
| h | h | f | g | p | q | e |

The isomorphism with the group of symmetry transformations of the equilateral triangle (Chapter 1, Section 3.3, Example 4) is immediately apparent.

**8.** This is the combination of an enlargement of factor $a$ with a translation of amount $b$.

$$l_2 l_1: x \rightarrow a_2 a_1 x + (a_2 b_1 + b_2),$$
$$l_1 l_2: x \rightarrow a_1 a_2 x + (a_1 b_2 + b_1).$$

The scale factor of $l_1 l_2$ is $a_1 a_2$. This foreshadows the 'chain rule' for differentiating composite functions (see Book 2, Chapter 17).

See the note on the term 'linear function' under Exercise C, Question 18.

**9.** $k = b/(1-a)$. This number is the 'fixed point' of the transformation.

An interesting sidelight on this is provided by starting with the number zero and applying the transformation $x \rightarrow ax + b$ repeatedly, thus generating the sequence defined inductively by

$$\begin{cases} u_1 = 0, \\ u_{n+1} = au_n + b. \end{cases}$$

Since the transformation is an enlargement of factor $a$ about $k$, it follows that if $|a| < 1$ successive values of $u_n$ converge on the fixed point as limit. Now these successive values are

$$0, \quad b, \quad ab + b, \quad a^2 b + ab + b, \quad a^3 b + a^2 b + ab + b, \quad \ldots;$$

which leads to the conclusion that the sum of the infinite geometric progression

$$b + ab + a^2 b + a^3 b + \ldots$$

is $b/(1-a)$ provided that $|a| < 1$.

This is a special case of a more general 'fixed point' theorem, that (if $f$ is continuous) the sequence defined by

$$u_{n+1} = f(u_n)$$

and any initial value converges on a root $\alpha$ of the equation $x = f(x)$ provided that $|f'(\alpha)| < 1$.

It is also interesting to notice that the inverse function is an enlargement of factor $1/a$ and fixed point $k$, so that this is given by the formula

$$x \rightarrow \frac{1}{a}(x-k) + k.$$

75

For example, the temperature which is measured by the same number in both Fahrenheit and Centigrade scales is $-40°$. Thus to convert $°C$ to $°F$ we have the rule

add 40,   multiply by $\tfrac{9}{5}$,   subtract 40;

and to convert $°F$ to $°C$,

add 40,   multiply by $\tfrac{5}{9}$,   subtract 40.

**10.** $\xi \to \dfrac{1}{a}(\xi - b)$.

**11.** (a) $\xi \to \sqrt{(4-\xi)}$;   (b) $\xi \to \cos^{-1}(\tfrac{1}{2}\xi)$;

(c) $\xi \to \tfrac{1}{3}\sin^{-1}\xi$;   (d) $\xi \to \dfrac{1}{2}\left(\dfrac{1}{\xi}+3\right)$;

(e) $\xi \to \sqrt{\left(\dfrac{4}{\xi}-1\right)}$.

**13.**

   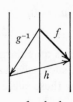   

$$fg = h \qquad\qquad f = hg^{-1} \qquad\qquad g = f^{-1}h$$

Fig. X

**14.** For example:

(a) $f: x \to x^2$,   $g: x \to x^3$ gives $fg = gf: x \to x^6$;

(b) permutations

$$\begin{pmatrix} a & b & c & d & e \\ b & c & a & d & e \end{pmatrix}, \quad \begin{pmatrix} a & b & c & d & e \\ c & a & b & e & d \end{pmatrix};$$

(c) a pair of translations.

**15.** $pq$ is $\begin{pmatrix} a & b & c & d \\ d & a & c & b \end{pmatrix}$.

The matrices are

$$\mathbf{M}_p = \begin{pmatrix} 0 & 0 & 1 & 0 \\ 0 & 0 & 0 & 1 \\ 0 & 1 & 0 & 0 \\ 1 & 0 & 0 & 0 \end{pmatrix}, \quad \mathbf{M}_q = \begin{pmatrix} 0 & 1 & 0 & 0 \\ 0 & 0 & 0 & 1 \\ 1 & 0 & 0 & 0 \\ 0 & 0 & 1 & 0 \end{pmatrix},$$

and

$$\mathbf{M}_{pq} = \begin{pmatrix} 0 & 0 & 0 & 1 \\ 1 & 0 & 0 & 0 \\ 0 & 0 & 1 & 0 \\ 0 & 1 & 0 & 0 \end{pmatrix},$$

and we observe that $\mathbf{M}_{pq} = \mathbf{M}_q \mathbf{M}_p$. Thus '$q$ followed by $p$', written as the permutation $pq$, is found from the product of the matrices $\mathbf{M}_q \mathbf{M}_p$ *in the natural order*.

This sometimes occasions surprise, since it is the reverse of the situation which arises with transformation matrices. There is, of course, no reason to expect the same pattern; for when we write the permutation $p$ symbolically as

$$\begin{pmatrix} a \\ b \\ c \\ d \end{pmatrix} \rightarrow \begin{pmatrix} 0 & 0 & 1 & 0 \\ 0 & 0 & 0 & 1 \\ 0 & 1 & 0 & 0 \\ 1 & 0 & 0 & 0 \end{pmatrix} \begin{pmatrix} a \\ b \\ c \\ d \end{pmatrix}$$

we are not thinking of $\begin{pmatrix} a \\ b \\ c \\ d \end{pmatrix}$ as an element of the domain of a

function, as when we write (for example)

$$\begin{pmatrix} x \\ y \end{pmatrix} \rightarrow \begin{pmatrix} 2 & 7 \\ 1 & 4 \end{pmatrix} \begin{pmatrix} x \\ y \end{pmatrix}.$$

The notation has in fact a quite different significance, and we must examine afresh the method of combination and its connection (if any) with the 'multiplication' of matrices.

The general result can be demonstrated as follows. Suppose that the set of elements permuted is denoted by $\{a_1, a_2, ..., a_n\}$, that the permutation $q$ maps some element $a_i \rightarrow a_j$, and that $p$ maps $a_j \rightarrow a_k$. Then $pq$ maps $a_i \rightarrow a_k$. Then the permutation $q$ is denoted by

$$\begin{pmatrix} a_1 \\ a_i \\ a_n \end{pmatrix} \underset{\text{row}}{\overset{\rightarrow}{\underset{i\text{th}}{}}} \begin{pmatrix} 0 & 0 & 0 \\ 0 & 1 & 0 \\ 0 & 0 & 0 \end{pmatrix} \begin{pmatrix} a_1 \\ a_j \\ a_n \end{pmatrix}$$

$$j\text{th} \atop \text{col}$$

and $p$ is denoted by

$$
\begin{pmatrix} a_1 \\ a_j \\ a_n \end{pmatrix}
\begin{matrix} \rightarrow \\ j\text{th} \\ \text{row} \end{matrix}
\begin{pmatrix} 0 & 0 & 0 \\ 0 & 1 & 0 \\ 0 & 0 & 0 \end{pmatrix}
\begin{matrix} \\ \\ k\text{th} \\ \text{col} \end{matrix}
\begin{pmatrix} a_1 \\ a_k \\ a_n \end{pmatrix}.
$$

The product $pq$ is described similarly by

$$
\begin{pmatrix} a_1 \\ a_i \\ a_n \end{pmatrix}
\begin{matrix} \rightarrow \\ i\text{th} \\ \text{row} \end{matrix}
\begin{pmatrix} 0 & 0 & 0 \\ 0 & 1 & 0 \\ 0 & 0 & 0 \end{pmatrix}
\begin{matrix} \\ \\ k\text{th} \\ \text{col} \end{matrix}
\begin{pmatrix} a_1 \\ a_k \\ a_n \end{pmatrix}
$$

and we see at once that $\mathbf{M}_{pq} = \mathbf{M}_q \mathbf{M}_p$.

# 5

# GRAPHS

The purpose of this chapter is to give the pupil a wide experience of the behaviour of standard types of function, notably power functions, circular functions and exponential functions, together with combinations of them by addition, multiplication and division.

It is therefore a long chapter, and rather a difficult one for most pupils, and it is worth considering ways of sharing the experiences of a number of individuals among a larger group. It may well be worth dividing a class into groups of three or four working together; or else dividing an exercise so that each individual does two or three questions, which are later collated and discussed.

But it is also important not to allow obsession with details. Most diagrams should probably be drawn freehand, on squared paper, without ruled axes or extensive scales; and the processes described here should be treated, like the rough approximations needed in slide rule work, as lightly as possible.

Positive and negative integral powers of 10 should be familiar from previous work, and so should positive powers, and square and cube roots, of other numbers. Other powers are avoided as far as possible until after Chapter 6, though the exponential functions, notably $2^x$, are quite widely used to point contrasts, and are included here for completeness.

It is worth following the example of the text in making an effort to use words like 'function' and 'relation' correctly, even if, at this stage, it is not practicable to insist on full clarity from the class.

# 1. GRAPHICAL REPRESENTATION
# OF FUNCTIONS
## *Exercise A (p. 123)*

**1.**

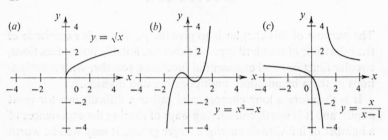

**2.**

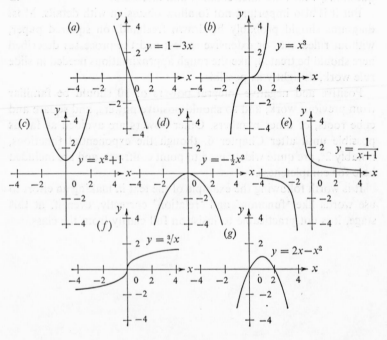

**3.**

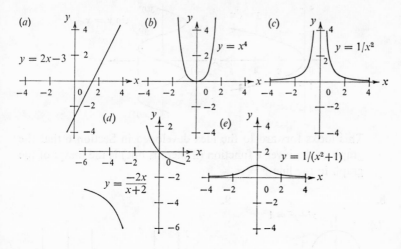

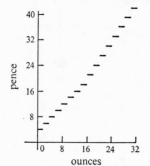

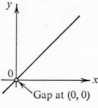

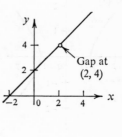

**4.**        **5.**        **6.**

**5, 6.** The values 0, 2 respectively are excluded from the domains. If $g_1(0)$ is defined as 0, and $f_1(2)$ as 4, the functions $g_1$ and $f_1$ are continuous.

These questions look forward to the finding of the derivatives of $x \to x^2$ at 0 and at 2, and throw light on the idea of a limit; compare also the footnote on p. 133 of the pupils' text.

**7.**

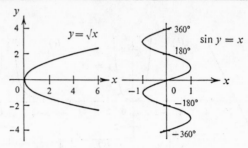

This looks forward to the idea developed in Section 6 that the graph of the inverse function (if there is one) is the image of the graph in the line $y = x$.

**8.**

(a)

(b)

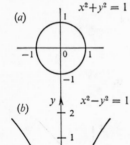

**9.**

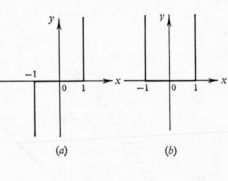

(a)                    (b)

**10.**

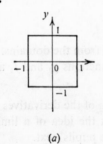

(a)                    (b)

82

**9, 10.** The shapes of these interesting graphs are predictable, because, for example,

$$(0 \cdot 9)^{100} = 2 \cdot 6 \times 10^{-5},$$

$$(1 \cdot 1)^{100} = 1 \cdot 4 \times 10^{4}.$$

## 2. GRAPHS OF STANDARD FUNCTIONS

It is worth having one or two of these standard graphs drawn by each pupil; the best can be displayed, and then the whole class should make small, quick but careful freehand sketches of them all from the display.

## 3. ASYMPTOTES AND DISCONTINUITIES

It is worth taking care at this stage to use accurately the language recommended in the pupils' text, with its suggestion of 'challenge and response'; it provides a very useful foundation for later studies of limits, continuity, and other fundamental ideas of analysis.

### Exercise B (p. 128)

**1.**

| $x$ | $+\infty$ | $-\infty$ | $0^+$ |
|---|---|---|---|
| (a) $x^2$ | $+\infty$ | $+\infty$ | $0^+$ |
| (b) $\sqrt{x}$ | $+\infty$ | — | $0^+$ |
| (c) $1/x^2$ | $0^+$ | $0^+$ | $+\infty$ |
| (d) $1/\sqrt[3]{x}$ | $0^+$ | $0^-$ | $+\infty$ |

Notice how much less the table tells us than the graphs in Figures 8 and 10. A scale of 'largeness' and 'smallness', based on powers of $x$, may be introduced here, as in Question 2, but the stress should still be laid on the idea of challenge and response.

Thus, '$x^2 + 2x$ behaves like $x^2$ when $x$ is large' may be interpreted as meaning 'for sufficiently large $x$, $(x^2 + 2x)/x^2$ can be made as close as we please to 1', and this in turn may be phrased in terms of a challenge.

6-2

**2.** (a) $x^2 + 2x$: like $x^2$ as $x \to \pm\infty$, like $2x$ as $x \to 0^{\pm}$; notice that the $x^2$ ensures that $x \neq 0 \Rightarrow x^2 + 2x > 2x$, giving an outline like Figure A near the origin.

(b) $1/(x+1)$: like $1/x$ as $x \to \pm\infty$, like $1 - x + x^2$ as $x \to 0^{\pm}$; see Figure B.

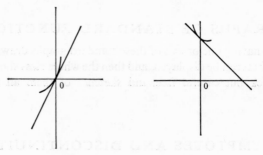

Fig. A                    Fig. B

(c) $\sqrt{(x+x^2)}$: this is only undefined for $\{x: -1 < x < 0\}$. Like $|x|$ as $x \to \pm\infty$, like $\sqrt{x}$ as $x \to 0^+$, undefined as $x \to 0^-$.

(d) $x - \sqrt{x}$: undefined for $\{x: x < 0\}$. Like $x$ as $x \to +\infty$, like $-\sqrt{x}$ as $x \to 0^+$.

(e) $x + 1/x$: like $x$ as $x \to \pm\infty$, like $1/x$ as $x \to 0^{\pm}$.

(f) $x\sqrt{x}$: undefined for $\{x: x < 0\}$: greater than $x$, but less than $x^2$, as $x \to \pm\infty$; conversely, as $x \to 0^+$. Compare its graph with the graph of $x \to x^2$.

(g) $x^2 + x^5$: like $x^5$ as $x \to \pm\infty$, like $x^2$ as $x \to 0^{\pm}$. (Note that $f(-1) = 0$.)

(h) $x^4 + 1/x^3$: like $x^4$ as $x \to \pm\infty$, like $1/x^3$ as $x \to 0^{\pm}$.

**3.** This question leads to the study of $y = x^m$ for all rational values of $m$. Although the class has not yet treated negative and fractional indices systematically, and it may be wise to consider a series of numerical values of $m$ first, it is interesting to see how the part of the curve in the first quadrant changes as $m$ takes values from $+\infty$ to $-\infty$, with landmarks at $m = 1$ and at $m = 0$. Notice that all the curves pass through $(1, 1)$.

A convenient sequence is $x^3$, $x^2$, $\sqrt{x^3}$, $x$, $\sqrt[3]{x^2}$, $\sqrt{x}$, $\sqrt[3]{x}$, $1$, $1/\sqrt[3]{x}$, $1/\sqrt{x}$, $1/\sqrt[3]{x^2}$, $1/x$, $1/\sqrt{x^3}$, $1/x^2$, $1/x^3$; this covers all the simplest rational powers, and suggests the conclusions listed below, besides the inter-relations between them.

As $x \to \pm\infty$, only the terms of highest degree are considered; as $x \to 0^{\pm}$, only the terms of lowest degree (though of course other terms will modify the basic shapes—see Figure B, for example).

Figures 8 and 10 give a fair indication of the behaviour of these functions as $x \to +\infty$; as $x \to -\infty$, remember that even integral powers give $y \to +\infty$, odd integral powers $y \to -\infty$; for rational powers $x^{p/q}$, if $q$ is even the domain contains no negative numbers: while if $q$ is odd, the parity of $p$ determines the sign of $y$ as $x \to -\infty$.

Figures 8 and 10 also indicate how $x^m$ behaves as $x \to 0^{\pm}$, and the sequence above is again a useful one for the purpose.

**4.** $[2^{(x+1)}/(x+1)^2] \div [2^x/x^2] = 2x^2/[(x+1)^2] > 1$ for $x > 1$, so that $2^x/x^2$ is large, for large $x$.

In fact $2^x$ tends to infinity faster than any power of $x$; and, indeed, if $a > 1$, $a^x$ tends to infinity *faster* than any power of $x$; and, correspondingly, $\log_a x$ tends to infinity more slowly than any positive power of $x$.

### 3.2 Approximations and asymptotes.

*Example* 7.
$$\frac{x^3}{x-1} = x^2 + \frac{x^2}{x-1} = x^2 + x + 1 + \frac{1}{x-1};$$

this goes to infinity like $y = x^2$, and the graph of $x^2 + x + 1$ cannot easily be distinguished from the graph of $x^2$ when $x$ is large. Although it is useful to pursue a second approximation for linear asymptotes, it is not so useful with parabolic asymptotes.

### Exercise C (p. 131)

**1.** See Figures 8 to 10.

One term is given to modify the equations of linear asymptotes; sketches are enough.

**2.** (a) $3/2 + 15/4x$;　　(b) $4 - 13/2x$;　　(c) $2 - 5/x$;
(d) $1 - 1/x$;　　(e) $-2 - 2/x$;　　(f) $-3/5 - 22/5x$.

3.  (a) $2/3x$;  (b) $3-4/x$;  (c) $3/4x$;
    (d) $x\sqrt{x}$ ($+\infty$ only);  (e) $-\sqrt{(-x)}$ ($-\infty$ only);
    (f) none;  (g) $-1/x$.

4.  (a) $1/2^x$;  (b) $x+1/x^2$;  (c) $(x-2)/3$ exactly;
    (d) $(x+4)$ exactly;  (e) $x-1/x$.

5.  (a) $x^2$;  (b) $1-1/x^2$;  (c) $1/x$;
    (d) $1/x$ ($+\infty$ only);
    (e) lower half of parabola, with axis $y = x$;
    (f) $1+(\log_e 10)/x$.

### Exercise D (p. 134)

**1.**

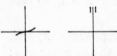    

(a) $x^5$;  (b) $1/x^2$;  (c) $x-\sqrt{x}$;  (d) $x+1/x$;  (e) $\sin(\sqrt[3]{x^2})$;  (f) $1+1/x$.

(c) $\sqrt{x}$ restricts the function to non-negative values of $x$.

(e) Since $\sin h \simeq h$, for small $h$, this behaves like $\sqrt[3]{x^2}$.

**2.**

(a) $x-x^2$;  (b) $x-x^3$;  (c) $-1+4x-8x^2$;  (d) $x+\frac{1}{2}x^3$;  (e) $1-x^2$;  (f) $-\frac{2}{5}-\frac{3}{5}x-\frac{8}{25}x^2$.

**3.**

 gap at (0, 4)

(a) $(x^4-1)/(x^3-1)$;  (b) $[(2+x)^2-2^2]/x$;  (c) $(x^3-1)/(x^2+x+1)$;  (d) $[(x+1)^3-1^3]/x$.

(b), (c), (d) are exact polynomials: (b), (d) are not defined at $x = 0$.

**4.**

(a) $x/(2-x)$;

(b) $x^2/(2-x)$;

(c) $(x-1)/(x+1)$;

(d) $1/(x^2-1)$;

(e) $x/(x^2-1)$.

**5.**

(a) $(x+1)/x(x+2)$;

(b) $x/\sqrt{(1-x)}$;

(c) $x/(1-x)^2$;

(d) $1/x\sqrt{(x+2)}$;

(e) $1/x^2(x-1)$;

(f) $1/x(x^2-1)$.

(d) Defined only for $\{x: x > -2\}$.

**6.**

(a) $\left[\dfrac{x}{2}\right]$

(b) $[x^2]$

(c) $\left[\dfrac{1}{x}\right]$

(d) $\dfrac{[x]}{x}$

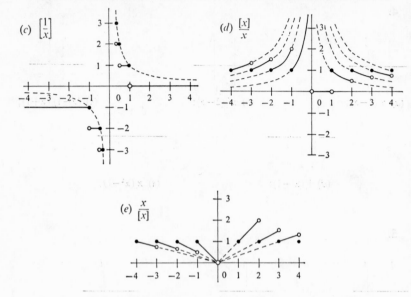

(e) $\dfrac{x}{[x]}$

The lightly marked lines show the method of construction.

7. The graph of (a) has points on the line $y = x$ which divide each interval between consecutive integers into $n$ equal parts.

(b) is indistinguishable from the pair of lines $y = \pm 1$, but it is of course everywhere discontinuous, and is undefined when $x$ is irrational—that is, at nearly all points of the line.

*Exercise E (p. 135)*

**1.**

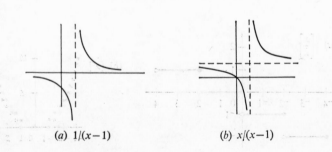

(a) $1/(x-1)$    (b) $x/(x-1)$

88

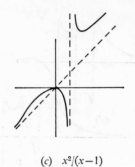

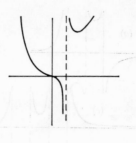

(c)  $x^2/(x-1)$          (d)  $x^3/(x-1)$

**2.**

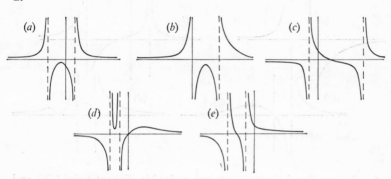

**3.**

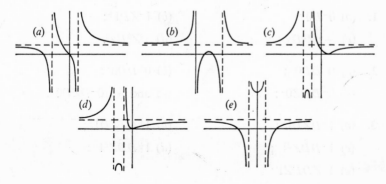

**4.**

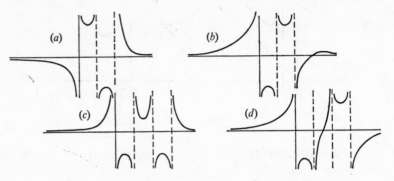

**5.**

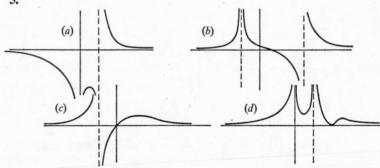

**6.** Notice the difference between a double discontinuity ($D^2$) and two separate discontinuities ($DD$); also between $Z^2$ and $ZZ$. Signs change at $D$ and $Z$.

**1.** (a) $0^-D0^+$;      (b) $1^-ZD1^+$;

    (c) $-xZ^2Dx+$;      (d) $x^2Z^3Dx^2$.

**2.** (a) $0^+DD0^+$;      (b) $0^+DD0^+$;

    (d) $0^-DDZ0^+$;      (c) and (e) $0^-DZD0^+$.

**3.** (a) $1^-DZD1^+$;      (b) $1^+DZZD1^+$;

    (c) $1^+DDZ^21^-$;      (d) $1^+DDZ^21^-$;

    (e) $1^-ZDDZ1^-$.

**4.** (a) $0^- DDD0^+$;  (b) $0^+ DDDZ0^+$;

(c) $0^+ DDDD0^+$;  (d) $0^+ DDZDD0^-$.

**5.** (a) $0^- D^2 D0^+$;  (b) $0^+ D^2 ZD0^+$;

(c) $0^+ D^3 Z0^+$;  (d) $0^+ D^2 D^2 Z^2 0^+$.

## 4. TRANSFORMATIONS APPLIED TO GRAPHS

In this text, instead of the usual movement of axes, we prefer to transform the plane in the manner familiar from the O-Level course. This creates more difficulties for the teacher than for the class, and, because the first approach to a topic is likely to be the lasting one, it is suggested that the questions which introduce each worked example should be:

(a) What is the parent graph?

(b) What transformation must we apply to it?

(c) Does the result check for an obvious key point?

Paragraph 4.4 of the pupils' text should be thoroughly understood; compare the questions set in Exercise F with the answers given below.

### Exercise F (p. 141)

In these answers, instructions are given for transforming the given graphs; **M** is a reflection, **R** a rotation, **S** a stretch, **T** a translation.

**1.** (a) $y = x^2$; $\mathbf{T}\begin{pmatrix}0\\1\end{pmatrix}$;  (b) $y = x^2$; $\mathbf{T}\begin{pmatrix}1\\0\end{pmatrix}$;

(c) $y = 1/x$; $\mathbf{T}\begin{pmatrix}-1\\0\end{pmatrix}$;  (d) $y = \dfrac{1}{x}$; $\mathbf{T}\begin{pmatrix}1\\1\end{pmatrix}$;

(e) $y = x^3$; $\mathbf{M}$, $y = 1$;  (f) $y = \sqrt{x}$; $\mathbf{T}\begin{pmatrix}\frac{1}{2}\\0\end{pmatrix}$, $\mathbf{S}\|Ox$, $\frac{1}{2}$;

(g) $y = \sqrt{x}$; $\mathbf{M}$, $x = 1$.

**2.** (a) $y = \cos x°$; $\mathbf{S}\|Oy$, 2;  (b) $y = \sin x°$; $\mathbf{S}\|Ox$, $\frac{1}{2}$;

(c) $y = \sin x°$; $\mathbf{T}\begin{pmatrix}-90\\0\end{pmatrix}$;  (d) $y = \cos x°$; $\mathbf{S}\|Ox$, 2;

(e) $y = \tan x°$; $\mathbf{S}\|Ox$, 2; $\mathbf{S}\|Oy$, $\frac{1}{2}$;

(f) $y = \cos x°$; $\mathbf{M}$, $x = 90$;

(g) $y = \cos x°$; $\mathbf{M}$, $x = 45$; $\mathbf{S}\|Ox\,\frac{1}{2}$.

**3.** (a) $y = x^2$; $\mathbf{T}\begin{pmatrix} -1 \\ -1 \end{pmatrix}$;

(b) $y = x^2$; $\mathbf{M}$, $y = 2$; $\mathbf{T}\begin{pmatrix} 2 \\ 0 \end{pmatrix}$;

(c) $y = \sqrt{x}$; $\mathbf{T}\begin{pmatrix} -\frac{1}{2} \\ 0 \end{pmatrix}$; $\mathbf{S}\|Ox, \frac{1}{2}$;

(d) $y = 2^x$; $\mathbf{T}\begin{pmatrix} -1 \\ 0 \end{pmatrix}$;

(e) $y = x^2$; $\mathbf{T}\begin{pmatrix} \frac{5}{4} \\ -\frac{9}{16} \end{pmatrix}$, $\mathbf{S}\|Oy, 2$;

(f) $y = 2^x$; $\mathbf{S}\|Ox, \frac{1}{2}$.

**4.** (a) $y = \sin x^\text{L}$; $\mathbf{S}\|Ox, 2$;

(b) $y = \cos x^{\text{rev.}}$; $\mathbf{S}\|Ox, \frac{1}{2}$;

(c) $y = \sin x^\frown$; $\mathbf{T}\begin{pmatrix} -1 \\ 0 \end{pmatrix}$;

(d) $y = \tan x^{\text{rev.}}$; $\mathbf{T}\begin{pmatrix} 1 \\ 0 \end{pmatrix}$;

(e) $y = \sin x^\frown$; $\mathbf{M}$, $x = \frac{1}{2}$;

(f) $y = \tan x^\text{L}$; $\mathbf{M}$, $x = \frac{1}{4}$; $\mathbf{S}\|Ox, \frac{1}{2}$.

**5.** (a) $y = x^2$; $\mathbf{T}\begin{pmatrix} -q \\ q-p^2 \end{pmatrix}$;

(b) $\mathbf{T}\begin{pmatrix} -b/2a \\ -(b^2-4ac)/4a^2 \end{pmatrix}$, $\mathbf{S}\|Oy, a$.

**6.**                                    **7.**

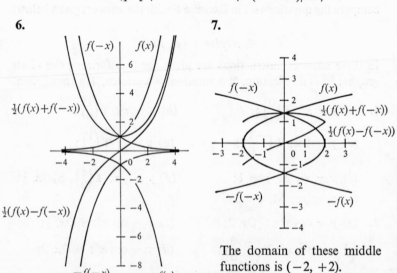

The domain of these middle functions is $(-2, +2)$.

Notice that (d) and (e) are even and odd respectively, in both questions.

**8.** $y^2 = -x$.           **9.** $xy = 1$.

**10.** (a) $y = x^3 + x$;    (b) $y = x + 1/x$;    (c) $y = x + \sin x^2$.

Notice that the gradient of (a) at $O$ is 1, and that $y = x$ becomes an asymptote of (b).

**11.** $y = (1/x)$. The fact that the integral

$$\int_a^b \frac{1}{x}\,dx = \int_{\frac{1}{2}a}^{\frac{1}{2}b} \frac{1}{x}\,dx$$

will be used in Chapter 20 (area).

**12.** $y = \frac{1}{2}x^2$. Rotation and translation reduces any parabola to the form $y = ax^2$, and an enlargement, factor $a$, from $O$ reduces it to the form $y = x^2$.

**13.** $\left( \dfrac{1+t}{(1-t)^2}, \dfrac{t(1+t)}{(1-t)^2} \right)$. When $t = 1$, this point is 'at infinity', and is the only one. When $t = -1$, the point is at $O$, and the gradient of the curve is $-1$. $t = 0$ and $t \to \infty$ give $(1, 0)$ and $(0, 1)$.

**14.** A rotation of $+45°$ turns this into the curve $y = \sqrt{2}.x^2$, and a stretch or an enlargement into $y = x^2$.

**15.** $x = \sqrt{\left( \dfrac{c}{a+bt^2} \right)}$, $y = t\sqrt{\left( \dfrac{c}{a+bt^2} \right)}$; there will be a 'point at infinity' on the line $y = tx$ if $a + bt^2 = 0$, that is, if $a$ and $b$ have opposite signs; asymptotes are then $y = \pm x\sqrt{\dfrac{-a}{b}}$.

## 5. SYMMETRIES OF GRAPHS

Odd and even functions are most useful for simplifying definite integrals; periodic functions, especially the trigonometrical functions, occur very frequently in physical problems of all types.

## Exercise G (p. 144)

1. (a) Odd;         (b) odd;         (c) neither;
   (d) even;        (e) even;        (f) odd;
   (g) even;        (h) neither;     (i) even;
   (j) odd;         (k) neither;     (l) even;
   (m) even;        (n) even;        (o) odd;
   (p) neither; $\cot x° + \operatorname{cosec} x°$ is, however, odd (and equal to $\cot \frac{1}{2}x°$).

2. $f(x)$ will be defined as $f(\{x\})$.

3. No reflections or rotations (consider points like $(\frac{1}{2}, -1)$); translations $\begin{pmatrix} n \\ 0 \end{pmatrix}$, where $n$ is any integer.

   $\sin x°$; reflections in $x = 90 + 180n$; half-turns about $(180n, 0)$; translations $\begin{pmatrix} 360n \\ 0 \end{pmatrix}$; where $n$ is any integer.

   $\cos x°$; reflections in $x = 180n$; half-turns about $(90 + 180n, 0)$; translations $\begin{pmatrix} 360n \\ 0 \end{pmatrix}$, where $n$ is any integer.

   $\tan x°$; half-turns about $(90n, 0)$, translations $\begin{pmatrix} 180n \\ 0 \end{pmatrix}$, where $n$ is any integer.

4.

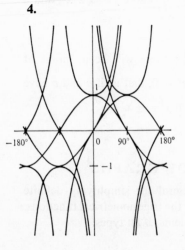

5.

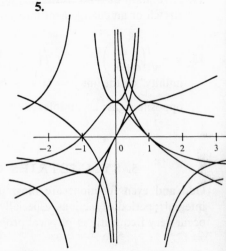

4. Symmetries of sec, csc, cot are the same as those of cos, sin, tan respectively; the pattern has reflectional symmetry in $x = 45+180n$; and is periodic with period 360.

5. The graphs are very similar to those of Question 4. Indeed, the six graphs cut the line $x = \tan(\tfrac{1}{2}t)°$ at precisely the same points as the line $x = t$ in the previous question, for if

$$x' = \tan\left(\tfrac{1}{2}x\right)°, \quad \sin x° = \frac{2x'}{1+x'^2} \quad \text{and} \quad \cos x° = \frac{1-x'^2}{1+x'^2}.$$

In fact, it may be regarded as the image of Question 4 under a 'variable stretch', under which $\pm 90 \to \pm 1$, $\pm 180 \to \pm \infty$.

6. $O = $ odd, $E = $ even, $N = $ neither.

| $\pm$ | $E$ | $O$ |
|---|---|---|
| $E$ | $E$ | $N$ |
| $O$ | $N$ | $O$ |

| $\times, \div$ | $E$ | $O$ |
|---|---|---|
| $E$ | $E$ | $E$ |
| $O$ | $E$ | $O$ |

Exceptions only occur when one of the functions is the zero function.

7. (a) Zero function only;     (b) $x \to x+1$.

   Any graph (such as $x^2+2y^2 = 1$) which has the symmetry group of the rectangle is both odd and even, but the two values of $y$ for each value of $x$ mean that it is not the graph of a function.

8. $g(x) = \tfrac{1}{2}(f(x)-f(-x))$,   $h(x) = \tfrac{1}{2}(f(x)+f(-x))$.
   This may be seen thus:

$$\left.\begin{array}{l} f(-x) = g(-x)+h(-x) = -g(x)+h(x) \\ f(x) = g(x)+h(x). \end{array}\right\}$$

9. Yes, if the domain does not include an interval whose mid-point is $O$; for example, $x \to \sqrt{x}$.

10. The graph is symmetrical about $x = 2$; a translation

$$\binom{-2}{0} \quad \text{converts it into} \quad \left(\frac{4}{x^2-9}\right),$$

an even function.

11. (a), (b) Symmetries of the rectangle.

12. (a), (b) All the symmetries of the circle.

**13.** $\begin{pmatrix} x \\ y \end{pmatrix} \rightarrow \begin{pmatrix} 2a-x \\ -y \end{pmatrix} \rightarrow \begin{pmatrix} 2b-2a+x \\ y \end{pmatrix}$ under reflections in $x = a$ and $x = b$. The curve is mapped onto itself by a translation

$$\begin{pmatrix} 2b-2a \\ 0 \end{pmatrix},$$

and therefore by any number of repetitions of this translation. It follows that the point

$$\begin{pmatrix} (2b-2a)n+2a-x \\ -y \end{pmatrix}$$

lies on the curve, which therefore maps onto itself under a half-turn about $(nb-(n-1)a, 0)$. The trigonometrical functions, especially, behave like this.

**14.** Frieze patterns symmetrical about their centre line must be excluded.

**15.** The graphs are all related to each other by translations; $y = f(x-ct)$ repeats itself every time $t$ increases by $l/c$; $c$ is the speed at which the wave travels, if $t$ represents the time. $p = l/c$ means that $cp$ is the wavelength. Many important physical equations have solutions of this form.

## 6. GRAPHS OF INVERSE FUNCTIONS
### *Exercise H (p. 146)*

**2.**   (a) $y = 1/x$;         (b) $y = \sqrt{x}$;         (c) $y = 1/\sqrt{x}$;
        (d) $y = x/(x-1)$;   (e) $y = 2x-6$;      (f) $y = \sqrt{(x-2)}$;
        (g) $y = \sqrt{(x+1)}-1$;   (h) $\log_2 x$ (not required by Question 2).

**3.**   $a = b$, provided that $a.b.c$ are not all zero and $ab \neq c$; the relation is then symmetrical in $x$ and $y$.

   (a) Asymptotes at $y = -a$, $x = -b$;

   (b) $\left[ -a\left( \dfrac{-ax-c}{x+b} \right) - c \right] \Big/ \left[ \left( \dfrac{-ax-c}{x+b} \right) + b \right]$

$$= [(a^2-c)x+(a-b)c]/[(b-a)x+(b^2-c)] = x$$

   if $a = b$ and $b^2 \neq c$.

**4.**   Any curve symmetrical about $y = x$.

96

**5.** The graph of the inverse relation, which can often be restricted to give an inverse function; thus, $x^2 + y^2 = 1$ is self-inverse, and inverse functions are $y = \pm \sqrt{(1 - x^2)}$.

# 7. CURVE SKETCHING

## *Exercise I (p. 149)*

**1.**

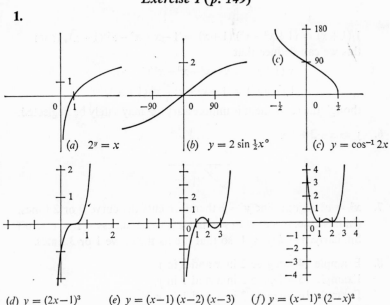

(a) $2^y = x$    (b) $y = 2 \sin \frac{1}{2} x°$    (c) $y = \cos^{-1} 2x$

(d) $y = (2x-1)^3$    (e) $y = (x-1)(x-2)(x-3)$    (f) $y = (x-1)^2(2-x)^2$

**2.**    **3.**

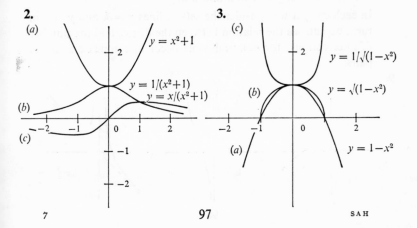

7    97

**4.**  (*a*)  (*b*)  (*c*)  (*d*)

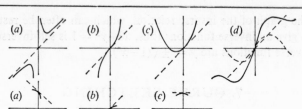

**5.**  (*a*)  (*b*)  (*c*)

$1/(1+x) = (1+x^3-x^3)/(1+x) = 1-x+x^2-x^3/(1+x)$; from this we can deduce that

$$x/(1+x) = x-x^2+x^3-x^4/(1+x);$$
$$1/(1+x^2) = 1-x^2+x^4-x^6/(1+x^2),$$

though the refinement is unnecessary; $x^3$ may safely be neglected.

**6.**  $y \simeq x+2+4/x.$

**7.**  $x^2 = c^2+1/c$; a line $y = c$ therefore cuts the curve 0 or 2 times. (In this case, it is easy to see that it is twice, unless $-1 < c < 0$.) Similarly, $y^3-k^2y = 1$, so that it cuts the curve 1 or 3 times.

**8.**  Example 14—degree 2 in $x$ and 3 in $y$.
Example 15—degree 2 in $x$ and 1 in $y$.
Example 16—degree 3 in $x$ and 1 in $y$.
Example 17—degree 2 in $x$ and 2 in $y$.

In each case, if we consider the sets of lines $x = k$ and $y = c$ in turn, we can see the relation between the degree and the number of intersections; for non-real roots occur in conjugate complex pairs.

**9.**

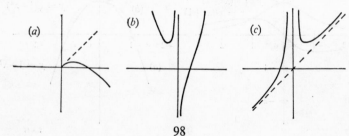

(*a*)  (*b*)  (*c*)

(d)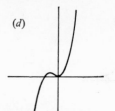

(e)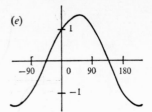

**10.**

(a)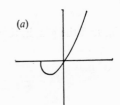

(b)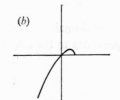

(c)

(d)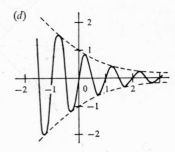

**11.**

(a)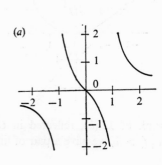

(b)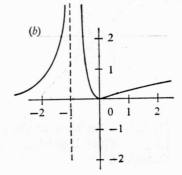

(c)

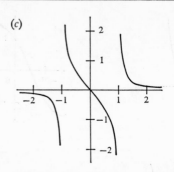

(d) The domain consists of the set {0}, and the graph, therefore, degenerates to the single point O.

**12.**

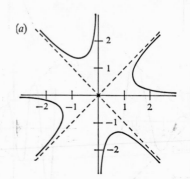

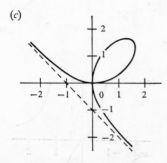

(d) This is the same as the graph of 12 (b), reflected in Ox.
(e) $y^2 = x^2((a-1)/(a+1))$, so, if $|a| > 1$, we have a pair of lines through O.

**13.**

(a), (b)

(c)

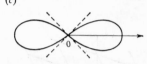

(d)

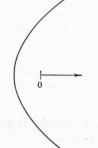

(d), (e)

**14.**

(c)

(a)

(b)

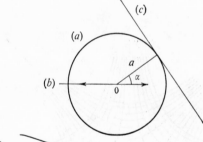

(f), (g)

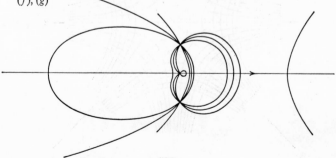

## 8. FUNCTIONS OF TWO VARIABLES
### *Exercise J (p. 154)*

**1.**

**2.**

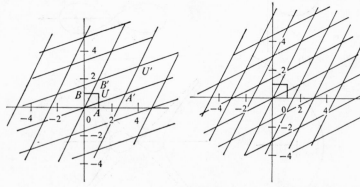

This is a stretch, factor 3, parallel to $x = y$.

**3.** A series of concentric circles, radius $y$, and of lines through $O$ at angles of $10x°$.

**4.**

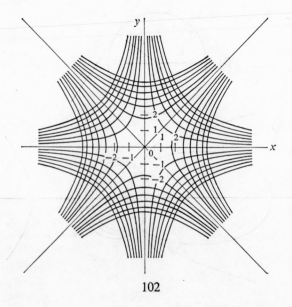

**5.** $j^2 = -1 \Rightarrow (x+jy)^2 = x^2-y^2+2jxy$, so that if $z$ is represented by the point $(x, y)$, $z^2$ is represented by the point $(x^2-y^2, 2xy)$.

**6.** The line $x = a$ is mapped onto $(a^2-y^2, 2ay) = (\xi, \eta)$, say, for any value of $y$. Then, eliminating $y$, $\eta^2+4a^2\xi = 4a^4$, a parabola whose focus is at $O$, vertex $(a^2, 0)$.

Similarly, $y = b$ is mapped onto $(x^2-b^2, 2bx)$.

So $\eta^2-4b^2\xi = 4b^4$, a parabola whose focus is at $O$, vertex $(-b^2, 0)$. The grid is therefore mapped onto:

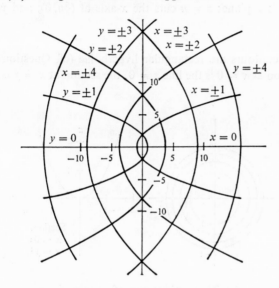

**7.**

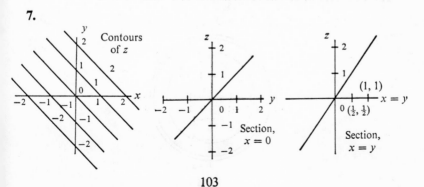

103

**8.**

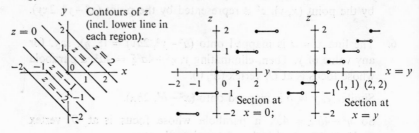

$z = 0$ Contours of $z$ (incl. lower line in each region).

Section at $x = 0$;

Section at $x = y$

**9.** This is a plane: $z = n$ cuts the $x$-axis at $(\frac{5}{3}n, 0)$, and $y$-axis at $(0, \frac{5}{4}n)$.

**10.** The contours are rectangular hyperbolae (cf. Question 4); the section at $x = 0$ is the line $z = 0$; the section at $x = y$ is $z = y^2$.

**11.**

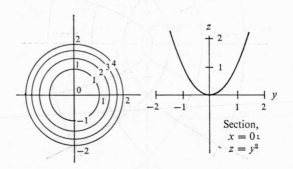

Section, $x = 0$: $z = y^2$

**12.** Contours of $z$. The sections are, of course, circles.

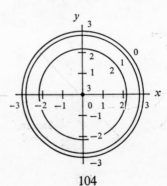

104

**13.** All contours of $z$ are circles, centre $O$.

**14.**

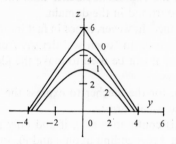

(Hyperbolae, with asymptotes on section $x = 0$.)

**15.** Equation is $x^2 + y^2 = \frac{2}{3}x(6-z)$, if the cone of Question 14 is sheared, with $(0, 0, 6)$ fixed, so that $(-4, 0, 0) \rightarrow (0, 0, 0)$. The contours are circles touching the $y$-axis.

## 9. CONTINUITY

This is generally found a difficult section, because it attempts to lead from the purely graphical picture of a jump in the value of the function towards a more abstract topological definition. Perhaps one of the most important things about it is that the need for such a step should be appreciated. See also the discussion on pp. 68–72.

It is useful to employ the notation established on p. 106 throughout. English letters are then used for members of the domain, and Greek letters for members of the codomain. This throws the emphasis on the difficult idea of an inverse image, which should be revised before this section is attempted. Unfortunately, this needs to be corrected in the text; see Exercise K, Questions 1–3.

The idea of a *neighbourhood*, which is an example of an *open* set—that is, one which does not contain its boundary points—is fundamental to this approach, and it is important to see why we must start with the member of the codomain and its neighbourhoods, rather than, as we would expect, with the original member of the domain.

Perhaps the essential point of doing this may be seen as follows. At a discontinuity, any neighbourhood of the point concerned can, of course, be mapped into a neighbourhood of the codomain; but the

105

size of the 'jump' at the discontinuity gives a size below which the neighbourhood in the codomain cannot fall. If therefore we take a neighbourhood in the codomain smaller than this, it cannot be the image of a neighbourhood in the domain.

The idea of distance, however, is not in fact indispensable; and the emphasis on the idea of an 'open set' derives from the fact that in more general spaces it can be used to make the idea of distance unnecessary.

It is useful, too, for the teacher to express the condition (for his own benefit) in the usual form:

The function $f$ is continuous at $c$, if and only if, for every value of $\epsilon$, we can find a $\delta$ (depending upon $\epsilon$ and $c$), such that

$$|x-c| < \delta \Rightarrow |f(x)-f(c)| < \epsilon.$$

## Exercise K (p. 159)

1. (a) The question should read $[1-x]$. $\{x: -1 < x \leqslant 0\}$; (b) $\{0\}$;

(c) $\{x: -0 \cdot 1 < x < +0 \cdot 1\}$;  (d) $\{x: 0 \leqslant x < 0 \cdot 1\}$;

(e) $\{x: -0 \cdot 01 < x < +0 \cdot 01\}$.

It is also helpful to use $\xi$ instead of $y$ as the typical member of the codomain (see also Questions 2 and 3).

2. $\{x: 0 \leqslant x < 0 \cdot 1\} \cup \{x: -0 \cdot 995 > x > -1 \cdot 005\}$.

3. This is a plane; $\{(x, y): 1 \cdot 99 < x+y < 2 \cdot 01\}$.

4. This is a 'staircase'; $\{(x, y): 2 \leqslant x+y < 3\}$.

6. Rotation and enlargement; the inverse image of

$\{(\xi, \eta): d((\xi, \eta), (1, 1)) < \sqrt{2}/100\}$   is   $\{(x, y): d((x, y), (1, 0)) < 0 \cdot 01\}$.

Both these neighbourhoods are circles.

7. The image is an isolated point in Question 1, in each case; in Question 2, $\{-1, 0\}$; in Question 3, $\{(x, y): x+y = 2\}$, and in Question 4 $\{(x, y): 2 \leqslant x+y < 3\}$. In each case, the point $(1, 1)$ is a boundary point, so that the mappings are discontinuous; indeed, using this, the *discrete* metric, all mappings are discontinuous.

8.  (i) The neighbourhood of $(1, 1)$, $\{(\xi, \eta): d((\xi, \eta), (1, 1)) < h\}$ is a diamond, and its inverse image is a square, which *contains* $\{(x, y): d((x, y), (1, 0)) < \frac{1}{2}h\}$; the mapping is continuous.

    (ii) The inverse image is $\{(1, 0)\}$, so that, as in Question 7, the mapping is discontinuous.

9.  The contours must run together; at such points, the relation between position and height is no longer a mapping, for the height is not unique. The 1:25000 O.S. map of Kilnsey Crag in Wharfedale (which overhangs) is interesting.

10. A mapping from $R^3$ to $R$, which will be discontinuous at interfaces between substances of different densities, though of course the density can also vary continuously.

11. The best that can be done is to have a point discontinuity only—consider the map made in the figure on the plane $\pi$ by projection from $O$.

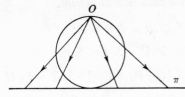

# REVISION EXERCISES

## 1. STRUCTURE (p. 160)

**1.** This question can be answered by direct computation, but also by considering the isomorphism

$$\{a, \oplus, \otimes\} \leftrightarrow \{a+1, +, \times\}.$$

The identity element for $\oplus$ is $-1$; for $\otimes$, 0.

**2.** (a) (iii); (b) (i); (c) (i); (d) (ii); (e) (iii); (f) (i).

**3.** (a), (e) and (g) are isomorphic; the other four are all different. Had (f) been *addition* mod 4 it would have been isomorphic to (c). Provided the identity elements are made to correspond, the remaining elements can be paired in any way—i.e. there are 6 isomorphisms for each pair of groups.

**4.** (a) (i) $S.T = S.Q.R = I.R = R;$

(ii) $T.U = S.P.U = S.I = S.$

(b) (i) $S.T = S.(Q+R) = S.Q+S.R = I+U = R;$

(ii) $T.U = T.(I+R) = T.I+T.R = T+I = S.$

$$P.x+Q = R \Leftrightarrow P.x+Q+Q = R+Q \Leftrightarrow P.x = T$$

$$\Leftrightarrow U.P.x = U.T = Q.Q.T = Q.P = S \Leftrightarrow x = S.$$

$$\left.\begin{array}{l} P.x+Q.y = R \\ T.x+U.y = S \end{array}\right\} \Leftrightarrow \left\{\begin{array}{l} U.P.x+U.Q.y = U.R \\ Q.T.x+Q.U.y = Q.S \end{array}\right\} \Leftrightarrow \left\{\begin{array}{l} x+R.y = P \\ P.x+R.y = I \end{array}\right.$$

$$\Rightarrow (I+P).x+(R+R).y = P+I$$

$$\Leftrightarrow Q.x+O = Q$$

$$\Leftrightarrow x = I$$

Hence

$$I+R.y = P \Leftrightarrow I+I+R.y = I+P$$

$$\Leftrightarrow \quad O+R.y = Q$$

$$\Leftrightarrow \quad\quad y = T.R.y = T.Q = P.$$

**5.** (*a*) (i) is immediate; for (ii) write

$$\alpha\gamma - \beta\delta = \alpha(\gamma - \delta) + \delta(\alpha - \beta).$$

(*b*) $aN \equiv bN \Rightarrow (a-b)N \equiv 0 \Rightarrow a-b$ is divisible by 7, since $N$ is not. Hence $N, 2N, ..., 6N$ must belong to different residue classes, and these classes must be those of $1, 2, ..., 6$ in some order. Hence $6!N^6 \equiv 6!$ and $N^6 \equiv 1$, since 6! is not divisible by 7. This is Fermat's Theorem for the case $p = 7$; the general theorem (proved in the same way) states that

If $a$ is not divisible by a prime $p$, $a^{p-1} \equiv 1 \pmod{p}$.

**6.** The identity is $e$; $g^{-1} = f$.
$e$ commutes with all; $f$ and $g$ commute with each other.

| o | e | f | g | h | j | k |
|---|---|---|---|---|---|---|
| e | e | f | g | h | j | k |
| f | f | g | e | j | k | h |
| g | g | e | f | k | h | j |
| h | h | k | j | e | g | f |
| j | j | h | k | f | e | g |
| k | k | j | h | g | f | e |

The operation o is 'followed by'.

$p$ could be $h, j$ or $k$; $q$ could be $f$ or $g$.

If $p = h$, $q = f$, then

$e = pp = qqq$,      $h = p$,

$f = q$,                $j = qp$,

$g = qq$,              $k = pq$.

The set is isomorphic to (*b*).

109

## 2. FLOW DIAGRAMS, NATURAL NUMBERS, INDUCTION (p. 162)

**1.** (a)                  (b)

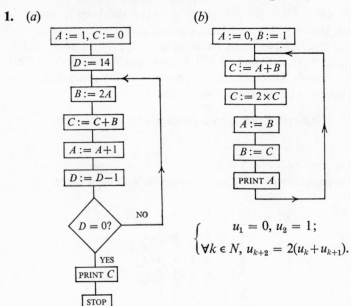

$$\begin{cases} \quad u_1 = 0,\ u_2 = 1; \\ \forall k \in N,\ u_{k+2} = 2(u_k + u_{k+1}). \end{cases}$$

**2.** (a) $1 \in T$.

$$k \in T \Rightarrow 1^2 - 2^2 + \ldots + (-1)^{k-1}k^2 + (-1)^k(k+1)^2$$
$$= (-1)^{k-1}\tfrac{1}{2}k(k+1) + (-1)^k(k+1)^2$$
$$= (-1)^k\{(k+1)^2 - k(k+1)/2\}$$
$$= (-1)^k(k+1)(k+2)/2$$
$$\Rightarrow (k+1) \in T.$$

Hence $n \in T$ for all natural numbers $n$.

(b) $7^{k+1} + 2 - (7^k + 2) = 6 \cdot 7^k$ which is divisible by 3.

Hence $k \in T \Rightarrow (k+1) \in T$, and clearly $1 \in T$. Hence $n \in T$ for all $n$.

**3.** $x,\ 2x,\ 4x,\ 7x,\ 11x$.

**4.** If $k \in T$, draw the $(k+1)$th line and change all the colours on one side of it. Then $(k+1) \in T$.

**5.** $(k+1)^3+5(k+1)-k^3-5k = 3k^2+3k+6 = 3k(k+1)+6 = 6N$,
since $k(k+1)$ is even. Hence if $P(n)$ is the statement '$n(n^2+5)$ is
divisible by 6', $P(k)$ and $P(k+1)$ are true or false together. But
$P(1)$ is true; hence $P(2)$, $P(3)$, ... and also $P(0)$, $P(-1)$, ... are
true, so that $P(n)$ is true for all integers $n$.

**6.**   (*a*) Data: $t_1, t_2, ..., t_6$.       (*b*) Data: $a_1, a_2, a_3, ..., a_n$.

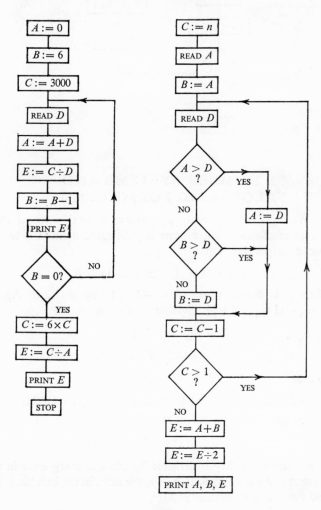

111

(*c*)

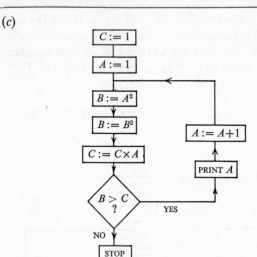

## 3. NUMBER SYSTEMS AND ALGEBRAIC FORMS (p. 163)

**1.** (*a*) We may simply write $p(x) = ax+b$, $q(x) = cx+d$, and equate coefficients, but a more sophisticated method is to use Euclid's algorithm. Let

$$(x^2-3x+2) = A, \quad (x^2+x+1) = B.$$

Then $A = B+R$, where $R = -4x+1$, by division. Again, $B = (-\frac{1}{4}x-\frac{5}{16}) R+\frac{21}{16}$, dividing once more. Hence

$$16B = R(-4x-5)+21$$

$$= (4x+5)(B-A)+21,$$

so that $\qquad (4x+5)A+(11-4x)B = 21.$

Accordingly, $p(x) = (4x+5)/21$, and $q(x) = (11-4x)/21$.

(*b*) $(x+y)^5 - x^5 - y^5 = 5x^4y+10x^3y^2+10x^2y^3+5xy^4$

$$= 5xy(x^3+2x^2y+2xy^2+y^3).$$

If $x, y$ are even, $5xy$ is divisible by 20, and every term in the bracket is divisible by 8. If $x = y$, the term in the bracket is $6x^3$ and the whole expression is $30x^5$.

**2.** (a) Yes; yes.

(b) $2x^4 + x^3 - 2x - 1$

$$= (2x+1)(x^3-1) = (2x+1)(x-1)(x^2+x+1).$$

**3.** (a) Difference $= \dfrac{x(x+4)}{2(x-2)(x+2)}$; product $= \dfrac{1}{(x-2)^2}$.

(b) Polynomial $= kx(x-2)(x+3)(4x+3)$

$$= k(4x^4 + 7x^3 - 21x^2 - 18x).$$

Least integral values are

$$a_4 = 4, \quad a_3 = 7, \quad a_2 = -21, \quad a_1 = -18, \quad a_0 = 0.$$

**4.** (a)

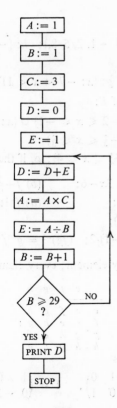

(b) $a10^3+b10^2+c10+d-(a+b10+c10^2+d10^3)$
$$= 999(a-d)+90(b-c).$$

To base $n$, the difference $= (n^3-1)(a-d)+n(n-1)(b-c)$ and is always divisible by $(n-1)$.

5. $x^3-3x+2 = (x+2)(x-1)^2 \leqslant 0$ if $x \leqslant -2$ or $x = 1$.

6. (a) $a = -\sqrt{3}$, polynomial $= (x-3)(x^2-3) = x^3-3x^2-3x+9$.

   (b) $\dfrac{x^3-3x+2}{x(x-1)(x+1)} = 0 \Rightarrow x = -2$ only.

## 4. FUNCTIONS (p. 163)

1. (a) $n \to (n+1)^2$;  (b) $n \to (n^2+3n+6)/2$.

2. (a) 6;  (b) 21.

3. If $x \in \{$integers$\}$,

   $f: \{0, 1, 4\}$;  $g: \{-4, -1, 2, 5, 8,\}$;  $h: \{-\frac{1}{5}, -\frac{1}{4}, -\frac{1}{3}, -\frac{1}{2}, -1\}$.

   If $x \in \{$reals$\}$,

   $f: \{x: 0 \leqslant x < 9\}$;  $g: \{x: -7 < x < 11\}$;  $h: \{x: x < -\frac{1}{6}\}$.

   The inverse image of $B$:

   under $f$ is $\{x: -2 \leqslant x \leqslant -1\} \cup \{x: 1 \leqslant x \leqslant 2\}$;

   under $g$,  $\{x: -\frac{1}{3} \leqslant x \leqslant \frac{2}{3}\}$;

   under $h$,  $\{x: 3\frac{1}{4} \leqslant x \leqslant 4\}$; ø, if the domain is $A$.

4. (a) $f.g: x \to 2x^2/3+3x-6$;   (b) $f+g: x \to 7x/3-1$;

   (c) $fg: x \to 2x/3+1$;   (d) $f^{-1}: x \to (x+3)/2$;

   (e) $g^{-1}: x \to 3(x-2)$;

   (f) $(fg)^{-1}: x \to 3(x-1)/2$;  $(fg)^{-1} = g^{-1}f^{-1}$.

5. Yes. $e$ is the identity element; every element is its own inverse. The table is

|   | $e$ | $f$ | $g$ | $h$ |
|---|-----|-----|-----|-----|
| $e$ | $e$ | $f$ | $g$ | $h$ |
| $f$ | $f$ | $e$ | $h$ | $g$ |
| $g$ | $g$ | $h$ | $e$ | $f$ |
| $h$ | $h$ | $g$ | $f$ | $e$ |

   that for the matrices

$$I = \begin{pmatrix} 1 & 0 \\ 0 & 1 \end{pmatrix}, \quad X = \begin{pmatrix} -1 & 0 \\ 0 & 1 \end{pmatrix}, \quad Y = \begin{pmatrix} 1 & 0 \\ 0 & -1 \end{pmatrix}, \quad H = \begin{pmatrix} -1 & 0 \\ 0 & -1 \end{pmatrix}$$

is

|   | I | H | X | Y |
|---|---|---|---|---|
| I | I | H | X | Y |
| H | H | I | Y | X |
| X | X | Y | I | H |
| Y | Y | X | H | I |

,

and there is isomorphism between the groups: $e \leftrightarrow I$, and $f, g, h \leftrightarrow X, Y, H$ in any order. Compare Section 1, Question 3.

**6.** (d) is a *homomorphism*, since $f$ maps two integers onto one. For the domain of positive integers, it is an isomorphism.

(e) and (f) are isomorphisms. (a), (b), (g) fail because the structure is not preserved; (c) fails because it is not a one-one correspondence.

## 5. GRAPHS (p. 165)

**1.**

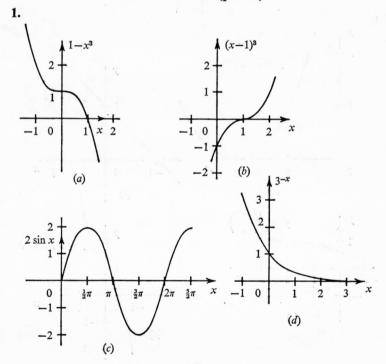

115

**2.**

| | (i) | (ii) | (iii) |
|---|---|---|---|
| (a) | $\sim 0 + 1/x$ | $\to +\infty$ | $\to -\infty$ |
| (b) | $\sim 1 + 1/x$ | $\to +\infty$ | $\to -\infty$ |
| (c) | $\sim 1 + 2/x$ | $\to +\infty$ | $\to +\infty$ |

**3.** $x \to x/(x^2 - 1)$ is an odd function: $f(-x) = -f(x)$.

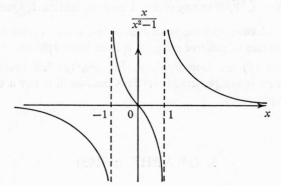

**4.**

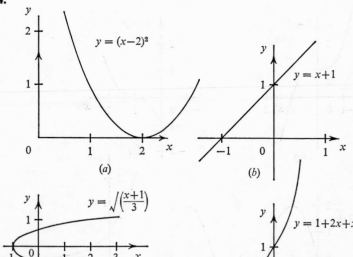

5. (*a*) This defines a function.

Domain: real numbers except $\frac{1}{2}$ and $-2$; range: real numbers.

Graph:

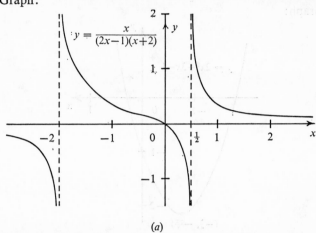

$$y = \frac{x}{(2x-1)(x+2)}$$

(*a*)

(*b*) $\sin x = \cos y \Rightarrow \cos y = \cos(\frac{1}{2}\pi - x) \Rightarrow y = 2n\pi \pm (\frac{1}{2}\pi - x)$ which is a one-many relation and not a function. Graph:

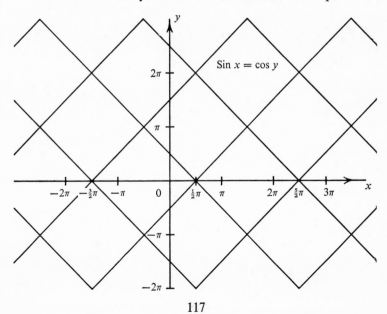

Sin $x = \cos y$

**6.** $2x^2+3x-1 = 2(x+\frac{3}{4})^2-\frac{17}{8}$; $p = \frac{3}{4}, q = -\frac{17}{8}$.
(*a*) The axis of symmetry is $x = -\frac{3}{4}$;
(*b*) the least value is $-\frac{17}{8}$.
Graph:

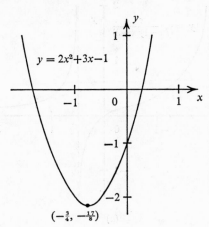

$(-\frac{3}{4}, -\frac{17}{8})$

118

# 6

# INDICES AND LOGARITHMS

## 1. INDICES

### Exercise A (p. 166)

1. 64, $2^6$.　　2. 243, $3^5$.　　3. 48.　　4. 36.

5. $-227$.　　6. 4096, $2^{12}$.　　7. 1,000,000.　　8. 9·72.

9. 49, $7^2$.

### Exercise B (p. 167)

1. (a) $5^6$;　　(b) $10^{11}$;　　(c) $3^6$;　　(d) $2^4$.

2. (a) $x$;　　(b) $x^4$;　　(c) $x^5 y^4$;
   (d) $xy$;　　(e) $xy^9$.

3. (a) $6x^5$;　　(b) $64x^{15}$;　　(c) $9/x$.

4. (a) 2;　　(b) 3;　　(c) 10.

5. (a) $n = 2$;　　(b) $n = 5$;　　(c) $n = 5$;
   (d) $x = a^2$;　　(e) $x = a$;　　(f) $n = 7$.

### Exercise C (p. 169)

1. (a) (i) 8,　(ii) 81,　(iii) 16,　(iv) 5;
   (b) (i) no,　(ii) no;
   (c) yes, provided we consider $2^x$ to be positive for all $x$. No, it is many-one if $b = 1$, and not a function if $b \leqslant 0$.

2. (a) Yes;　　(b) yes;　　(c) yes;　　(d) no;　　(e) no.

### Exercise D (p. 170)

1. (a) $2^0$, 1;　(b) $2^0$, 1;　　(c) $3^0$, 1;　　(d) $7^0$, 1;
   (e) $x^0$, 1;　(f) $x^0$, 1.　$b^0 = 1$.

119

**2.** (a) $2^1, 2$;          (b) $2^{-1}, \frac{1}{2}$,    $2^{-1} = \frac{1}{2}$;

    (c) $3^{-2}, \frac{1}{9}$,    $3^{-2} = \frac{1}{9}$;          (d) $5^{-4}, \frac{1}{625}$,    $5^{-4} = \frac{1}{625}$;

    (e) $x^{-2}, 1/x^2$;                (f) $x^{-1}, 1/x$;

    (g) $x^{-p}, 1/x^p$,    $x^{-p} = 1/x^p$.

**3.** (a) $n = 2$;    (b) $n = 3$;    (c) $n = 5$;    (d) $n = \frac{1}{5}$    (e) $n = 1/q$.
  $x^{\frac{1}{2}} = \sqrt{x}$,    $x^{\frac{1}{3}} = \sqrt[3]{x}$,    $x^{1/q} = \sqrt[q]{x}$.

### Exercise E (p. 171)

**1.** (a) The mapping $x \to b^x$ from $(Q, +)$ to $(B, \times)$ is one-one and preserves the operations, since the property $b^x \times b^y = b^{x+y}$ holds for all rational numbers $x, y$.

(b) (i)                            (ii)

| + | $-1$ | $-\frac{1}{2}$ | $0$ | $\frac{1}{2}$ | $1$ |
|---|---|---|---|---|---|
| $-1$ | $-2$ | $-1\frac{1}{2}$ | $-1$ | $-\frac{1}{2}$ | $0$ |
| $-\frac{1}{2}$ | $-1\frac{1}{2}$ | $-1$ | $-\frac{1}{2}$ | $0$ | $\frac{1}{2}$ |
| $0$ | $-1$ | $-\frac{1}{2}$ | $0$ | $\frac{1}{2}$ | $1$ |
| $\frac{1}{2}$ | $-\frac{1}{2}$ | $0$ | $\frac{1}{2}$ | $1$ | $1\frac{1}{2}$ |
| $1$ | $0$ | $\frac{1}{2}$ | $1$ | $1\frac{1}{2}$ | $2$ |

| $\times$ | $\frac{1}{4}$ | $\frac{1}{2}$ | $1$ | $2$ | $4$ |
|---|---|---|---|---|---|
| $\frac{1}{4}$ | $\frac{1}{16}$ | $\frac{1}{8}$ | $\frac{1}{4}$ | $\frac{1}{2}$ | $1$ |
| $\frac{1}{2}$ | $\frac{1}{8}$ | $\frac{1}{4}$ | $\frac{1}{2}$ | $1$ | $2$ |
| $1$ | $\frac{1}{4}$ | $\frac{1}{2}$ | $1$ | $2$ | $4$ |
| $2$ | $\frac{1}{2}$ | $1$ | $2$ | $4$ | $8$ |
| $4$ | $1$ | $2$ | $4$ | $8$ | $16$ |

**2.** (a) $5^2$;      (b) $2^6$;      (c) $7^{\frac{1}{3}}$;      (d) $5^{-4}$;      (e) $3^{\frac{3}{2}}$.

**3.** (i) (a) $2^3$;      (b) $2^{\frac{1}{2}}$;      (c) $2^{-2}$;      (d) $2^{\frac{2}{3}}$;      (e) $2^{-\frac{1}{3}}$.

    (ii) (a) $4^{\frac{3}{2}}$;      (b) $4^{\frac{1}{4}}$;      (c) $4^{-1}$;      (d) $4^{\frac{3}{4}}$;      (e) $4^{-\frac{1}{6}}$.

**4.** (a) $0.45$;      (b) $23$;      (c) $1.8$;      (d) $1.8$;      (e) $0.15$.

**5.** (a) $6$;      (b) $1\frac{1}{2}$;      (c) $1$;      (d) $32$.

**6.** (a) $x^{-1}$;      (b) $x^{\frac{5}{3}}$;      (c) $x$;      (d) $x^{-3}$;      (e) $x^{-1}$.

### Exercise F (p. 173)

**1.**

| $x$ | $-1\frac{1}{4}$ | $-1.6$ | $0.59$ | $2\frac{1}{4}$ | $2.58$ |
|---|---|---|---|---|---|
| $y$ | $0.42$ | $\frac{1}{3}$ | $1\frac{1}{2}$ | $4.75$ | $6$ |

**2.**

| | 10.30 | 11.00 | 11.30 | 12.00 | 12.30 | 1.00 | 1.30 | 2.00 |
|---|---|---|---|---|---|---|---|---|
| $\times 10^6$ | 1.6 | 2.0 | 2.4 | 3.0 | 3.7 | 4.5 | 5.5 | 6.8 |

**3.** $m = 50 \times 0.8^t$;    2 years ago;    2 years hence.

120

*Exercise G (p. 175)*

1. 2·9.　　　　2. 4·4.　　　　3. 7·9.

4. 2·22.　　　　5. 1·95.　　　　6. 0·95.

# 2. LOGARITHMIC FUNCTIONS
## *Exercise H (p. 179)*

1. (a) $\log a = 1, \log b = 2$;　　(b) 2, i.e. $2 \log a$;
   (c) $b = a^2$;　　　　　　　　(d) $c = a^3; d = a^4$;
   (e) $a$;　　　　(f) $1\frac{1}{2}$;　　　　(g) $-4$.

2. $p = 4, q = 3, r = 128$.

3. (a) 4;　　　　(b) $\frac{1}{25}$;　　　　(c) 2;
   (d) 6;　　　　(e) $1/\sqrt{10}$;　　　(f) 64.

4. (a) 1·79;　(b) $-0·69$;　(c) 0·41;　(d) 3·30;　(e) 2·89;
   (f) 0·28;　(g) 0·35;　(h) 1·65;　(i) 0·46;　(j) 0·62.

5. (a) 7;　(b) 27;　(c) 6;　(d) 16;　(e) 2;　(f) $1/\sqrt{5}$.

6. $2^{10} = 1024 \Rightarrow 2^{10} \simeq 10^3 \Rightarrow \dfrac{2^{10}}{10^3} \simeq 1$

   $$\Rightarrow 10 \log 2 \simeq 3 \log 10$$

   $$\Rightarrow \log 2 \simeq \tfrac{3}{10}.$$

7. (a) 1·477;　(b) 0·699;　　(c) 3·301;　　(d) 0·523;
   (e) $-0·398$;　(f) $-0·398$;　(g) 0·826.

# 3. APPLICATIONS OF LOGARITHMS
## *Exercise I (p. 183)*

1. 6·2.　　　　2. 2·8.　　　　3　4·9.

4. 2·0.　　　　5. 7·6.　　　　6. 1·8

### Exercise J (p. 184)

1. (a) 2·4972;  (b) 5·4972;  (c) $\bar{1}$·4972;  (d) $\bar{3}$·4972.

2. (a) 271·8;  (b) 0·02718;  (c) 271,800;  (d) 0·2718.

3. (a) 0·2176;  (b) 3·9924;  (c) $\bar{2}$·8213;  (d) 0·1193;
   (e) $\bar{1}$·0238.

4. (a) (i) 4·4019, (ii) 0·4891;  (b) (i) $\bar{9}$·6543, (ii) $\bar{1}$·0727;
   (c) (i) $\bar{6}$·5298, (ii) $\bar{1}$·3922;  (d) (i) 13·8042, (ii) 1·5338;
   (e) (i) $\overline{10}$·4303, (ii) $\bar{2}$·9367.

5. (a) 1·0828;  (b) 1·0828;  (c) $\bar{1}$·6020;
   (d) 1·6020;  (e) 2·6848;  (f) $\bar{1}$·4808;
   (g) 0·6712;  (h) $\bar{1}$·8702;  (i) 2·7126;
   (j) $\bar{5}$·9444.

### Exercise K (p. 186)

1. 39·6.  2. 18·1.  3. 0·115.  4. 0·464.

5. 0·949.  6. 2·43.  7. 7900.  8. 1·17.

9. $3·01 \times 10^{14}$.  10. $2·00 \times 10^{-9}$.  11. 19·0.

12. 0·408.  13. $4·08 \times 10^{-9}$.  14. $7·13 \times 10^{-14}$.

15. 25300.  16. $1·24 \times 10^{-2}$.  17. $9·45 \times 10^{12}$ km.

18. $1·08 \times 10^{12}$ km$^3$;  $5·10 \times 10^8$ km$^2$.

19. 6010 cm$^2$.  20. 4·79.  21. 35.

### Exercise L (p. 193)

Most answers have been given correct to 3 S.F.

1. (a) 2·57;  (b) $4·76 \times 10^{-5}$;  (c) $3·58 \times 10^{-5}$;  (d) 57·2.

2. $y = 2·718, 1·649, 1, 0·6065, 0·3679, 0·2231, 0·1353$.
   Gradient, $dy/dx = -y$.

3. (a) 2·10;  (b) 4;  (c) 1·08;  (d) $-190$.

4. £328;  £344 12s.;  19 years.

5. (a) 18 years;  (b) 15 years;  (c) 11 years.

6. £232.

**7.** $12\frac{1}{2}\%$ since $1\cdot04^3 = 1\cdot125$ (4 s.f.). This assumes that the earnings over the first three years (and therefore over every run of three years) are the same. But if the two salaries are the same to start with then the one with the annual review will give higher total earnings in the long run.

$$1500 \times \frac{(1\cdot04)^{12}-1}{0\cdot04} = 22{,}500 \quad \text{and} \quad 1500 \times \frac{(1\cdot12)^4-1}{0\cdot12} = 21{,}500,$$
$$£1000 \text{ difference.}$$

**8.** See Exercise F, Question 3. **9.** $t = 13\cdot15$.

**10.** See Figure A. Values in the order given are: $0\cdot954$, $1\cdot404$, $1\cdot09$, $0\cdot631$, $1\cdot995$.

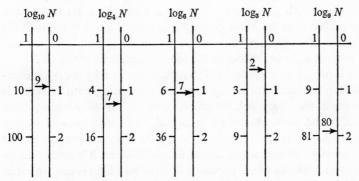

Fig. A. The scale on the image line is the same in each case. The positions of the 'base' points are therefore fixed in the domain. The positions of the required points have been estimated relative to these fixed points.

**11.** 128; $n = 11$ since we require $2^n \geqslant 1500$.

**12.** 5; 6; 8. If $N = 2^x$ where $p < x \leqslant p+1$ then there will be $(p+1)$ rounds for $N$ people. 236. $N-1$.

**13.** (a) 5; (b) 3; (c) 25.

**14.** Plot $\log y$ against $x$. $b = 2\cdot14$, $k = 1\cdot36$.

**15.** $y = 2^{(x-2)}$.

**16.** (a) On the paper, add the distance from 1 to $1\cdot5$ to that from 1 to 2. This gives the point for 3, and so on.
(b) $\sqrt{2}$ or $1\cdot41$, $\sqrt{6}$ or $2\cdot45$.

**17.** $1\cdot06$ times.

# 7

# DERIVATIVES

The idea of a scale factor will be less familiar to most teachers than the idea of a gradient. Indeed, all the preliminary work on rates of change in the O-Level course has been based upon interpreting the gradient of a graph; the Additional Mathematics course (for those pupils who have studied it) depends heavily upon the same idea; and even in this chapter, no sooner is the idea of a scale factor well established than the whole concept is presented again in terms of the gradient of a graph.

Why then do we introduce the idea of a scale factor at all?

It is not, of course, intended to replace one idea by the other completely; but there are strong arguments for using both pictures to illustrate the analytical definition, and, as far as possible, both teacher and pupil should be bi-lingual. Both stronger and weaker pupils do in fact find it helpful to regard the same process in two apparently different ways, and at the point where it becomes necessary to review the whole process a flood of new light is thrown on its meaning if pupils are encouraged to develop both illustrations alongside each other in class discussion. But there are special circumstances, discussed below, when there are definite advantages in talking about mappings and scale factors rather than about graphs and gradients.

(a) This treatment follows very naturally from the careful discussion of Function in Chapter 4, and not only from the diagrams used there; and the generalization to the Jacobian, for example, or to the differentiation of vectors, will later be easily made.

(b) The analytical definition $[f(b)-f(a)]/(b-a)$ is illustrated one stage more directly by the scale factor than by the gradient, and it can be built, in general, on the familiar ideas of average speed, average cost, and so on, without the need for translation to and from the graph. It is also possibly easier to approach the limit by thinking of drawing part of the mapping diagram on a larger and larger scale, than by thinking of one point travelling down the graph until, when it meets the other, the chord becomes the tangent.

124

On the other hand, a mapping diagram looks essentially discrete, while a graph looks essentially continuous; it is much easier to appreciate how the gradient is changing than how the scale factor is changing, so that graphs are more useful for the consideration of maxima and minima, and for any study of higher derivatives.

Moreover, the teacher has to be very careful to notice that if the function is not monotonic over the interval, it may actually be incorrect to identify $[f(b)-f(a)]/(b-a)$ with the ratio of the lengths of the intervals; consider, for example, the function $x \to x^2$, for which $\{x: -1 < x < +1\}$ maps onto $\{y: 0 \leqslant y < +1\}$; the 'average scale factor' is zero, but the ratio of the lengths of the intervals is $\frac{1}{2}$. (These lengths must, of course, both be signed.)

(c) Differentiation of a composite function (unhappily called 'function of a function' in many texts) can be illustrated with a very convincing diagram, which a graph cannot match. Indeed, the simplest cases, such as differentiating $\sin(ax+b)$, become virtually obvious when seen in these terms.

On the other hand, the analytical difficulties are no less, and, although it may seem to be glossed over more easily in this setting, the problem of dealing with $(\delta y/\delta u) \times (\delta u/\delta x)$ when $\delta u$ may vanish is, of course, in no way simplified.

(d) Inverse functions are particularly easily visualized by this means; it is much simpler to appreciate the interchange of domain and codomain than to appreciate the effect of reflection of a graph in $y = x$.

Products, however, can only be handled by this means by a *tour de force*.

(e) The discrete appearance of the mapping diagram is a help in several ways. It is at least as easy to appreciate the meaning of $\delta y \simeq (dy/dx)\delta x$ on a mapping diagram as on a graph, and, because it brings out the similarity between differentiation and differencing, it compares well with the numerical methods which must be used to simulate differentiation in a computer, and leads on to numerical methods which proceed by finite differences.

Indeed, it is possible to consider realistically the approximate differentiation of functions which we cannot yet handle analytically—compare Section 4—or for which only a table of values is available; and, conversely, it provides a very good indication of how to use tables (such as the S.M.P. Advanced Tables) which need interpolation. In fact, a session with the square tables, and, later, with the tables of circular functions, can be most illuminating.

On the other hand, with Newton's method of successive approximation, which may well be regarded as the prediction of $\delta x$, instead of $\delta y$, from $\delta y \simeq (dy/dx)\,\delta x$, the $x$-axis appears much more significant to the eye than does the point $y = 0$ of the codomain; and though some pupils find Newton's method, in the first instance, easier to grasp from a mapping diagram than from a graph, the difficulties associated with the size of $d^2y/dx^2$ can really only be illustrated by a graph.

It is advisable, therefore, to aim at being completely bi-lingual, and teachers should consider how each illustration can be used at each new step of the course, even if they decide only to use one on that occasion.

## 1. AVERAGE SCALE FACTORS: DERIVATIVES

**1.1 Scale factors for a linear function.** The inverse mapping $x \to (x+2)/3$ has scale factor $\frac{1}{3}$, and even at this stage it is worth pointing out why.

The invariant point of $x \to 4-3x$ is 1, so that the mapping diagram will simply be that of Figure 1 twisted about a line drawn from $x = 1$ to $y = 1$.

(a) 2; (b) $-\frac{1}{2}$; (c) $a$; inverses, (a) $\frac{1}{2}$; (b) $-2$; (c) $1/a$. The point is, of course, that the scale factor of the inverse mapping is the reciprocal of the scale factor of the original mapping, and this will be a very useful point to be able to take up later. Compare Exercise A, Question 12, and the differentiation of $\tan^{-1} x$ in the next volume.

**1.2 Scale factors of a quadratic function.** (a) 65·6; (b) 64·16; (c) 62·4; (d) 64·0; $64-16h$. The answer to (d) suggests that a symmetrical interval, even if its length is greater, will give a better estimate of the derivative; this is true, in the sense that (using the first few terms of Taylor's expansion)

$$\frac{f(a+h)-f(a)}{h} = f'(a)+\frac{h}{2}f''(a)+\frac{h^2}{6}f'''(a)+\dots$$

while
$$\frac{f(a+h)-f(a-h)}{2h} = f'(a)+\frac{h^2}{6}f'''(a)+\dots$$

126

so that, when $h$ is small, the error in the latter is an order of magnitude smaller. It will, however, be exact (except for a coincidence) only for quadratic functions.

**1.5   Alternative forms for the average scale factor.** Each of the forms given in this section is important in its own right, and a careful balance should be kept between them. The first is often the easiest to use for 'first principles' work; the second provides a natural lead to Taylor's series; the third is fundamental to numerical work. It is also worth noticing that for some purposes other choices may be even more useful—for example, when we differentiate $\log_a x$, the interval $(b, bk)$, considered as $k$ tends to 1, is the simplest.

The use of the third form is, of course, not only legitimate but vital. The teacher should, however, be aware that

$$\lim_{h \to 0} \frac{f(a+h) - f(a-h)}{2h}$$

may exist when the derivative does not exist—consider $x \to |x|$ at $x = 0$. But if the derivative exists (as the text assumes) it is equal to this limit.

### Exercise A (p. 202)

1.   (a) 3·0301;      (b) 2·9701;      (c) 3·0001;
     (d) $3+3h+h^2$;   (e) $3-3h+h^2$;      (f) $3+h^2$.

2.   (a) 4;   (b) $-\frac{1}{4}$;   (c) $-\frac{1}{16}$;   (d) $-\frac{1}{16}$ $\left(\text{translation} \begin{pmatrix} 0 \\ 1 \end{pmatrix}\right)$.

3.   (a) $-2$;      (b) 3;      (c) 8;      (d) $-6$;
     (e) 9;      (f) 18.

4.   (a) $2a$;      (b) $2a+2$;   (c) $4a-5$;   (d) $1-2a$;
     (e) $2pa+q$;   (f) $-1/(a+2)^2$;      (g) $-1/(a+2)^2$.

5.   (a) $f': x \to 1$;      (b) $g': x \to 2x$;      (c) $h': x \to 3x^2$;
     (d) $r': x \to -1/x^2$;   (e) $s': x \to -3/x^4$;   (f) $t': x \to 0$;
     (g) $S': x \to f'(x)+g'(x)$;      (h) $M': x \to mf'(x)$.

Pupils should be encouraged to look back at their answers to this question as long as there is any need to do so.

It is worth insisting on a logical presentation at this stage; thus, pupils should either tabulate $f$ and $f'$ (as in the tables), or write

$$f(x) = x^3 \Rightarrow f'(x) = 3x^2;$$

or say 'The derived function is $f': x \to 3x^2$'.

Abbreviations such as '$x^3 \Rightarrow 3x^2$' or, worse still, '$x^3 = 3x^2$', must be firmly discouraged. '$f: x \to x^3 \Rightarrow f': x \to 3x^2$' is possible, though strictly incorrect. It may be read 'if $f$ maps $x$ to $x^3$, then $f'$ maps $x$ to $3x^2$', though it is better to use $f: x \to x^3$ as the name of the function—'$f$, such that $x$ is mapped to $x^3$'.

6.  (a) $f': x \to 1 - 1/x^2$;  (b) $g': x \to 4x$;
    (c) $h': x \to 3x^2 + 2x + 1$;  (d) $k': x \to 1 + x + x^2/2 + x^3/6$.

(There is a lead here towards the series solution of $k'(x) = k(x)$, if any pupils have met $e^x$ previously.)

7.  $f'(x) = 3x^2 - 1$, so $f'(-1) = f'(+1) = 2, f'(0) = -1$. This gives the gradients at the three zeros of the function.

$$h(x) = fg(x) = 8x^3 - 2x,$$
so that
$$h'(x) = 24x^2 - 2; \quad h'(\pm 1) = 22, h'(0) = -2.$$
$$h'(x) = f'g(x) \cdot g'(x),$$

of course; it is perhaps surprising that the two sets of gradients are not more closely related.

8.  $f': x \to 2x; \quad g': x \to 2; \quad fg: x \to 4x^2 - 4x + 1; \quad gf: x \to 2x^2 - 1;$
    $g^{-1}: x \to \frac{1}{2}(x+1); \quad p: x \to 8x - 4; \quad q: x \to 4x; \quad r: x \to \frac{1}{2}.$

The numerical examples are meant to suggest the possibility of the chain rule, the product rule, and the inverse rule, and some of the corresponding relations which are *not* true, perhaps, might also be introduced here.

(a) 12;  (b) 12;  (c) 12;  (d) 12;  (e) $\frac{1}{2}$;  (f) 1.

9.  3(a), none; (b) $1\frac{1}{2}$; (c) 0; (d) 0; (e) 0; (f) $\pm\sqrt{3}$.
    4(a) 0;  (b) $-1$;  (c) $\frac{5}{4}$;  (d) $\frac{1}{2}$;
    (e) $-q/2p$;  (f) none;  (g) none.

At this point, the question may well be asked, 'Why is $f'(a) = 0$ so important?'

10. $g(b) = b^2+b+1$, if $b \neq 1$; define $g(1) = 3$; this is the value
which gives the value of the derivative of $f$ there. Similarly, we
might use $b^2+ba+a^2$, and here the limit would be $f'(a) = 3a^2$.

11. There is a step from $-1$ for $x < 0$ to $+1$ for $x > 0$. No value
$g(0)$ can make this continuous, and the derivative cannot exist
there.

12. The diagrams are connected by a reflection $f'(p) = 1/g'(a)$, so
that the scale factor for the square root function is $1/2p = 1/2\sqrt{a}$.
This is a more important method than the 'first principles'
method suggested to differentiate this particular inverse function,
but the other makes a pretty example, since

$$\frac{\sqrt{b}-\sqrt{a}}{b-a} = \frac{1}{\sqrt{b}+\sqrt{a}}.$$

## 2. GRADIENT OF A CURVE
### Exercise B (p. 206)

1. (a) $-4$; (b) 0; (c) $+4$.

2. (a) 3; (b) $\frac{3}{2}$; (c) $-4$; (d) 0, 0; (e) 0; (f) 0.

3. The tangent at $P(h, \frac{1}{2}h^2)$ cuts $Ox$ at $T(\frac{1}{2}h, 0)$; the gradient at $P$ is
in fact $h$, which proves this. The lines from the focus $S(0, \frac{1}{2})$ to
the points $T$ are perpendicular to the tangents, since the gradient
of $ST$ is $-1/h$. To draw the tangent, find $Q$ on the negative
$y$-axis so that $SQ = SP$; join $PQ$. There are many variations
upon this theme.

   The question suggests the very attractive *envelope* (easily drawn
with geo-liner or set-square) of the lines $TP$ drawn perpendicular to $ST$.

4. The velocity is $-14$ m/s, so that the car is approaching the
camera at this speed; filming stops about $\frac{3}{7}$ seconds before impact.

5. The scale factor is $4\pi r^2$ cm³/cm, which may be called $4\pi r^2$ cm².
This represents the surface area of the sphere, because the
average scale factor gives the volume of a spherical shell divided
by its thickness, which can be made as close as we please to the

surface area. Similar relations may be found between the area and the circumference of a circle, the volume and the base area of a prism of constant cross-section; a cylinder expanding but retaining its shape, a cone expanding but with constant vertical angle, and an expanding regular solid give further examples which may be profitably studied.

6. $dE/dx = 2000x$ newtons; when $x = 0.02$, the energy stored is 0·4 joules and the thrust exerted 40 newtons. This suggests the fact that energy measures the capacity of a force to move its point of application through a particular distance; the unfamiliar idea of a thrust representing a rate of change may be introduced through this idea, and potential energy stored when the centre of mass is raised may also be compared.

7. $dC/dn = 5 - \frac{1}{50}n$; the marginal cost is (approximately) the cost of producing one extra article. When $n = 250$, it is actually cheaper to produce more of them (since this point gives the maximum cost); it is not likely, therefore, that this will be a good model for so large a value of $n$, though it may well be adequate for (say) $n$ from 0 to 50. The legitimacy of replacing $n \in Z$ by $n \in R$ is a point for discussion.

8. $v = 12 - 10t$; $dv/dt = -10$. The velocities are $+12$, $+7$, 0, $-12$ m/s; this suggests that it was thrown vertically at 12 m/s, reached its highest point (at a height of 7·2 m) at $t = 1·2$ s, and fell to the point of projection at $t = 2·4$ s.

9. Angular velocity is $(5-t)/9$ rev/s, and angular acceleration $-\frac{1}{9}$ rev/s². The initial angular velocity was $\frac{5}{9}$ rev/s ($33\frac{1}{3}$ rev/min), and it took 5 s to stop.

10. The average scale factor is also the average height of the curve over that interval, and the derivative is simply $f(c)$, the height of the curve. This example paves the way for the 'fundamental theorem of analysis'.

11. A graphical treatment is probably enough at this stage, though a consideration of $x \to a + bx + cx^2 + dx^3$ near the origin leads to

the reflection that the error is reduced by $\frac{1}{2}hf''(a)$+terms of order $h^3$, where $h$ is the length of the original interval—in fact, by $\dfrac{1}{h}\times$ the even terms of the Taylor series. This is no help if $c$ (above) $= 0$, i.e. near a point of inflexion.

## 3. DERIVED FUNCTIONS OF POLYNOMIALS AND OF $1/x$

The results at the head of Section 3.1 should be written out so as to emphasize that
$$f(x) = x^m \Rightarrow f'(x) = mx^{m-1}.$$

This result must, of course, be known thoroughly.

The idea of *linearity*, mentioned here, is of great importance in this course, though it is not necessary for the pupil to appreciate it. Compare the comments on Chapter 4, Exercise C, Question 18. It occurs in two main groups of topics:

(1) *Matrices.* Transforming vectors $\mathbf{x}$, $\mathbf{y}$, say, by a matrix $\mathbf{M}$ is a linear process, for
$$\mathbf{M(x+y)} = \mathbf{Mx+My}$$
and (for scalar k)
$$\mathbf{M}(k\mathbf{x}) = k(\mathbf{Mx}).$$

This has several consequences: the geometrical property that parallelograms are transformed into parallelograms, the possibility of describing the solution sets of linear simultaneous equations, and the ideas of linear dependence.

(2) *Summation.* $\Sigma$-algebra and $E$-algebra (of expectations), integration, and thus (as here) differentiation, are all linear; from this there follows the finding of solution sets of linear differential equations, in particular, for they also form a vector space.

(For a full development of this idea, see Sawyer, *A Path to Modern Mathematics* (Penguin, 1966).)

### Exercise C (*p. 209*)

1. (*a*) 40, 34; (*b*) $3\frac{1}{4}$, 8; (*c*) $\mp 2$, 0; (*d*) 0, $u$; (*e*) $-1$, 3; use the gradients to sketch the parabola.

2. (*a*) $3x^2-6x+2$; (*b*) $1-2/x^2$; (*c*) $4x^3$;

   (*d*) $\frac{1}{2}+\dfrac{1}{2x^2}$; (*e*) $3(x+2)^2$; (*f*) $8x(x^2+1)^3$.

131

**3.**

| | $-\infty$ | $-3$ | $-2$ | $-1$ | $-\frac{1}{2}$ | $0\pm$ | $+\frac{1}{2}$ | $+1$ | $+2$ | $+3$ | $+\infty$ |
|---|---|---|---|---|---|---|---|---|---|---|---|
| $x^3+x$ | $-\infty$ | $-30$ | $-10$ | $-2$ | $-\frac{5}{8}$ | $0$ | $+\frac{5}{8}$ | $+2$ | $+10$ | $+30$ | $+\infty$ |
| $3x^2+1$ | $+\infty$ | $+27$ | $+13$ | $+4$ | $+1\frac{3}{4}$ | $1$ | $+1\frac{3}{4}$ | $+4$ | $+13$ | $+27$ | $+\infty$ |
| $x^3-x$ | $-\infty$ | $-24$ | $-6$ | $0$ | $+\frac{3}{8}$ | $0$ | $-\frac{3}{8}$ | $0$ | $+6$ | $+24$ | $+\infty$ |
| $3x^2-1$ | $+\infty$ | $+26$ | $+11$ | $+2$ | $-\frac{1}{4}$ | $-1$ | $-\frac{1}{4}$ | $+2$ | $+11$ | $+26$ | $+\infty$ |
| $x+1/x$ | $-\infty$ | $-3\frac{1}{3}$ | $-2\frac{1}{2}$ | $-2$ | $-2\frac{1}{2}$ | $\mp\infty$ | $+2\frac{1}{2}$ | $+2$ | $+2\frac{1}{2}$ | $+3\frac{1}{3}$ | $+\infty$ |
| $1-1/x^2$ | $+1^-$ | $+\frac{8}{9}$ | $+\frac{3}{4}$ | $0$ | $-3$ | $-\infty$ | $-3$ | $0$ | $+\frac{3}{4}$ | $+\frac{8}{9}$ | $+1^-$ |
| $x^2-1/x$ | $+\infty$ | $+9\frac{1}{3}$ | $+4\frac{1}{2}$ | $+2$ | $+2\frac{1}{4}$ | $+\infty$ | $-1\frac{3}{4}$ | $0$ | $+3\frac{1}{2}$ | $+8\frac{2}{3}$ | $+\infty$ |
| $2x+1/x^2$ | $-\infty$ | $-5\frac{8}{9}$ | $-3\frac{3}{4}$ | $-1$ | $+3$ | $\mp\infty$ | $+5$ | $+3$ | $+4\frac{1}{4}$ | $+6\frac{1}{9}$ | $+\infty$ |

**4.** (a) $4x^2-12x+10$;  (b) $2x^3-3x^2+2x-3$;

(c) $2x^2-1$;  (d) $4x-6$;  (e) $8x-12$;

(f) $6x^2-6x+2$;  (g) $5$;  (h) $8x-12$;

(i) $6x^2-6x+2$.

Thus, $(fg)' = f'g \cdot g'$;  $(f.g)' = f'.g + f.g'$.

**5.** (a) $dy/dx = 3(x^2+2ax+b)$; two zeros if $a^2 > b$.

(b) If the graph is to cut $Ox$ three times, the maximum must be positive and the minimum negative; since $a = 0$, $x = \pm\sqrt{(-b)}$ for max/min, and $y = \pm 2b\sqrt{(-b)}+c$. The product of the $y$'s is therefore negative, and thus $4b^3+c^2 > 0$.

# 4. EXPONENTIAL FUNCTIONS

## *Exercise D (p. 210)*

(For most pupils, it is sensible to omit this exercise, or to make the points rather lightly; it is included to give some indication of the character of numerical differentiation.)

**1.**

| Date | 1925 | 1930 | 1935 | 1940 | 1945 | 1950 | 1955 | 1960 | |
|---|---|---|---|---|---|---|---|---|---|
| Rate of growth | 24·5 | 27·1 | 29·9 | 33·0 | 36·5 | 40·4 | 44·6 | 49·2 | thou./10 yr |
| Percentage of Pop. | 20·0 | 20·0 | 20·0 | 20·0 | 20·0 | 20·0 | 20·0 | 20·0 | %/10 yr |

This reminds us of the exponential nature of a function which increases so that $f'(x) = k.f(x)$, typical of unhindered population growth.

2. The average scale factor is $8[(2^h - 2^{-h})/2h]$. Slide-rule accuracy gives values 5·55 and 5·5 respectively; 5·545 is a better value; though, since the quantities to be subtracted are very close together, accuracy is inevitably lost. The local scale factor is

$$\lim_{h \to 0} 8 \left( \frac{2^h - 2^{-h}}{2h} \right) = 8 \log_e 2.$$

Values for $f'(4)$ and $f'(5)$ are 11·1, 22·2; the important point here is that $f'(x)$ is proportional to $f(x)$, although no explicit formula for the limit should be mentioned at this stage.

3. The limit is here expressed in the form

$$\lim_{h \to 0} \left( 2^a \frac{2^h - 2^{-h}}{2h} \right) = 2^a . k_1.$$

Similarly, the second limit is

$$\lim_{h \to 0} \left( 8^a \frac{8^h - 8^{-h}}{2h} \right) = \lim_{3h \to 0} \left( 8^a \frac{2^{3h} - 2^{-3h}}{\frac{1}{3}.2.3h} \right)$$

and this is equal to $3k_1 . 8^a$. Thus, $k_2 = 3k_1$.

4. 10, 31·62, 100, 316·2, 1000; using $h = 0·05$, we find for $f'(x)$ the approximate values: 23·1, 73·0, 231, 730, 2310.

$$f'(x)/f(x) \simeq 2·3026.$$

5. The scale factor of $f$ is $k_1 . 2^a = k_1 b$; the scale factor of $F$ is therefore its reciprocal, $1/k_1 b$.

6. 0·036% per year, approximately, on $(0·82)^4$ gm, gives

$$0·00016 \text{ gm/year.}$$

7. (Although this does not refer to exponential functions, this question indicates that numerical methods can be devised to handle the differentiation of functions not so far considered in the text.)

Taking 0·1° above and below, and using the form

$$\frac{\sin (a+h)° - \sin (a-h)°}{2h},$$

133

we obtain the values:

| Angle | 0° | 10° | 20° | 30° | 40° |
|---|---|---|---|---|---|
| Scale f. | 0·0175 | 0·0172 | 0·0164 | 0·0151 | 0·0133 |
| Cosine | 1·0000 | 0·9848 | 0·9397 | 0·8660 | 0·7660 |

| Angle | 50° | 60° | 70° | 80° | 90° |
|---|---|---|---|---|---|
| Scale f. | 0·0112 | 0·0088 | 0·0059 | 0·0030 | 0·0000 |
| Cosine | 0·6428 | 0·5000 | 0·3420 | 0·1736 | 0·0000 |

The factor of proportionality should be $\pi/180$; agreement is quite fair.

It is worth noticing throughout this exercise that the difficulties of calculating the average scale factor with only slide-rule and four-figure tables available become increasingly formidable as the interval decreases; compare this with the difficulty of measuring small lengths on a graph or a mapping diagram with sufficient accuracy to make their ratio accurate to two significant figures.

## 5. APPLICATIONS OF DIFFERENTIATION
### Exercise E (p. 214)

1. (a) $-5$; (b) 2; (c) $\frac{5}{4}$; (d) $\pm 1$;

   (e) 2, 1; (f) $\pm 2, 0$; (g) $\pm 1$; (h) 2;

   (i) $-b/2a$; (j) $\pm \sqrt{a}$; (k) 1 (thrice); (l) none.

2. (a) $(-5, 25)$, min; (b) $(2, 0)$, min; (c) $(\frac{5}{4}, -\frac{9}{8})$, min;

   (d) $(1, 2)$, max; $(-1, -2)$ min;

   (e) $(2, 5)$, max; $(2, 4)$, min; (f) $(\pm 2, -4)$, min; $(0, 12)$, max;

   (g) $(\pm 1, 2)$, min; (h) $(2, 12)$, min;

   (i) $(-b/2a, c-b^2/4a)$, max/min;

   (j) $(\pm \sqrt{a}, b \mp 2a \sqrt{a})$, both;

   (k) $(1, -1)$, min; (l) none.

**3.**

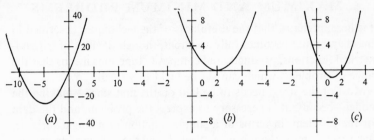

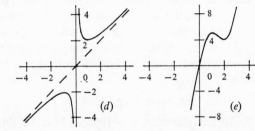

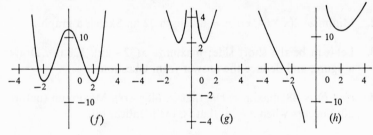

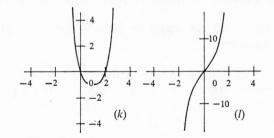

135

## 6. MAXIMUM AND MINIMUM PROBLEMS

It is here, perhaps, that the usefulness of the techniques described in this chapter first becomes fully apparent, though the lack of trigonometrical functions, products, and composite functions means that the range of problems which can yet be tackled is small.

Most of the stress needs to be laid on the first stage—making the model—because it is necessary to express the problem, and the data for the problem, in terms of a simple function of a single variable. One variable must therefore be selected, and the data used to express the others in terms of it; the simplifications and assumptions made should constantly be emphasized; and the relation of the answer to the physical reality is important. Thus, in Example 9, since we know that $r^2h = 128$, we should regard an answer such as $r = 1$ with the gravest suspicion.

### Exercise F (p. 216)

1. $dx/dt = 5 - 10t$; acceleration $= -10$ m/s². Max. height, 2·25 m.

2. Minimize $2(x + 64/x)$; $x = 8$, length 32 m. Sketch a graph.

3. Let $x$ m be the short side; maximize $x(32 - 2x)$. 128 m². Draw a figure, and deduce the answer from Question 2.

4. $r(r + h) = 48$, maximize $r^2h$, that is, $(48r - r^3)$. Maximum (naturally) occurs when $r = 4$, that is, the identical tin.

5. If $x$ cm is a short side, minimize $(4x^2 + 729/x)$; height 6 cm.

6. $A = 4x\sqrt{(25 - x^2)}$, so maximize $(400x^2 - 16x^4)$. $x = 2\frac{1}{2}\sqrt{2}$ cm, giving a square.

7. Average cost, £$(100/n + 5 + n)$; marginal cost, £$(5 + 2n)$. $n = 10$ minimizes the average cost; both are then £25. In the graph, the average cost is represented by the gradient of $OP$; the marginal cost, by the gradient of $PT$. The former is minimized at $M$, where the tangent passes through $O$ and the marginal cost is equal to the average cost. For the cricketer, this shows that if another innings with a score higher than average is added, or one with lower than average discounted, the average rises.

136

Alternatively, if

$$A = C/n, \quad \frac{dA}{dn} = \frac{n(dC/dn) - C}{n^2},$$

so that there is a maximum or a minimum when

$$(dC/dn) = (C/n).$$

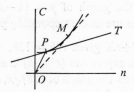

**8.** Maximize $2p(1-p)$ and $3p(1-p)^2$. The values of $p$ are $\frac{1}{2}$, $\frac{1}{3}$.

**9.** Minimize $(2\pi k/r + \pi r^2)$; a graph shows that this has a minimum, but no maximum.

**10.** $dM/dx = 4x - 3, 4x - 12$. $x = \frac{3}{4}$, gives $-\frac{9}{8}$, but $x = 2$ gives $+2$, and the bending moment is numerically greater at the latter point.

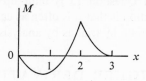

**11.** Minimize $u^2/(u-f)$. If $x = u-f$, minimize $(x + 40 + 400/x)$, so that $x = 20$, and $u = 40$. $v = 40$ also, so the minimum distance is 80 cm.

**12.** Maximize $144R/(R+12)^2$, or, if $x = R+12$, $144(1/x - 12/x^2)$; so that $x = 24$ and $R = 12$ ohms. In general, $RE^2/(R+r)^2$ has a maximum when $R = r$.

**13.**

| Day | 1 | 2 | 3 | 4 | 5 | 6 | 7 | 8 | 9 | 10 |
|---|---|---|---|---|---|---|---|---|---|---|
| Admissions | 37 | 58 | 73 | 82 | 85 | 82 | 73 | 58 | 37 | 10 |
| Beds | | 37 | 95 | 168 | 250 | 335 | 380 | 395 | 380 | 335 | 260 |

Total admissions, 595; greatest number of admissions, 85; of beds, 395. (The maximum number of beds is reached when $(10 + 30n - 3n^2)$ is first smaller than $10 + 30(n-5) - 3(n-5)^2$; that is, roughly when $225 - 30n = 0$.)

137

**14.** The graph of $y = 64/x$ has the same gradient as $2x+2y = k$ when $x = y = 8$, which is therefore the point of the curve which minimizes the total length needed. A shear $y \to y+x$ $\Big($i.e. with matrix $\begin{pmatrix} 1 & 0 \\ 1 & 1 \end{pmatrix}\Big)$ turns the graph of $y = 64/x$ into the graph of $y = 64/x+x$; and the graph of $y = \frac{1}{2}k-x$ into the graph of $y = \frac{1}{2}k$. The minima are at corresponding points.

**15.** (a) To minimize $r^2+rh$, given $r^2h = 128$, we take $x = r^2$ and $y = rh$ (to make the expression $(r^2+rh)$ linear in the variables); then $xy^2 = 128^2$. Draw the graph of $128/\sqrt{x}$, and minimize $(x+y)$ at $(16, 32)$; the answer follows.

(b) This problem, to maximize $xy$ while $2x+y$ is constant, may be reduced to the problem of minimizing $2x+y$ while $xy$ is constant. If $xy = 32$, say, $(4, 8)$ minimizes $2x+y$; if, therefore, we enlarge with a factor 2 from 0, $xy = 128$ at $(8, 16)$ gives the actual solution to the problem.

**16.** The sequence of Question 13 is built up by differences. The point of the question is that it is often as easy, with a computer, to find the maximum by trial as by analysis.

## 7. HIGHER DERIVATIVES

### Exercise G (p. 219)

**1.** If $f''(x)$ is positive, the curve is 'concave upwards', because the gradient is increasing; and if $f''(x)$ is negative, it is 'concave downwards'.

**2.** (a) $(0, 0)$;       (b) none;       (c) $(0, 1)$;
   (d) $(1, 0)$;       (e) $(0, -4)$;       (f) $(\pm 1, 0)$.

**4.** $f: x \to p(x^3-3ax^2+3bx-c)$ may be converted by a stretch $1/p$ parallel to $Oy$ and then a translation $\begin{pmatrix} -a \\ 0 \end{pmatrix}$ into

$$x \to x^3+3hx+k,$$

and by a further translation $\begin{pmatrix} 0 \\ -k \end{pmatrix}$ into an odd function, symmetrical about $O$, its point of inflexion.

**5.** $c^2 < 4b^3$ (adapt Exercise C, Question 5).

Under the translation, the curve becomes
$$x^3 - 3(a^2 - b)\,x - (2a^3 - 3ab + c) = 0,$$
so that the condition is
$$(2a^3 - 3ab + c)^2 < 4(a^2 - b)^3,$$
which reduces to
$$3a^2b^2 - 4b^3 - 4a^3c + 6abc - c^2 > 0.$$

## 8. THE $d$, $\delta$ NOTATION
### *Exercise H (p. 222)*

**1.** (a) 12;           (b) $-3, 0, 0$;           (c) $t = \pm 4$; $t = 0$;
   (d) $4\pi r^2$ (surface area);       (e) $-1, +1$; maximum and
                                                           minimum.

**2.** $y = x^{\frac{1}{3}} \Leftrightarrow x = y^3$;   $x = 8 \Leftrightarrow y = 2$.
   (a) $\frac{1}{12}$;   (b) 12;   (c) $-\frac{1}{144}$;   (d) $+\frac{1}{144}$;   (e) 12.
   (i) This is always true; (ii), (iii) these are only exceptionally true.

**3.** $y = x^{\frac{2}{3}}$;   (a) 3;   (b) $\pm 2$;   (c) $\pm \frac{2}{3}$;   (d) $\pm 6$;   (e) 2;   (f) $-\frac{2}{9}$.
   (i) This is always true; (ii) this is rarely true.

**4.** $v = 10\, t = 2\sqrt{(5x)}$; (c) 10; (d) 1; (e) 10; (f) 10.
   $dv/dt = 10$, $v(dv/dx) = 10$, whatever the value of $t$.

**5.** $v = \frac{1}{2}t^2 = \frac{1}{2}(6x)^{\frac{2}{3}}$; (c) 1;   (d) 2;   (e) 1;   (f) 1.
   Here, $dv/dt = t$; $v(dv/dx) = (6x)^{\frac{1}{3}} = t$. In fact, the statement is
   true, and the expressions
$$\frac{dv}{dt}, \quad \frac{dv}{dx} \times \frac{dx}{dt}, \quad v\frac{dx}{dv}, \quad \frac{d^2x}{dt^2}$$
are all equal.

139

# 8

# CIRCULAR FUNCTIONS

## 1. TRIGONOMETRIC FUNCTIONS

### Exercise A (p. 227)

**1.** (a) $\frac{4}{5}, \frac{3}{5}, \frac{12}{13}, \frac{5}{13}$;  (b) $\mathbf{OP} = 48\mathbf{i} + 36\mathbf{j}$;
   (c) $\mathbf{PQ} = -15\mathbf{i} + 20\mathbf{j}$;  (d) $\mathbf{OQ} = 33\mathbf{i} + 56\mathbf{j}$;
   (e) $\cos(\alpha+\beta) = \frac{33}{65}$, $\sin(\alpha+\beta) = \frac{56}{65}$;
   (f) $\alpha = 36° 52'$, $\beta = 22° 37'$, $\cos(\alpha+\beta) = 5\cdot5078$,
   $\sin(\alpha+\beta) = 0\cdot8615$.

**2.** $\frac{7}{25}, \frac{24}{25}, \frac{5}{13}, \frac{12}{13}$;  (b) $\mathbf{OP} = 7\mathbf{i} + 24\mathbf{j}$;
   (c) $\mathbf{PQ} = -57\cdot6\mathbf{i} + 16\cdot8\mathbf{j}$;
   (d) $\mathbf{OQ} = -50\cdot6\mathbf{i} + 40\cdot8\mathbf{j}$, $OQ = 65$;
   (e) $\cos(\alpha+\beta) = -\frac{253}{325}$, $\sin(\alpha+\beta) = \frac{204}{325}$;
   (f) $\alpha = 73° 44'$, $\beta = 67° 23'$,
   $\alpha+\beta = 180° - \cos^{-1} 0\cdot7784 = 141° 07'$.

**3.** (a) $\frac{3}{5}, \frac{4}{5}, \frac{4}{5}, \frac{3}{5}$;  (b) $\mathbf{OP} = 12\mathbf{i} + 16\mathbf{j}$;
   (c) $\mathbf{PQ} = -12\mathbf{i} + 9\mathbf{j}$;  (d) $\mathbf{OQ} = 25\mathbf{j}$;
   (e) $\cos(\alpha \times \beta) = 0$, $\sin(\alpha+\beta) = 1$, $\alpha+\beta = 90°$.

Angles $\alpha$ and $\beta$ are complementary since the triangles $ONP$, $QPO$ are similar.

**4.** $-\sin\theta$, $\sin\theta$, $-\cos\theta$, $-\cos\theta$.

**5.** $1, \sqrt{3}$; $\sin 30° = \cos 60° = \frac{1}{2}$, $\cos 30° = \sin 60° = \frac{1}{2}\sqrt{3}$.

$$\sin(60° + 30°) = \frac{\sqrt{3}}{2}\cdot\frac{\sqrt{3}}{2} + \frac{1}{2}\cdot\frac{1}{2} = 1 = \sin 90°.$$

$$\cos(60° + 30°) = \frac{1}{2}\cdot\frac{\sqrt{3}}{2} - \frac{\sqrt{3}}{2}\cdot\frac{1}{2} = 0 = \cos 90°.$$

$$\sin(60° - 30°) = \frac{\sqrt{3}}{2}\cdot\frac{\sqrt{3}}{2} - \frac{1}{2}\cdot\frac{1}{2} = \frac{1}{2} = \sin 30°.$$

$$\cos(60° - 30°) = \frac{1}{2}\cdot\frac{\sqrt{3}}{2} + \frac{1}{2}\cdot\frac{\sqrt{3}}{2} = \frac{\sqrt{3}}{2} = \cos 30°.$$

**6.** $\sin \theta = \cos \phi.$   $\sin (\theta + \phi) = \cos^2 \phi + \sin^2 \phi = 1.$

**7.** $\cos \theta = \frac{4}{5}.$                      **8.** $\sin \phi = \frac{15}{17}.$

**9.** $\sin (\theta + \phi) = \frac{84}{85}, \cos (\theta + \phi) = -\frac{13}{85}, \sin (\phi - \theta) = \frac{36}{85}.$

**10.** $\pm \frac{20}{29}.$

**11.** $\sin 2A = 2 \sin A \cos A;$   $\cos 2A = \cos^2 A - \sin^2 A.$

**12.** $\cos 2A = 2 \cos^2 A - 1.$

**13.** $\tan 2x = \dfrac{\sin 2x}{\cos 2x} = \dfrac{2 \sin x \cos x}{\cos^2 x - \sin^2 x} = \dfrac{\dfrac{2 \sin x \cos x}{\cos^2 x}}{\dfrac{\cos^2 x}{\cos^2 x} - \dfrac{\sin^2 x}{\cos^2 x}}$

$\qquad = \dfrac{2 \tan x}{1 - \tan^2 x}.$

**14.** $\sin 61° = \frac{1}{2}\sqrt{3} \cos 1° + \frac{1}{2} \sin 1° \simeq 0\cdot8660 + 0\cdot0087 = 0\cdot8747.$
Tables give $0\cdot8746.$

$\cos 59° = \frac{1}{2} \cos 1° + \frac{1}{2}\sqrt{3} \sin 1° \simeq 0\cdot5000 + 0\cdot0152 = 0\cdot5152.$
Tables give $0\cdot5150.$

($\cos 1°$ is actually $0\cdot9998$.)

**15.** $\sin 44° = \frac{1}{2}\sqrt{2} \cos 1° - \frac{1}{2}\sqrt{2} \sin 1° = 0\cdot7071 \times 0\cdot9825 = 0\cdot6947.$
$\cos 44° = \frac{1}{2}\sqrt{2} \cos 1° + \frac{1}{2}\sqrt{2} \sin 1° = 0\cdot7071 \times 1\cdot0175 = 0\cdot7195.$

**16.** (*a*) $\sin A;$        (*b*) $2 \sin P \cos Q;$     (*c*) $2 \sin P \sin Q;$
(*d*) $\cos Y;$        (*e*) $\cos x;$         (*f*) $-\cos x;$
(*g*) $\tan x$ if $0 < x < 90°, 270° < x < 360°;$ $-\tan x$ otherwise.

**17.** $\dfrac{\sin (A+B)}{\cos A \cos B} = \dfrac{\sin A \cos B}{\cos A \cos B} + \dfrac{\cos A \sin B}{\cos A \cos B} = \tan A + \tan B.$

**18.** $\dfrac{\sin (A-B)}{\cos A \cos B} = \tan A - \tan B$ similarly; divide.

## 2. ANGLE MEASURE
### *Exercise B (p. 229)*

**1.** 10.        **2.** Yes, 0·5.        **3.** 3.

**4.** 6. See Figure A.        **5.** About 60°.

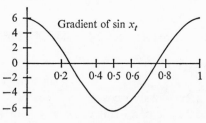

Fig. A

**6.**

| $x$ | 0 | 1 | 30 | 31 | 45 |
|---|---|---|---|---|---|
| $\sin x°$ | 0 | 0·0175 | 0·5000 | 0·5150 | 0·7071 |
| Average gradient | — | 0·0175 | 0·0150 | 0·0122 | 0·0086 |
| $\cos x$ | — | 1 | 0·866 | 0·707 | 0·5 |

| $x$ | 46 | 60 | 61 | 89 | 90 |
|---|---|---|---|---|---|
| $\sin x°$ | 0·7193 | 0·8660 | 0·8746 | 0·9998 | 1·0000 |
| Average gradient | 0·0002 | — | — | — | — |
| $\cos x$ | 0·0 | — | — | — | — |

The average gradient is about $0·0175 \times \cos x$.

(The proportionality is most easily tested on a slide-rule.)

## 2. CIRCULAR MEASURE

Fundamentally, the reason for using circular measure is that the differential equation $d^2y/dx^2 + y = 0$ has a solution $y = s(x)$ where $s(x+2\pi) = s(x)$; if we choose the initial conditions $s(0) = 0$ and $s'(0) = 1$, then $s(x)$ is the sine of an angle which is measured by $x$ in terms of a unit which will ascribe the measure $2\pi$ to a whole turn. But of course it is impossible to appreciate this until a much later stage in learning mathematics, and some temporarily convincing reason has to be given. It seems that the reasons often put first— that the formulae for arc length and sectorial area are simplified— are rather remote from the truth and correspondingly unconvincing.

142

They are therefore put in the second place in this section, and the gradient is brought to the forefront of the discussion. The gradient of sin $x$ is easily seen to be proportional to cos $x$, and it is obviously convenient to arrange that this shall be a strict equality;

$$d(\sin x)/dx = \cos x.$$

This determines the unit to be used, and the true nature of the gain which accrues from this choice of unit appears as the subject is developed.

### *Exercise C (p. 232)*

1. $\dfrac{3\pi}{4}$, $\dfrac{3\pi}{2}$, $\dfrac{5\pi}{3}$, $\dfrac{13\pi}{6}$, $4\pi$, $\dfrac{17\pi}{4}$, $\dfrac{3\pi}{8}$, $\dfrac{1\pi}{5}$, $\dfrac{3\pi}{5}$, $\dfrac{11\pi}{18}$.

2. $22\frac{1}{2}°$, 54°, 630°, 150°, 165°, 72°, 540°, 405°, 130°, 243°.

3. $1, \frac{1}{2}, -1, -\frac{1}{2}\sqrt{3}, 0, 0, -\sqrt{3}, 1$.

4. $\cos\theta, -\cos\theta, -\tan\theta$.

5. $\sin(2\pi+x) = \sin x, \quad \tan(\pi+x) = \tan x$.

6. Area $= \frac{1}{2}r^2(\theta-\sin\theta)$.

7. A solid angle subtended by an area $A$ at a point $O$ is the area cut off on the unit sphere surrounding $O$ by the rays drawn from $O$ to the points of $A$ (see Figure B).

   The solid angle subtended by the whole sphere is $4\pi$.

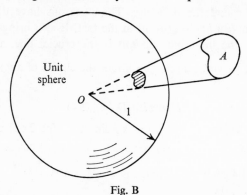

Fig. B

8. Area of cap $= r^2\omega$; volume of sector $= \frac{1}{3}r^3\omega$.

143

## 3. THE DERIVATIVES OF
### $\sin x$ AND $\cos x$

Many students find difficulty in grasping that the $x$ in $\sin x$ is just as much a number as the $x$ in $x^2$ or in $\log x$, and even at a much later stage are capable of writing

$$\int_0^1 \frac{dx}{1+x^2} = 45°.$$

Insistence on good habits of thought at the start, and an occasional problem like 'find $x$ if $x = 2 \sin x$' (to be solved graphically) can help to overcome it, but it often indicates lack of appreciation of the true nature of a function.

If a symmetrical neighbourhood is not chosen for evaluating the gradient of $\sin x$, there is more difficulty with the limits.

$$\lim_{h \to 0} \frac{\sin (x+h) - \sin x}{h} = \lim_{h \to 0} \frac{\sin x (\cos h - 1) + \cos x \sin h}{h}$$

necessitates dealing with

$$\lim_{h \to 0} \frac{\cos h - 1}{h},$$

and the half-angle formula is not at present available. Nor are we yet familiar with the formula

$$\sin (x+h) - \sin x = 2 \cos (x+h/2) \sin (h/2)$$

which gets round the difficulty. These reasons have dictated the choice of $\sin (a+h) - \sin (a-h)$ in the text. It also brings out more clearly that the limit $\lim_{h \to 0} (\sin h/h)$ is the crucial one, and throws light on the previous discussion about the choice of angle measure.

### Exercise D (p. 234)

1. (a) $-3 \sin x$;     (b) $\cos x - \sin x$;     (c) $2 \cos x$;
   (d) $\sin x$;     (e) $-\sin x$;     (f) $\cos x$.

2. $3 \sin x + 4 \cos x = 5$ when $\cos x = \frac{4}{5}$, $\sin x = \frac{3}{5}$;
   $x = 2n\pi + 0.6435$.

3. $1, -1$.

**4.** 7 cm, 3 cm. Its velocity $= 2 \sin t$ cm/s, and has a maximum of 2 cm/s when $t = (2n+\frac{1}{2})\pi$, when it is moving up; when

$$t = (2n-\frac{1}{2})\pi$$

it is moving down with the same speed. It is then 5 cm above the table. When $t = \frac{5}{6}\pi$, velocity $= 2 \sin \frac{5}{6}\pi = 1$ cm/s.

**5.** See Figure C. 0·185. **7.** See figure D.

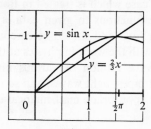

Fig. C

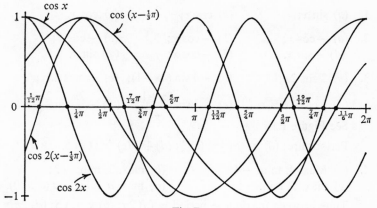

Fig. D

**8.** $y = 3 \sin (x-2)$.

**9.** (a) Arc $UP = t$ m.;
(b) velocity of $P = 1$ m/s along tangent at $P$;
(c) $NP = \sin t$ m.;
(d) vertical component of velocity of $P = 1$ m/s cos $t$

$$= \frac{d}{dt}(NP) = \frac{d}{dt}\sin t \text{ m/s} \Rightarrow \frac{d}{dt}(\sin t) = \cos t.$$

## 4. MORE GENERAL
## CIRCULAR FUNCTIONS

Paragraph 4 of Chapter 5 should be revised before tackling this section. We cannot of course use 'composite function' methods to obtain the derivative of $\sin(ax+b)$, but the idea of the effect of a simple scale factor on gradient is not difficult, and is a helpful guide to the more general case which is treated in Book 2.

Constructing sine functions to given data is a valuable piece of mathematical 'modelling' and should be carefully explained. There may be useful links with the work in physics at this point; if students are familiar with wave motion of various kinds—ripples, sound waves in strings and pipes, light waves, and so on—it will be profitable to discuss their appropriate mathematical expression.

### *Exercise E (p. 237)*

1. (a) $\sin x$;　　(b) $\cos x$;　　(c) $\cos x$.

2. (a) $-\cos x$;　　(b) $-\cos x$;　　(c) $-\cos x$;
   (d) $-\sin x$.　　(e) $-\cos x$;　　(f) $\sin x$.

3. (a) $2\cos 2x$;　　(b) $-4\sin(4x-1)$;　(c) $4\pi\cos 4\pi x$;

   (d) $\frac{1}{2}\cos\frac{1}{2}x$;　　(e) $-\frac{3}{2}\sin\frac{3x+1}{2}$;　(f) $-\frac{2\pi}{5}\sin\frac{2\pi x}{5}$.

   See Figure E.

   Periods are: (a) $\pi$; (b) $\frac{1}{2}\pi$; (c) $\frac{1}{2}$; (d) $4\pi$; (e) $\frac{4}{3}\pi$; (f) 5.

4. (a) Max. 4, min. $-4$;　　　(b) max. 3, min. $-3$;
   (c) max. 5, min. $-5$;　　　(d) max. $a$, min. $-a$ ($a > 0$).

   Time between maxima = period = (a) $2\pi$; (b) $\pi$; (c) 5; (d) $2\pi/p$ seconds.

5. (a) 4;　(b) 0;　(c) $-2\pi\sin\frac{1}{5}\pi$;　(d) $-pa\sin\alpha$.

6. (a) $\pm 4$;　(b) $\pm 6$;　(c) $\pm 2\pi$;　(d) $\pm pa$.

   In each case $dy/dt = k\cos\theta$ where $y = l\sin\theta$ for some $\theta$; when $y = 0$, $\theta = 0$ or $\pi$, and $\cos\theta = \pm 1$; hence $dy/dt = \pm k$.

7. (a) 11 m, 1m; (b) $2+\pi$h after noon, about 5·8; (c) $4\pi$ h, about 12·6 h; (d) 7·5 m/h.

**8.** $x = 5 \sin \pi t$ cm.  **9.** See Figure F.

**10.** $V = 325 \sin 100\pi t$ volts.

$dv/dt = 32500 \pi \cos 100 \pi t$ volt/s $= 32500\pi$ volt/s at maximum.

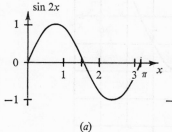

(a)

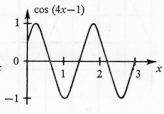

(b)

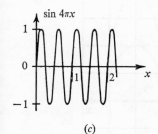

(c)

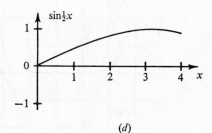

(d)

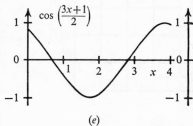

(e)

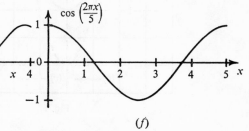

(f)

Fig. E

**11.** (a) $a$;  (b) $2\pi/p$;  (c) $pa \cos pt$;  (d) $-p^2 a \sin pt$.

$d^2x/dt^2 = -p^2 x$, which is proportional to $x$, and is negative when $x$ is positive, positive when $x$ is negative. Hence the acceleration is always along **PO**.

**12.** $v = pa \cos pt$,  $u = v_{max} = pa$.

$u^2 - v^2 = p^2 a^2 (1 - \cos^2 pt) = p^2 a^2 \sin^2 pt = p^2 x^2.$

147

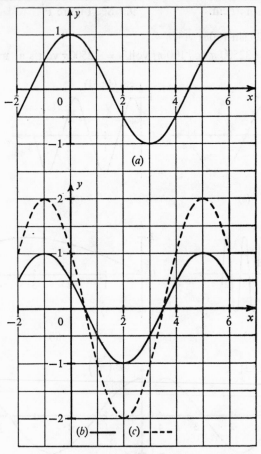

Fig. F

## 5. FORMAL PROOFS OF THE DERIVATIVES
### OF sin $\theta$ AND cos $\theta$

If we have introduced sine and cosine geometrically as ratios of lengths, we are bound to treat their derivatives by geometrical argument in the first place, and analytical rigour is beside the point. That is the position adopted in this chapter. If we wish to be rigorous, a geometrical start involves us in rigorous treatment of such geometric ideas as distance, arc length, area of curved regions

148

and so on. We can obtain the interesting periodic properties of the circular functions more easily by starting with an analytical definition: for example, we may define $\sin x$ as the solution of $d^2y/dx^2 + y = 0$ for which $y = 0$ and $dy/dx = 1$ for $x = 0$. Or we can define $\sin x$ as the sum of the series

$$x - x^3/3! + x^5/5! - x^7/7! + \ldots.$$

Alternatively we may remain nearer to the geometric approach and define $\sin x$ by the equation

$$x = \int_0^{\sin x} \frac{du}{\sqrt{(1 - u^2)}}.$$

All demand a level of analytical sophistication which is at best on the fringe of attainability in an advanced school course. The first is probably the simplest; from the definition the addition formulae and the periodicity are easy to establish, followed by $\cos^2 x + \sin^2 x = 1$, the connection with the circle $x^2 + y^2 = 1$, and with the matrix of a rotation. Finally, when arc-length has been rigorously defined, we may connect it with this rotational measure. And this is where we came in.

# 9

# VECTORS

## 1. THE GEOMETRICAL VECTOR

It is easy for pupils to be muddled in the distinctions between
vectors, bound vectors and position vectors, and to have a feeling of
insecurity when using vectors through failing to realize that when a
position vector is expressed in terms of base position vectors, as, for
example, in $k\mathbf{OP} = l\mathbf{OA}+m\mathbf{OB}+n\mathbf{OC}$, the point $P$, for fixed
$A, B, C$, may or may not be independent of the position of $O$ (here
it is independent if and only if $k = l+m+n$).

A geometrical vector is defined as an equivalence class, so that it is
a set of directed line segments, whereas a bound vector is an element
of such a set. (It is worth remarking here that a position vector is a
vector and not a bound vector; the position vector $\mathbf{OP}$ of the point
$P$ has the directed line segment $OP$ as one of its elements.) It is
common practice to write bound vectors as vectors, because of the
implied vector law for combining them. For example, in finding the
resultant of forces represented by line segments $AB$, $AC$, one adds
the vectors $\mathbf{AB}$, $\mathbf{AC}$ and then selects from the vector sum the line
segment through $A$.

Most teachers, it is thought, will want to use Section 2, or part of
it, to add interest to the work of the chapter and to show at an early
stage some need for vector addition.

### Exercise A (p. 243)

**2.** $\mathbf{d} = \mathbf{e}$ is 4·9 cm, N $22\frac{1}{2}°$ W $(337\frac{1}{2}°)$; $\mathbf{f} = \mathbf{h}$ is 5·3 cm, S 86° W
$(266°)$; $\mathbf{g}$ is 8·7 cm, S $68\frac{1}{2}°$ W $(248\frac{1}{2}°)$.

**3.** $\mathbf{p}+\mathbf{q}$ is 1 cm due east; $\mathbf{q}+\mathbf{p} = \mathbf{p}+\mathbf{q}$.

**4.** $\mathbf{r}$ is 4 cm due west.

5. $(a+b)+c = a$; $a+f = 0$; $a+b+c+d+e+f = 0$;
$(a+f)+(b+c)+(d+e) = 0$. This question is designed to illustrate the associative and commmutative laws, as in

$$(a+b)+c = e+c = a,$$

or $\qquad (a+b)+c = a+(b+c) = a+0 = a.$

6. 0.

7. In (b) the figure might be 'crossed over'. Yes.

8. (a) **AC** or **A'C'**; (b) **AB'** or **DC'**; (c) **AB'** or **DC'**;
(d) **BA'** or **CD'**; (e) **AC'**; (f) **B'D'** or **BD**.

9. No. Replacing $\pm$**BC** by $\pm$(**BA**+**AC**), $\pm$**CD** by $\pm$(**CA**+**AD**),
$\pm$**DB** by $\pm$(**DA**+**AB**), the sum of the six vectors is

$$\lambda AB + \mu AC + \nu AD,$$

where $\lambda = \pm 1 \pm 1 \pm 1$, and similarly for $\mu$, $\nu$. Hence $\lambda$, $\mu$, $\nu$ are not zero. Three such non-coplanar vectors do not sum to a zero vector.

# 2. PHYSICAL VECTOR QUANTITIES
## Exercise B (p. 249)

1. 0·68 N (2 sin 20°).

2. 3·9 m/s. In a direction of $22\frac{1}{2}°$ with the direction of the train's movement ($\tan^{-1} \frac{5}{12}$).

3. 37° (36° 52′).      **4.** 3·7° above the horizontal.

5. N 15° E, 160 km/h (15° 4′, 163·2).

6. $076\frac{1}{2}°$, 22 minutes.

7. 3 minutes; 0·3 km. 53° (53° 8′) upstream from the bank, $3\frac{3}{4}$ minutes.

8. 4° 24′.

9. 49 N at right-angles to the string.

## 3. EXTENDING VECTOR ALGEBRA

The point of Questions 3 and 4 of the next exercise will be lost if the drawing is not very accurate. If this is thought likely, the vectors **a** and **b** could be modified to, say,

$$\begin{pmatrix} 12 \\ 0 \end{pmatrix}, \quad \begin{pmatrix} 8 \\ 16 \end{pmatrix},$$

$O'$ taken at $(-12, 20)$, and the work done on graph paper.

### Exercise C (p. 252)

**2.** $R$ and $R'$ are each the mid-point of $PQ$.

**3.** In ($b$), $Q$ lies on $AB$ such that $AQ:QB = 1:3$. In ($c$), $R$ lies on $AB$ produced such that $BR:RA = 1:3$.

**4.** In ($b$), ($c$), $Q'$, $R'$ are the same points as $Q$, $R$ of Question 3; but in ($a$) $P'$ is not the same point as $P$.

**5.** $\mathbf{AB} = \mathbf{b} - \mathbf{a}$.          **6.** $P$ is the mid-point of $AB$.

**7.** $Q$ is the point such that $A$ is the mid-point of $BQ$.

**8.** $\mathbf{OR} = \frac{1}{3}\mathbf{a} + \frac{2}{3}\mathbf{b} = \mathbf{a} + \frac{2}{3}(\mathbf{b} - \mathbf{a})$. No; it is the same expression for all positions of $O$.

**9.** ($a$) $\mathbf{BC} = \mathbf{c} - \mathbf{b}$;    ($b$) $\mathbf{AD} = \mathbf{c} - \mathbf{b}$;      ($c$) $\mathbf{d} = \mathbf{a} + \mathbf{c} - \mathbf{b}$;
$\mathbf{AD} = \mathbf{d} - \mathbf{a}$;      ($d$) $\frac{1}{2}\mathbf{a} + \frac{1}{2}\mathbf{c}, \frac{1}{2}\mathbf{a} + \frac{1}{2}\mathbf{c} = \frac{1}{2}\mathbf{b} + \frac{1}{2}(\mathbf{a} + \mathbf{c} - \mathbf{b})$.
The diagonals bisect each other.

**10.** ($a$) $P$ is the mid-point of $CG$;

    ($b$) $X \equiv D$;

    ($c$) $Q$ is on $DH$ such that $HQ = \frac{2}{3}HD$;

    ($d$) $Y$ is such that $\mathbf{HD} = \mathbf{DY}$.

## 4. THE RATIO THEOREM
### Exercise D (p. 256)

**1.** $1:1$; $3:1$; $2:-1$ (or externally in the ratio $2:1$); $-3:5$ (or, externally in the ratio $3:5$).

**2.** ($a$) $\mathbf{a} = \frac{1}{3}(2\mathbf{q} + \mathbf{s})$;          ($b$) $\mathbf{q} = \frac{1}{6}(5\mathbf{p} + \mathbf{r})$;
    ($c$) $\mathbf{s} = \frac{1}{5}(14\mathbf{q} - 9\mathbf{r})$;        ($d$) $\mathbf{b} = \frac{1}{3}(5\mathbf{a} - 2\mathbf{s})$.

**3.** *A*, *B*, *C* are collinear and $2\mathbf{AC} = \mathbf{CB}$.

**4.** (*a*) Mid-point of *BC*;
(*b*) point of trisection furthest from *A* of the join of *A* to the mid-point of *BC*;
(*c*) point of trisection furthest from *B* of the join of *B* to the mid-point of *CA*.

No. The medians of a triangle are concurrent at a point which is the point of trisection of each median furthest from its vertex.

**5.** (*a*) $\frac{2}{3}\mathbf{b}+\frac{1}{3}\mathbf{c}$;          (*b*) $\frac{2}{3}\mathbf{a}+\frac{1}{3}\mathbf{c}$;
(*c*) $\frac{1}{2}\mathbf{a}+\frac{1}{6}\mathbf{b}+\frac{1}{3}\mathbf{c}$;       (*d*) $\frac{1}{3}\mathbf{a}+\frac{1}{2}\mathbf{b}+\frac{1}{6}\mathbf{c}$.

**6.** The point of trisection nearest to *C* of the median through *C*.
$\frac{1}{3}(\frac{1}{2}\mathbf{b}+\frac{1}{2}\mathbf{a})+\frac{2}{3}\mathbf{c}$.

**7.** (*a*) $\mathbf{b}-\mathbf{a}$; $\frac{2}{3}(\mathbf{b}-\mathbf{a})$;        (*b*) $\frac{1}{3}\mathbf{a}+\frac{2}{3}\mathbf{b}$; $\frac{1}{6}\mathbf{a}+\frac{1}{3}\mathbf{b}+\frac{1}{2}\mathbf{c}$;
(*c*) $\frac{1}{4}\mathbf{a}+\frac{3}{4}\mathbf{c}$; *N* lies on *AC* (dividing it in the ratio 3:1).

**8.** (*a*) $\mathbf{p}-\mathbf{a} = k(\mathbf{b}-\mathbf{p})$ and $\mathbf{q}-\mathbf{a} = k(\mathbf{q}-\mathbf{b})$, from which the results follow;
(*b*) from (*a*), *A*, *B* divide *PQ* in the ratios

$$-\frac{k-1}{k+1} \quad \text{and} \quad \frac{k-1}{k+1};$$

that is, one internally and the other externally in the same ratio.

**9.** *A*, *B*, *C* are collinear; $\overline{AB}/\overline{BC} = r/p$ (unless $p = q = r = 0$, when nothing can be said about *A*, *B*, *C*).

**10.** On the graph of $y = 1/x$ draw the line $y = -1$ to meet the curve at *A* and the *y*-axis at *B*. The graph is the locus of *P* in relation to *AB*. At *B* the ratio is 'infinite'.

## 5. CENTROIDS

In Question 2 of the next Exercise, it may be worth showing that different methods lead to the same result. In (*a*), the position of *P* can be found as the centroid of *A*, *B*, *C* with associated numbers 2, 1, 1, *or* by writing $\mathbf{p} = \frac{1}{2}\mathbf{a}+\frac{1}{2}(\frac{1}{2}\mathbf{b}+\frac{1}{2}\mathbf{c})$, *or* by taking *A* as the origin, since the position is independent of the origin.

### Exercise E (p. 260)

1. (a) 9 cm, 15 cm; (b) 14 cm, 10 cm; (c) 54 cm, 30 cm.

2. With reference to axes $BC$ and $BA$:
   (a) (1, 2);　　　(b) (2, 3);　　　(c) (4, 4).

3. (a) $R$;　(b) $S$;　(c) mid-point of $SR$;　(d) mid-point of $QR$.
   Yes. Yes. Planes $ABC$, $PQR$ cut $OS$ at its points of trisection; and these points are the centroids of triangles $ABC$ and $PQR$.

4. $\mathbf{g} = (2\mathbf{a} - \mathbf{b} + 3\mathbf{c} - \mathbf{d})/3$; $\mathbf{d} = \mathbf{a} + \mathbf{c} - \mathbf{b}$. $G$ is the point of trisection of $AC$ nearer $C$.

5. (a) Masses at $B$, $C$ are equivalent to a mass of 3 at (10, 2). Hence $G$ is (7, 3).
   (b) Masses at $A$, $B$ are equivalent to a mass of 4 at $(4\frac{1}{2}, 4\frac{1}{2})$. Hence $G$ is (7, 3).
   (c) Masses at $C$, $A$ are equivalent to a mass of 5 at $(7\cdot2, 2\cdot4)$. Hence $G$ is (7, 3).

6. $\Sigma \mathbf{GA} = \Sigma(\mathbf{a} - \mathbf{g}) = \Sigma\mathbf{a} - 3\mathbf{g} = \mathbf{0}$.

7. $\Sigma \mathbf{AA}' = \Sigma(\mathbf{G}'\mathbf{A}' - \mathbf{G}'\mathbf{A}) = \Sigma(\mathbf{G}'\mathbf{A}' - \mathbf{GA} + \mathbf{GG}') = \Sigma\mathbf{GG}'$
   $= 3\mathbf{GG}'$. Yes.

8. $\Sigma \mathbf{GA} = \Sigma(\mathbf{a} - \mathbf{g}) = \Sigma\mathbf{a} - 4\mathbf{g} = \mathbf{0}$.

9. $\mathbf{x} = 3\mathbf{b} - 2\mathbf{c}$;　$y = \frac{1}{8}(5\mathbf{c} + 3\mathbf{a})$;　$\mathbf{z} = \frac{1}{7}(2\mathbf{a} + 5\mathbf{b})$.
   $X$, $Y$, $Z$ are collinear since $5 + 16 - 21 = 0$ (see Exercise D, Question 9).

10. $\mathbf{x} = \dfrac{1}{\lambda + 1}(\lambda\mathbf{c} + \mathbf{b})$;　$\mathbf{y} = \dfrac{1}{\mu + 1}(\mu\mathbf{a} + \mathbf{c})$;　$\mathbf{z} = \dfrac{1}{\nu + 1}(\nu\mathbf{b} + \mathbf{a})$.

11. $X$ divides $AU$ in the ratio $q + r : p$, where $U$ divides $BC$ in the ratio $r : q$. Hence $X$ is in the plane of $ABC$. (That $X$ is in the plane of $ABC$ follows also from a result of Section 5.1.)
    Let $AF$, $BG$, $CH$ meet at $X$; choose $p$, $q$, $r$ so that
    $$BF : FC = r : q \quad \text{and} \quad AX : XF = q + r : p.$$
    Then
    $$\mathbf{x} = \frac{p\mathbf{a} + q\mathbf{b} + r\mathbf{c}}{p + q + r}.$$
    Hence $G$ divides $CA$ in the ratio $p : r$ and it divides $AB$ in the ratio $q : p$. The result follows.

# 6. SOME GEOMETRICAL THEOREMS

## *Exercise F (p. 263)*

**1.**  $\mathbf{PS} = \frac{1}{2}(\mathbf{a}+\mathbf{d}) - \frac{1}{2}(\mathbf{a}+\mathbf{b}) = \frac{1}{2}(\mathbf{d}-\mathbf{b}) = \mathbf{QR}$ (similarly). Hence $PQRS$ is a parallelogram.

**2.**  With origin $O$, $\mathbf{a}' = -\mathbf{a}$, etc. Centroid of $ABC$ is $\frac{1}{3}(\mathbf{a}+\mathbf{b}+\mathbf{c})$; centroid of $A'B'C'$ is $\frac{1}{3}(\mathbf{a}'+\mathbf{b}'+\mathbf{c}') = -\frac{1}{3}(\mathbf{a}+\mathbf{b}+\mathbf{c})$. Hence the result. It also follows by point symmetry.

**3.**  $\lambda = \dfrac{bc}{c-b}$, so $\mathbf{x} = \dfrac{bc}{c-b}\left(\dfrac{\mathbf{b}}{b} - \dfrac{\mathbf{c}}{c}\right)$. Therefore $BX/XC = -b/c$. Similarly $CY/YA = -c/a$ and $AZ/ZB = -a/b$. Hence $X$, $Y$, $Z$ are collinear by Menelaus's Theorem.

**4.**  $(p+1)\,\mathbf{DP} = \mathbf{a}+p\mathbf{b}$; $(q+1)\,\mathbf{DQ} = \mathbf{b}+q\mathbf{c}$; $(r+1)\,\mathbf{DR} = \mathbf{c}$; $(s+1)\,\mathbf{DS} = s\mathbf{a}$. If $P$, $Q$, $R$, $S$ are coplanar,

$$s(p+1) - ps(q+1) + pqs(r+1) - (s+1) = 0,$$

that is $pqrs = 1$.

# 7. LINEAR DEPENDENCE

At a first reading of this section attention might well be restricted to the 'general' situations, so that the simplicity of the ideas is not lost through relentless pursuit of the 'special' cases.

## *Exercise G (p. 266)*

**1.**  $\mathbf{AB} + \mathbf{BC} + \mathbf{CA} = 0$.

**2.**  (*a*) $\mathbf{BC} - \mathbf{AB}$;  (*b*) $\mathbf{AC} - 2\mathbf{AB}$, no.

**3.**  $p = \frac{3}{5}, q = \frac{2}{5}$. $A$ divides $BC$ in the ratio $2:3$.
(*a*) $O$, $A$, $B$, $C$ are coplanar;  (*b*) $O$, $A$, $B$, $C$ are not coplanar.

**4.**  $O$, $P$, $Q$, $R$ are not collinear. Suppose $P$, $Q$, $R$ are collinear, then each pair of $\mathbf{p}$, $\mathbf{q}$, $\mathbf{r}$ is a pair of linearly independent vectors. But $\lambda\mathbf{p} + \mu\mathbf{q} + \nu\mathbf{r} = 0$, and therefore none of $\lambda$, $\mu$, $\nu$ is zero. Now $(\mu+\nu)\,\mathbf{s} = \mu\mathbf{q} + \nu\mathbf{r}$; so $S$, $Q$, $R$ are collinear and as $(\mu+\nu)\,\mathbf{s} = -\lambda\mathbf{p}$, $S \equiv P$. Hence $\lambda + \mu + \nu = 0$. Conversely, if $\lambda + \mu + \nu = 0$, then $(\mu+\nu)\,\mathbf{p} = \mu\mathbf{q} + \nu\mathbf{r}$, and $P$, $Q$, $R$ are collinear.

5. An argument similar to that for Question 4 can be used. An alternative method: Suppose $P$, $Q$, $R$, $S$ are coplanar, then **PQ**, **PR**, **PS** are linearly dependent; so $\alpha$, $\beta$, $\gamma$ exist such that $\alpha(\mathbf{q}-\mathbf{p})+\beta(\mathbf{r}-\mathbf{p})+\gamma(\mathbf{s}-\mathbf{p}) = \mathbf{0}$. Compare this with

$$\lambda\mathbf{p}+\mu\mathbf{q}+\nu\mathbf{r}+\tau\mathbf{s} = \mathbf{0}$$

(noting that if this relation were not unique then $O$, $P$, $Q$, $R$, $S$ would be coplanar); then $k\lambda = -\alpha-\beta-\gamma$, $k\mu = \alpha$, $k\nu = \beta$, $k\tau = \gamma$; and hence $\lambda+\mu+\nu+\tau=0$.

Conversely, if $\lambda+\mu+\nu+\tau = 0$, we have

$$(-\mu-\nu-\tau)\,\mathbf{p}+\mu\mathbf{q}+\nu\mathbf{r}+\tau\mathbf{s} = \mathbf{0},$$

i.e. $\mu(\mathbf{q}-\mathbf{p})+\nu(\mathbf{r}-\mathbf{p})+\tau(\mathbf{s}-\mathbf{p}) = \mathbf{0}$, so that $P$, $Q$, $R$, $S$ are coplanar.

6. (Remember that $\tau^2 = \tau+1$.)

$$\mathbf{AB} = \frac{1}{\tau}\mathbf{EA} = \frac{1}{\tau}(\mathbf{OA}-\mathbf{OE}) = \frac{1}{\tau}(\mathbf{OA}+\tau\mathbf{OD}) = \frac{1}{\tau}\mathbf{OA}+\mathbf{OD}.$$

$$\mathbf{BC} = \frac{1}{\tau}(\mathbf{OD}-\mathbf{OA}); \quad \mathbf{CD} = -\mathbf{OA}-\frac{1}{\tau}\mathbf{OD}.$$

7. (a) $\mathbf{AB}+0.\mathbf{BC}+\mathbf{CD}+0.\mathbf{CC'} = \mathbf{0}$;

(b) $\mathbf{AB}-\mathbf{BC}+\mathbf{CC'}+\mathbf{B'D} = \mathbf{0}$;

(c) $-\mathbf{AB}-\mathbf{BC}+\mathbf{CC'}+\mathbf{A'C} = \mathbf{0}$;

(d) $\mathbf{AB}+\mathbf{BC}+0.\mathbf{CC'}+\mathbf{C'A'} = \mathbf{0}$;

(e) $2\mathbf{AB'}+4\mathbf{B'C}+3\mathbf{CA'}-\mathbf{BD'} = \mathbf{0}$.

# 10

# GROUPS

## 1. SETS WITH BINARY OPERATION

This section is designed to remind the reader of the various group laws, before a group itself is actually defined. It may be omitted without any loss of continuity.

### *Exercise A (p. 269)*

1. $S_2$ is not closed: $2 \times 2 = 0$ (mod 4) and $0 \notin S_2$. A glance at the various tables shows that all the others are closed.

2. In $S_6$ $(2 \sim 1) \sim 1 = 0$, while $2 \sim (1 \sim 1) = 2$.

   Multiplication is associative over the integers, and hence is associative over the classes of integers given in $S_1$, $S_2$, $S_3$, $S_9$ and $S_{10}$. Addition is also known to be associative over the integers, and $\cap$ is known to be an associative operation for sets. (To be precise, the *table* in $S_2$ cannot be said to exhibit associativity since $(2 \times 2) \times 3$ is undefined in the table. However, for multiplication modulo 4,

   $$(2 \times 2) \times 3 = 0 \times 3 = 0 \quad \text{and} \quad 2 \times (2 \times 3) = 2 \times 2 = 0.)$$

3. (*a*) 1, 1, 1, $D$, 0, 0, $w$, $d$, 1, 6;
   (*b*) 1, 1, 1, $D$, 0, 0, $-$, $d$, 1, 6.
   $S_1$ to $S_6$, $S_8$ to $S_{10}$.

4. $S_1$, $S_3$, $S_5$, $S_6$, $S_8$, $S_{10}$. Note that although the universal set is an identity element under $\cap$, inverses cannot exist.

5. $S_1$ to $S_6$, $S_8$ to $S_{10}$ are commutative under the operation given. Symmetry about the leading diagonal is an obvious test for this property, although if, as in $S_8$, the elements are listed in a different order in the rows and columns, this will not appear until they are reordered. Note also that it is not a test for $S_3$.

157

**6.**

| | Closed | Associative | Has neutral element | Has unique inverse | Commutative |
|---|---|---|---|---|---|
| $S_1$ | ✓ | ✓ | ✓ | ✓ | ✓ |
| $S_2$ | ✗ | ✗ | ✓ | ✗ | ✓ |
| $S_3$ | ✓ | ✓ | ✓ | ✓ | ✓ |
| $S_4$ | ✓ | ✓ | ✓ | ✗ | ✓ |
| $S_5$ | ✓ | ✓ | ✓ | ✓ | ✓ |
| $S_6$ | ✓ | ✗ | ✓ | ✓ | ✓ |
| $S_7$ | ✓ | ✗ | ✗ | ✗ | ✗ |
| $S_8$ | ✓ | ✓ | ✓ | ✓ | ✓ |
| $S_9$ | ✓ | ✓ | ✓ | ✗ | ✓ |
| $S_{10}$ | ✓ | ✓ | ✓ | ✓ | ✓ |

$S_1$, $S_3$, $S_5$, $S_8$ and $S_{10}$ satisfy the first four conditions.

**7.**  (a) $p = 4$, $q = 4$;  (b) no solution, $q = 2$;
(c) $p = 3$, $q = 2$;  (d) neither has a solution;
(e) $p = 2$, $q = 3$;  (f) $p = 2$, $q = 2$;
(g) $p = x$, $q = w$;  (h) $p = a$, $q = b$;
(i) $p =$ anything, no solution for $q$;
(j) $p = 2$, $q = 2$.

**8.** All, but only associativity if 0 is included; two, if $a > b$. $x = a+b$ only if $a < b$.

## 2. GROUPS

The previous exercise should enable pupils to handle the group laws with reasonable efficiency; now they have to apply them all simultaneously. The idea that a group table must be a Latin square, but that this is not a sufficient condition should be stressed. One single failure is enough to show that a set is not a group; for example, $(\{1, 2, 3\}, \times (\mathrm{mod}\ 4))$ is not a group since 2 has no inverse.

### Exercise B (p. 273)

**1.**  (a) No inverse;  (b) no inverse of 0;
(c) not associative: $3 - (4 - 5) \neq (3 - 4) - 5$;
(d) no inverse of 0;
(e) not closed: $2 \div 3$ is not an integer;
(f) not associative;  (g) yes, if $n \in Z$;
(h) no identity;  (i) yes, if 0 is included;
(j) no identity.

2. (*a*) No inverse of 0;       (*b*) no inverse of 2;
   (*c*) no inverse of 0;       (*d*) yes;
   (*e*) yes;              (*f*) no inverse of 2, 3, or 4;
   (*g*) yes.

   $n$ is prime, otherwise there are elements $a, b$: $ab = 0 \pmod{n}$.

3. (*a*) Yes;
   (*b*) no inverse of 2, 3, 4, 6, 8, 9, 10 (which is the set of numbers which are not relatively prime to 12);
   (*c*) no inverses;    (*d*) no inverses;    (*e*) yes;
   (*f*) yes;          (*g*) not closed;    (*h*) no identity;
   (*i*) no inverses;     (*j*) no inverses;    (*k*) not associative;
   (*l*) no inverses.

4. $\{1\}$, $\{1, E\}$, $\{1, 5, 7, E\}$, $\{1, 5\}$, $\{1, 7\}$, $\{3, 9\}$.

5. $(a \circ b) \circ (b^{-1} \circ a^{-1}) = (a \circ (b \circ b^{-1})) \circ a^{-1}$ (using the associative law twice)

   $$= (a \circ e) \circ a^{-1} = a \circ a^{-1} = e.$$

   Similarly $(b^{-1} \circ a^{-1}) \circ (a \circ b) = e$.

6. Any non-commutative group; for instance, non-singular $2 \times 2$ matrices.

7. If $e$ and $f$ are both neutral elements, then $e \circ f = e$ (using $f$ as a right identity) and $e \circ f = f$ (using $e$ as a left identity).

8. $a \circ y = b \Leftrightarrow a^{-1} \circ a \circ y = a^{-1} \circ b \Leftrightarrow (a^{-1} \circ a) \circ y = a^{-1} \circ b$
   $$\Leftrightarrow e \circ y = a^{-1} \circ b \Leftrightarrow y = a^{-1} \circ b.$$

9. $a \circ e = a \circ (a^{-1} \circ a)$    (iv)
           $= (a \circ a^{-1}) \circ a$    (ii)
           $= e \circ a$           (iv)
           $= a.$             (iii*b*)

10. Suppose that $a \circ a^{-1} = g$(i). By (iv*b*), there is a $b$ such that $b \circ a^{-1} = f$. Then

    $$
    \begin{aligned}
    g &= f \circ g &&\text{(iii}a\text{)} \\
    &= (b \circ a^{-1}) \circ g = b \circ (a^{-1} \circ g) &&\text{(ii)} \\
    &= b \circ (a^{-1} \circ (a \circ a^{-1})) = b \circ ((a^{-1} \circ a) \circ a^{-1}) &&\text{(ii)} \\
    &= b \circ (f \circ a^{-1}) &&\text{(iv}b\text{)} \\
    &= b \circ a^{-1} &&\text{(iii}a\text{)} \\
    &= f.
    \end{aligned}
    $$

    These axioms for a group, which are those given in the Advanced Tables, are a minimum possible set.

**11.**   Consider first $p = 7$. The multiplicative group is cyclic, as can be seen by taking 3 as a generator; $3^0 = 1$, $3^1 = 3$, $3^2 = 2$, $3^3 = 6$, $3^4 = 4$, $3^5 = 5$, $3^6 = 1$. Since $10 = 3 \pmod 7$, $10^d = 1$ for $d = 6$ and for no lower value of $d$. Now consider

$$\tfrac{1}{7} = 0 \cdot \dot{1}4285\dot{7}.$$

The successive remainders in the division are just these six group elements in order: 1, 3, 2, 6, 4, 5. Hence the blocks of recurring

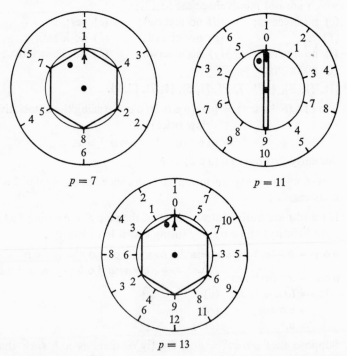

$p = 7$   $p = 11$

$p = 13$

Fig. A. The fixed ring carries the $(p-1)$ remainders on its outer edge, and the decimal digits on its inner edge. The inner polygonal rotor selects the appropriate digits and locates the decimal point when the arrow points at the selected remainder $q$.

digits in $\tfrac{1}{7}, \tfrac{3}{7}, \tfrac{2}{7}, \tfrac{6}{7}, \tfrac{4}{7}, \tfrac{5}{7}$, are obtained from those for $\tfrac{1}{7}$ by repeated application of the permutation $P$ (142857) which changes 1 to 4, 4 to 2, etc. We can show this on a circular disc (Figure A). Now consider $p = 11$. The multiplicative group is again cyclic and we can choose 2 as a generator; the elements are now 1, 2, 4, 8, 5,

160

$10, 9, 7, 3, 6$. But now $10^2 = 1 \pmod{11}$, and $\frac{1}{11} = 0.0\dot{9}$ with only two remainders appearing, 1 and 10. These form a subgroup of index 5 in the multiplicative group and the 4 cosets, $(2, 9)$, $(4, 7)$, $(8, 3)$, $(5, 6)$ give rise to different recurring blocks, all of length 2. Thus $\frac{2}{11} = 0.\dot{1}\dot{8}$, $\frac{9}{11} = 0.\dot{8}\dot{1}$, and so on. On the circular disc the subgroup operation is a half-turn and there are five separate digons carrying the decimal digits. For $p = 3$ the multiplicative group is simply $\{1, 2\}$, and $10^1 = 1$, so that there are two blocks $\{1\}$, the subgroup, and $\{2\}$, its coset. $\frac{1}{3} = 0.\dot{3}$ and $\frac{2}{3} = 0.\dot{6}$. For $p = 5$ there is no root of $10^d = 1$ and the decimals do not recur. $p = 13$ is discussed in *Some Lessons in Mathematics*, ed. T. J. Fletcher, pp. 65–71. It can be proved that the multiplicative group is always cyclic; the number of digits in a recurring block must be a divisor of $p-1$, and is equal to $d$, the smallest integer for which $10^d = 1 \pmod{p}$. See Hardy and Wright, *Theory of Numbers*, pp. 84 and 113–14.

**12.** For $n = 6$, the multiplication table is

|   | 1 | 2 | 3 | 4 | 5 |
|---|---|---|---|---|---|
| 1 | 1 | 2 | 3 | 4 | 5 |
| 2 | 2 | 4 | 0 | 2 | 4 |
| 3 | 3 | 0 | 3 | 0 | 3 |
| 4 | 4 | 2 | 0 | 4 | 2 |
| 5 | 5 | 4 | 3 | 2 | 1 |

and contains two groups, $\{1\}$, and $\{1, 5\}$.

For $n = 10$, there are three groups $\{1\}$, $\{1, 9\}$, $\{1, 3, 7, 9\}$.

For $n = 14$, there are four groups: $\{1\}$, $\{1, 13\}$, $\{1, 9, 11\}$, $\{1, 3, 5, 9, 11, 13\}$.

The elements are the integers coprime to $n$.

**13.** Continuing the process suggested in the hint we shall either find an element which is its own inverse or have just two elements left one of which will be the identity. The other must be its own inverse.

**14.** Let $a, b, \ldots$ be positive integers less than $n$ and relatively prime to $n$.

Then $\{a, b, \ldots, x\}$ is a group. For:

(i) closure: $ab$ is relatively prime to $n$;

(ii) multiplication is associative;

(iii) 1 is the identity element;

(iv) Consider $aa, ab, ac, \dots.$ No two can be equal, since

$$ab = ac \Rightarrow a(b-c) = 0 \Rightarrow b-c = 0,$$

since $a$ is prime to $n$. One of them must therefore be 1.

**15.** If $n$ is a prime $p$, *all* positive integers less than $n$ are prime to $n$. Hence $\{Z_p^*, \times\}$ is a group of order $p-1$.


# 3. TRANSFORMATION GROUPS

This section introduces a number of important ideas. The symmetries of any figure will provide a group (ranging from unsymmetrical figures which have only the identity symmetry to the circle which has an infinite number of symmetry transformations). The rotational symmetries on their own always provide a cyclic group, which is a simple example of a subgroup of the full symmetry group. The idea that in a cyclic group of prime order all the elements except the identity can act as generators, whereas in those of composite order only the relatively prime powers can be generators, needs to be brought out.

### Exercise C (p. 278)

**1.**   (a) Yes;         (b) yes;         (c) no, not closed;

    (d) yes;         (e) not closed;

    (f) no, not closed without the glide reflection.

    (a) and (b) are commutative, but not (d).

**2.**   (a) 4 elements: two reflections, half and whole turn. Three subgroups of order 2.

    (b) 2 elements: reflection in axis of symmetry and identity. No subgroups other than the identity and the full group.

    (c) 8 elements: rotations through multiples of 90° and reflections in the 4 axes of symmetry. Five subgroups of order 2; three of order 4, one of which is cyclic.

    (d) 6 elements: rotations through multiples of 60°. One subgroup of order 2, one of order 3.

**3.**   (a) $F, F^2, F^3, F^4$;

    (b) $S$ and $S^5$ (Note: 1 and 5 are prime to 6; 2, 3 and 4 are not.)

**4.**   (a) $(rm)^2 = r(mr)\,m = rr^2mm = r^3m^2 = I$;

    (b) $rmr = rr^2m = Im = m$;

    (c) $r^2mrm = r^2(r^2m)\,m = r^4m^2 = rI = r$.

**5.**   8, 4, 2, 2. ($rm$ is obviously a reflection.) The elements can be expressed at $I$, $r$, $r^2$, $r^3$, $m$, $rm$, $r^2m$, $r^3m$.

**6.**   The 10 elements can be similarly expressed as $I$, $r$, $r^2$, $r^3$, $r^4$ and $m$, $mr$, $mr^2$, $mr^3$, $mr^4$. The periods are 5, 2, 2.

**7.**   One would expect the number of elements in a group to be a multiple of the number of elements in a subgroup (see Lagrange's Theorem in Section 6).

**8.**   The order of a subgroup is a factor of the order of the parent group.

    (Note that, strictly speaking, all groups have two trivial subgroups—the group itself and the group consisting of just the identity element. The number of subgroups listed in the text of this question is the number of *proper subgroups*.)

**9.**   Since all the elements can be expressed in the form $r^n$, and $r^n.r^m = r^{m+n} = r^m.r^n$, cyclic groups are commutative. Not all commutative groups are cyclic (the symmetries of the rectangle, for example).

**10.**   If $a \in H$ then $a^{-1} \in H$, and $a \circ a^{-1} = e \in H$.

**11.**   (1) If two isometries leave a line fixed, or have some such property, so will their product. Hence we have *closure*.

    (2) The *identity* obviously has this property as it leaves everything fixed.

    (3) If $Q$ preserves some property but $Q^{-1}$ does not, then $Q \circ Q^{-1} (= I)$ does not. Hence $Q^{-1}$ is in the set, for every $Q$.

    (4) The *associative* law must be satisfied by a subset if it is satisfied by the whole set.

## 4. ISOMORPHISM

It is very important to grasp the techniques used in Example 5 thoroughly. The 'sledge hammer approach' must be avoided at all costs. The idea of comparing the structure of two groups by looking at their subgroups is very elegant and helps to emphasize the importance of subgroups.

## Exercise D (p. 281)

1. (a) See Chapter 1, Exercise H, Question 3.

   (b) The proof follows identical lines to 1(a). The symmetry group of the rectangle and the rotational symmetry group of the square have the same order, but are not isomorphic. No. If two groups are isomorphic they must have the same order.

2. $1 \to 0$, $3 \to 3$, $9 \to 2$, $7 \to 1$.

3. Yes; refer back to Chapter 1, Exercise H, Question 2.

4. (a) No. If $a$ and $b$ are inverse elements, then $c$ must be its own inverse.

   (b)

   | $*$ | $e$ | $a$ | $b$ | $c$ |
   |-----|-----|-----|-----|-----|
   | $e$ | $e$ | $a$ | $b$ | $c$ |
   | $a$ | $a$ | $e$ | $c$ | $b$ |
   | $b$ | $b$ | $c$ | $a$ | $e$ |
   | $c$ | $c$ | $b$ | $e$ | $a$ |

   (Note that there is, of course, another type of group of order 4—the Klein group.)

5. If $a$ corresponds to $a'$ and if $e$, the neutral element of $(G, *)$, corresponds to $e'$, then $a * e$ corresponds to $a' \circ e'$. Thus $a$ corresponds to $a'$ and to $a' \circ e'$; so that $e'$ is the neutral element of $(H, \circ)$.

6. $2n + 2m = 2(n + m)$ is an adequate proof. Clearly such results can hold only in the realm of infinite groups as finite groups which are isomorphic have the same number of elements.

## 5. PERMUTATION GROUPS

This section summarizes and includes much that has gone before. The symmetry group of the regular tetrahedron, while complicated, is general enough to provide an exciting discussion about subgroups, isomorphism, permutations and Lagrange's Theorem. Obviously a geometrical model is highly desirable. Permutations themselves are very simple and provide a satisfying way of unravelling some of the awkward symmetries of the regular tetrahedron. Here we meet for the first time a symmetry, for instance the permutation

$$\begin{pmatrix} 1 & 2 & 3 & 4 \\ 2 & 3 & 4 & 1 \end{pmatrix},$$

which cannot be thought of in terms of just a reflection or just a rotation.

*Some general comments.* If we consider the subgroup $\{I, X, Y, Z\}$ of the symmetries of the tetrahedron we see that it can be represented by the four permutations

$$\begin{pmatrix} 1 & 2 & 3 & 4 \\ 1 & 2 & 3 & 4 \end{pmatrix}, \quad \begin{pmatrix} 1 & 2 & 3 & 4 \\ 2 & 1 & 4 & 3 \end{pmatrix}, \quad \begin{pmatrix} 1 & 2 & 3 & 4 \\ 3 & 4 & 1 & 2 \end{pmatrix}, \quad \begin{pmatrix} 1 & 2 & 3 & 4 \\ 4 & 3 & 2 & 1 \end{pmatrix}.$$

These four permutations can also represent the symmetries of the rectangle. Thus the two groups are *isomorphic* but they are not identical. Geometrically, the symmetry group of the rectangle does not contain the same operations as the $\{I, X, Y, Z\}$ subgroup of the symmetries of the regular tetrahedron; the former contains reflections where the latter has half-turns.

The teacher is warned that it is very easy to get confused in talking about permutations. As here defined,

$$\begin{pmatrix} 1 & 2 & 3 & 4 \\ 2 & 1 & 3 & 4 \end{pmatrix}$$

interchanges the vertices which are in places 1 and 2. If this is the *first* permutation to be applied to $ABCD$, then it interchanges $A$ and $B$. But if it follows another permutation (and is written before it, in accordance with our rule for operators), then it interchanges the vertices which happen now to be in positions 1 and 2, and these may be any two vertices.

It is of course possible to define the permutation the other way, so that

$$\begin{pmatrix} 1 & 2 & 3 & 4 \\ 2 & 1 & 3 & 4 \end{pmatrix}$$

interchanges $A$ and $B$ wherever they happen to be. It will be found that this is equivalent to combining the permutations in the reverse order; i.e. if $p_1 p_2 = p_3$ when $p$'s operate on the positions (as here), then $p'_2 p'_1 = p'_3$ for the corresponding $p$'s operating on the vertices.

The genius who can see this at once needs no explanation; others will not be helped by an attempt to explain the situation verbally.

To them we offer the advice we adopt ourselves—try it in a number of cases, and see what happens.

The pattern of the group of rotational symmetries of the regular tetrahedron is more clearly seen if the table is displayed in terms of $I, X, Y, Z$ and one rotation through $120°$. If we select $A_1$ (here written simply as $A$), we have

$$A_2 = A^2, \; B_1 = AY, \; B_2 = A^2Z, \; C_1 = AZ, \; C_2 = A^2X,$$
$$D_1 = AX, \; D_2 = A^2Y.$$

The table now has the following form:

| | $I$ | $X$ | $Y$ | $Z$ | $A$ | $AX$ $=D_1$ | $AY$ $=B_1$ | $AZ$ $=C_1$ | $A^2$ $=A_2$ | $A^2X$ $=C_2$ | $A^2Y$ $=D_2$ | $A^2Z$ $=B_2$ |
|---|---|---|---|---|---|---|---|---|---|---|---|---|
| $I$ | $I$ | $X$ | $Y$ | $Z$ | $A$ | $AX$ | $AY$ | $AZ$ | $A^2$ | $A^2X$ | $A^2Y$ | $A^2Z$ |
| $X$ | $X$ | $I$ | $Z$ | $Y$ | $AZ$ | $AY$ | $AX$ | $A$ | $A^2Y$ | $A^2Z$ | $A^2$ | $A^2X$ |
| $Y$ | $Y$ | $Z$ | $I$ | $X$ | $AX$ | $A$ | $AZ$ | $AY$ | $A^2Z$ | $A^2Y$ | $A^2X$ | $A^2$ |
| $Z$ | $Z$ | $Y$ | $X$ | $I$ | $AY$ | $AZ$ | $A$ | $AX$ | $A^2X$ | $A^2$ | $A^2Z$ | $A^2Y$ |
| $A$ | $A$ | $AX$ | $AY$ | $AZ$ | $A^2$ | $A^2X$ | $A^2Y$ | $A^2Z$ | $I$ | $X$ | $Y$ | $Z$ |
| $AX = D_1$ | $AX$ | $A$ | $AZ$ | $AY$ | $A^2Z$ | $A^2Y$ | $A^2X$ | $A^2$ | $Y$ | $Z$ | $I$ | $X$ |
| $AY = B_1$ | $AY$ | $AZ$ | $A$ | $AX$ | $A^2X$ | $A^2$ | $A^2Z$ | $A^2Y$ | $Z$ | $Y$ | $X$ | $I$ |
| $AZ = C_1$ | $AZ$ | $AY$ | $AX$ | $A$ | $A^2Y$ | $A^2Z$ | $A^2$ | $A^2X$ | $X$ | $I$ | $Z$ | $Y$ |
| $A^2 = A_2$ | $A^2$ | $A^2X$ | $A^2Y$ | $A^2Z$ | $I$ | $X$ | $Y$ | $Z$ | $A$ | $AX$ | $AY$ | $AZ$ |
| $A^2X = C_2$ | $A^2X$ | $A^2$ | $A^2Z$ | $A^2Y$ | $Z$ | $Y$ | $X$ | $I$ | $AY$ | $AZ$ | $A$ | $AX$ |
| $A^2Y = D_2$ | $A^2Y$ | $A^2Z$ | $A^2$ | $A^2X$ | $X$ | $I$ | $Z$ | $Y$ | $AZ$ | $AY$ | $AX$ | $A$ |
| $A^2Z = B_2$ | $A^2Z$ | $A^2Y$ | $A^2X$ | $A^2$ | $Y$ | $Z$ | $I$ | $X$ | $AX$ | $A$ | $AZ$ | $AY$ |

The intelligent pupil might well wonder, if the permutations of 3 elements are isomorphic to the symmetries of the equilateral triangle, and the permutations of four elements are isomorphic to the symmetries of the regular tetrahedron, what geometrical configuration corresponds to the permutation of 5 elements. We need a fourth dimension, and require a configuration of points which are all equidistant from each other. It is called a regular pentatope.

A basic theorem of more advanced group theory is that every finite group is isomorphic to a group of permutations.

## Exercise E (p. 285)

1. The set of permutations which keep the element 3 fixed is the set of the 3! permutations which permute the other 3 elements, and hence forms a subgroup isomorphic to the full permutation

group of 3 elements. The set of permutations which map 3 onto 2 is not closed and hence does not form a subgroup. For example

$$\begin{pmatrix} 1 & 2 & 3 & 4 \\ 1 & 3 & 2 & 4 \end{pmatrix} \begin{pmatrix} 1 & 2 & 3 & 4 \\ 3 & 4 & 2 & 1 \end{pmatrix} = \begin{pmatrix} 1 & 2 & 3 & 4 \\ 2 & 4 & 3 & 1 \end{pmatrix}$$

which does not map 3 onto 2. The relevance of Question 11 in Exercise C is that it is an example of a dual result—in this case the set of transformations which keep a point fixed form a subgroup.

**2.** It is isomorphic to the symmetry group of the equilateral triangle.

|   | $e$ | $a$ | $b$ | $c$ | $f$ | $g$ |
|---|---|---|---|---|---|---|
| $e$ | $e$ | $a$ | $b$ | $c$ | $f$ | $g$ |
| $a$ | $a$ | $e$ | $f$ | $g$ | $b$ | $c$ |
| $b$ | $b$ | $g$ | $e$ | $f$ | $c$ | $a$ |
| $c$ | $c$ | $f$ | $g$ | $e$ | $a$ | $b$ |
| $f$ | $f$ | $c$ | $a$ | $b$ | $g$ | $e$ |
| $g$ | $g$ | $b$ | $c$ | $a$ | $e$ | $f$ |

The isomorphism can be effected in a number of ways. The 3 reflections can be made to correspond to $(a, b, c)$ in 3! ways. Note, however, that once 2 of the reflections have been made to correspond then their products *must* correspond and so there are 6 and not 12 isomorphisms.

**3.** The symmetry group of the regular hexagon is isomorphic to a subgroup of order 12 of the permutation group of 6 elements, which has 720 elements.

**4.** (*a*) $I$ has period 1; $A_1 \ldots D_2$ have period 3; $X, Y, Z$ have period 2. (*b*) $(I, X)$; $(I, A_1, A_2)$; $(I, X, Y, Z)$ are subgroups of order 2, 3, 4 respectively.

It is worth noting that 2, 3, 4 are some but not all of the factors of 12. It should be fairly obvious that subgroups must have an order which is a factor of the order of the parent group; but this question suggests indirectly that the converse is false. We shall show later that there is no subgroup of order 6.

167

## 6. LAGRANGE'S THEOREM

This is one of the fundamental theorems of group theory and though outside the A-Level syllabus should be proved. The proof given in the text is straightforward and provides a good example of the technique of listing, by which many of the more advanced theorems on groups can be proved.

### *Exercise F (p. 287)*

*(Alternative approach to Lagrange's Theorem)*

1. Note first that, in general, $Hx \neq xH$.

   $H1 = \{1, 9\}; \quad H3 = \{3, 7\}; \quad H9 = \{9, 1\}; \quad H7 = \{7, 3\}.$

   Thus $H1$ and $H9$ are identical and complementary to $H3$ and $H7$.

2. If $y \in Hx$ then $y = wx$, where $w$ is some element in $H$. Then $yx^{-1} = w$; or $yx^{-1} \in H$.

3. If $x\,R\,y$ is $yx^{-1} \in H$, where $H$ is a subgroup of $G$, then it follows that
   $$x\,R\,x \qquad \text{(since } e \in H\text{)},$$
   $$x\,R\,y \Rightarrow y\,R\,x \qquad \text{(since } yx^{-1} \in H \Rightarrow (yx^{-1})^{-1} = xy^{-1} \in H\text{)};$$
   and finally
   $$x\,R\,y \text{ and } y\,R\,z \Leftrightarrow yx^{-1} \in H \text{ and } zy^{-1} \in H$$
   $$\Rightarrow zy^{-1}yx^{-1} = zx^{-1} \in H$$
   $$\Leftrightarrow x\,R\,z.$$

   Hence the three conditions for an equivalence relation are satisfied.

4. If there are $n$ elements in $H$, then there must be $n$ elements in each equivalence class. If $z \in Hx$ and $Hy$, then $zx^{-1}$ and $zy^{-1}$ are both in $H$, as also are $yz^{-1}$ and $(yz^{-1}).(zx^{-1}) = yx^{-1}$. But if $yx^{-1} \in H$ then $Hx = Hy$. Equally every element must occur in some equivalence class ($z \in Hz$ if nothing else!). Thus the total number of elements in the group is $n \times$ number of equivalence classes, and $n$, the order of the subgroup, is a factor of the order of the parent group.

5. No. $SB_1 = \{B_1, D_2, I, D_1\}$; $SX = \{X, D_1, D_2, I\}$; and these are not disjoint. The partitioning property is a property of subgroups and their cosets.

168

## Exercise G (*p. 288*)

1. The table has a 'subgroup' of order 2, but the group is apparently of order 5; these two facts are contradictory.

2. A subgroup of order 6 would have to have a subgroup of order 3, such as $\{I, A_1, A_2\}$; also it would have to have an element of order 2, such as $X$. This would give us a potential subgroup consisting of the elements $\{I, A_1, A_2, X, A_1X \text{ (i.e. } D_1), A_2X(C_2)\}$. But this set is not closed; for instance, $XD_1 = B_1$.

3. If an element $a$ has period $k$, then the set $\{e, a, a^2, ..., a^{k-1}\}$ is a subgroup of order $k$; consequently $k$ is a factor of the order of the parent group.

4. This is an obvious error as 3 and 5 divide 15 but not 16. If $a^3 = e$, $b^5 = e$ and $ab = ba$; then $(ab)^2 = a^2b^2$ and

$$(ab)^3 = a^3b^3 = b^3.$$

Hence $(ab)^{15} = b^{15} = e$. Thus the group is cyclic, generated by $ab$, and of order 15. There are no other elements, as any product can ultimately be expressed in the form $a^ib^j$ where $1 \leqslant i \leqslant 3$ and $1 \leqslant j \leqslant 5$.

5. If $a^2 = b^2 = c^2 = ... = e$ and $ab = c$, then $b = ac$, $bc = a$, $c = ba$, $ca = b$, $a = cb$. Consequently $\{a, b, c, e\}$ is a subgroup of order 4, and the total number of elements is a multiple of 4, with the two possible exceptions of the groups with orders 1 and 2.

6. 'is isomorphic to' is an equivalence relation for all groups. There are just two abstract groups of order 6: the cyclic group $C_6$, and the group $D_3$ isomorphic to the symmetry group of the equilateral triangle.

7. (*a*) The order of the group is $p-1$ (see Exercise B, Question 15).
(*b*) $a^2 = 1 \pmod p \Rightarrow a^2 - 1 = 0 \Rightarrow (a-1)(a+1) \Rightarrow a = 1$ or $a = -1 \pmod p$.
(*c*) $1, p-1$, using (*b*).
(*d*) 2 is not its own inverse. Indeed, if $r$ is its own inverse then $r^2 = 1 \pmod p$ and $r = 1$ or $p-1$.

(e) 2, 3, 4, ..., $p-2$ are an even number of integers, inverse in pairs. Hence $2 \times 3 \times 4 \times \ldots \times (p-2) = 1 \pmod{p}$.

(f) Thus $(p-1)! = (p-1) = -1 \pmod{p}$.

(g) $2! = 2 = -1 \pmod 3$, $4! = 24 \equiv -1 \pmod 5$, $6! = 720 = -1 \pmod 7$.

This is a useful theorem in number theory. Another is Fermat's Theorem that, for any integer $a$, $a^p \equiv a \pmod{p}$ ($p$ prime). The proof of this is simple.

Consider the group 1, 2, 3, ..., $p-1$ under multiplication mod $p$.

By Exercise G, Question 3, the period of every element divides $p-1$. Thus $a^{p-1} = 1 \pmod p$ for all $a \neq 0 \pmod p$; and hence for all integers, $a$, $a^p = a \pmod p$.

### Miscellaneous Exercise H (p. 289)

1. $(a), (h);$ $(b), (j);$ $(c), (f);$ $(g), (i)$.

2. $(a + b\sqrt3)(a - b\sqrt3) = a^2 - 3b^2$, and so the inverse of $a + b\sqrt3$ is $a/(a^2 - 3b^2) - b\sqrt3/(a^2 - 3b^2)$; hence the set forms a group under multiplication. The set also forms a group under addition if $0 + 0\sqrt3$ is included. The set forms a field if $0 + 0\sqrt3$ is included.

3. $(ab)^2 = (ab)(b^2a) = ab^3a = e$.

   $(ab^2)^2 = (ab^2)(ab^2) = (ab^2)(b^2ab) = abab = e$.

   Thus the group is the set of 6 elements $\{e, a, b, b^2, ab, ab^2\}$ and is isomorphic to the symmetry group of the equilateral triangle.

4. 0 is the neutral element. $-1$ does not have an inverse ($\{Q, \circ\}$ is isomorphic to $\{Q, \times\}$ under the correspondence $n \leftrightarrow n+1$). Thus the largest subset which forms a group is the set $Q$ without the element $-1$.

5. If $f: x \to ax + b$ and $g: x \to cx + d$ ($a$ and $c \neq 0$), then

$$fg: x \to acx + ad + b$$

which is a member of the set. Also $h: x \to (x - b)/a$ is the inverse of $f$, which is also in the set. The identity function $e: x \to x$ is the neutral element and the associative law is satisfied by all sets of functions. Thus the set forms a group under the operation of combining functions.

170

**6.** The group table is as follows:

| o | $f_1$ | $f_2$ | $f_3$ | $f_4$ | $f_5$ | $f_6$ |
|---|---|---|---|---|---|---|
| $f_1$ | $f_1$ | $f_2$ | $f_3$ | $f_4$ | $f_5$ | $f_6$ |
| $f_2$ | $f_2$ | $f_1$ | $f_5$ | $f_6$ | $f_3$ | $f_4$ |
| $f_3$ | $f_3$ | $f_4$ | $f_1$ | $f_2$ | $f_6$ | $f_5$ |
| $f_4$ | $f_4$ | $f_3$ | $f_6$ | $f_5$ | $f_1$ | $f_2$ |
| $f_5$ | $f_5$ | $f_6$ | $f_2$ | $f_1$ | $f_4$ | $f_3$ |
| $f_6$ | $f_6$ | $f_5$ | $f_4$ | $f_3$ | $f_2$ | $f_1$ |

Note that $f_3 \circ f_4$ means apply $f_4$ first.

$f_4$ is of period 3 and $f_6$ is of period 2. The group is isomorphic to the group of symmetries of the equilateral triangle (under the isomorphism $f_2, f_3, f_6 \leftrightarrow$ the three reflections and $f_4, f_5 \leftrightarrow$ the two rotations).

**7.**
$$\begin{pmatrix} a & -b \\ b & a \end{pmatrix} \begin{pmatrix} c & -d \\ d & c \end{pmatrix} = \begin{pmatrix} ac-bd & -(ad+bc) \\ ad+bc & ac-bd \end{pmatrix}$$

so the set is closed.

$$\begin{pmatrix} a & -b \\ b & a \end{pmatrix} \begin{pmatrix} \dfrac{a}{a^2+b^2} & \dfrac{b}{a^2+b^2} \\ \dfrac{-b}{a^2+b^2} & \dfrac{a}{a^2+b^2} \end{pmatrix} = \begin{pmatrix} 1 & 0 \\ 0 & 1 \end{pmatrix};$$

thus inverses exist. (Note that $a^2+b^2 \neq 0$.)

$$\begin{pmatrix} 1 & 0 \\ 0 & 1 \end{pmatrix}$$

is a member of the set and matrix multiplication is associative. The group corresponds to the group of rotational enlargements about the origin, and has the group of rotations about the origin (when $a^2+b^2 = 1$) as a subgroup. See Chapter 34 (Complex Numbers).

**8.** Let $x$ be an element of $S$. Then since $(S, \circ)$ is closed $x \circ x \in S$. Indeed all finite powers of $x$ are contained in $S$. But since $S$ is a finite subset $x^n = e$ for some integer $n$. But this shows that $e \in S$. Also since $x^{-1} = x^{n-1}$, $x^{-1} \in S$; consequently

$$x, y \in S \Rightarrow y \circ x^{-1} \in S;$$

which is the condition for $S$ to be a subgroup under o.

9. Let $c, d$ be elements of the set $C$. Then

$$a(cd) = (ac)d = (ca)d = c(ad) = c(da) = (cd)a.$$

Thus $cd \in C$ and $C$ is closed. Now

$$(ca)c^{-1} = (ac)c^{-1} = a(cc^{-1}) = ae = a.$$

But $\quad (ca)c^{-1} = a \Rightarrow c(ac^{-1}) = a \Rightarrow ac^{-1} = c^{-1}a$

and thus $c^{-1} \in C$.

Evidently $e \in C$ and the elements of $C$ must obey the associative law. Thus $C$ is a subgroup.

10. The resulting hexagon has alternate sides equal. There are three axes of symmetry and rotational symmetry through any multiple of 120°.

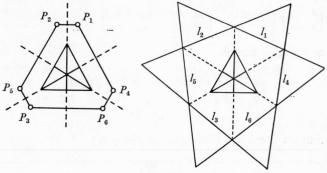

Fig. B

*Groups of small order.* It is worthwhile to have a list of these.

| Order | | Description of group(s) |
|---|---|---|
| 1 | $C_1$ | Identity |
| 2 | $C_2$ | Symmetries of parallelogram |
| 3 | $C_3$ | The rotational symmetry group of the equilateral triangle |
| 4 | $C_4$ | The group of rotational symmetries of the square |
| | $D_2$ | The full symmetry group of the rectangle |
| 5 | $C_5$ | The group of rotational symmetries of the the regular pentagon |
| 6 | $C_6$ | The group of rotational symmetries of the regular hexagon |
| | $D_3$ | The full symmetry group of the equilateral triangle |

172

Generally, for every natural number $n$ there is at least one group of order $n$, the group of rotational symmetries of the regular $n$-sided polygon. This is the cyclic group $C_n$. If $n$ is prime, since there can be no subgroups, this is the only group. On the other hand there are exactly two of order $2p$ ($p$ prime): the group of rotational symmetries of the regular $2p$-sided polygon ($C_{2p}$) and the full symmetry group of the regular $p$-sided polygon ($D_p$). A study of the groups of order $pq$ (both prime) is entertaining and not too difficult (see Birkhoff and Maclane, *A Survey of Modern Algebra*, Revised Edition, p. 150, Example 16). In fact if neither $p = 1 \pmod{q}$ nor $q = 1 \pmod{p}$ there is only one such group. For instance, all groups of order 15 are cyclic (and thus isomorphic!). There are 5 groups of order 8, including the full symmetry group of the square and the quaternion group. It is instructive to see why there are only two possible groups of order 6. Question 5 of Exercise G shows that not every element can be its own inverse and the only possible cases that remain are that two or four of the elements are their own inverses. The first leads uniquely to the cyclic group of rotational symmetries of the regular hexagon and the latter leads uniquely to the full symmetry group of the equilateral triangle.

# REVISION EXERCISES

## 6. INDICES AND LOGARITHMS (p. 292)

1.

|       | $a$ | $b$ | $c$ | $d$ | $e$ | $f$ |
|-------|-----|-----|-----|-----|-----|-----|
| (i)   | $\frac{1}{4}$ | $\frac{1}{2}$ | 2 | 4 | 8 | 16 |
| (ii)  | $\frac{1}{9}$ | $\frac{1}{3}$ | 3 | 9 | 27 | 81 |
| (iii) | 25 | 5 | $\frac{1}{5}$ | $\frac{1}{25}$ | $\frac{1}{125}$ | $\frac{1}{625}$ |

2. (a) 3·303;  (b) $-1·303 = \bar{2}·697$;
   (c) 3;  (d) 1·151;  (e) 7·409;
   (f) $-0·721 = \bar{1}·279$;  (g) $-2·303 = \bar{3}·697$;
   (h) $-0·651 = \bar{1}·349$.

3. (a) $x = 3$;  (b) $x = 1\frac{1}{2}$;  (c) $x = 1·16$;  (d) $x = 18·9$.
   The answer to (d) shows that money invested at 6% trebles in value in about 19 years.

4. Just under 1%. 73 years.

5. (i) $A = bx^c$,  $y = bx^c$;
   (ii) $A = y/b$,  $y = b10^{cx}$;
   (iii) $y = 10^{\frac{1}{2}x}$;  (a) $y = 1·92$;  (b) $y = 70·8$.

6. (a) The first graph is the bell-shaped Normal curve, with the $x$-axis as asymptote and $y$-axis an axis of symmetry. The second graph consists of isolated points, with $y$ tending to 0 as $x$ tends to infinity.

   (b) and (c) give straightforward exponential curves.

7. (a) 84·4;  (b) 1570;  (c) 0·952;  (d) 0·00311.

8. (a) 3·74;  (b) 643,000;  (c) 5·44;  (d) 287,000.

9. (a) 0·632;  (b) 0·436;  (c) 3·62;  (d) 29·6.

10. (a) $4·62 \times 10^8$;  (b) $9·30 \times 10^{-4}$;
    (c) $1·91 \times 10^5$;  (d) $2·06 \times 10^{-3}$.

11. (a) $4·43 \times 10^{-5}$;  (b) $3·84 \times 10^{-3}$;
    (c) 0·360;  (d) 112.

12. (a) 11·2;  (b) 8·54;  (c) 1·73;  (d) 1·32.

## 7. DERIVATIVES (p. 294)

**1.** $f'(a) = \lim\limits_{b \to a} \left( \dfrac{f(b)-f(a)}{b-a} \right)$. $\quad f': x \to 6x-2$.

**2.** (a) (i) 1, $-1$; (ii) 0.
(b) $(2, 4)$ is a minimum point and $(-2, -4)$ is a maximum point. $x = 0$ and $y = x$ are asymptotes.

**3.** $y = 2x^2 + 3x$.

(a) $\dfrac{dx}{dt} = 2t$, $\quad \dfrac{d^2x}{dt^2} = 2$;

(b) $\dfrac{dy}{dt} = 8t^3 + 6t$, $\quad \dfrac{d^2y}{dt^2} = 24t^2 + 6$;

(c) $\dfrac{dy}{dx} = 4x + 3$, $\quad \dfrac{d^2y}{dx^2} = 4$.

**4.** $20 \times 60 \times 30$.

**5.** (a) False. $g$ is continuous at $x = 0$, but $f$ is not.
(b) False. $f$ and $g$ are continuous but not differentiable at $x = 1, 3$; and $g$ at $x = 2$ also.

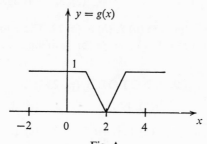

Fig. A

**6.** Assume (without loss of generality) that $b > a$. Then
$$\frac{-(a-b)^2}{b-a} < \frac{f(b)-f(a)}{b-a} < \frac{(a-b)^2}{b-a},$$
i.e.
$$-(b-a) < \frac{f(b)-f(a)}{b-a} < (b-a).$$

When $b$ tends to $a$, this gives $0 \leqslant f'(a) \leqslant 0$, so $f$ is differentiable for all $x$, and $f'(x) = 0$.

## 8. CIRCULAR FUNCTIONS (p. 295)

**1.** (a) $\begin{pmatrix} \dfrac{1}{2} & -\dfrac{\sqrt{3}}{2} \\ \dfrac{\sqrt{3}}{2} & \dfrac{1}{2} \end{pmatrix}$, $\begin{pmatrix} \dfrac{1}{\sqrt{2}} & -\dfrac{1}{\sqrt{2}} \\ \dfrac{1}{\sqrt{2}} & \dfrac{1}{\sqrt{2}} \end{pmatrix}$.

(i) $\sin \frac{2}{3}\pi = \frac{1}{2}\sqrt{3}$;  (ii) $\cos \frac{5}{6}\pi = -\frac{1}{2}\sqrt{3}$;

(iii) $\cos \frac{11}{12}\pi = -(1+\sqrt{3})/2\sqrt{2}$.

(b) $\cos A = \pm \frac{24}{25}$,  $\sin B = \pm \frac{20}{29}$.

**3.** (a) (i) $-\frac{7}{25}$;  (ii) $\frac{47}{72}$;  (iii) $\dfrac{47}{120} \pm \dfrac{\sqrt{119}}{18}$;  (iv) $\frac{7}{25}$.

(b) $f'(x) = 4\cos 4(x+3)$.

$f$ and $f'$ both have period $\frac{1}{2}\pi$; their greatest values are 1 and 4.

**4.** If the domain is restricted to $\{x: -1 \leqslant x \leqslant 1\}$, the greatest value of $3x - x^2$ is 2. If the domain is unrestricted, the greatest value is $2\frac{1}{4}$.

**5.** (a) $dy/dx = 2\cos x - 6\sin 2x$;

(b) $9 \cdot 6°$, $90°$, $170 \cdot 4°$;  (c) $3\frac{1}{6}$, $-1$, $3\frac{1}{6}$.

**6.** The greatest values are (a) 8, (b) 6, (c) 12. These first occur when (a) $t = \frac{1}{4}\pi$, (b) $t = 0$, (c) $t = \frac{3}{4}\pi$ (or $\frac{1}{4}\pi$ if sign is irrelevant).

## 9. VECTORS (p. 295)

**1.** (a) $0°$;  (b) $49 \cdot 1°$;  (c) $39 \cdot 2°$.

**2.** (a) $(3, 3)$;  (b) $(2\frac{2}{3}, 4)$;  (c) $(5, -3)$.

$A, B, C, D, E$ are collinear. $F$ lies on the line if $\lambda = 1$.

**3.** (a) $2 \cdot 2$ min; (b) craft must steer courses between $277°$ and $316°$.

**4.** $t = \frac{2}{3}$.

**5.** (a) $(4, 4\frac{2}{3})$;  (b) $(3, 4)$.

**6.** $\mathbf{AX} = \dfrac{c\mathbf{b} \times b\mathbf{c}}{2(b+c)}$,  $m = \dfrac{b}{b+c}$,  $n = \dfrac{c}{b+c}$.

## 10. GROUPS (p. 297)

1. $\{e, 1\}$, $\{e, m\}$, $\{e, n\}$ are subgroups of order 2; $\{e, d, c\}$ is a subgroup of order 3.

   The group is not commutative, but every subgroup is.

2.

|       | $D_0$ | $D_1$ | $D_2$ | $D_3$ |
|-------|-------|-------|-------|-------|
| $D_0$ | $D_0$ | $D_1$ | $D_2$ | $D_3$ |
| $D_1$ | $D_1$ | $D_2$ | $D_3$ | $D_0$ |
| $D_2$ | $D_2$ | $D_3$ | $D_0$ | $D_1$ |
| $D_3$ | $D_3$ | $D_0$ | $D_1$ | $D_2$ |

3. The matrices form a group under multiplication, isomorphic to the group of Question 2. Other groups isomorphic to these include the group of symmetries of the swastika and the addition group, modulo 4.

4. It is only necessary to show that $A_6 = I$, and $A_n \neq I$ for $n = 2, 3$.

5. Taking $f$ and $g$ as

$$f: x \to \frac{ax+b}{cx+d}, \quad g: x \to \frac{ex+f}{gx+h},$$

we find

$$fg: x \to \frac{(ae+bg)x+(af+bh)}{(ce+dg)x+(cf+dh)}.$$

This suggests a connection between these bilinear functions and $2 \times 2$ matrices since

$$\begin{pmatrix} a & b \\ c & d \end{pmatrix} \begin{pmatrix} e & f \\ g & h \end{pmatrix} = \begin{pmatrix} ae+bg & af+bh \\ ce+dg & cf+dh \end{pmatrix}.$$

It is admissible to quote results about determinants to show (as we have to) that

$$(ae+bg)(cf+dh)-(af+bh)(ce+dg) \neq 0$$

if $ad-bc \neq 0$ and $eh-fg \neq 0$.

The neutral element is

$$x \to \frac{1x+0}{0x+1},$$

and the inverse of $f$ maps $x$ onto $(dx-b)/(-cx+a)$. Composition of functions may be assumed to be associative.

$f: x \to \dfrac{x-1}{x}$ generates a group of order 3.

**6.** The set is obviously closed. $(0, 1)$ is the neutral element, and

$$\left(-\frac{x_1}{y_1}, \ \frac{1}{y_1}\right)$$

is the inverse of $(x_1, y_1)$. To establish associativity, it must be shown that

$$(x_1, y_1) \oplus [(x_2, y_2) \oplus (x_3, y_3)] = (x_1 + x_2 y_1 + x_3 y_1 y_2, \ y_1 y_2 y_3)$$
$$= [(x_1, y_1) \oplus (x_2, y_2)] \oplus (x_3, y_3).$$

The group is not Abelian, but the subset of all pairs of the form $(0, y)$ forms an Abelian subgroup.

Compare with the set of matrices of the form $\begin{pmatrix} 1 & 0 \\ x_1 & y_1 \end{pmatrix}$.

# 11

## Σ-NOTATION AND FINITE SERIES

### 1. THE Σ-NOTATION

Sigma-notation is, of course, widely used throughout mathematics. It has been used loosely in the statistics chapters of earlier books, and a more precise treatment and investigation of the main properties of Σ-algebra here prepares for the following chapter. In particular, some of the examples are designed to make subsequent manipulations of formulae for the variance of a population easier and more meaningful.

Foundations are also laid for later work on area (Exercise B, Questions 15, 16, 17), and the brief discussion of finite series is made the excuse for further practice in using the method of proof by induction. Finite series are given less emphasis than in most traditional texts, but several of the standard techniques are suggested in Exercise B. Geometric series have practical importance, and are of interest mathematically in discussing convergence of infinite series.

### Exercise A (p. 307)

**1.** (a) 9;    (b) 36;    (c) 30;    (d) 30;    (e) 44;    (f) 20;
    (g) $-x^2+2x^3-3x^4+4x^5-5x^6$.

**2.** (a) $\sum\limits_{1}^{9}(i+1)(i+3) = \sum\limits_{1}^{10} i(i+2) = \sum\limits_{0}^{10} i(i+2)$;

    (b) $\sum\limits_{0}^{n-4} \dfrac{1}{i+4} = \sum\limits_{1}^{n-3} \dfrac{1}{i+3}$;

    (c) $\sum\limits_{0}^{5} 64(\tfrac{3}{4})^i = \sum\limits_{1}^{6} 64(\tfrac{3}{4})^{i-1}$;

    (d) $\sum\limits_{0}^{4}(-1)^i(i+1)x^{i+1} = \sum\limits_{1}^{5}(-1)^{i-1}ix^i$;

179

(e) $\displaystyle\sum_0^n (-x)^i = \sum_1^{n+1} (-x)^{i-1};$

(f) $\displaystyle\sum_0^q ar^{p+i} = \sum_1^{q+1} ar^{p+i-1};$

(g) $\displaystyle\sum_0^{n-p+1} ar^{p+i-1} = \sum_1^{n-p+2} ar^{p+i-2}.$

3. All are true except (c), (d), and (h).

4. (a) 86;  (b) 41;  (c) 86;  (d) 45;  (e) 37.

5. (a) 4;  (b) 80;  (c) 43;  (d) 166;  (e) 37.

$$\sum_1^4 (u_i - 3) f(u_i) = \sum_1^4 u_i f(u_i) - 3 \sum_1^4 f(u_i).$$

6. 72, 276, 1024.

7. (a) 54; (b) $61\frac{1}{2}$. The answer to (b) equals the sum of the areas of eight rectangles of width $\frac{1}{2}$ drawn under the graph of $y = x^2$ between $x = 2$ and $x = 6$.

(c) 11·985. In the same way, this is a lower bound for the area under the graph of $y = x^2$ between $x = 3$ and $x = 4$.

8. 15, the sum of the elements in the third column of the matrix; 20.

9. $\displaystyle\sum_1^3 a_{2i} b_{i3}; \quad \sum_{k=1}^{k=3} a_{ik} b_{kj}.$

10. $c_{ij} = \displaystyle\sum_{k=1}^{k=m} a_{ik} b_{kj}.$

## 2. SOME FINITE SERIES

### Exercise B (p. 311)

1. $k \in T \Rightarrow (k+1) \in T$ in all parts except for (d). Note that (c) and (e) are alternative forms of the same question; the factorized form is easier to handle.

2. $1 \in T$ in all parts except for (b). The results of (a), (c) and (e) are thus proved by induction.

3. 
| $n$: | 1 | 2 | 3 | 4 | 5 | 6 |
|------|---|---|----|-----|-----|-----|
| $S_n$: | 1 | 9 | 36 | 100 | 225 | 441 |

$S_n = \frac{1}{4} n^2 (n+1)^2.$

**4.**

| $n$: | 1 | 2 | 3 | 4 | 5 | 6 | 7 | 8 | 9 | 10 | 11 |
|---|---|---|---|---|---|---|---|---|---|---|---|
| $S_n$: | 1 | 5 | 14 | 30 | 55 | 91 | 140 | 204 | 285 | 385 | 506 |

$S_n = \frac{1}{6}n(n+1)(2n+1)$.

**5.** This is a concise version of the familiar method of summing an arithmetic progression by reversing the series and adding pairs of terms.

$$S_n = \quad 1 \;+\; 2 \;+\; 3 \;+...+\; n$$
$$S_n = \quad n \;+(n-1)+(n-2)+...+\; 1$$
$$\overline{S_n = \tfrac{1}{2}((n+1)+(n+1)+(n+1)+...+(n+1))} = \tfrac{1}{2}n(n+1).$$

Variations on this theme are

(i) $\sum_0^n i^2 = \sum_0^n (n-i)^2 = n^2(n+1) - 2n\sum_0^n i + \sum_0^n i^2,$

whence $\sum_1^n i = \sum_0^n i = \frac{1}{2}n(n+1)$ as before.

(ii) $\sum_0^n i^3 = \frac{1}{2}\left(\sum_0^n i^3 + \sum_0^n (n-i)^3\right)$

$\qquad = \frac{1}{2}\sum_0^n (n^3 - 3n^2 i + 3ni^2)$

$\qquad = \frac{1}{2}n^3(n+1) - \frac{3}{2}n^2\sum_0^n i + \frac{3}{2}n\sum_0^n i^2,$

giving $\sum_0^n i^2$ once $\sum_0^n i^3$ is known, or vice versa.

**6.** (a) 195;   (b) 341;   (c) $rn + \frac{3}{2}n(n+1)$;   (d) $\frac{1}{2}(n-1)n$.

**7.** (a) $\frac{1}{2}n(3n+1)$;   (b) $\frac{1}{2}(n-1)n$;   (c) $n(2k+1)$.

**8.** (a) $\sum_1^{32} (3i-2) = \sum_0^{31} (3i+1) = 1520$;

(b) $\sum_1^{11} (27-5i) = -33$;      (c) $\sum_1^{39} (10+2i) = 1950$;

(d) $\sum_1^{14} (89-9i) = 301$.

**9.** $u_n = n^3 - (n-1)^3 = 3n^2 - 3n + 1$; $u_i = 3i^2 - 3i + 1$. So

$$n^3 = \sum_1^n u_i = 3\sum_1^n i^2 - 3\sum_1^n i + n,$$

giving $\sum_1^n i^2 = \frac{1}{6}n(n+1)(2n+1)$.

**10.** As in Question 9, we obtain $n^4 = \sum_1^n (4i^3 - 6i^2 + 4i - 1)$, and the formula for $\sum_1^n i^3$ follows if the result for $\sum_1^n i^2$ is assumed.

**11.** $\frac{1}{4}n(n+1)(n+2)(n+3)$; $\quad \dfrac{1}{r+2}n(n+1)(n+2) \dots (n+r+1)$.

**12.** $a = 1, \quad b = 9, \quad c = 6.$

$$\sum_1^n (i^3 + 12i^2 + 17i) = \tfrac{1}{4}n(n+1)(n+2)(n+3) + 3n(n+1)(n+2)$$
$$+ 3n(n+1)$$
$$= \tfrac{1}{4}n(n+1)(n^2 + 17n + 42).$$

**13.** (a) 3800;     (b) 2124;     (c) $n(n+1)(n^2 - 3n - 2)$;

(d) $\tfrac{1}{4}(n+2)^2(n+3)^2 - 9$;     (e) $\tfrac{1}{6}(n-1)n(2n-1)$.

$n = 2$ gives $-24$ in (c), and 91 in (d).

**14.** $n(n+1)(2n+1) = 6\sum_1^n i^2$, which is a multiple of 6.

**15.** The diagram is as in Exercise A, Question 7(a), but with $n$ rectangles.

$$\sum_{i=0}^{n-1} h.g(x_i) = \frac{4}{n}\sum_0^{n-1}\left(2 + \frac{4i}{n}\right)^2 = \frac{4}{n}\left[4n + 8(n-1) + \frac{8}{3n}(n-1)(2n-1)\right].$$

The limit as $n \to \infty$ is $69\frac{1}{3}$, the exact area under the graph from $x = 2$ to $x = 6$ (see Chapter 22).

**16.** $\displaystyle\sum_{i=0}^{i=n-1} h.g(x_i) = a^2hn + ah^2(n-1)n + \tfrac{1}{6}h^3(n-1)n(2n-1),$

where $hn = b - a$. As $n \to \infty$,

$$\sum_0^{n-1} h.g(x_i) \to a^2(b-a) + a(b-a)^2 + \tfrac{1}{3}(b-a)^3 = \tfrac{1}{3}(b^3 - a^3).$$

**18.** (i) A single line divides a plane into 2 regions, and when $n = 1$ $\frac{1}{2}(n^2 + n + 2) = 2$, so that $1 \in T$.

(ii) The $(k+1)$th line increases the number of regions by $(k+1)$.

$$\tfrac{1}{2}(k^2 + k + 2) + (k+1) = \tfrac{1}{2}(k^2 + 3k + 4)$$
$$= \tfrac{1}{2}((k+1)^2 + (k+1) + 2).$$

So $k \in T \Rightarrow k+1 \in T$.

(i) and (ii) together prove the result for all $n$.

**19.** There are $(i-1)$ points on one side of $QP_i$, and $(k-i)$ points on the other side of $QP_i$, so $QP_i$ crosses $(i-1)(k-i)$ existing lines. The increase in the number of regions is one more than the number of lines crossed.

$$u_k = \sum_{i=1}^{i=k} ((i-1)(k-i)+1)$$
$$= k \sum_{1}^{k} (i-1) - \sum_{1}^{k} i(i-1) + \sum_{1}^{k} 1$$
$$= \frac{k^2(k-1)}{2} - \frac{(k-1)k(k+1)}{3} + k = \frac{k(k-1)(k-2)}{6} + k.$$
$$S_n = \tfrac{1}{24}n(n-1)(n-2)(n-3) + \tfrac{1}{2}n(n-1) + 1.$$

*Alternative method.* The previous analysis leads to the statement:
$S_n = $ (total number of intersections) + (total number of lines) + 1. Hence

$$S_n = \binom{n}{4} + \binom{n}{2} + 1,$$

using the notation of Chapter 25. The sequence

$$1, 2, 4, 8, 16, 31, 57, \ldots$$

is now seen to arise from adding the first, third and fifth numbers in the rows of Pascal's Triangle.

### Exercise C (p. 314)

**1.** (a) $7(2^{10}-1)$;      (b) $\tfrac{8}{3}(1-(\tfrac{1}{4})^{12})$;
   (c) $1+2^{19}$;      (d) $-\tfrac{9}{4}(1-(\tfrac{1}{3})^{16})$.

**2.** Total investment $= 40+40x+\ldots+40x^{10}$, where $x = 1{\cdot}05$,
$$= 800\,(1{\cdot}05^{11}-1)$$
$$= \pounds569.$$

**3.** (a) After 20 years, amount owed $= 4000x^{20}-y(x^{19}+x^{18}+\ldots+1)$
$$= 0 \text{ when } y = 349.$$

(b) After 10 years, amount owed $= \pounds2570$.

6 % of £4000 $= \pounds240$. In the first year the debt is reduced by £110. 6 % of £2570 $\simeq \pounds154$. In the tenth year the debt is reduced by £190.

During the first ten years the debt is reduced by about £150 a year on average; this accords with the answer to (b). During the second decade, the debt is paid off much more rapidly.

**4.** $S_n = 2(1-(\tfrac{1}{2})^n)$.

$S_n \to 2$ as $n \to \infty$.

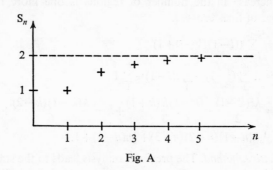

Fig. A

**5.** (a) $S_n = \tfrac{2}{3}(1-(-\tfrac{1}{2})^n)$.

$S_n \to \tfrac{2}{3}$ as $n \to \infty$.

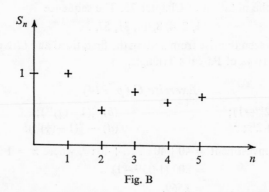

Fig. B

(b) $S_n = \tfrac{3}{2}(1-(\tfrac{2}{3})^n)$.

$S_n \to \tfrac{3}{2}$ as $n \to \infty$.

**6.** $S_3 = 1+\tfrac{2}{3}+\tfrac{4}{9} = 2\tfrac{1}{9}$ seconds.

$S_{10} = 1+\tfrac{2}{3}+\ldots+(\tfrac{2}{3})^9 = \dfrac{1-(\tfrac{2}{3})^{10}}{1-\tfrac{2}{3}} = 2\cdot95$ seconds.

$S_n \to 3$ as $n \to \infty$.

The same issues are raised here as in the famous paradox of Achilles and the tortoise.

# 12

# POSITION AND SPREAD

In the elementary course we were concerned merely with Descriptive Statistics. This chapter seems to be an extension of this work, but in fact we should already be looking ahead. The great merit of standard deviation and variance as measures of spread does not emerge until the analogous definitions are made for discrete and continuous probability models, when many simple but important results follow. The table overleaf shows how the definitions and notation of this chapter link up with those of later parts of the course.

As well as re-casting the elementary ideas in the exact notation now at our disposal, we take the opportunity early on of stressing two points which will be vital later. First, the fact that in a histogram frequencies are represented by *areas*; in the elementary course histograms and frequency diagrams may well have been confused. Secondly, the distinction between populations drawn from *discrete* and *continuous* domains is emphasized.

Correct and precise statements in Probability and Statistics require the use of a special vocabulary which must be learnt. For most pupils this will be a gradual process, but it is important that teachers from the outset should set an example in this respect. Confusion is often caused because many of the technical terms are words which in non-mathematical contexts carry somewhat different meanings.

The use of functional ideas and notation from the beginning may not appear to bring tangible advantages at this stage (particularly as we choose to graph frequency density functions in a different way from other functions), but again the table illustrates the benefits to be gained later.

This is the first of six chapters which together form an introduction to statistical inference. Chapter 20 aims at strengthening fundamental ideas of probability and few new problem-solving techniques emerge. The initial difficulties of defining probability are faced, and mathematical definitions are given for *independent*, *exclusive* and *exhaustive* events (which were treated intuitively hitherto). Chapter 25

185

| | Statistical populations |
|---|---|
| Basic symbols and terms | Population: the quantities $x_1, x_2, ..., x_n$ occurring with frequencies $f(x_1), f(x_2), ..., f(x_n)$<br>Relative frequency $q(x_i) = f(x_i)/N$<br>Frequency density $= f(x_i)/\delta x_i$ where<br>$\delta x_i$ = length of class interval |
| Histograms | Frequency density<br><br>$x_i$  $x$<br>Shaded area $= f(x_i)$ |
| Total area of histogram | Population size $= N = \Sigma f(x_i)$<br>$\Sigma q(x_i) = 1$ |
| Mean | $m = \bar{x} = (1/N)\,\Sigma x_i f(x_i)$  or  $\Sigma x_i q(x_i)$ |
| Variance and standard deviation | $\begin{aligned} s^2 &= (1/N)\,\Sigma(x_i - m)^2 f(x_i) \\ &= (1/N)\,\Sigma x_i^2 f(x_i) - m^2 \\ \text{or} \quad & \Sigma(x_i - m)^2 q(x_i) \\ &= \Sigma x_i^2 q(x_i) - m^2 \end{aligned}$ |
| References | $m$ and $s$ are *statistics*<br>Chapter 12 |

(Binomial Probability Functions), Chapter 26 (Probability Parameters), and Chapter 37 (Probability Density Functions) develop some important special probability models and show how the parameters of a general model are defined and calculated. From time to time, comparisons between statistical populations and appropriate probability models are made, and intuitive ideas about estimation and inference are encouraged. Chapter 38 (Sampling and Estimation) brings together the ideas of all previous chapters and considers the size of likely errors in the estimation of parameters of parent populations from samples.

Few of the techniques and tests used by practising statisticians are included, but it is felt that these can be learnt quickly once a sound understanding of fundamentals has been developed.

Probability models

| Discrete domain | Continuum |
|---|---|
| Possibility space $\{x_1, x_2, ..., x_n\}$ | Probabilities associated with sub-intervals of $\{x : L \leqslant x \leqslant R\}$ |
| Associated probabilities $p(x_1), p(x_2), ..., p(x_n)$ | Probability density $\rho = \phi(x)$ |

Probability density

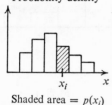

Shaded area $= p(x_i)$

Probability density

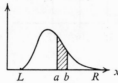

Shaded area $= p(a < x \leqslant b)$

$\Sigma p(x_i) = 1$ $\qquad\qquad \int_L^R \phi(x)\,dx = 1$

Expected value or 'theoretical mean'

$\mu = E[x] = \Sigma x_i p(x_i)$ $\qquad\qquad \mu = E[x] = \int_L^R x\phi(x)\,dx$

$$\sigma^2 = E[(x-\mu)^2]$$
$$= \Sigma(x_i-\mu)^2\, p(x_i)$$
$$= \Sigma x_i^2\, p(x_i) - \mu^2$$

$$\sigma^2 = E[(x-\mu)^2]$$
$$= \int (x-\mu)^2\, \phi(x)\,dx$$
$$= \int x^2\, \phi(x)\,dx - \mu^2$$

$\mu$ and $\sigma$ are *parameters*

| Chapter 26 | Chapter 37 |
|---|---|

# 2. FREQUENCY FUNCTIONS

## *Exercise A (p. 319)*

**1.** See Exercise B, Question 2.

**2.**

Age $(x_i)$ 14 15 16 } $N = 13$, $n = 3$.
$f(x_i)$ 1 4 8

No. of brothers/sisters $(y_i)$ 0 1 2 3 4 6 } $N = 13$, $n = 6$
$g(y_i)$ 3 3 3 2 1 1

No. of letters in Christian name $(z_i)$ 4 5 6 7 8 11 } $N = 13$, $n = 6$
$h(z_i)$ 5 4 1 1 1 1

Height $(w_i)$ 62 63 65 66 67 69 70 } $N = 13$, $n = 7$.
$j(w_i)$ 1 1 2 4 2 1 2

187

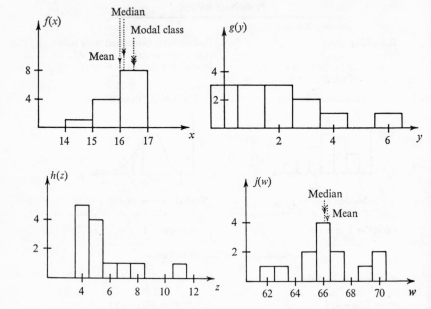

Note that an age of 15 means $15 < x < 16$, whereas a height of 65 inches means $64.5 < w < 65.5$. Care must be taken in marking the axes of the frequency diagrams, and the same considerations are vital in the calculations of Exercise B, Question 1.

## 3. POSITION AND AVERAGE

### *Exercise B (p. 325)*

**1.** The numbers of brothers and sisters, and the number of letters in the Christian names are discrete; ages and heights are continuous.

|  | Mean | Median |
|---|---|---|
| Age | 16·0 | 16·2 |
| No. of brothers/sisters | 1·9 | 2 |
| No. of letters in Christian name | 5·5 | 5 |
| Height | 66·3 | 66·1 |

If every child had just had a birthday, the mean age would be 15·5 years. If every child had a birthday the next week, the mean age would be 16·5 years.

188

All we can say with certainty about the median is

$$16 \cdot 0 \leqslant \text{median age} \leqslant 17 \cdot 0.$$

Similarly    $65 \cdot 8 \leqslant \text{mean height} \leqslant 66 \cdot 8,$

and    $65 \cdot 5 \leqslant \text{median height} \leqslant 66 \cdot 5.$

These answers neglect the effect of rounding errors.

**2.**

| Frequency function | Mean | Median | Modal class |
|---|---|---|---|
| $f$ | 5 | 5 | 5 |
| $g$ | 6·1 | 6·4 | 7 |
| $h$ | 6·5 | 6·8 | 8 |

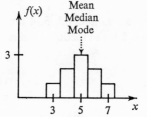

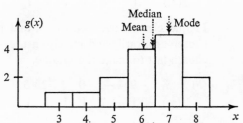

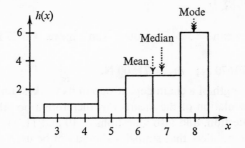

The frequency diagrams are the same shape as the histograms for these populations. The calculation of each median results in a line bisecting the area of the histogram; the line $x = m$ passes through the centre of mass of the histogram. The fact that the mean is less than the median in a negatively-skewed or negatively-J-shaped population is best discussed in terms of moments. If the histogram is cut out of cardboard of uniform thickness and

189

placed on a knife-edge at the median, it would turn anticlock-wise. The knife-edge must be moved to the left to achieve a balance. The connections between first moments in Statistics and moments in Mechanics, and between second moments in Statistics and moments of inertia, are illuminating, and may be discussed at an appropriate stage.

If the domain is discrete, it is possible for the mean to be greater than the median in a negatively-skewed or negatively-J-shaped population.

3. There are infinitely many possible solutions. For example:

(a)

| $x_i$ | −8 | −1 | 1 | 2 | 3 | 4 |
|-------|----|----|---|---|---|---|
| $f(x_i)$ | 1 | 2 | 1 | 1 | 1 | 1 |

Frequencies are ascribed to −1 and 1; the numbers 2, 3, 4 are chosen arbitrarily and merely ensure that 1 is the median. −8 is chosen last to make the mean 0.

(b)

| $x_i$ | −9 | −2 | 0 | 1 | 2 | 3 |
|-------|----|----|---|---|---|---|
| $f(x_i)$ | 1 | 2 | 1 | 1 | 1 | 1 |

This population is the same as in (a) except that each x is reduced by 1.

4. Zena's mean = 3·245 minutes. Ann's mean = 3·28 minutes.

5. $m_1 = 70670$ N; $m_2 = 71500$ N.

The strength of a chain depends upon its weakest link, of course. The calculation of the means was therefore a pointless exercise. This question, and also Questions 6, 10 and 11, are intended as gentle reminders that statistics should not be used uncritically.

6.

| Monthly rainfall at P.R. | 5 | 7 | 9 | | | |
|--------------------------|---|---|---|---|---|---|
| Frequency | 9 | 2 | 1 | | | |
| Monthly rainfall at Ll. | 3 | 4 | 6 | 9 | 10 | 11 |
| Frequency | 3 | 3 | 1 | 3 | 1 | 1 |

Llandrwnch has the higher average monthly rainfall but is drier during the summer months.

**7.**

| Class interval | Frequency | Class interval | Frequency | Class interval | Frequency |
|---|---|---|---|---|---|
| $2\frac{1}{2}$– $7\frac{1}{2}$ | 8 | $\frac{1}{2}$– $7\frac{1}{2}$ | 8 | $2\frac{1}{2}$– $9\frac{1}{2}$ | 8 |
| $7\frac{1}{2}$–$12\frac{1}{2}$ | 3 | $7\frac{1}{2}$–$14\frac{1}{2}$ | 5 | $9\frac{1}{2}$–$16\frac{1}{2}$ | 8 |
| $12\frac{1}{2}$–$17\frac{1}{2}$ | 7 | $14\frac{1}{2}$–$21\frac{1}{2}$ | 9 | $16\frac{1}{2}$–$23\frac{1}{2}$ | 7 |
| $17\frac{1}{2}$–$22\frac{1}{2}$ | 5 | $21\frac{1}{2}$–$28\frac{1}{2}$ | 4 | $23\frac{1}{2}$–$30\frac{1}{2}$ | 3 |
| $22\frac{1}{2}$–$27\frac{1}{2}$ | 3 | $28\frac{1}{2}$–$35\frac{1}{2}$ | 0 | $30\frac{1}{2}$–$37\frac{1}{2}$ | 1 |
| $27\frac{1}{2}$–$32\frac{1}{2}$ | 0 | $35\frac{1}{2}$–$42\frac{1}{2}$ | 1 | | |
| $32\frac{1}{2}$–$37\frac{1}{2}$ | 1 | | | | |
| $m_1 = 14\cdot3$ | | $m_2 = 14\cdot4$ | | $m_3 = 15\cdot1$ | |

This question illustrates the errors to be expected whenever grouping is used.

**8.**

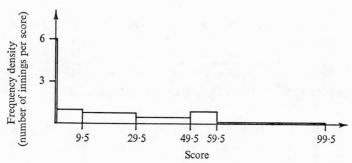

**9.** $m = £1005$. Only 15 out of 100 men earn more than the mean.

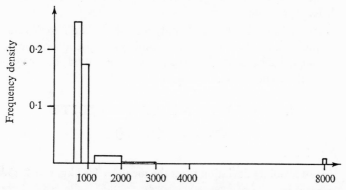

The one £8,000 salary can be shown in a variety of ways. Whichever is chosen, the rectangle should have area 1.

191

10. We could imagine a newspaper reporter wishing to convey an indication of the ages of the party in the event of a coach crash. He might write 'the median age is 14' (assuming an educated reading public) or '60 % of the party are about 14 years old' or '60 % of the party are between the ages of 13 and 15 inclusive'.

The last statement is similar to giving an inter-quartile range.

11. (a)

|  | A | B | C | D | E | F | G | H | I | J | K |
|---|---|---|---|---|---|---|---|---|---|---|---|
| Judge 1 | 30 | 22 | 12 | 8 | 6 | 6 | 6 | 4 | 2 | 2 | 0 |
| Judge 2 | 36 | 45 | 30 | 18 | 15 | 21 | 15 | 24 | 18 | 24 | 18 |
|  | 66 | 67 | 42 | 26 | 21 | 27 | 21 | 28 | 20 | 26 | 18 |

Order B, A, C, H, F, D and J equal, E and G equal, I, K.

(b)

| A | B | C | D | E | F | G | H | I | J | K |
|---|---|---|---|---|---|---|---|---|---|---|
| 60 | 44 | 24 | 16 | 12 | 12 | 12 | 8 | 4 | 4 | 0 |
| 60 | 75 | 50 | 30 | 25 | 35 | 25 | 40 | 30 | 40 | 30 |
| 120 | 119 | 74 | 46 | 37 | 47 | 37 | 48 | 34 | 44 | 30 |

Order A, B, C, H, F, D, J, E and G equal, I, K.

(c)

| A | B | C | D | E | F | G | H | I | J | K |
|---|---|---|---|---|---|---|---|---|---|---|
| 1 | 2 | 3 | 4 | 6 | 6 | 6 | 8 | $9\frac{1}{2}$ | $9\frac{1}{2}$ | 11 |
| 2 | 1 | 3 | 8 | $10\frac{1}{2}$ | 6 | $10\frac{1}{2}$ | $4\frac{1}{2}$ | 8 | $4\frac{1}{2}$ | 8 |
| 3 | 3 | 6 | 12 | $16\frac{1}{2}$ | 12 | $16\frac{1}{2}$ | $12\frac{1}{2}$ | $17\frac{1}{2}$ | 14 | 19 |

Order A and B equal, C, D and F equal, H, J, E and G equal, I, K.

It is not surprising that different methods yield different results. Combining marks from different subjects to give a form order is a similar exercise; method (a) is commonly used, but may not give 'the right order'.

## 4. SPREAD AND VARIABILITY
### Exercise C (p. 329)

1. $s = 2 \cdot 36$.

2. Mean absolute deviation from the mean $= 1 \cdot 87$ kg. $s = 2 \cdot 25$ kg.

3. $2 \cdot 5$ years.

## Exercise D (p. 333)

**1.**

|   | f | g | h | p | q | r |
|---|---|---|---|---|---|---|
| m | 4 | 2·87 | 4·4 | 4 | 3·75 | 3·5 |
| s | 1·22 | 1·36 | 1·56 | 2·26 | 1·58 | 1·71 |
| Percentage of population within 1 s.d. of the mean | 78 | 70 | 50 | 60 | 55 | 67 |
| Percentage of population within 2 s.d. of the mean | 97 | 94 | 95 | 100 | 95 | 100 |

The means of the symmetrical populations can be written down immediately, and formula (3) of Section 4.4 is better than (4) for the first and fourth populations.

**2.** Mean absolute deviation from the mean $= 1·08$.

**3.** For both populations, $m = 7·46$. For the first, $s = 3·48$. For the second, $s = 3·38$.

When the standard deviation is calculated from grouped data, the answer is not the same as if the numbers were uniformly spread in each interval.

**4.** One simple solution is

| $x_i$ | 1 | 2 | 3 | 4 | 5 | 6 | 7 |
|---|---|---|---|---|---|---|---|
| $f(x_i)$ | 1 | 7 | 11 | 26 | 11 | 7 | 1 |

**5.** Two small populations with these statistics are $(-5, -2, -1, 1, 7)$ and $(-6, -2, -2, 0, 4, 6)$. Perhaps the easiest way to provide a solution is to start with the population

$$(-a, -2, -1, 3, a),$$

say, with mean 0 and choose $a$ so that $\Sigma x_i^2 = N.4^2 = 80$.

**6.** Males: $m = 2$, $s = 0·77$.
Females:

First group, $m = 0·67$, $s = 0·79$ 
Second group, $m = 2$, $s = 0·77$ combined $\begin{cases} m = 1·5, \\ s = 1·00. \end{cases}$

**7.**

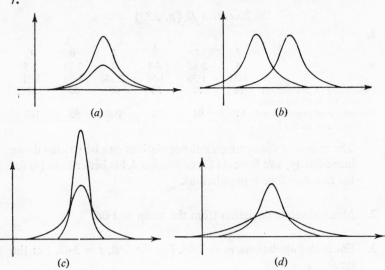

(a)　　　　　　　　(b)

(c)　　　　　　　　(d)

**8.** Total square deviation from the mean $= 100 \times 30^2 + 400 \times 20^2$

$$= 250\,000 \text{ g}^2;$$

$$s = \sqrt{\left(\frac{250\,000}{500}\right)} = 22 \cdot 4 \text{ g}.$$

**9.** (a) $m = 15$, $s = 5 \cdot 1$;　　　　　　(b) $m = 14$, $s = 4 \cdot 5$;

(c) $m = 15$, $s = 5 \cdot 8$.

In (a), the standard deviation is clearly expected to be between 4 and 6, and is in fact the root-mean-square of these numbers. The standard deviation in (b) is at first sight surprising, but a little reflection shows that an answer greater than 4 is correct.

Two methods of working (c) are set out below:

(i)　$m = \dfrac{12 \times 10 + 16 \times 30}{40} = 15.$

$$\frac{\Sigma x_i^2}{10} - 12^2 = 4^2 \quad \text{and} \quad \frac{\Sigma y_i^2}{30} - 16^2 = 6^2.$$

$$s^2 = \frac{\Sigma x_i^2 + \Sigma y_i^2}{40} - 15^2 = 34; \quad s = 5 \cdot 8.$$

194

(ii) $m = 15$ as before.

$$s^2 = \frac{\Sigma(x_i-15)^2+\Sigma(y_i-15)^2}{40}$$

$$= \frac{10(4^2+3^2)+30(6^2+1^2)}{40}$$

$$= 34.$$

Method (ii) illustrates the use of the formula in Question 11(d). Question 12 is answered in the same way.

10. $m_1 = 5$, $s_1^2 = 2$;  $m_2 = 7$, $s_2^2 = 12\cdot4$;

$m_3 = 8$, $s_3^2 = 34\cdot4$;  $m_4 = 2$, $s_4^2 = 6\cdot8$.

Average variance within classes  $= 13\cdot9$,

average variance between classes $= 5\cdot25$,

variance of the whole population $= 19\cdot15$.

Proving the result in general is a good exercise in $\Sigma$-algebra which will extend the best pupils.

11. (c) $\dfrac{1}{N}\Sigma(x_i-k)f(x_i)+k = \dfrac{1}{N}\Sigma x_i f(x_i)-\dfrac{k}{N}\Sigma f(x_i)+k$

$$= m-k+k = m.$$

(d) $\dfrac{1}{N}\Sigma(x_i-k)^2 f(x_i)-(m-k)^2$

$$= \dfrac{1}{N}\Sigma x_i^2 f(x_i)-\dfrac{2k}{N}\Sigma x_i f(x_i)+\dfrac{k^2}{N}\Sigma f(x_i)-(m-k)^2$$

$$= \dfrac{1}{N}\Sigma x_i^2 f(x_i)-2km+k^2-m^2+2km-k^2$$

$$= \dfrac{1}{N}\Sigma x_i^2 f(x_i)-m^2.$$

(a) and (b) are special cases of (c) and (d) taking $k$ equal to $m$. (a) proves the alternative formula for variance quoted in Section 4.3. (b) shows that the sum of the deviations from the mean is zero. (c) and (d) prove the formulae for mean and variance using a working zero $k$ (see Section 5.2).

12.  $m = 172$ cm, $s = 10\cdot0$ cm.

**13.** *(a)* $\bar{x} = \dfrac{1}{N} \Sigma(k + ct_i) f(x_i) = \dfrac{k}{N} \Sigma f(x_i) + \dfrac{c}{N} \Sigma t_i f(x_i) = k + c\bar{t};$

*(b)* $\sqrt{\left( \dfrac{1}{N} \Sigma(x_i - \bar{x})^2 \right)} = \sqrt{\left( \dfrac{1}{N} \Sigma(k + ct_i - k - c\bar{t})^2 \right)}$

$$= \sqrt{\left( \dfrac{c^2}{N} \Sigma(t_i - \bar{t})^2 \right)} = c\sqrt{\left( \dfrac{1}{N} \Sigma(t_i - \bar{t})^2 \right)}.$$

Section 5.3 deals with the application of these results.

**14.** $m = 0$, $s = 1 \cdot 2$ for each population.

**15.** This should be the same as that in Section 4.5 except that the instructions within the loop should be replaced by these.

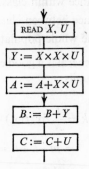

# 5. AIDS TO CALCULATION

## *Exercise E (p. 341)*

**1.** *A*'s marks seem to be negatively-skewed with probably several very low scores (to account for the low mean). *B*'s marks must be positively-skewed with many marks between 35 and 45, and a considerable number of high scores.

*D* and *E* probably had about the same proportion of failures, but *E*'s better girls scored more highly than *D*'s. *C* had a smaller proportion of failures, but also a smaller proportion of high scorers than *E*.

*C* will have had most girls scoring over 80 %, followed closely by *E*, then *B*.

$E$ had the largest proportion getting over 80%, followed by $B$ or $C$.

|          | A  | B  | C  | D  | E  | F  |
|----------|----|----|----|----|----|----|
| Failures: | 15 | 30 | 15 | 15 | 10 | 20 |

All answers to this question are necessarily approximate and uncertain. For school $F$, the reasoning is as follows: the pass-mark is 1 standard deviation below the mean, so if the marks were normally distributed this would imply about $\frac{1}{6} \times 160$ failures. But the value of the median suggests a positively-skewed population, so the number of failures would be less than 27. For the other schools we have even less information, but we can make guesses in much the same way.

The statistics for $G$ must be wrong. The marks of half the girls are apparently more than 10 below the mean, so there must be a large number of high marks to compensate. If the mean and median are correct, the standard deviation must be much greater than 10.

2. $m = 16.8$ mm; $s = 0.48$ mm.

   10 cubits $= 198 \pm 11$ inches. 1 pole $= 5\frac{1}{2}$ yards $= 198$ inches.

3. The means are 1.8, 3.5, 6.9, 13.7, 27.3, 54.3, 135.7 grams.

   These are approximately in the ratio $1:2:4:8:16:32:80$.

   Notice that we could make the same deductions about the number system used by inspecting the modes. The calculation of the means (though good practice in the use of working zeros) is unnecessary for this purpose.

4. Taking $1\frac{1}{2}$–$8\frac{1}{2}$ as the first interval, we get $m = 14.6$, $s^2 = 73$.
   Taking $2\frac{1}{2}$–$9\frac{1}{2}$ as the first interval, we get $m = 15.1$, $s^2 = 51$.

   The contrast between these answers shows clearly the possible effects of grouping. With a desk calculator, it is easy to work out the statistics from the ungrouped data. We get $m = 14.6$ and $s^2 = 51$, so by a curious coincidence the first mean and the second variance are correct!

5. $s = 9.8$ cm.

6. $m = 169.4$ cm; $s = 3.8$.

**7.** The theoretically ideal frequency tables are:

| $x_i$ | 1 | 2 | 3 | 4 | 5 | 6 | | | | |
|---|---|---|---|---|---|---|---|---|---|---|
| $f(x_i)$ | 12 | 12 | 12 | 12 | 12 | 12 | | | | |

| $y_i$ | 1 | 1·5 | 2 | 2·5 | 3 | 3·5 | 4 | 4·5 | 5 | 5·5 | 6 |
|---|---|---|---|---|---|---|---|---|---|---|---|
| $g(y_i)$ | 2 | 4 | 6 | 8 | 10 | 12 | 10 | 8 | 6 | 4 | 2 |

The mean is 3·5 in each case. The variances are $\frac{35}{12}$ and $\frac{35}{24}$. With 7200 throws the differences between the statistics calculated from experimental data and the parameters of the probability model are expected to be much smaller. This is discussed quantitatively in Chapter 38.

# 6. MEAN VALUE
## *Exercise F (p. 345)*

**1.** (a)

| $k$ | 2 | 3 | 4 | 5 | 6 | 7 | 8 | 9 |
|---|---|---|---|---|---|---|---|---|
| $p(k)$ | 4 | 3 | 2 | 1 | 0 | −1 | −2 | −3 |
| $q(k)$ | 4 | 3 | 2·4 | 2·2 | 2 | 1·8 | 2 | 3 |
| $r(k)$ | 20·4 | 13·4 | 8·4 | 5·4 | 4·4 | 5·4 | 8·4 | 13·4 |

The graph of $p$ is a straight line, that of $q$ consists of five straight line segments, while that of $r$ is a parabola.

(b) $q(k)$ is least when $k = 7$, the median of the population. $r(k)$ is least when $k = 6$, the mean of the population.

(c) The positive and negative deviations cancel each other when $k = 6$, the mean.

**2.** $r(k) = s^2 + (m-k)^2$. So the minimum value of $r(k)$ is $s^2$, and this occurs when $k = m$. For the population of Question 1, the variance is therefore 4·4.

**3.**

| $k$ | 5 | 6 | $6\frac{1}{2}$ | 7 |
|---|---|---|---|---|
| $q(k)$ | 2 | $1\frac{2}{3}$ | $1\frac{2}{3}$ | $1\frac{2}{3}$ |

If the median is now defined as a value of $k$ minimizing $q(k)$— a perfectly acceptable definition—it may be indeterminate if the population size is even. See Section 3.2.

**4.** (b) $x_i = 0$, $y_i = 0$,
$\Sigma x_i^2 = 60$, $\Sigma y_i^2 = 174·72$, $\Sigma x_i y_i = 101·7$.
$\Sigma(kx_i + l - y_i)^2 = 60k^2 + 9l^2 + 174·72 - 203·4k$.

(c) The expression is a minimum when $l = 0$, $k = 1.7$. This gives $z$ (as defined in Section 6.1) equal to $0.5$, representing an 'average' distance from the regression line measured parallel to the $y$-axis.

5.  We wish to minimize

$$a^2 \Sigma X_i^2 + Nb^2 + \Sigma Y_i^2 - 2a \Sigma X_i Y_i + 2ab \Sigma X_i - 2b \Sigma Y_i,$$

i.e.    $a^2 \Sigma X_i^2 + Nb^2 + \Sigma Y_i^2 - 2a \Sigma X_i Y_i.$

This clearly implies $b = 0$, and the remaining quadratic function of $a$ has minimum value when

$$a = \frac{\Sigma X_i Y_i}{\Sigma X_i^2}$$

$$= \frac{\frac{1}{N} \Sigma (x_i - \bar{X})(y_i - \bar{Y})}{\frac{1}{N} \Sigma (x_i - \bar{X})^2} = \frac{v_{xy}}{v_x}.$$

So the regression line has equation $Y = (v_{xy}/v_x)X$, which gives the required equation immediately.

### Exercise G (p. 346)

1.

|          | f     | g    | h     |
|----------|-------|------|-------|
| Skewness | 0     | 0    | −0·69 |
| Kurtosis | −0·92 | 0·94 | −0·22 |

The origin of the term 'negatively-skewed' now becomes apparent.

2.  $Nm_3 = \Sigma (x_i - \bar{x})^3 f(x_i)$

$= \Sigma x_i^3 f(x_i) - 3\bar{x} \Sigma x_i^2 f(x_i) + 3\bar{x}^2 \Sigma x_i f(x_i) - \bar{x}^3 \Sigma f(x_i)$

$= Nm_3' - 3\bar{x}(Ns^2 + N\bar{x}^2) + 3\bar{x}^2 . N\bar{x} - \bar{x}^3 . N.$

Hence $m_3 = m_3' - 3s^2\bar{x} - \bar{x}^3.$

The other result is obtained similarly.

|          | f     | g     | h     | p     | q     | r     |
|----------|-------|-------|-------|-------|-------|-------|
| Skewness | 0     | 0·71  | −0·60 | 0     | 0·19  | 0     |
| Kurtosis | −0·33 | −0·12 | −0·83 | −1·56 | −0·78 | −1·27 |

3.    $\Sigma x_i^3 f(x_i) + \Sigma x_i^2 f(x_i) = \Sigma x_i^2 (x_i + 1) f(x_i)$.

The terms on the left-hand side of the identity are required in calculating $m_2'$ and $m_3'$. The right-hand side comes from summing an extra column added to the table.

4.    $m = 0 \cdot 61$,   $s^2 = 0 \cdot 61$,   skewness $= 1 \cdot 23$.

5.    On this occasion,

$$m = \frac{1}{N} \Sigma i f(i), \quad s^2 = \frac{1}{N} \Sigma i^2 f(i) - m^2.$$

$$G(t) = \Sigma f(i) \, t^i$$
$$\Rightarrow G'(t) = \Sigma i f(i) \, t^{i-1}$$
$$\Rightarrow G''(t) = \Sigma i(i-1) f(i) \, t^{i-2}.$$

Hence,

$$G'(1) = \Sigma i f(i) = mN; \quad G''(1) = \Sigma i^2 f(i) - \Sigma i f(i)$$
$$= Ns^2 + Nm^2 - Nm.$$

$G$ is a 'frequency generator'. Probability generators (often called probability generating functions) are discussed in some detail in Chapter 26.

6.    $G(1) = 2^6$,   $G'(1) = 6 \times 2^5$,   $G''(1) = 6 \times 5 \times 2^4$.

Hence $m = 3$, $s^2 = 1 \cdot 5$, as before.

7.    $G'''(t) = \Sigma i(i-1)(i-2) f(i) \, t^{i-3}$,
$$G'''(1) = \Sigma i^3 f(i) - 3\Sigma i^2 f(i) + 2\Sigma i f(i)$$
$$= N(m_3 + 3s^2 m + m^3) - 3(Ns^2 + Nm^2) + 2Nm.$$

Skewness $= m_3/s^3 = \left( \dfrac{1}{N} G'''(1) - 3s^2 m - m^3 + 3s^2 + 3m^2 - 2m \right) \Big/ s^3$,

where

$$N = G(1), \quad m = \frac{G'(1)}{G(1)}, \quad s^2 = \frac{G''(1)}{G(1)} - \left( \frac{G'(1)}{G(1)} \right)^2 + \frac{G'(1)}{G(1)}.$$

# 13

# FURTHER VECTORS

## 1. BASE-VECTORS AND COORDINATES

### Exercise A (*p. 347*)

1.  (*a*) $3\mathbf{a}+\mathbf{b}$;        (*b*) $3\mathbf{b}$;        (*c*) $2\mathbf{b}-2\mathbf{a}$;
    (*d*) $-\mathbf{a}-2\mathbf{b}$;      (*e*) $\mathbf{a}-2\mathbf{b}$;      (*f*) $-4\mathbf{a}-3\mathbf{b}$;
    (*g*) $4\mathbf{b}-3\mathbf{a}$;      (*h*) $\mathbf{a}-3\mathbf{b}$;      (*i*) $-3\mathbf{a}-\mathbf{b}$;
    (*j*) $3\mathbf{b}$.

2.  (*a*) $\mathbf{OP}=5\mathbf{i}-3\mathbf{j}$;   (*b*) $Q$ is $(-7, 4)$;   (*c*) $\mathbf{PQ}=-12\mathbf{i}+7\mathbf{j}$.

3.  $\mathbf{OP}+\mathbf{OR}=\mathbf{OU}=\mathbf{a}+3\mathbf{b}$.    4.  $(x_1+x_2, y_1+y_2)$.

This section is mainly revision of earlier work. There are several ways of drawing rectangular axes in three dimensions on a plane sheet of paper. In theory, rays drawn in any direction could be a perspective view of a tri-rectangular set, as can easily be seen by turning a box into various positions; but it is not always easy to see what the appropriate units of length should be when the rays have been drawn. In practice we do not use perspective, but parallel projections, in which parallel lines are represented by parallel lines, in whatever direction they may be. The two main projections are seen in Figures 3 and 4; they are called *axonometric* and *isometric* respectively. In axonometric projection, two axes are depicted at right-angles, with their true scales, in the plane of the paper. The third axis is drawn to make an angle, usually 30°, with one of these axes, and its scale is reduced, usually by a factor of $\frac{1}{2}$. Such a projection will be completely described by the phrase 'axonometric, 30°.$\frac{1}{2}$'. Figure A shows two right-handed sets of axes under this projection.

In isometric projection the axes are drawn with angles of 60° or 120° between them and all the scales are true. This is widely used for engineering drawings, and isometric paper, ruled in equilateral triangles, is available for such purposes. Two common ways of drawing cartesian axes in this projection are shown in Figure B.

Time is well spent in practising the use of these projections, and the later questions in Exercise B provide useful examples. It is easy, using squared or isometric paper, to produce convincing drawings of the rhombic dodecahedron by the two methods, and the final effects should be compared.

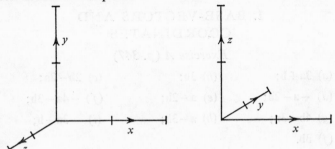

Fig. A. Axonometric axes (30°. ½).

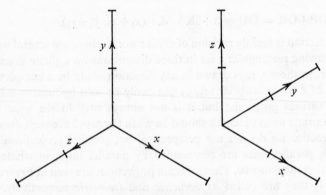

Fig. B. Isometric axes.

### Exercise B (p. 350)

1.  **OP** $= 5\mathbf{i} - \mathbf{j} + 3\mathbf{k}$,    **OQ** $= -2\mathbf{i} + 4\mathbf{j} - \mathbf{k}$,    **OR** $= 3\mathbf{i} + 3\mathbf{j} + 2\mathbf{k}$.
    $R$ is (3, 3, 2).

2.  **PQ** $=$ **OQ** $-$ **OP** $= -7\mathbf{i} + 5\mathbf{j} - 4\mathbf{k}$.

3.  (a) (5, 6, 0);   (b) (5, 6, 2);   (c) (1, −1, 0);   (d) (0, 6, −2).

**4.**  $\mathbf{i} = \begin{pmatrix} 1 \\ 0 \\ 0 \end{pmatrix}$, $\mathbf{j} = \begin{pmatrix} 0 \\ 1 \\ 0 \end{pmatrix}$, $\mathbf{k} = \begin{pmatrix} 0 \\ 0 \\ 1 \end{pmatrix}$.

**5.**  $A(-1, -1, 1)$; $\quad B(1, -1, 1)$; $\quad C(1, 1, 1)$; $\quad D(-1, 1, 1)$;

   $A'(-1, -1, -1)$; $\quad B'(1, -1, -1)$; $\quad C'(1, 1, -1)$;

   $D'(-1, 1, -1)$.   Plane $BCC'B'$.   Plane $A'B'C'D'$.

**6.**  A cube of side 1 unit. The centroid $G$ of the triangle $ABC$. The plane $ABC$ trisects $OH$ at $G$ (see Figure C). Yes, it is true for any parallepiped.

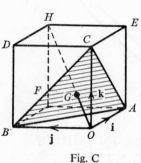
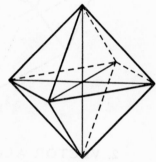

Fig. C   Fig. D

**7.**  The points are $C$, $B'$, $D'$, $A$ in Figure 5, and form the vertices of a regular tetrahedron. The mid-points of $PQ$ and $RS$ are images in the centre of the figure.

**8.**  $4\mathbf{p} + \mathbf{q} = \begin{pmatrix} 10 \\ 5 \\ 15 \end{pmatrix} = 5\mathbf{r}$. $P$, $R$, $Q$ are collinear, and $\mathbf{PR} = \tfrac{1}{4}\mathbf{RQ}$.

**9.**  A regular octahedron (see Figure D).

**10.**  The diagonal vectors, $(2\mathbf{i} - 2\mathbf{j})$ and $2\mathbf{k}$, are perpendicular and their lengths are in the ratio $\sqrt{2}:1$. $\mathbf{i} + \mathbf{j}$ gives the mid-point of each. Hence the figure is a rhombus, and the 14 points are vertices of a rhombic dodecahedron (see Figure E). Since it is a cube+6 pyramids which themselves make an equal cube, its volume is twice that of the cube = 16 cubic units.

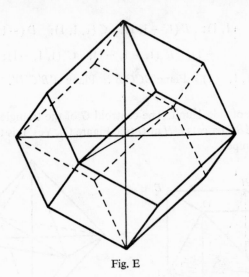

Fig. E

## 2. VECTOR ALGEBRA IN TERMS OF COMPONENTS

This section revises Chapter 9; the results are trivial if the earlier work is well known.

*Exercise C (p. 352)*

1. $\begin{pmatrix} x \\ y \\ z \end{pmatrix}$.

2. $\begin{pmatrix} -1 \\ 0 \\ 2 \end{pmatrix}$.

3. The points are collinear, and the middle point divides the join of the outer pair in the ratio $2:3$.

4. $(\frac{1}{2}, 1)$.

5. $(\frac{1}{2}, 1, 5\frac{1}{2})$.

6. $\left( \dfrac{x_1+x_2+x_3}{3}, \ \dfrac{y_1+y_2+y_3}{3} \right)$.

**7.** (a) $(2, 3\frac{1}{2}, 2)$;　　　(b) $(-\frac{1}{2}, 2, \frac{1}{2})$;　　　(c) $(\frac{3}{4}, 2\frac{3}{4}, 1\frac{1}{4})$;

(d) $(\frac{2}{3}, 2\frac{2}{3}, 2\frac{1}{3})$.　$\frac{3}{4}(\frac{2}{3}, 2\frac{2}{3}, 2\frac{1}{3}) + \frac{1}{4}(1, 3, -2) = (\frac{3}{4}, 2\frac{3}{4}, 1\frac{1}{4})$.

**8.** $(a, 5a/7)$.　　　　　　　**9.** $(-\frac{1}{13}, 0, -\frac{2}{13})$.

# 3. PARAMETERS IN ONE DIMENSION

Underlying this section is the idea of dimensionality. A plane is two-dimensional and every vector in it can be expressed in terms of two base vectors **i** and **j**; this is because any three vectors in a plane are linearly dependent. Further, this expression is unique; if it were not so, then there would be a linear relation between the two independent vectors **i** and **j**, which is not the case. A line through the origin is a one-dimensional vector space; all vectors in it are multiples of a single vector. If **r** is any vector in such a line, and **b** is one particular vector in the line, then **r** = $t$**b**, where $t$ is an arbitrary scalar. Vectors (or points) on the line are thus isomorphic with the real numbers. A parametric equation is simply a one-one mapping from the real numbers onto the points of the line.

The idea of a parameter representing a 'degree of freedom'—that is, the mapping of the points of a locus onto $R$ or a subset of $R$—two parameters representing two degrees of freedom, mapping onto $R \times R$, and so on—is of vital importance, and needs careful emphasis. The next section considers two-parameter equations, which give rise to planes.

The technique of finding the intersection of two lines by expressing the position vector in two ways in terms of **i** and **j**, and equating coefficients, is of course justified by the independence of **i** and **j** and the resulting uniqueness of such an expression. This is a method of widespread use in mathematics and especially in geometry, but some people find it difficult to master. A simple elementary example would be to find the line joining $(3, 0)$ to $(0, 5)$ as the common member of the sets of lines $y = t(x-3)$ and $x = u(y-5)$. We meet it again when we express $3\cos\theta + 4\sin\theta$ in the form $r\cos(\theta - \alpha)$, where again the essential idea is that $\cos\theta$ and $\sin\theta$ are independent functions so that the expression is really unique.

### Exercise D (p. 355)

1. (a) $\mathbf{r} = t\mathbf{b} = 3t\mathbf{i} + t\mathbf{j}$;       (b) $\mathbf{r} = 2t\mathbf{i} + 3t\mathbf{j}$;
   (c) $\mathbf{r} = -t\mathbf{i} + t\mathbf{j}$;       (d) $\mathbf{r} = 2\mathbf{i} + (1+t)\mathbf{j}$;
   (e) $\mathbf{r} = (1+3t)\mathbf{i} + (1+t)\mathbf{j}$.

2. (a) $\mathbf{r} = t\mathbf{i}$;       (b) $\mathbf{r} = t\mathbf{i} + t\mathbf{j} + 2t\mathbf{k}$;
   (c) $\mathbf{r} = 2\mathbf{i} + (1+t)\mathbf{k}$;       (d) $\mathbf{r} = \mathbf{i} + t\mathbf{j} + (1-t)\mathbf{k}$;
   (e) $\mathbf{r} = \mathbf{i} + t\mathbf{j} + t\mathbf{k}$;       (f) $\mathbf{r} = t\mathbf{i} + (1-2t)\mathbf{j} + \mathbf{k}$.

3. (a)   (i) $P$ is $(1, 3)$;       (ii) $Q$ is $(3, 7)$;
   (iii) $x = t$, $y = 3t$; $y = 3x$;       (iv) $x = 4t$, $y = 3t$;
                                              $y = 3x/4$;
   (v) $x - 2 = y = t$;       (vi) $x = 1 + t$, $y = 3(1+t)$;
                                              $y = 3x$.
   (b)   (i) $\mathbf{r} = t(\mathbf{i} + 2\mathbf{j})$;       (ii) $\mathbf{r} = t(\mathbf{i} - \mathbf{j})$;
   (iii) $\mathbf{r} = t(5\mathbf{i} + 4\mathbf{j})$;       (iv) $\mathbf{r} = \mathbf{j} + t(\mathbf{i} + 3\mathbf{j})$.

   These answers are not unique.

4. (i) $\sqrt{2}, 2\sqrt{2}$;    (ii) $\sqrt{29}, 2\sqrt{29}$;    (iii) $\sqrt{38}, 2\sqrt{38}$.

5. $\mathbf{r} = 6\mathbf{i} + 3\mathbf{j}$.

6. The lines are $\mathbf{r} = \mathbf{i} + u(-2\mathbf{i} + \mathbf{j} + \mathbf{k})$ and $\mathbf{r} = t(\mathbf{i} + \mathbf{j} + \mathbf{k})$. If they intersect, then $1 - 2u = t$ and $u = t$; hence $t = \frac{1}{3}$, and the point of intersection is $(\frac{1}{3}, \frac{1}{3}, \frac{1}{3})$.

7. By symmetry, the point found in Question 6 lies on them all.

8. (a) No;    (b) no;    (c) yes, at $(\frac{1}{2}, \frac{1}{2}, \frac{1}{2})$.

# 4. PARAMETERS IN TWO DIMENSIONS
### Exercise E (p. 358)

1. (a) $\mathbf{r} = t\mathbf{i} + s\mathbf{k}$;       (b) $\mathbf{r} = t\mathbf{i} + s(\mathbf{i} + \mathbf{j} + \mathbf{k})$;
   (c) $\mathbf{r} = t(\mathbf{i} + \mathbf{k}) + s(\mathbf{i} + \mathbf{j})$.

2. (a) $\mathbf{r} = \mathbf{k} + t\mathbf{i} + s\mathbf{j}$;       (b) $\mathbf{r} = \frac{1}{2}\mathbf{i} + (t + \frac{1}{2})\mathbf{j} + s\mathbf{k}$;
   (c) $\mathbf{r} = t\mathbf{i} + s\mathbf{j} + (2 - t - s)\mathbf{k}$;       (d) $\mathbf{r} = t\mathbf{i} + s\mathbf{j} + (1 - s)\mathbf{k}$.

3. $(\frac{1}{3}, \frac{1}{3}, \frac{1}{3})$.

4. $(\frac{1}{4}, \frac{1}{4}, \frac{1}{4})$. $4\mathbf{OG}/3 = \mathbf{OP}$, where $P$ is $(\frac{1}{3}, \frac{1}{3}, \frac{1}{3})$, the centroid of the triangle $IJK$.

5. The plane is
$$\mathbf{r} = \mathbf{k} + \tfrac{1}{2}\mathbf{j} + t(\mathbf{i}+\mathbf{j}) + s(\mathbf{i}-\mathbf{k}) = (t+s)\mathbf{i} + (t+\tfrac{1}{2})\mathbf{j} + (1-s)\mathbf{k}$$
and the point $\mathbf{i} + u\mathbf{k}$ lies on it if
$$t+s = 1,$$
$$t+\tfrac{1}{2} = 0,$$
$$1-s = u;$$
which equations give $t = -\frac{1}{2}$, $s = \frac{3}{2}$, $u = -\frac{1}{2}$. The point divides $CI$ in the ratio $-3:1$.

6. Plane $BCD$ is $\mathbf{r} = t\mathbf{i} + s\mathbf{j} + (2-t-s)\mathbf{k}$ (see Question 2($c$)); plane $OKAD$ is $\mathbf{r} = u(\mathbf{i}+\mathbf{j}) + v\mathbf{k}$. (Note that we must use different parameters.)

For common points
$$t = u,$$
$$s = u,$$
$$2-t-s = v;$$
whence $\mathbf{r} = u(\mathbf{i}+\mathbf{j}) + 2(1-u)\mathbf{k}$, the line of intersection.

7. Yes, $s = \frac{1}{2}$, $t = \frac{1}{3}$.

8. ($a$) $x+y+z = 1$;    ($b$) $x+y+z = 2$;    ($c$) $y = z$.

# 5. SCALAR PRODUCT

Up to this section there has been no reason why the base vectors $\mathbf{i}$, $\mathbf{j}$ and $\mathbf{k}$, should have had any particular length or direction. The geometry has been *affine*, that is to say it deals with properties of incidence, ratios of lengths in the same direction, and parallelism, which are not changed by linear transformations. If the base vectors are replaced by any other independent triplet of vectors, there will not be any difference in results based on these properties.

With the introduction of the scalar product the geometry changes. We require now that $\mathbf{i}.\mathbf{i} = 1$, $\mathbf{i}.\mathbf{j} = 0$, and so on. Logically, these are postulates about our vector space; in terms of the scalar product, defined simply as a number depending on the two vectors which satisfies certain axioms, we may define length, angle, right-angle, and all the fundamental concepts of Euclidean geometry.

Here the approach is still based on intuitive knowledge of the properties of space. The definition of scalar product has to be motivated by physical considerations and stated in terms of lengths and angle. The abstract algebraic properties are developed from this, and machinery set up for dealing with these Euclidean ideas in terms of the new product. The length of the vector $\mathbf{r}$ is seen to be $\sqrt{(\mathbf{r}.\mathbf{r})}$, and the angle between $\mathbf{p}$ and $\mathbf{q}$ is found as $\cos^{-1}(\mathbf{p}.\mathbf{q})/\sqrt{\{(\mathbf{p}.\mathbf{p})(\mathbf{q}.\mathbf{q})\}}$. From an abstract point of view we should take these as definitions; here they are simply useful formulae. The student should begin to realize that any geometrical theorem involving right-angles, angle-bisectors, isosceles triangles, and so on, is going to require the use of the scalar product in some form. For perpendiculars, it is the natural tool.

The scalar product is so called because there is another product of two vectors, the vector product, defined in Exercise H, Question 6. This latter product is often written $\mathbf{p}\times\mathbf{q}$; the notation $\mathbf{p}.\mathbf{q}$ for scalar product is therefore *de rigueur* and must be insisted on. Care must also be taken not to confuse it with 'multiplication by a scalar'; $k\mathbf{p}$ should not be called the scalar product of the vector $\mathbf{p}$ with the scalar $k$.

## Exercise F (p. 364)

1. (a) 10; (b) $-15\sqrt{3}/2$; (c) 0; (d) 0; (e) $-2\sqrt{3}$; (f) $-2\sqrt{3}$.

2. The positive directions of $\mathbf{u}$ and $\mathbf{v}$ have an obtuse angle between them.

3. $(\mathbf{a}+\mathbf{b}).(\mathbf{a}-\mathbf{b}) = \mathbf{a}.\mathbf{a}-\mathbf{b}.\mathbf{b} = 0$ since $\mathbf{a}$ and $\mathbf{b}$ have equal lengths.

   If the sides of a rhombus are along the vectors $\mathbf{a}$ and $\mathbf{b}$, its diagonals are segments representing $\mathbf{a}+\mathbf{b}$ and $\mathbf{a}-\mathbf{b}$; since the scalar product is zero, the diagonals are at right-angles.

4. Vertically opposite angles are equal.

5. If $\theta$ is the angle between $\mathbf{F}$ and $\mathbf{x}$,
$$\mathbf{F}.\mathbf{x} = Fx\cos\theta = F(x\cos\theta)$$
   = force $F$ multiplied by the component of $\mathbf{x}$ in the direction of $\mathbf{F}$.
   $4\times180\cos60° \text{ mN} = 720 \text{ J}$.

6. Work done by tension = 480 J.
   Work done by weight = $-320$ J.
   Work lost in overcoming friction = 160 J.

7. Not if the track is smooth. $\Sigma W.s = -1000$ kJ always, since it can be written $W.\Sigma s = W.AB$, where $A$ and $B$ are initial and final positions.

8. (a) $OP = 17$, $OQ = 9$, $POQ = \cos^{-1}\frac{88}{153} = 55°$;
   (b) $OP = 9$, $OQ = 9$, $POQ = \cos^{-1}\frac{56}{81} = 46.2°$;
   (c) $OP = 11$, $OQ = 7$, $POQ = \cos^{-1}\frac{27}{77} = 110.5°$;
   (d) $OP = 5\sqrt{2}$, $OQ = 13\sqrt{2}$, $POQ = \cos^{-1}\frac{41}{130} = 108.4°$;
   (e) $OP = \sqrt{89}$, $OQ = 5\sqrt{2}$, $POQ = 90°$.

9. The eight alternatives of $(\pm 1, \pm 1, \pm 1)$. $\cos^{-1}\frac{1}{3} = 70.5°$.

10. Symmetry requirements show at once that it is equilateral. The
   vectors of the three sides are $\begin{pmatrix} 0 \\ 1 \\ -1 \end{pmatrix}$, $\begin{pmatrix} -1 \\ 0 \\ 1 \end{pmatrix}$, $\begin{pmatrix} 1 \\ -1 \\ 0 \end{pmatrix}$.

11. (a) 2;  (b) $-3$;  (c) 9;  (d) 5;  (e) 26;  (f) 3.

12. $a = 0$, $b = 0$, or $a$ is perpendicular to $b$.

13. $(x\mathbf{i}+y\mathbf{j}+z\mathbf{k}).(x\mathbf{i}+y\mathbf{j}+z\mathbf{k}) = x^2+y^2+z^2$, since $\mathbf{i}.\mathbf{i} = 1$, etc., $\mathbf{i}.\mathbf{j} = 0$, etc.

14. If $\mathbf{p} = \begin{pmatrix} 3 \\ -4 \end{pmatrix}$, $\mathbf{q} = \begin{pmatrix} 4 \\ 3 \end{pmatrix}$, $\mathbf{p}.\mathbf{q} = 0$. Hence

$$\mathbf{i} = \frac{(\mathbf{i}.\mathbf{p})\mathbf{p}}{p^2} + \frac{(\mathbf{i}.\mathbf{q})\mathbf{q}}{q^2} = (3\mathbf{p}+4\mathbf{q})/25;$$

$$\mathbf{j} = (-4\mathbf{p}+3\mathbf{q})/25 \quad \text{similarly.}$$

15. $x = 3p+4q$, $y = -4p+3q$; $p = (3x-4y)/25$, $q = (4x+3y)/25$.

16. $\mathbf{u}.\mathbf{v} = \mathbf{v}.\mathbf{w} = \mathbf{w}.\mathbf{v} = 0$; $\mathbf{u}.\mathbf{u} = \mathbf{v}.\mathbf{v} = \mathbf{w}.\mathbf{w} = 9$.

17. $a+2b+2c = 1$;  $2a-2b+c = 0$;  $2a+b-2c = 0$.
   $a = \frac{1}{9}$,  $b = \frac{2}{9}$,  $c = \frac{2}{9}$.  $\mathbf{i} = (\mathbf{u}+2\mathbf{v}+2\mathbf{w})/9$.

18. Since $\mathbf{u}.\mathbf{v} = \mathbf{u}.\mathbf{w} = 0$, etc.,

$$\mathbf{i} = \frac{\mathbf{i}.\mathbf{u}}{u^2}\mathbf{u} + \frac{\mathbf{i}.\mathbf{v}}{v^2}\mathbf{v} + \frac{\mathbf{i}.\mathbf{w}}{w^2}\mathbf{w}$$

and so on.
Hence
$\mathbf{i} = (\mathbf{u}+2\mathbf{v}+2\mathbf{w})/9$,  $\mathbf{j} = (2\mathbf{u}-2\mathbf{v}+\mathbf{w})/9$,  $\mathbf{k} = (2\mathbf{u}+\mathbf{v}-2\mathbf{w})/9$.
$3\mathbf{i}+4\mathbf{j}-\mathbf{k} = \mathbf{u}-\frac{1}{3}\mathbf{v}+\frac{4}{3}\mathbf{w}$.

**19.** $\hat{u} = \begin{pmatrix} \frac{1}{3} \\ \frac{2}{3} \\ \frac{2}{3} \end{pmatrix}$  $\hat{v} = \begin{pmatrix} \frac{2}{3} \\ -\frac{2}{3} \\ \frac{1}{3} \end{pmatrix}$  $\hat{w} = \begin{pmatrix} \frac{2}{3} \\ \frac{1}{3} \\ -\frac{2}{3} \end{pmatrix}$,

$$\mathbf{i}.\hat{u} = \tfrac{1}{3}, \quad \mathbf{i}.\hat{v} = \tfrac{2}{3}, \quad \mathbf{i}.\hat{w} = \tfrac{2}{3},$$
$$\mathbf{j}.\hat{u} = \tfrac{2}{3}, \quad \mathbf{j}.\hat{v} = -\tfrac{2}{3}, \quad \mathbf{j}.\hat{w} = \tfrac{1}{3},$$
$$\mathbf{k}.\hat{u} = \tfrac{2}{3}, \quad \mathbf{k}.\hat{v} = \tfrac{1}{3}, \quad \mathbf{k}.\hat{w} = -\tfrac{2}{3}.$$

**20.** $QR = \begin{pmatrix} 11 \\ 4 \\ -5 \end{pmatrix}$, $RP = \begin{pmatrix} -4 \\ -8 \\ +1 \end{pmatrix}$, $PQ = \begin{pmatrix} -7 \\ 4 \\ 4 \end{pmatrix}$.

$PR = PQ = 9; \quad QR = 9\sqrt{2}.$

$\cos P = 0; \quad P = \tfrac{1}{2}\pi; \quad \cos Q = 1/\sqrt{2} = \cos R; \quad Q = R = \tfrac{1}{4}\pi.$

**21.** $QR = \begin{pmatrix} -1 \\ 7 \\ 0 \end{pmatrix}$, $RP = \begin{pmatrix} 4 \\ -11 \\ -5 \end{pmatrix}$, $PQ = \begin{pmatrix} -3 \\ 4 \\ +5 \end{pmatrix}$.

$QR = 5\sqrt{2}, \quad RP = 9\sqrt{2}, \quad PQ = 5\sqrt{2}.$

$\cos P = \cos R = \tfrac{9}{10}; \quad \cos Q = -\tfrac{31}{50};$

$P = R = 25 \cdot 8°, \quad Q = 128 \cdot 3°.$

**22.** $a^2 = b^2 + c^2 - 2bc \cos A$. Largest angle $= \cos^{-1}\left(-\tfrac{1}{2}\right) = \tfrac{2}{3}\pi$.

**23.** $BC = 20$ cm, $CA = 18 \cdot 36$ cm, $AB = 15$ cm.

$\cos A = 81/bc = 0 \cdot 294; \quad A = 72 \cdot 9°; \quad \cos B = 0 \cdot 48, \quad B = 61 \cdot 3°;$

$\cos C = 256/ab = 0 \cdot 698, \quad G = 45 \cdot 8°.$

**24.** $x = p \cos \alpha$, etc. $x^2 + y^2 + z^2 = \mathbf{p}.\mathbf{p} = p^2$.

**25.** $p_1 p_2 \cos \theta$

$= \mathbf{p}_1.\mathbf{p}_2 = x_1 x_2 + y_1 y_2 + z_1 z_2$

$= p_1 p_2 \cos \alpha_1 \cos \alpha_2 + p_1 p_2 \cos \beta_1 \cos \beta_2 + p_1 p_2 \cos \gamma_1 \cos \gamma_2.$

## 6. PERPENDICULARITY

The proofs in 6.2 and 6.3 are often found difficult to follow. It may help to consider the vector $\begin{pmatrix} a \\ b \end{pmatrix}$ as a free vector at right-angles to the line; the point $Q$ is irrelevant, and may confuse.

The angle between two lines is not uniquely defined; there are two such angles, whereas the angle between the normal vectors is unique once the normal vectors have been defined. The normal vectors, however, are themselves not unique. $3x+4y = 5$ has $\binom{3}{4}$ or any scalar multiple of this as normal vector. If we take the normal vector $\binom{-3}{-4}$ we alter the angle as found in Example 6. If there is any doubt about which angle is intended, a figure should be drawn. In three dimensions, however, it may not be easy to see which of the two angles between two planes, for example, is the acute angle, and the normal vectors will have to be carefully examined.

### Exercise G (p. 371)

| | Parallel | Perpendicular |
|---|---|---|
| **1.** (a) | $3x-y = 3$ | $x+3y = 11$ |
| (b) | $x+y+4 = 0$ | $x-y+2 = 0$ |
| (c) | $2x+y = 3$ | $x-2y = 14$ |
| (d) | $x = -3$ | $y = 4$ |
| (e) | $7x+5y = 2$ | $5x-7y = 12$ |
| (f) | $13x-8y = 32$ | $8x+13y = -52.$ |

**2.** $PP_1$ is perpendicular to $PP_2$. The circle on $P_1P_2$ as diameter.

**3.** (a) $x^2+y^2+2x-3y-13 = 0$;

(b) $x^2+y^2+(q-p)x-(p+q)y = 0$.

**4.** (a) $\cos^{-1}\frac{9}{50}\sqrt{10} = 55\cdot3°$;    (b) $90°$;

(b) $\cos^{-1}\frac{120}{169} = 44\cdot8°$;    (d) $\cos^{-1}\frac{4}{5} = 36\cdot9°$;

(e) $\cos^{-1}1/\sqrt{2} = 45°$.

**5.** (a) 1;    (b) $\frac{3}{13}$;    (c) 3;    (d) $13/\sqrt{2}$.

**6.** The line through $(3, 2)$ perpendicular to $\binom{5}{5\frac{1}{2}}$ is $10x+11y = 52$.

The line through $(-2, 2\frac{1}{2})$ perpendicular to $\binom{10}{5}$ is
$$2x+y = -1\frac{1}{2}.$$
The line through $(-7, -3)$ perpendicular to $\binom{5}{-\frac{1}{2}}$ is
$$10x-y = -67.$$

Solve any two of these and check in the third: $x = -\frac{137}{24}$, $y = \frac{119}{12}$. A proof that the altitudes do in general meet in a point is given in the next section.

## 6.8 Orthocentres.

*The orthocentric tetrahedron.* This is an interesting configuration. Other results about it which may be easily proved include the following:

$BC^2 + AD^2 = CA^2 + BD^2 = AB^2 + CD^2$;

$HG = GO$, where $G$ is its centroid and $O$ its circumcentre;

$A, B, C, D$ are alternate vertices of a rhombohedron;

The centroids of the four faces and the four points $K_1, K_2, K_3, K_4$, which are the orthocentres of the faces, lie on a sphere.

### Exercise H (p. 375)

1.  $\mathbf{OP.OQ} = \mathbf{OP.OR} = 0$;  $\mathbf{OP.OS} = 0$ also;  $\mathbf{s} = \mathbf{q} + \mathbf{r}$.

2.  $\mathbf{AB} = \begin{pmatrix} 2 \\ 5 \\ 3 \end{pmatrix}$,  $\mathbf{CD} = \begin{pmatrix} -10 \\ 10 \\ -10 \end{pmatrix}$: $\mathbf{AB.CD} = 0$.

    $\mathbf{AC} = \begin{pmatrix} -2 \\ -3 \\ 2 \end{pmatrix}$,  $\mathbf{DB} = \begin{pmatrix} 14 \\ -2 \\ 11 \end{pmatrix}$: $\mathbf{AC.DB} = 0$.

    Use theorem in Section 7.8.

3.  These are alternate vertices of a cube, centred on the origin.
    If $P = (1, 1, 1)$, $Q = (1, -1, -1)$, $R = (-1, 1, -1)$,
    $S = (-1, -1, 1)$, then

    $$\mathbf{PQ} = \begin{pmatrix} 0 \\ -2 \\ -2 \end{pmatrix} \quad \text{and} \quad \mathbf{RS} = \begin{pmatrix} 0 \\ -2 \\ 2 \end{pmatrix};$$

    hence $\mathbf{PQ.RS} = 0$, and so on.

    The other four vertices also form a congruent tetrahedron. The two tetrahedra together ('twinned' tetrahedra) form Kepler's *stella octangula*.

4.  $2x + 3y - 4z = 0$;  $2x + 3y - 4z = 2$.

**5.** Solve $5a+2b+3c = 0$ and $3a+4b+c = 0$ to get
$$a:b:c = 5:-2:-7.$$

**6.** Either verify that
$$a_1(b_1c_2-b_2c_1)+b_1(c_1a_2-c_2a_1)+c_1(a_1b_2-a_2b_1)$$
$$= a_2(b_1c_2-b_2c_1)+b_2(c_1a_2-c_2a_1)+c_2(a_1b_2-a_2b_1) = 0,$$
or solve for $p:q:r$ the two equations
$$pa_1+qb_1+rc_1 = 0, \quad pa_2+qb_2+rc_2 = 0.$$
This vector is called the VECTOR PRODUCT of the two given vectors. Fuller consideration of it is given in the Further Mathematics text.

**7.** $4\mathbf{g} = \mathbf{a}+\mathbf{b}+\mathbf{c}+\mathbf{d}$. Since $2\mathbf{h} = \mathbf{a}+\mathbf{b}+\mathbf{c}+\mathbf{d}$ also, $\mathbf{h} = 2\mathbf{g}$ and $G$ is the mid-point of $OH$. $OGH$ is called the *Euler Line* of the tetrahedron.

## 7. LINES AND PLANES
### *Exercise I (p. 379)*

**1.** $4x-y-3z = 0$.

**2.** $x+y+z = -1$, $-x+y+z = 1$, $x-y+z = 1$, $x+y-z = 1$. These can be obtained by the method of Example 2, or, more quickly, by observing that (for example) the plane through $BCD$ is normal to $OA$. All perpendiculars are equal to $1/\sqrt{3}$.

**3.** (*a*) $\sqrt{3}$; (*b*) 0; (*c*) $\frac{1}{5}$; (*d*) 1; (*e*) 3; (*f*) $3\sqrt{10}/5$.

**4.** $7\times 3-10\times(-8)+13\times(-9)+15 = -1$, so that this point is on the opposite side to the origin. On the same side.

**5.** Making the perpendiculars from the origin each positive, the locus is
$$\{(x, y, z): (-2x-8y+4z+11)/\sqrt{84} = (4x-y+2z+7)/\sqrt{21}\}.$$
This equation reduces to
$$-2x-8y+4z+11 = 8x-2y+4z+14,$$
and finally to $10x+6y+3 = 0$.

**6.** $5x-2y+7z = 15-2-14 = -1$.

**7.** The normal vector is perpendicular to

$$\begin{pmatrix} 1 \\ 1 \\ -3 \end{pmatrix} \quad \text{and to} \quad \begin{pmatrix} 1 \\ -1 \\ 1 \end{pmatrix}.$$

Such a vector is

$$\begin{pmatrix} -2 \\ -4 \\ -2 \end{pmatrix}$$

(see Exercise H, Question 6). We therefore choose the simpler vector

$$\begin{pmatrix} 1 \\ 2 \\ 1 \end{pmatrix} \quad \text{and the plane} \quad x+2y+z = -1.$$

**8.** $ax+by+cz = d$ and
$ax_1+by_1+cz_1 = d \Rightarrow a(x-x_1)+b(y-y_1)+c(z-z_1) = 0$,
which can be interpreted as

$$\mathbf{n.PP_1} = 0, \quad \text{where } \mathbf{n} \text{ is the vector} \quad \begin{pmatrix} a \\ b \\ c \end{pmatrix}.$$

**9.** Any plane with normal vector

$$\begin{pmatrix} -1 \\ 3 \\ \lambda \end{pmatrix}$$

has an equation of the form $-x+3y+\lambda z = k$, and will meet the plane $x = 0$ where it is met by the plane $3y+\lambda z = k$. This can only be $6y-5z = 30$ if $k = 15$ and $\lambda = -2\frac{1}{2}$. The plane is then $-2x+6y-5z = 30$ and it meets $y = 0$ in the line $y = 0$, $2x+5z+30 = 0$.

### Exercise J (p. 382)

**1.** $x = 1, y = 1+t, z = 1+t; \quad x = -1, y = -1+t, z = 1-t;$
$y = 1, z = 1+t, x = 1+t; \quad y = -1, z = -1+t, x = 1-t;$
$z = 1, x = 1+t, y = 1+t; \quad z = -1, x = -1+t, y = 1-t.$

The form of these equations shows clearly that the edges are diagonals of the cube-faces, $x = \pm 1, y = \pm 1, z = \pm 1$, and that opposite edges are non-parallel diagonals.

**2.** $x = u-tu$, $y = t$, $z = tu$; $x+z = u \Rightarrow z = y(x+z)$.

If we take $u$ as parameter and put $t = v$ we have $x = u(1-v)$, $y = v$, $z = uv$, so that $(x, y, z) = (0, v, 0)+u(1-v, v, v)$.

The first line is parallel to the plane $x+z = 0$ for all $u$. The second line is parallel to $y = 0$ for all $v$. These two families of lines are the *generators* of this ruled surface, which is a hyperbolic paraboloid.

**3.** (*a*) $(0, 1, 0)$; (*b*) $(-\frac{1}{2}, \frac{17}{4}, \frac{15}{4})$; (*c*) $(0, \frac{1}{3}, \frac{14}{3})$;

(*d*) line is parallel to the plane;

(*e*) line lies in the plane.

**4.** $\begin{pmatrix} 9 \\ 7 \\ -11 \end{pmatrix}$.   $9x+7y-11z = 0$.   No.

**5.** $d = \mathbf{p} . \mathbf{n} = \mathbf{p}_1 . \mathbf{n} + t(\mathbf{u} . \mathbf{n}) \Rightarrow t = \dfrac{d - \mathbf{p} . \mathbf{n}}{\mathbf{u} . \mathbf{n}}$

$$\Rightarrow \mathbf{p} = \frac{\mathbf{p}_1(\mathbf{u} . \mathbf{n}) - \mathbf{u}(\mathbf{p}_1 . \mathbf{n}) + d\mathbf{u}}{\mathbf{u} . \mathbf{n}}.$$

**7.7   A sheaf and a prism of planes.** A full discussion of this can be given more easily when linear dependence is understood and the theory of determinants has been developed. Essentially the condition for either a sheaf or a prism is that all three, but no two, of the left-hand sides of the equations of planes shall be linearly dependent. If the entire equations are linearly dependent, the planes form a sheaf; if not, a prism. When we come to solve linear equations in Chapter 21, we shall find that there are many more special cases arising in three dimensions than in two. Two lines in a plane meet in a point, are parallel, or coincide; with three planes in space the possibilities are far more numerous.

A. M. Macbeath, *Elementary Vector Algebra,* is a useful companion to the work of this chapter.

### Exercise K (*p. 385*)

**1.**   $x = 1+(3\lambda+4\mu)\,t$, $y = 2+(4\lambda-2\mu)\,t$, $z = 3+(5\lambda+3\mu)\,t$ lies in the plane if and only if

$$2+(6\lambda+8\mu)\,t+2+(4\lambda-2\mu)\,t-6-(10\lambda+6\mu)\,t+2 = 0,$$

215

which is seen to be true for all values of $\lambda$, $\mu$ and $t$. This line passes through $(1, 2, 3)$ and has a vector which is a linear combination of the direction vectors of the two lines in Section 7.6.

**2.** $x = 0$, $y = t$, $z = -t$; $x = -t$, $y = 0$, $z = t$ and $x = t$, $y = -t$, $z = 0$. They all lie in $x + y + z = 0$.

**3.** For different values of $k$ the planes form a sheaf with the common line $\frac{1}{3}x = \frac{1}{4}y = \frac{1}{5}z$.

**4.** (a) The vector

$$\begin{pmatrix} 3 \\ 4 \\ 5 \end{pmatrix}$$

is parallel to all three planes.

(b) Putting $z = 0$, we find that the point $(\frac{11}{5}, -\frac{7}{5}, 0)$ lies on the first two planes. It does not satisfy the third equation. Hence the planes form a prism.

**5.** (a) The vector

$$\begin{pmatrix} 14 \\ -27 \\ -11 \end{pmatrix}$$

is parallel to all three planes.

(b) Putting $z = 0$, the line common to the first two planes pass through $(\frac{25}{11}, -\frac{27}{11}, 0)$.

(c) This point lies on the third plane if $k = -3$.

Alternatively, knowing what we are expected to prove, we may observe that

$$3x + 4y - 6z - k = (5x + 3y - z - 4) - (2x + y + 5z - 7)$$

identically, provided that $k = -3$.

**6.** Evidently

$$\begin{pmatrix} 1 \\ -1 \\ 1 \end{pmatrix} \text{ is perpendicular to both } \begin{pmatrix} 1 \\ 1 \\ 0 \end{pmatrix} \text{ and } \begin{pmatrix} 0 \\ 1 \\ 1 \end{pmatrix}.$$

**7.** The plane parallel to $x = z$ through the intersection of the first two planes is obviously

$$(x+y)-(y+z) = 0,$$

i.e. $\qquad\qquad\qquad x = z.$

$x = z+1$ is parallel to this, so the planes form a prism. Its axis is in the direction of the vector

$$\begin{pmatrix} 1 \\ -1 \\ 1 \end{pmatrix},$$

from the result of Question 6.

**8.** $c = b-a,$ by subtracting the equations of the first two planes.

# 14

# FURTHER TRIGONOMETRY

The material in this chapter is mostly traditional, but is treated in a modern way in places where this seems appropriate. Chapter 13 on Vectors leads naturally into this one where the theory of vectors is applied, and the development of the subject follows the lines suggested by the O-Level course, with emphasis on wave-motion rather than on surveying.

Throughout there has been attention to functions, and the solution of equations is treated in rather more detail than is usual, as the reader now has a familiarity with set language and the various number systems. A section on Polar Coordinates follows naturally from the idea of functional dependence, and the chapter closes with a section on the solution of triangles, which now takes its place as a subsidiary idea in the main development of trigonometry. Perhaps the central core, both in content and attitude, is found in Section 3 on simple Harmonic Analysis.

Throughout the chapter it must be understood that the traditional use of this subject as a mine of examination exercises in manipulation was very far from the writers' mind. We have only included such manipulation as we consider to be entirely necessary to the understanding of what is being done.

## 1. THE ADDITION FORMULA FOR TANGENTS

*Example* 2. We say that the method cannot be used to find the angle between the two vectors

$$\begin{pmatrix} 1 \\ 1 \\ 3 \end{pmatrix} \quad \text{and} \quad \begin{pmatrix} 2 \\ 3 \\ 1 \end{pmatrix},$$

but this invites discussion. Could we ever find the angle between three-dimensional vectors by this method? Certainly two three-dimensional

218

vectors are always in one plane, but to find anything corresponding to gradient in this plane involves heavy arithmetic except when the plane is one of the axial planes. The scalar product method is superior when this is not so. See Exercise A, Question 5.

### Exercise A (p. 387)

1.  $\tan 2A = \dfrac{2 \tan A}{1 - \tan^2 A}.$

2.  Expand $\tan(\tfrac{1}{4}\pi + \theta)$, using $\tan \tfrac{1}{4}\pi = 1$.

3.  (a) $\tan^{-1}(\tfrac{1}{3}) = 18 \cdot 4°$;

    (b) $\tan^{-1}(-1) = 135°$ (or $45°$);

    (c) $\tan^{-1}(-\tfrac{9}{5}) = 119°$ (or $61°$);

    (d) $\tan^{-1}(-38/9) = 103 \cdot 3°$ (or $76 \cdot 7°$);

    (e) these lines are parallel to those of (d); the angle between them is therefore the same.

4.  (a) $\tan^{-1}(\tfrac{1}{41})$.

    (b) These lines are of course perpendicular. The scalar product method of the previous chapter gives this, since it is zero and the lengths of the vectors themselves are not zero. The method of this section gives $\tfrac{2 \cdot 5}{0}$ which is undefined.

5.  Either angle can be found. One line is parallel to

$$\begin{pmatrix} 1 \\ 2 \\ 0 \end{pmatrix} \quad \text{and the other to} \quad \begin{pmatrix} 2 \\ 1 \\ 0 \end{pmatrix}.$$

These are therefore in the $xy$-plane, and the methods of this section can easily be applied to the two vectors

$$\begin{pmatrix} 2 \\ 1 \end{pmatrix} \quad \text{and} \quad \begin{pmatrix} 1 \\ 2 \end{pmatrix}.$$

$\theta = 36 \cdot 9°$.

### 2. MULTIPLE ANGLES

The development of the graphs of $\sin^2$ and $\cos^2$ should be straightforward after the work on transformations in Chapter 5 of the pupil's text. A one-way stretch of the function cos in Figure A(a) gives the graph shown in Figure A(b), and is followed by another to give $\frac{1}{2} \cos 2\theta$ in Figure A(c). This is reflected in the $\theta$-axis to give $-\frac{1}{2} \cos 2\theta$, Figure A(d), and finally, Figure A(e), is translated $\frac{1}{2}$ upwards to give Figure 2 on p. 389 of the pupil's text. Similar stages, omitting the reflection, give $\cos^2 \theta$.

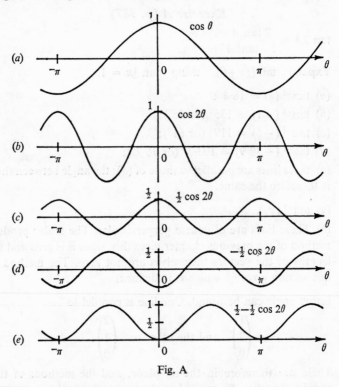

Fig. A

The subject of the graphs of $\sin \theta$ and $\cos \theta$ as functions of $t$ and their extensions beyond $t = 1$ can be taken as far as the teacher wishes, giving opportunities for further curve sketching, bringing in asymptotic states ($t \to \infty$), discontinuities, and the related domain of $\theta$.

### Exercise B (p. 390)

2.   (a) $\cos 2x$;       (b) $\tan^2 x$;       (c) $1 + \sin 2x$;

     (d) this is $\frac{1}{4} \sin^2 2x = \frac{1}{8}(1 - \cos 4x)$.

4.  $\tan \theta = 1$ has solution set $\{\theta : \theta = (4n+1)\frac{1}{4}\pi, n \in Z\}$ and, for this set, $2\theta = 2n\pi + \frac{1}{2}\pi$ and $\tan 2\theta$ is undefined.

When $\tan \theta = \sqrt{3}$, $\tan 2\theta = -\sqrt{3}$, which is perhaps well illustrated by the diagram, which shows up the half-turn rotational symmetries of the function 'tan' (see Figure B).

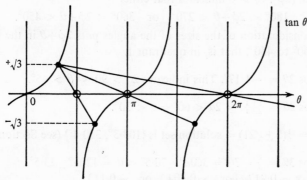

Fig. B

5.  See Figure C. $\tan A = \dfrac{a}{b}$, $\tan B = \dfrac{b}{a} \Rightarrow \tan A \tan B = 1$.

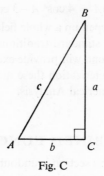

Fig. C

6.  $\tan \theta = \frac{1}{5} \Rightarrow \tan 4\theta = \frac{120}{119} \Rightarrow \tan 4\theta > 1 \Rightarrow 4\theta > 45°$.

7.  $\cos \theta = \frac{3}{5}$, $\sin \theta = \frac{4}{5}$, $\sin \phi = \frac{5}{13}$, $\cos \phi = -\frac{12}{13}$,
    $\sin 2\theta = \frac{24}{25}$, $\sin 2\phi = -\frac{60}{169}$, $\cos 2\phi = \frac{119}{169}$.
    (a) $-33/65$; (b) $-7/25$; (c) $-36/325$; (d) $-120/119$;
    (e) $+116/837$.

221

Consideration of the ranges for $\theta$ and $\phi$ given does not, of itself, define the quadrants for $2\theta + \phi$ and $2\phi + \theta$.

$\cos(2\theta + \phi)$ is negative so that $90° < (2\theta + \phi) < 270°$, and more detailed consideration of the angles shows that $2\theta + \phi$ is in the third quadrant. $180° < 2\phi + \theta < 450°$ from the ranges given, but $\tan(2\phi + \theta) > 0$ indicates that either

$$180° < 2\phi + \theta < 270° \quad \text{or} \quad 360° < 2\phi + \theta < 450°.$$

Consideration of the sizes of the angles puts $2\phi + \theta$ in the range $360°$ to $450°$, that is, in quadrant 1.

8. $\cos 2\theta = -1/17^2$. This indicates $2\theta > 90° \Leftrightarrow \theta > 45°$.

9. $\cos 2\theta = \frac{113}{225}. \Rightarrow 2\theta < 60° \Leftrightarrow \theta < 30°$.

10. $t = \frac{1}{6}(3 \pm \sqrt{21}) \Rightarrow$ solution set is $\{103.3°, 330.4°\}$ (see Section 6.3).

11. $\cos 3\theta = \frac{1}{3} \Rightarrow 3\theta = 360n° \pm 70.5° \Leftrightarrow \theta = 120n° \pm 23.5°$.
$\Leftrightarrow x = 0.917,$ or $-0.804,$ or $-0.113.$

The use of this substitution itself is limited since in this particular example there was no term in $x^2$, and even so the coefficients of the other two terms were closely related to those of

$$\cos 3A = 4 \cos^3 A - 3 \cos A.$$

However, this does open up a whole field of methods of solution by substitution, and standard traditional texts on trigonometry for A-Level and beyond will provide examples for the interested student. With computerization these methods have rather given way to those of Numerical Analysis.

## 3. COMBINED FUNCTIONS

The best way to follow this section is undoubtedly to do the practical work oneself, and the whole section could well be done as a project. This, of course, will take time, but it is isolated from the rest of the book and so can conveniently and usefully be spread over a long period. There is good opportunity for discovery, in analysis and synthesis as well as display, and for further reading.

The graph of $\sin 3x + \sin 5x$ is shown in Figure D and covers one full period.

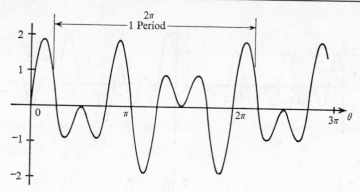

Fig. D

## Exercise C (p. 393)

1. Phase-difference $\frac{1}{2}\pi$; (a) $\sqrt{2}$; (b) $2\pi$; (c) $-\frac{1}{4}\pi$.

2. Phase-difference $\frac{1}{3}\pi$; (a) $\sqrt{3}$; (b) $2\pi$; (c) $-\frac{1}{6}\pi$. Yes.

3. Yes. 7. $2\pi$. (Phase-difference from $\sin x$ is about $+38°$.)

4. $a = \frac{11}{2}$, $b = \dfrac{-5\sqrt{3}}{2}$.         5. $\sqrt{65}$, $n\pi + 29°\,45'$.

6. (a) $\sqrt{65}$, $60°\,15'$;

   (b) $4\sin\theta + 7\cos\theta$, $\sqrt{65}\sin(\theta + 60°\,15')$;

   (c) $\sqrt{65}$, $29°\,45'$;         (d) $k = \sqrt{65}$, $\alpha = 60°\,15'$.

7.

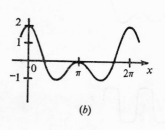

(b)

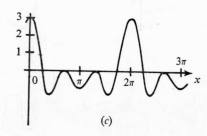

(c)

223

**8.**

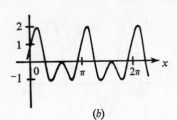

(b)

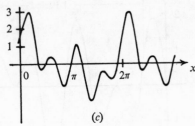

(c)

**9.**

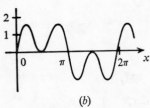

(b)

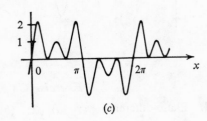

(c)

**10.**

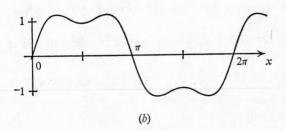

(b)

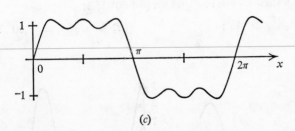

(c)

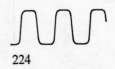

## 4. FUNCTION $a \sin x + b \cos x$

### Exercise D (p. 396)

1. $5 \sin (x + 0.643)$. Check when $x = 0$ or $-0.643$.

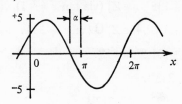

2. 17.

3. $\{0, \tfrac{1}{2}\pi, 2\pi\}$.

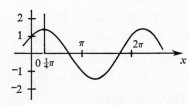

4. $25 \cos (x + 0.284)$; $\{0.961, 4.754\}$.

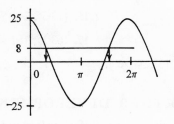

5. (a) Almost $1.2$ m; (b) $19\tfrac{1}{2}°$.

6. $2n\pi + 0.81$; no.

## 5. SIMPLE TRIGONOMETRICAL EQUATIONS

### Exercise E (p. 400)

1. $\{x: x = 360n° \pm 27°, n \in Z\}$.

2. $\{x: x = 360n° - 63°, n \in Z\} \cup \{x: x = 360n° + 243°, n \in Z\}$.

**3.** $\{x: x = 180n° + 57°, n \in Z\}$.

**4.** $\{x: x = 180n° + 53\cdot1°, n \in Z\}$ (via $\tan x = \frac{4}{3}$).

**5.** $\{x: x = 360n° \pm 94\cdot2°, n \in Z\}$.

**6.** $\{x: x = 180n° + 135°, n \in Z\}$ (via $\tan x = {}^-1$).

**7.** $\{x: x = 360n° + 330°, n \in Z\} \cup \{x: x = 360n° + 210°, n \in Z\}$.

**8.** $\{x: x = 360n° \pm 101\cdot5°, n \in Z\}$.

**9.** $\{22°, 68°, 202°, 248°\}$.

**10.** $\{48°, 72°, 168°, 192°, 288°, 312°\}$.

**11.** $\{9°, 45°, 81°, ..., 333°\}$.

In nos. 9, 10 and 11 it may well be easier to say that

$$0 \leqslant x < 360 \Leftrightarrow 0 \leqslant nx < 360n°,$$

in which case a sketch of the appropriate curve soon shows up the values of $nx$ and hence of $x$, on division by $n$.

**12.** $\{0°, 36°, 108°, 180°, 252°, 324°\}$.

**13.** $\{18°, 30°, 90°, 150°, 162°, 234°, 270°, 306°\}$.

**14.** $\{0°, 90°\}$.             **15.** $\{13\cdot3°, 240\cdot5°\}$.

**16.** $\{0°, 126\cdot8°\}$.           **17.** $\{63\cdot1°, 187\cdot9°\}$.

**18.** $\{135°, 161\cdot6°, 315°, 341\cdot6°\}$.

## 6. FURTHER DEVELOPMENTS

The work of this section is straightforward; vectors illuminate some traditional methods.

**6.1    The factor formulae.** The proof of

$$\cos v - \cos u = 2 \sin \frac{u+v}{2} \sin \frac{u-v}{2}$$

runs thus:

$$\text{In } \begin{pmatrix} \cos x \\ \sin x \end{pmatrix} + \begin{pmatrix} \cos y \\ \sin y \end{pmatrix} = 2 \cos \left( \frac{x-y}{2} \right) \begin{pmatrix} \cos \dfrac{x+y}{2} \\ \sin \dfrac{x+y}{2} \end{pmatrix}$$

substituting $y+\pi$ for $y$ we have

$$\begin{pmatrix}\cos x\\ \sin x\end{pmatrix}+\begin{pmatrix}-\cos y\\ -\sin y\end{pmatrix}=2\cos\left(\frac{x-y}{2}-\frac{\pi}{2}\right)\begin{pmatrix}\cos\left(\dfrac{x+y}{2}+\dfrac{\pi}{2}\right)\\[2mm] \sin\left(\dfrac{x+y}{2}+\dfrac{\pi}{2}\right)\end{pmatrix}$$

and equating first coefficients

$$\cos x-\cos y=2\cos\left(\frac{x-y}{2}-\frac{\pi}{2}\right)\cos\left(\frac{x+y}{2}+\frac{\pi}{2}\right)$$

$$\Rightarrow \cos x-\cos y=2\cos\left(\frac{\pi}{2}-\frac{x-y}{2}\right)\cos\left(\frac{x+y}{2}+\frac{\pi}{2}\right)$$

(since 'cos' is even)

$$=-2\sin\frac{x-y}{2}\sin\frac{x+y}{2}$$

$$=2\sin\frac{y-x}{2}\sin\frac{y+x}{2}\quad\text{(since 'sin' is odd).}$$

**6.3 Use of $\tan\frac12 x$ formulae in equations.** The method of solution of $a\cos x+b\sin x=c$ given in Section 6.3 is safe to use if the difficulties are appreciated. The treatment accorded here is unusually full, but we believe that the difficulties should be squarely faced by the student, and not glossed over as has often been customary in texts at this level.

### Exercise F (p. 405)

3. (a) $2\cos 2x\sin x$;     (b) $2\cos 4x\cos x$;
   (c) $2\sin 45°\cos 9°$;     (d) $-2\sin 45°\sin 30°$.

4. $x=a\cot\theta,\ y=a\csc\theta.$    5. $x=a\sec\theta,\ y=a\tan\theta.$

6. $\dfrac{1+\cos 2x}{\sin 2x}=\cot x=\dfrac{\sin 2x}{1-\cos 2x}\quad(x\neq n\pi/2,\ n\in Z).$

7. $\{45°,\ 60°,\ 135°,\ 225°,\ 300°,\ 315°\}.$

8. *Hint*: $\sin(x+\pi)=-\sin x;\quad \cos\frac13\pi=\frac12.$

9. The middle term is a common factor of the first simplified form. The remaining factor is easily evaluated as 0, so the expression has value zero. See Question 12 for a simple visual demonstration.

10. $\{x: x=360n°-53\cdot1°,\ n\in Z\}\cup\{x: x=360n°-67\cdot4°,\ n\in Z\}.$

15-2

**11.** (*a*) Angle $DCB = 2x$. $|\mathbf{OA}| + |\mathbf{OB}| = 2|\mathbf{OC}|$ remembering signed directions.

(*b*) $\cot x - \tan x = 2 \cot 2x$;     (*c*) $2 \csc 2x$.

**12.** See comment on Question 9 above. $\mathbf{AB} + \mathbf{BC} + \mathbf{CA} = 0$.

$$\mathbf{AB} = AB \begin{pmatrix} \cos x \\ \sin x \end{pmatrix}, \quad \mathbf{BC} = AB \begin{pmatrix} \cos (x + \frac{2}{3}\pi) \\ \sin (x + \frac{2}{3}\pi) \end{pmatrix},$$

$$\mathbf{CA} = AB \begin{pmatrix} \cos (x + \frac{4}{3}\pi) \\ \sin (x + \frac{4}{3}\pi) \end{pmatrix}$$

$$\Rightarrow \begin{pmatrix} \cos x \\ \sin x \end{pmatrix} + \begin{pmatrix} \cos (x + \frac{2}{3}\pi) \\ \sin (x + \frac{2}{3}\pi) \end{pmatrix} + \begin{pmatrix} \cos (x + \frac{4}{3}\pi) \\ \sin (x + \frac{4}{3}\pi) \end{pmatrix} = 0$$

$$\Rightarrow \cos x + \cos (x + \tfrac{2}{3}\pi) + \cos (x + \tfrac{4}{3}\pi) = 0$$

as well as the result of Question 9.

**13.** See Figure E. $OABC \ldots N$ is a regular polygon of $n$ sides, and having an external angle of $2\pi/n$ as shown.

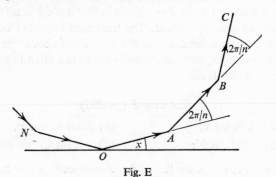

Fig. E

$$\mathbf{OA} + \mathbf{AB} + \mathbf{BC} + \ldots + \mathbf{NO} = 0$$

$$\Leftrightarrow OA \left[ \begin{pmatrix} \cos x \\ \sin x \end{pmatrix} + \begin{pmatrix} \cos \left( x + \dfrac{2\pi}{n} \right) \\ \sin \left( x + \dfrac{2\pi}{n} \right) \end{pmatrix} \right.$$

$$\left. + \begin{pmatrix} \cos \left( x + \dfrac{2 \cdot 2\pi}{n} \right) \\ \sin \left( x + \dfrac{2 \cdot 2\pi}{n} \right) \end{pmatrix} + \ldots + \begin{pmatrix} \cos \left( x + (n-1)\dfrac{2\pi}{n} \right) \\ \sin \left( x + (n-1)\dfrac{2\pi}{n} \right) \end{pmatrix} \right] = 0$$

$$\Rightarrow \cos x + \cos\left(x + \frac{2\pi}{n}\right) + \cos\left(x + \frac{2.2\pi}{n}\right) + \dots$$

$$+ \cos\left(x + (n-1)\frac{2\pi}{n}\right) = 0$$

$$\Leftrightarrow \sum_{k=0}^{n-1} \cos\left(x + \frac{2k\pi}{n}\right) = 0.$$

**14.** For $\sum_{k=0}^{n-1} \sin\left\{x + \frac{2k\pi}{n}\right\}$ proceed as in method on p. 407. Thus:

(a) Multiply $\sin\left\{x + \frac{2k\pi}{n}\right\}$ by $2\sin\frac{\pi}{n}$ and use formula (viii).

(b) Prove that

$$2\sin\frac{\pi}{n}\sum_{k=0}^{n-1}\sin\left\{x+\frac{2k\pi}{n}\right\} = \sum_{k=0}^{n-1}\left[\cos\left\{x+\frac{2k+1}{n}\pi\right\} - \cos\left\{x+\frac{2k-1}{n}\pi\right\}\right]$$

$$= \cos\left\{x+\frac{2n-1}{n}\pi\right\} - \cos\left\{x-\frac{\pi}{n}\right\} = 0.$$

Hence

$$\sum_{k=0}^{n-1}\sin\left\{x+\frac{2k\pi}{n}\right\} = 0.$$

## 7. POLAR COORDINATES

### *Exercise G (p. 411)*

**1.** $r = f(\cos\theta)$.

For $\theta_1$, $r_1 = f(\cos\theta_1)$.

For $\theta_2 = -\theta_1$, $r_2 = f(\cos{}^-\theta_1) = f(\cos\theta_1) = r_1$.

For $r = f(\sin\theta)$, $r_1 = f(\sin\theta_1)$, $r_2 = f(\sin{}^-\theta_1) = f(-\sin\theta_1)$ $= -r_1$ if $f$ is odd, $+r_1$ if $f$ is even.

Hence, when $f$ is odd, there is symmetry about a line perpendicular to $OU$ through $O$; when $f$ is even, there is symmetry about $OU$.

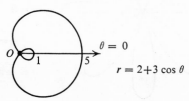

229

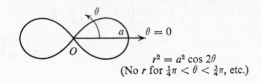

$r^2 = a^2 \cos 2\theta$
(No $r$ for $\frac{1}{4}\pi < \theta < \frac{3}{4}\pi$, etc.)

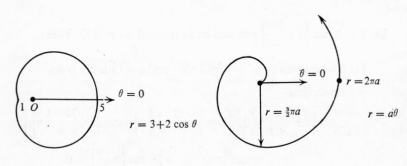

$r = 3 + 2\cos\theta$

$r = 2\pi a$

$r = \frac{3}{2}\pi a$

$r = a\theta$

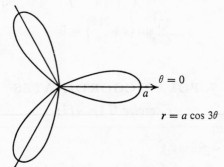

$r = a\cos 3\theta$

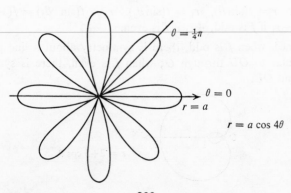

$r = a\cos 4\theta$

230

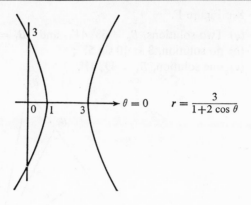

$$\theta = 0 \qquad r = \frac{3}{1+2\cos\theta}$$

# 8. THE SOLUTION OF TRIANGLES

The work of this section requires little commentary, being completely traditional in content. It seems an ideal opportunity for vector methods, the scalar product being used to derive both the sine and cosine rules. The slide-rule can be brought into service, to assist computation.

### *Exercise H (p. 415)*

**1.** (a) $75°\ 31'$;                  (b) $120°$;
    (c) $90°$ [$9:40:41$ triangle];     (d) $77°\ 55'$.

**2.** $a^2 > b^2 + c^2$.

**3.** (a) $A = 60°$,    $b = 8·85$ cm,     $c = 10·85$ cm;
   (b) $C = 47°$,    $a = 12·3$ cm,      $c = 9·35$ cm;
   (c) $C = 47°$,    $b = 2·92$ cm,      $c = 4·54$ cm;
   (d) $A = 22°$,    $a = 4·96$ km,      $b = 6·01$ km.

**4.** $\left.\begin{array}{l} 7^2 = 4^2 + AM^2 + 2.4.AM\cos\theta \\ 6^2 = 4^2 + AM^2 - 2.4.AM\cos\theta \end{array}\right\} \Rightarrow AM = 5·15$ cm.

**5.** (a) $6·86$ cm;     (b) $12·3$ cm;     (c) $17·1$ cm.

**6.** See Figure F.

  (a) Two solutions, $B_2 = 68°\ 44'$  and  $B_1 = 111°\ 16'$;
  (b) no solution, $8 < 10 \sin 57°$;
  (c) one solution, $B_3 = 49°\ 41'$.

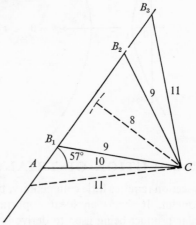

Fig. F

**7.** (a) No solution;
  (b) two possible solutions;  } these are exemplified in Question 6
  (c) one solution;  (b), (a) and (c) in that order.

There is never more than one solution if $A$ is obtuse.

**8.** Very slightly more than $90°$ ($90·3°$).
Slightly more than $8·8$ units ($8·85$) (see Question 12).

**9.** $700$ km/h at $49·6°$ east of north.

**10.** $81$ N about $4°$ to windward.

**11.** $044°$ approximately.

**12.** *Hint.* By the sine rule, if

$$\frac{a}{\sin A} = \frac{b}{\sin B} = \frac{c}{\sin C} = k,$$

then $b - c = k \sin B - k \sin C$, etc.

  (a) $63·3°$;  (b) $35·6°$;  (c) $B = 98·9°$, $C = 27·7°$.

**13.** *Hint.* Symmetry of tangents from an external point to a circle.

$$\tfrac{1}{2}(b+c-a), \quad \tfrac{1}{2}(c+a-b), \quad \tfrac{1}{2}(a+b-c).$$

**14.** *Hint*: as 13.

**15.** *Hint.* Write

$$\tan \tfrac{1}{2}C = \tan\left(90° - \frac{A+B}{2}\right) = \frac{1}{\tan \tfrac{1}{2}(A+B)}.$$

$$\Leftrightarrow \frac{1}{\tan \tfrac{1}{2}C} = \tan\frac{A+B}{2} = \frac{\tan \tfrac{1}{2}A + \tan \tfrac{1}{2}B}{1 - \tan \tfrac{1}{2}A \cdot \tan \tfrac{1}{2}B}.$$

**16.** Adding the equations of Question 13, we obtain

$$2u + 2v + 2w = a+b+c = 2s,$$

$$s = u+v+w \quad \text{and} \quad \tan^2\frac{A}{2} = \frac{v^2}{u^2} = \frac{uvw}{u^2 s} = \frac{vw}{us}.$$

Using the result of Question 13:

$$u = 1 \cdot 60, \quad v = 4 \cdot 48, \quad w = 1 \cdot 25, \quad s = 7 \cdot 33, \quad A = 69 \cdot 2°.$$

This is a convenient method for finding the angles of a triangle, given the three sides. Since

$$\tan^2\frac{B}{2} = \frac{wu}{vs} \quad \text{and} \quad \tan^2\frac{C}{2} = \frac{uv}{ws},$$

all these angles can be found with the minimum of additional computation.

# 15

# THE QUADRATIC FUNCTION

## 1. GRAPHS OF QUADRATIC FUNCTIONS

### Exercise A (p. 422)

1. (1) Translation $\begin{pmatrix} 0 \\ -3 \end{pmatrix}$;

   (2) Stretch 2 parallel to $y$-axis, $\begin{pmatrix} 1 & 0 \\ 0 & 2 \end{pmatrix}$;

   (3) Reflection in $x$-axis;

   (4) $\begin{pmatrix} 1 & 0 \\ 0 & 2 \end{pmatrix}$ followed by $\begin{pmatrix} 0 \\ -3 \end{pmatrix}$;

   (5) Reflection in line $y = 2$;

   (6) Translation $\begin{pmatrix} 3 \\ 0 \end{pmatrix}$.

2. (a) $x = \pm 0\cdot577$;   (b) $x = \pm 0\cdot8165$;   (c) $x = \pm 1\cdot53$.

3.

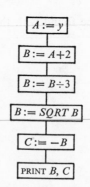

$$A := y$$
$$B := A + 2$$
$$B := B \div 3$$
$$B := SQRT\ B$$
$$C := -B$$
$$\text{PRINT } B, C$$

4. $x = \sqrt{[\frac{1}{2}(5-y)]}$;   $1\cdot058$.     5. $k = -14$.

6. (a) $(x-1)^2+2$;     (b) $(x+2)^2-7$;     (c) $(x-\frac{3}{2})^2-4\frac{1}{4}$.

7. $k = -4\frac{3}{4}$.

8. (a) $5(x+1)^2-7$;     (b) $3(x+\frac{1}{3})^2+\frac{2}{3}$;     (c) $-2(x-\frac{3}{2})^2-2\frac{1}{2}$.

234

## 2. COMPLETING THE SQUARE
### Exercise B (p. 425)

1. (a) $(x-4)^2-11$;   (b) $3(x+\frac{4}{3})^2-6\frac{1}{3}$;   (c) $5(x^2+\frac{2}{5})^2-2\frac{4}{5}$;
   (d) $6-(3x+1)^2$  or  $6-9(x+\frac{1}{3})^2$.

2. $(x+5)(x+1)$.

3. (a) $x^2-x-6 = (x-\frac{1}{2})^2-6\frac{1}{4}$
   $$= (x-\frac{1}{2}-\frac{5}{2})(x-\frac{1}{2}+\frac{5}{2}) = (x-3)(x+2);$$
   (b) $(3x-2)(2x+1)$.

4. (a) Least value 2, $x = 4$;   (b) greatest value 4, $x = 1$;
   (c) least value $-\frac{1}{8}$, $x = -\frac{3}{4}$;   (d) greatest value $2\frac{1}{4}$, $x = -\frac{1}{2}$;
   (e) greatest value 1, $x = 1$.

   $y = x^2$ mapped onto (a) by translation $\begin{pmatrix} 4 \\ 2 \end{pmatrix}$.
   $$\begin{pmatrix} x' \\ y' \end{pmatrix} = \begin{pmatrix} x \\ y \end{pmatrix} + \begin{pmatrix} 4 \\ 2 \end{pmatrix}.$$

5. (a) $(x+3)(x+2)$;   (b) $(x-3)(x+2)$;   (c) $(3x-5)(x+2)$.

6. (a) $(x-4)(x-3)$,   12, 6, 2, 0, 0, 2, 6, 12;
   (b) $(x+1)(x-5)$,   $-5, -8, -9, -8, -5, 0, 7, 16$.

7. (c) $(2x+1)(x+1)$,   at $x = -\frac{1}{2}$ and $x = -1$;
   (d) $(2+x)(1-x)$,   at $x = -2$ and $x = 1$;
   (e) $(2-x)x$,   at $x = 2$ and $x = 0$.

8. $(x-2)^2+(y+1)^2 = 25$;   translation $\begin{pmatrix} 2 \\ -1 \end{pmatrix}$.

9. See Figure A.
   $$\begin{pmatrix} x' \\ y' \end{pmatrix} = \begin{pmatrix} x \\ y \end{pmatrix} + \begin{pmatrix} 2 \\ -1 \end{pmatrix}$$
   $$\Rightarrow x = x'-2 \quad \text{and} \quad y = y'+1$$
   $$\Rightarrow \frac{(x'-2)^2}{4}+\frac{(y'+1)^2}{9} = 1.$$

   So $(x', y')$ satisfies
   $$9(x-2)^2+4(y+1)^2 = 36.$$

10. $(-2\frac{1}{2}, \frac{1}{2})$.

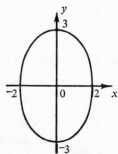

Fig. A

### 3. QUADRATIC EQUATIONS
#### *Exercise C (p. 429)*

**1.**  $x = 4$ or $-1\frac{1}{2}$.  **2.**  $x = 1 \cdot 317$ or $-5 \cdot 317$.

**3.**  $x = 2$.  **4.**  $x = -2$ or $-1$.

**5.**  No real roots, $x = -1 \pm \sqrt{2}\,j$.

**6.**  No real roots, $x = \frac{1}{3} \pm \frac{1}{3}\sqrt{2}\,j$.

**7.**  No real roots, $x = -\frac{3}{5} \pm \frac{1}{5}\sqrt{11}\,j$.

**8.**  $x = 0$ or $\frac{3}{5}$.  **9.**  $x = 0$ or $-\frac{3}{5}$.  **10.**  $x = \pm 0 \cdot 7746$.

**11.** 175 m. After $7 \cdot 3$ s (or $17 \cdot 3$ s *before* the start if the formula held then).

**12.** (*a*) $p, q$ both positive or both negative;
(*b*) $p$ or $q$ (or both) zero;
(*c*) one positive and the other negative.

**13.** (*a*) $x > 2$ or $x < -1$;  (*b*) $x = -1$ or $x = 2$;
(*c*) $-1 < x < 2$.

**14.** Q.3 $x^2 - 4x + 4 < 0$ for no value of $x$;
Q.4 $x^2 + 3x + 2 < 0$ for $-2 < x < -1$.

**15.** The two equations are symmetrical in $s$, $t$ which are the roots of $x^2 - 3x + 2 = 0$, i.e. $s = 1$, $t = 2$ or $s = 2$, $t = 1$.

**16.** $p = 3$, $q = -1$ or $p = -1$, $q = 3$.

### 4. QUADRATIC INEQUALITIES
#### *Exercise D (p. 431)*

**1.**  (*a*) $\{x : (2x+5)(x-1) > 0\}$
$= [\{x : (2x+5) > 0\} \cap \{x : x-1 > 0\}]$
$\cup [\{x : 2x+5 < 0\} \cap \{x : x-1 < 0\}]$;
(*b*) $\{x : (2x+5)(x-1) = 0\}$
$= \{x : 2x+5 = 0\} \cup \{x : x-1 = 0\}$.

**2.**  $-3 < x < \frac{1}{3}$.

3.   (a) $-1 < x < 2$;                        (b) $-1 \leqslant x \leqslant 2$.

4.   $x < -\frac{1}{2}$ or $x > 1\frac{1}{2}$.        **5.**   $-\frac{1}{2} < x < 1\frac{1}{2}$.

6.   $-0.77 < x < 3.27$ (correct to 2 decimal places).

7.   True for all $x$ except $x = 1$, since it becomes $(x-1)^2 > 0$.

8.   $-3 < x < 2$.

9.   $x \leqslant 1.38$ or $x \geqslant 3.62$ (correct to 2 decimal places).

10. True for no value of $x$.

*Note.* In cases such as Questions 6 and 9, where the quadratic form does not factorize, it is necessary first to find where it is zero by the method of Section 3.3 or of 6.1. These values of $x$ will be where the quadratic function changes sign.

## 5. DOMAIN AND RANGE

### *Exercise E (p. 434)*

1.   Suppose $\sqrt{5} = m/n$ where $m, n$ are integers with no common factor (i.e. suppose $\sqrt{5}$ is rational), then

$$5 = m^2/n^2$$
$$\Rightarrow 5n^2 = m^2$$
$$\Rightarrow m \text{ has a factor of 5, } m = 5p, \text{ say}$$
$$\Rightarrow 5n^2 = 25p^2$$
$$\Rightarrow n^2 = 5p^2$$
$$\Rightarrow n \text{ has a factor of 5. Contradiction.}$$

2.   (a) Yes.

(b) No, since 1 is the identity and 0 has no inverse. If 0 is excluded we have $(R^*, \times)$, and this is a group.

3.   $(a+b\sqrt{2})+(c+d\sqrt{2}) = (a+c)+(b+d)\sqrt{2}$;
$(a+b\sqrt{2})\times(c+d\sqrt{2}) = (ac+2bd)+(ad+bc)\sqrt{2}$;
$-2-3\sqrt{2}, \quad -\frac{1}{7}+\frac{3}{14}\sqrt{2}$.

*Note:* $\dfrac{1}{2+3\sqrt{2}} = \dfrac{2-3\sqrt{2}}{(2+3\sqrt{2})(2-3\sqrt{2})} = -\frac{1}{14}(2-3\sqrt{2})$.

**4.** $p^2$ and $q^2$ each have an even number of prime factors (including repeats). So $kp^2$ has an odd number of prime factors. This factorization is unique, so $kp^2 = q^2$ is impossible. Thus $\sqrt{k} = q/p$ is impossible for integers $p, q$.

## 6. THE GENERAL QUADRATIC FUNCTION

### *Exercise F (p. 436)*

**1.** (*a*) $x = 0 \cdot 768$ or $-0 \cdot 434$ (3 S.F.);

(*b*) $x = \frac{1}{3}$ or $-1$;

(*c*) no real roots.

**2.** When: (*a*) $a < \frac{1}{3}$;

(*b*) $a = \frac{1}{3}$;  (*c*) $a > \frac{1}{3}$.

**3.** See Exercise C.

**4.** (*d*) $x^2 + 5x - 2 = 0$.

$-3, -2$ satisfy the sum check but not the product check.

**5.** $x^2 - 7x + 3 = 0$; sum 14, product 12, $x^2 - 14x + 12 = 0$.

**6.** $2x^2 - 9x + 8 = 0$.

**7.** $-0 \cdot 43, 0 \cdot 77$.

**8.** The answer should be the same.

**9.** Roots $-2$ and $1\frac{1}{2}$.

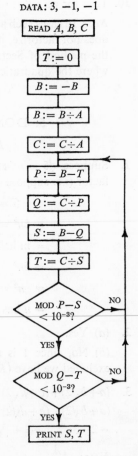

DATA: 3, $-1$, $-1$

READ $A, B, C$

$T := 0$

$B := -B$

$B := B \div A$

$C := C \div A$

$P := B - T$

$Q := C \div P$

$S := B - Q$

$T := C \div S$

MOD $P - S$ < $10^{-3}$?  NO

YES

MOD $Q - T$ < $10^{-3}$?  NO

YES

PRINT $S, T$

## 7. COMPLEX NUMBERS

### *Exercise G (p. 439)*

**1.** Yes.

**2.** See Figure B. The four points form a parallelogram.

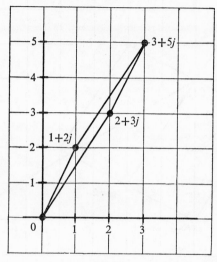

Fig. B

**3.** $(3+2j).j = -2+3j$. See Figure C. A quarter-turn about the origin.

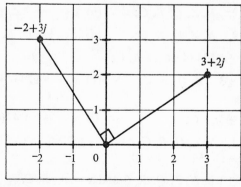

Fig. C

239

**4.** See Figure D.

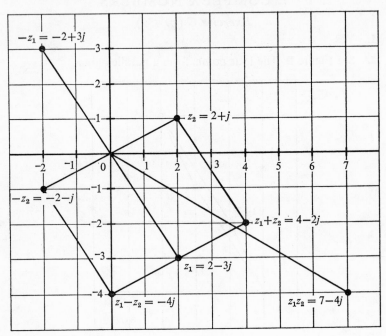

Fig. D

**5.** $a = c$ and $d = b$.    **6.** No.

**7.** (a) $x = 2$,   $N, Z, Q, R, C$;    (b) $x = -5$,   $Z, Q, R, C$;

(c) $x = 9$,   $N, Z, Q, R, C$;    (d) $x = \frac{1}{3}$,   $Q, R, C$;

(e) $x = \pm 4 \cdot 123$ (4 s.f.),   $R, C$;

(f) $x = \pm 3$,   $Z, Q, R, C$;    (g) $x = \pm 4 \cdot 243$ (4 s.f.),
                                        $R, C$;

(h) $x = \pm 5j$,   $C$;    (i) $x = \pm 1 \cdot 414j$ (4 s.f.),   $C$;

(j) $x = 1$,   $N, Z, Q, R, C$. Also $-\frac{1}{2} \pm 0 \cdot 866j$ in $C$. The equation
is $(x-1)(x^2+x+1) = 0$.

(k) $x = \pm 1$ in $N, Z, Q, R, C$ and $x = \pm j$ in $C$.

### Miscellaneous Exercise (p. 440)

**1.** $(x+1)(2x-1)(x-1)$; $-1, \frac{1}{2}, 1$.

**2.** (a) $x = -2$ or $\frac{1}{2}$;        (b) $x = 0$ or $-1\frac{1}{2}$;

(c) $x = -2\cdot35$ or $0\cdot85$ (2 dec. pl.);

(d) $x = 1$ or $-2\frac{1}{2}$;        (e) $x = -\frac{3}{4}$.

**3.** Shading in the region satisfying the inequalities.

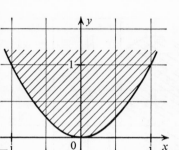

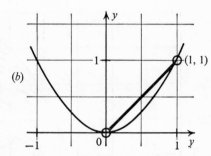

(b)

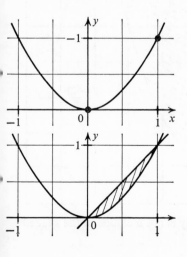

(d)

(f)

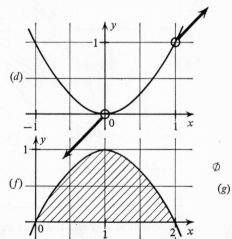

$\emptyset$

(g)

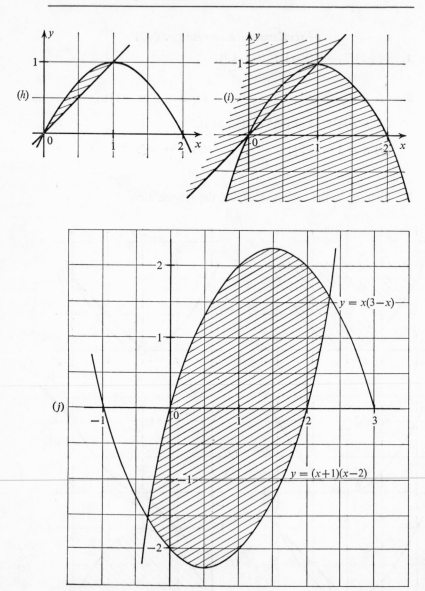

*Note* that in all cases the boundary is not included in the shaded area.

242

4. (a) $-0.434 < x < 0.768$;      (b) ø;

   (c) $-1 < x < \frac{1}{3}$;           (d) all $x$;

   (e) $-1 < x < 3$;          (f) $x < -1$ or $x > 3$;

   (g) $0 < x < 3$;    (h) $x = 1$ since it becomes $(x-1)^2 \leqslant 0$.

5. $x = 3$ or $1$;   $x = 2 \pm \sqrt{3}$; no real roots.

6. (i) $-2 - 16j$,    (ii) $2 + 11j$.

7. (a) $\dfrac{1}{1+j} = \dfrac{1-j}{(1+j)(1-j)}$;      (b) $\dfrac{1}{3-4j} = \dfrac{3+4j}{(3-4j)(3+4j)}$.

(Compare with Exercise E, Question 3.)

# REVISION EXERCISES

## 11. $\Sigma$-NOTATION AND FINITE SERIES (p. 441)

1.    (a) $\sum_{1}^{10} (59 - 7i) = \sum_{0}^{9} (52 - 7i) = 205;$

     (b) $(2^{n+1} - 2) - \frac{3}{2}n(n+1).$

2.   $\sum_{i=0}^{i=n} i = 0 + 1 + 2 + \ldots + n; \quad \sum_{i=0}^{i=n} (n-i) = n + (n-1) + \ldots + 2 + 1 + 0.$

   $\sum_{i=0}^{i=n} n = n(n+1).$

     (a) $\sum_{i=0}^{i=n} i = \sum_{i=0}^{i=n} n - \sum_{i=0}^{i=n} i \Rightarrow 2\sum_{i=0}^{i=n} i = n(n+1).$

3.   $4\sum_{1}^{n} i(i+1)(i+2) = n(n+1)(n+2)(n+3).$

4.    (a) $\sum_{0}^{n-1} i^2(i+1)^2 = 0^2 . 1^2 + 1^2 . 2^2 + \ldots + (n-1)^2 n^2$

                    $= \sum_{1}^{n} (i-1)^2 i^2;$

     (c) $4\sum_{1}^{n} i^3 = \sum_{1}^{n} i^2(i+1)^2 - \sum_{1}^{n} (i-1)^2 i^2$

               $= n^2(n+1)^2 + \sum_{0}^{n-1} i^2(i+1)^2 - \sum_{1}^{n} (i-1)^2 i^2$

               $= n^2(n+1)^2.$

5.   (b) and (c) are true. $n = 2$ gives a counter-example for each of the other parts.

6.    (a) $\Sigma(x_i - \alpha)f_i = \Sigma x_i f_i - \alpha\Sigma f_i = \Sigma x_i f_i - \alpha.$
   Hence $\Sigma x_i f_i = \alpha.$

     (b) $\beta^2 = \Sigma(x_i - \alpha)^2 f_i = \Sigma(x_i^2 f_i - 2\alpha x_i f_i + \alpha^2 f_i)$

          $= \Sigma x_i^2 f_i - 2\alpha^2 + \alpha^2$

          $= \Sigma x_i^2 f_i - \alpha^2.$

## 12. POSITION AND SPREAD (p. 442)

**1.** $s_1 = 3\sqrt{2}$;  $s_2 = 30\sqrt{2}$.

**2.** $m = 27$;  $s = 7$ (to the nearest integer).

**3.** $m = 16\cdot0$ years;  $s = 1\cdot4$ years.

**4.** (a) $m = 52$ cm;  $s = 7\cdot8$ cm;  (b) 17;  (c) 11.

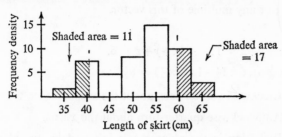

Fig. A

**5.** $m = 49\cdot8$,  $s = 19\cdot6$;

median $= 47\cdot8$; the other sextiles are 32·1, 40·9, 56·2, 71·8.

The standard deviation is approximately half the difference between the outer sextiles.

**6.**

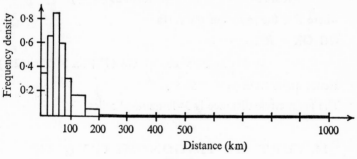

Fig. B

The median bisects the area of the histogram.

The mean is greater than the median. The deviations from the median of the larger distances far outweigh those of the shorter distances.

### 13. FURTHER VECTORS (p. 443)

1. (a) $\mathbf{r} = (-1+3t)\mathbf{i}+(1-4t)\mathbf{j}-2\mathbf{k}$;

   (b) $2x-y+z = 5$;  (c) $(2, -3, -2)$.

2. The lines are perpendicular and intersect at $(2, 1, 3)$.

3. $\begin{pmatrix} 3 \\ 11 \\ 9 \end{pmatrix}$ or any multiple of this vector.

4. $-4x+y+z = 1$;  $-4x+y+z = 6$.

   $V = \frac{1}{6}(6\times 6\times 1\frac{1}{2}-1\times 1\times \frac{1}{4}) = 8\frac{23}{24}$.

5. (a) Clockwise quarter-turn about the $x$-axis.

   (b) Anticlockwise quarter-turn about the $x$-axis.

   (c) Reflection in the plane $x = z$ followed by an enlargement with centre the origin and scale factor $-2$. Alternatively, a spiral enlargement with angle $180°$ and scale factor 2, the axis being the line joining the origin to $(1, 0, -1)$.

6. $\mathbf{OG} = \begin{pmatrix} R\cos 51\cdot5° \\ 0 \\ R\sin 51\cdot5° \end{pmatrix}$  $\mathbf{OK} = \begin{pmatrix} R\cos 25°\cos 67° \\ R\cos 25°\sin 67° \\ R\sin 25° \end{pmatrix}$,

   where $R$ is the radius of the earth.

   $\mathbf{OG}.\mathbf{OK} = R^2\cos\theta$

   $\qquad = R^2(\cos 51\cdot5°\cos 25°\cos 67°+\sin 51\cdot5°\sin 25°)$.

   Hence angle $GOK = \theta = 56\cdot5°$.

   The great circle distance is 3400 nautical miles.

### 14. FURTHER TRIGONOMETRY (p. 444)

1. $n\pi \pm \frac{1}{6}\pi$.

2. (a) $\tan A$.

   (b) $2\cos 4A\cos A$. Zero when $A = (2m+1)\pi/2$, and when $A = (2n+1)\pi/8$ ($m$ and $n$ any integers).
   (c) See Figure C.

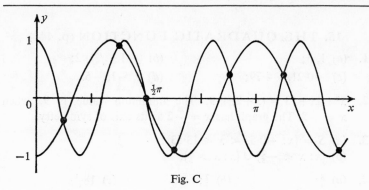

Fig. C

3. $2n\pi < x < (2n+1)\pi$. Greatest value $= \frac{1}{2}(3\sqrt{3})$.

4. For any line through $O$, $OA = OB + OC$ and $OD = OB - OC$.

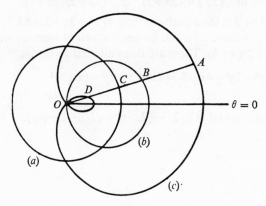

Fig. D

5. The sum $= \dfrac{\sin (N+\frac{1}{2}) x}{2 \sin \frac{1}{2}x}$ unless $x = 2n\pi$.

When $x = 0$, the sum $= \frac{1}{2} + \sum\limits_{n=1}^{n=N} 1 = N + \frac{1}{2}$. This is also the limit of $[\sin (N+\frac{1}{2}) x]/[2 \sin \frac{1}{2}x]$ as $x$ tends to 0.

6. $3\frac{1}{2}$ inches. The radius of the in-circle ($r$) is found from one of the formulae $rs = \Delta$ and $r = a/(\cot \frac{1}{2}B + \cot \frac{1}{2}C)$, which are easily derived.

($\Delta$ is the area of the triangle, and $s$ is half its perimeter.)

247

### 15. THE QUADRATIC FUNCTION (p. 444)

**1.** (a) 1, 3;  (b) $(-1 \pm \sqrt{3}j)/2$;
   (c) $-0.21$, $-4.79$;  (d) 0, $-1$, $-5$.

**2.** $x^2+4x+13 = (x+2)^2+9$. The minimum value is 9, when $x = -2$. The graph has $x = -2$ as its axis of symmetry.

**3.** (a) $S = \{x: -0.53 < x < 13.53\}$;
   (b) $\{x: x < -\frac{2}{5}\} \cup \{x: x > \frac{4}{3}\}$.

**4.** (a) $\frac{5}{4}$;  (b) $\frac{7}{4}$;  (c) $18\frac{1}{16}$.

**5.** In arithmetic, modulo 5,
$$x^2+2x+2 = (x+3)(x+4) \quad \text{or} \quad (2x+1)(3x+2)$$
$$\text{or} \quad (3x+4)(2x+3) \quad \text{or} \quad (4x+2)(4x+1).$$
$4x^2+3x+3$ is the additive inverse of $x^2+2x+2$, and $4x+2$ is the additive inverse of $x+3$. So one factorized form of $4x^2+3x+3$ is $(4x+2)(x+4)$. There are three alternative forms.

**6.** $x^4+2x^3+2x^2-4x-8 = (x^2+x+1)^2-(x+3)^2$
$$= (x^2-2)(x^2+2x+4).$$
The solution set is $\{\sqrt{2}, -\sqrt{2}, -1+\sqrt{3}j, -1-\sqrt{3}j\}$.

# 16

# LOCAL APPROXIMATION

The authors of the S.M.P. Advanced Mathematics course have not thought it appropriate to develop numerical analysis as a separate 'topic' at this level. Nevertheless, the advent of the electronic computer has brought numerical methods into prominence in many applications of mathematics, and it is important for pupils to acquire a feeling for numerical approximation. The natural place for this is within the framework of analysis: but whereas the concern of the pure analyst is to establish that a sequence approximates with arbitrary closeness to its limit for all terms beyond a certain point, the numerical analyst may regard the limit itself as of little significance—for it will often be a number which is not part of his equipment (since he can only handle numbers with a limited number of digits when expressed in the scale of notation in which he is operating) and he is looking for the number in his armoury which most nearly fits the conditions he wants to satisfy. These are two sides of the same coin: numerical analysis is of no avail unless the sequence does in fact converge, whilst the fact that the limit exists has little practical use unless a numerical approximation to its value can be found.

In this chapter we are concerned with linear approximations to functions mapping $R \to R$, but the illustration in Section 1 points to the fact that the concept is one of greater generality than this. Indeed, an important aspect of the work on linear approximation is that it opens up the possibility of extending differentiation, so far restricted to functions $R \to R$, to more general situations. Thus the central result of this chapter may be re-stated as follows:

If it is possible to approximate to a function $f$ in the neighbourhood of $p$ by a linear function $l$, such that

$$l(x) = f(p) + a(x-p),$$

then $f$ is said to be differentiable at $p$, and we write

$$a = f'(p).$$

249

Consider now a function $f$ which maps, say, $R \times R \to R$. Then we may look for a function $l$ which approximates to $f$ in the neighbourhood of $(p, q)$ such that

$$l(x, y) = f(p, q) + a(x - p) + b(y - q),$$

and define $a, b$ as the partial derivatives of $f$ at $(p, q)$.

An appropriate geometrical picture here is of a two-dimensional surface (or 'manifold') with equation $z = f(x, y)$ embedded in three-dimensional space, and of a local linear approximation (a plane $z = l(x, y)$) at the point for which $x = p$ and $y = q$. From this the concept can be generalized to higher dimensions and to differentiable manifolds in more general topological spaces; the study of these constitutes the branch of mathematics known as differential geometry.

A simple account of the possibilities opened up by such generalizations will be found in W. W. Sawyer, *A Path to Modern Mathematics*, Penguin, Chapter 7.

## 2. LINEAR APPROXIMATION TO A FUNCTION
### Exercise A (p. 453)

**1.** $\sqrt{(49 + \alpha)} \simeq 7 + \frac{1}{14}\alpha$, so that $\sqrt{50} \simeq 7 \cdot 071$, $\sqrt{48} \simeq 6 \cdot 929$. Hence
$$\sqrt{2} = \tfrac{1}{5}\sqrt{50} \simeq 1 \cdot 414, \quad \sqrt{3} = \tfrac{1}{4}\sqrt{48} \simeq 1 \cdot 732.$$

**2.** (i) $\dfrac{1}{10 + \alpha} \simeq \dfrac{1}{10} - \dfrac{1}{100}\alpha$;　(ii) $\dfrac{1}{a + \alpha} \simeq \dfrac{1}{a} - \dfrac{1}{a^2}\alpha$.
$$\dfrac{1}{9 \cdot 9} \simeq 0 \cdot 101.$$

**3.** $L(x) = 1 + \tfrac{1}{2}(x - 1) = \tfrac{1}{2}(x + 1)$.

**4.** $\cos(p + \alpha) \simeq \cos p - \alpha \sin p$. Taking $p = \tfrac{1}{3}\pi \simeq 1 \cdot 047$, this gives $\cos 1 \simeq 0 \cdot 541$. The approximate value is too high because the cosine graph is concave downwards.

**5.** Estimated value $\tfrac{1}{3}\pi + 0 \cdot 068 \simeq 1 \cdot 115$. (Correct value $1 \cdot 120$ to 3 decimal places.)

**6.** Near $x = 2$, $1/x^2 \simeq \tfrac{1}{4} - \tfrac{1}{4}(x - 2)$. This gives
$$\dfrac{1}{2^2} - \dfrac{1}{2 \cdot 05^2} \simeq \tfrac{1}{4} \times 0 \cdot 05,$$
so that $1/x^2$ can be relied on to within about $5\%$ accuracy.

**7.** $y = 8+12(x-2) = 12x-16$; accurate within 0·1 over the interval $\{x: 1\cdot87 < x < 2\cdot13\}$.

**8.** $(5+\alpha)^2 \simeq 25+10\alpha$ for small $\alpha$, so that $\sqrt{27} \simeq 5\cdot2$. $(5\cdot2+\beta)^2 \simeq 27\cdot04+10\cdot4\beta$ for small $\beta$, so that

$$\sqrt{27} \simeq 5\cdot2-\frac{0\cdot04}{10\cdot4} \simeq 5\cdot196.$$

**9.** The use of the derivative to give a linear approximation is valid for any power of $x$ whose derivative is known, and therefore

$$(p+\alpha)^n \simeq p^n+np^{n-1}\alpha \quad \text{(for small } \alpha)$$

can be used for any rational $n$. But unless $n$ is a positive integer the alternative method of obtaining the result cannot be used.

**10.** See Figure A.

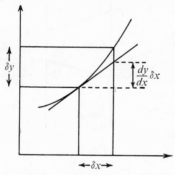

Fig. A

**11.** $v = 1000/t$. If $\delta t = \pm0\cdot0005$, $\delta v \simeq \mp0\cdot013$.

Land speed records are often quoted in km/h to three places of decimals, calculated from a time given in seconds to three places of decimals. The result given above shows this practice to be quite unjustified.

**12.** The time of each swing is increased by 0·05 %, so that the clock loses 43 seconds in 24 hours.

**13.** Volume $3\alpha$ %, surface area $2\alpha$ %, density $-3\alpha$ % approximately.

**14.** Time saved $\simeq 0\cdot25$ hours, or about 15 minutes. Extra cost per passenger $= 40$ p.

# 3. SOLUTION OF EQUATIONS

## *Exercise B (p. 460)*

1. With first estimate 1·9, a better approximation is found to be 1·8955.

2. 0·91, 3·19. In Chapter 35 a special algorithm is developed for calculating $f(p)$ and $f'(p)$ in cases where $f$ is a polynomial function.

3. See Figure B.

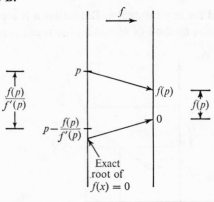

Fig. B

4. The function $x \to x^3 + x - 1$ is continuous and its derivative is always positive. The root is approximately 0·683.

5. 2·236.   6. 0·824.   7. 0·59, −7·07.

8. If the sign of $f''(x)$ in the interval under consideration is the same as the sign of $f(p_1)$, then we have a diagram such as Figure C. The sequence of successive approximations is monotonic, so that each term is on the same side of the limit.

If the sign of $f''(x)$ is opposite to that of $f(p_1)$, then the first two terms straddle the limit (see Figure D), but the sequence $p_2, p_3, p_4, \dots$ is monotonic.

Difficulty may arise if $f''(x)$ vanishes in the neighbourhood of the root.

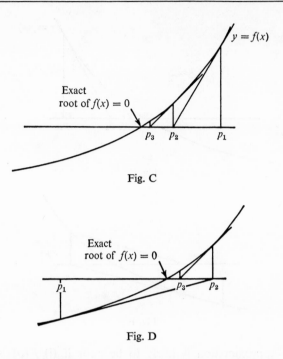

Fig. C

Fig. D

9. In this algorithm the derivative at $p_1$ is used in place of the derivatives at $p_2, p_3, \ldots$ to obtain subsequent approximations. This simplifies the calculation, since it is not necessary to re-calculate the derivative at each stage. There is an obvious loss of efficiency in the converging process, but if the first approximation is a good one the derivative will not change very much over the interval, and it is possible that the answer will be reached with little increase in the number of iterations.

If $f''(x)$ and $f(p_1)$ have the same sign the method can work well (compare Figure C with Figure E); but if the first approximation is on the 'wrong' side of the root (see Figure F) then the modified method as described may give very slow convergence, and may not even converge at all. In this case it would be better to find $p_2, p_3$ by the standard method and then to use

$$q_4 = p_3 - \frac{f(p_3)}{f'(p_2)}, \quad q_5 = q_4 - \frac{f(q_4)}{f'(p_2)}, \text{ etc.}$$

253

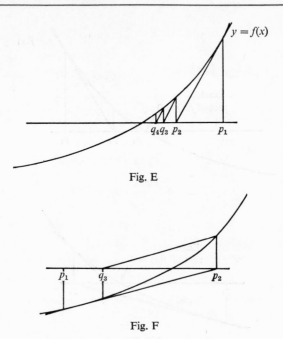

Fig. E

Fig. F

**10.** The approximation is likely to be poor if (i) $f'(p)$ is small, (ii) $f''(x)$ is large in the interval (so that the gradient is changing rapidly).

The method will certainly give a better approximation if $f''(x)$ has constant sign over the interval and the sign of $f(p)$ is the same as that of $f''(x)$.

**11.** There could be difficulty only if the graph of $y = f(x)$ has a discontinuity or a point of inflexion in the relevant interval. Otherwise $p_2, p_3, p_4, \ldots$ form a monotonic sequence which certainly has a limit and this limit is a root of $f(x) = 0$.

**12.** The Newton–Raphson formula applied to the equation $x^2 - k = 0$ gives

$$p_{n+1} = p_n - \frac{p_n^2 - k}{2p_n} = \frac{1}{2}\left(p_n + \frac{k}{p_n}\right).$$

For the flow diagram see Figure G.

254

**13.** See Figure H. The area beyond the line is $\theta - \frac{1}{2}\sin 2\theta$, and for the median distance this must be half the area of the semi-circle, so that

$$f(\theta) = \theta - \tfrac{1}{2}\sin 2\theta - \tfrac{1}{4}\pi = 0.$$

The root is 1·155, so that the median distance is 0·404 mm.

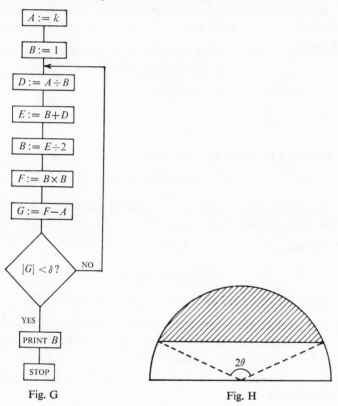

Fig. G          Fig. H

## 4. OTHER LINEAR APPROXIMATIONS

We have not discussed in the text how the numbers $x_i$ were selected in the calculation of the root-mean-square difference. In fact ten numbers were taken as giving reasonable coverage of the interval without excessive computation. The interval (4, 6) was therefore divided into ten equal subintervals, and the functions evaluated at the middle point of each subinterval.

A better measure would, of course, be

$$\sqrt{\left(\frac{1}{6-4}\int_4^6 \{r(x)-l(x)\}^2\, dx\right)},$$

but this is not yet available. Indeed, the function $l_2$ defined in the text was selected as the linear function which makes this expression (or, which comes to the same thing, the integral contained in it) as small as possible.

### Exercise C (p. 465)

1. The tangent is $y = 0.54x+0.30$.

    By comparison with the linear equation

    $$y = 0.49x+0.22$$

    (obtained by selecting $a, b$ so that

    $$\int_0^2 (ax+b-\sin x)^2\, dx$$

    is a minimum) the integral root-mean-square difference is $0.176$ as against $0.113$.

2. For example, the mean absolute deviation

    $$\frac{1}{n}\sum_{i=1}^n |r(x_i)-l(x_i)|,$$

    giving values $0.0027$ and $0.0021$ for $l_1$ and $l_2$ respectively.

3. The graph of this linear approximation lies mid-way between the chord joining the end-points $(4, \frac{1}{4})$ and $(6, \frac{1}{6})$, whose equation is
    $$y = 0.4167-0.0417x,$$
    and the tangent parallel to this at the point $(\sqrt{24}, 1/\sqrt{24})$, whose equation is
    $$y = 0.4082-0.0417x \quad \text{(see Figure I)}.$$

    The root-mean-square difference (taken from the values at $4.1, 4.3, \ldots, 5.9$ as in the text) is $0.0029$; smaller than that for the tangent, but larger than that for $l_2(x)$. It is important to realize, however, that this does not *prove* that $l_2(x)$ is a better approximation than $l_3(x)$. Indeed, since $l_2$ was defined so as to minimize the value of

    $$\int_4^6 \{r(x)-l(x)\}^2\, dx,$$

256

which is a similar criterion to the root-mean-square difference as calculated above, the result is to be expected. Notice that for the function $l_2$ the maximum deviation from the value of $r$ is $0.0041$, which is the same as for $l_3$ to this degree of accuracy.

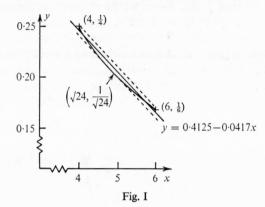

Fig. I

**4.** Minimize

$$E = (a+b-2\cdot3)^2 + (3a+b-3\cdot4)^2 + (4a+b-4\cdot0)^2$$
$$+ (7a+b-6\cdot0)^2 + (9a+b-8\cdot1)^2.$$

This gives $a = 0\cdot71$, $b = 1\cdot33$.

This technique, known as the *method of least squares*, is also discussed in Chapter 12, Section 6.

## 5. HIGHER DEGREE APPROXIMATIONS

The treatment of polynomial approximations in this course is an essentially practical one. Power series as such are not discussed; for the interest is not in the precise delineation of the interval of values of $\alpha$ for which an infinite Taylor series converges (however slowly), but in the efficient use of a finite Taylor polynomial to approximate to a given function around a certain point.

A numerical analyst is, of course, interested to have an upper bound for the error involved in his computation, and thus some of the formulae which have been derived for the 'remainder after $n$ terms' in Taylor's series are important practically; but to obtain these requires the use of sophisticated mathematics beyond the scope of most of the pupils for which this course is written. We have therefore been content to take as intuitive that a polynomial having its first few derivatives in common with a function at a point of its domain is likely to approximate closely to that function in a neighbourhood of that point. Since we have $n+1$ coefficients at our disposal for a polynomial of degree $n$, we can arrange for the values of the functions and their first $n$ derivatives to coincide at the point. It is a stroke of good fortune that increasing $n$ merely adds further terms to the polynomial, and does not necessitate modification of those already calculated; and thus the $n$th degree polynomial approximation is the infinite Taylor series truncated after the term of degree $n$.

### Exercise D (p. 468)

**1.** $q(x) = 1+3(x-1)+3(x-1)^2 \doteq 3x^2-3x+1$ (see Figure J).

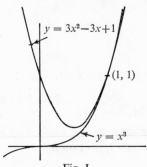

$y = 3x^2-3x+1$

$(1, 1)$

$y = x^3$

Fig. J

**2.** $\sqrt{(1+\alpha)} \simeq 1+\tfrac{1}{2}\alpha-\tfrac{1}{8}\alpha^2+\tfrac{1}{16}\alpha^3.$

$\sqrt{(4+\beta)} \simeq 2+\tfrac{1}{4}\beta-\tfrac{1}{64}\beta^2+\tfrac{1}{512}\beta^3,$

which could also be obtained as $2\sqrt{(1+\tfrac{1}{4}\beta)}$, substituting $\tfrac{1}{4}\beta$ for $\alpha$ in the first result.

**3.** $\cos(\tfrac{1}{3}\pi+\alpha) \simeq \cos\tfrac{1}{3}\pi-\alpha\sin\tfrac{1}{3}\pi-\tfrac{1}{2}\alpha^2\cos\tfrac{1}{3}\pi.$

Substituting $\alpha = 1\cdot4\times(\pi/180) = 0\cdot02443$ gives

$$\cos 61\cdot4° \simeq 0\cdot47869.$$

**4.** $\dfrac{1}{(10+\alpha)^2} \simeq \dfrac{1}{100}-\dfrac{1}{500}\alpha+\dfrac{3}{10{,}000}\alpha^2.$

Error $= \dfrac{40\alpha^3+3\alpha^4}{10{,}000(10+\alpha)^2}.$

258

5. $\sin \alpha \simeq \alpha - \frac{1}{6}\alpha^3$. Accurate to within $5\%$ approximately over the interval $\{\alpha: -1.45 < \alpha < 1.45\}$.

6. We require $\alpha$ so that

$$f(p_1) + \alpha f'(p_1) + \tfrac{1}{2}\alpha^2 f''(p_1) \simeq 0.$$

Thus
$$\alpha \simeq -\frac{f(p_1)}{f'(p_1)} - \tfrac{1}{2}\alpha^2 \frac{f''(p_1)}{f'(p_1)}$$

$$\simeq -\frac{f(p_1)}{f'(p_1)} - \frac{f''(p_1)\{f(p_1)\}^2}{2\{f'(p_1)\}^3}.$$

Notice that the final term is large if $f''(p_1)$ is large and $f'(p_1)$ is small. Also the correction term has the same sign as $\alpha$ (so that the second approximation under-corrects) if $f''(p_1)$ and $f(p_1)$ have the same sign as each other. Compare the note above on Exercise B, Question 10.

For the given equation $p_1 = 3$ gives $p_2 = 3 + \frac{1}{31} \simeq 3.0323$, with residual error of about $18/(2 \times 31^3) \simeq 0.0003$, and the second approximation over-corrects. Give answer as $3.032$ to three decimal places.

# 17

# THE TECHNIQUE OF DIFFERENTIATION

## 1. COMPOSITE FUNCTIONS

### Exercise A (p. 471)

**1.** (a) $2(x-1)$;   (b) $6(3x+2)$;   (c) $3(x-3)^2$;
   (d) $6(2x+5)^2$;   (e) $4x(x^2+3)$;   (f) $12x(2x^2-1)^2$.

**2.** (a) $-1/(x+3)^2$;   (b) $-2/(2x-1)^2$;   (c) $-2x/(x^2+1)^2$;
   (d) $2\cos 2x$;   (e) $3/\{2\sqrt{(3x+1)}\}$;   (f) $-x/\sqrt{(1-x^2)}$.

**3.** (a) $6(2x-1)^2$;   (b) $16(4x+1)^3$;   (c) $-2/(x+3)^3$;
   (d) $-4x/(x^2+1)^3$;   (e) $4\cos 4x$;   (f) $2x\cos x^2$;
   (g) $-3\sin(3x+\pi)$;   (h) $2\sin x\cos x$;   (i) $-6\cos 3x\sin 3x$.

**4.** The point is that the flow diagram does not branch, whereas the flow diagram for a product or a quotient does (see Exercise C, Question 5).

**5.** $ap; f'(a); f'(a).g'(b) = f'(a).g'f(a)$.

**6.** This attractive graphical method illustrates the chain rule well, in cases in which the first function to be applied is linear. Thus, the gradient of $\sin x$ at $(2a, \sin 2a)$ is $\cos 2a$; and under the stretch $(2a, \sin 2a)$ is mapped to $(a, \sin 2a)$ and the gradient to $2\cos 2a$ (see Figure A).

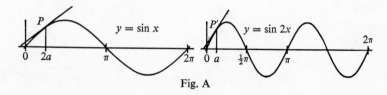

Fig. A

260

## 2. COMPOSITE FUNCTIONS— THE CHAIN RULE

It has always taken a long time for students to learn to apply the chain rule confidently, and it is useful to base the explanation firmly on the idea that lies behind Figure 1 in the pupils' text. It will then be possible at a later stage of their career to recall the technique by means of a simple sketch like Figure B, which applies the idea to $e^{-x^2}$ and to $\frac{1}{2}v^2$.

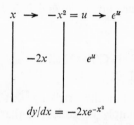 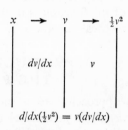

$$x \to -x^2 = u \to e^u$$
$$-2x \qquad e^u$$
$$dy/dx = -2xe^{-x^2}$$

$$x \to v \to \frac{1}{2}v^2$$
$$dv/dx \qquad v$$
$$d/dx(\frac{1}{2}v^2) = v(dv/dx)$$

Fig. B

### Exercise B (p. 475)

1.  (a) $8(2a+3)^3$;  (b) $10a(a^2-1)^4$;  (c) $-2/(2a+1)^2$;
    (d) $-(4a+5)/(2a^2+5a+1)^2$;  (e) $-1/\sqrt{(3-2a)}$;
    (f) $-2a(2a^2+3)^{-1\frac{1}{2}}$;  (g) $4\cos 4a$;  (h) $\frac{3}{2}\sin^2 \frac{1}{2}a \cos \frac{1}{2}a$.

2.  (a) $6(x-1)(x^2-2x+4)^2$;  (b) $-24x^2(1-2x^3)^3$;
    (c) $-2x/(1+x^2)^2$;  (d) $-x/\sqrt{(1-x^2)}$;
    (e) $x(1-x^2)^{-\frac{3}{2}}$;  (f) $4\sin^3 x \cos x$;
    (g) $-6\cos 3x \sin 3x$;  (h) $0$;
    (i) $3(\cos x-\sin x)(\cos x+\sin x)^2$.

3.  (a) $4(x-1/x)^3(1+1/x^2)$;  (b) $-(2x+1)/x^2(x+1)^2$;
    (c) $x^2(x^3-1)^{-\frac{2}{3}}$;  (d) $\sec x \tan x$;
    (e) $2\sec^2 x \tan x$;
    (f) $\sec^2 x \tan x/\sqrt{(\sec x^2-1)} = \sec^2 x$.
    The conclusion to be drawn from (f) is that $d/dx (\tan x) = \sec^2 x$.

261

4. $f(x) = \sin 3x - 2x$ ⎱ $f(0·5) = -0·0025,$ ⎱
   $f'(x) = 3 \cos 3x - 2,$ ⎰ $f'(0·5) = -1·7879.$ ⎰

   Correction, $-0·0014$; the answer, $0·4986$, cannot be improved by the use of four-figure tables.

5. $2 \sin x \cos x = 0$, so $x = \frac{1}{2}n\pi$; $y = 0$ or $1$. For sketch, see p. 389 of the pupils' text.

6. $-(2x-3)/(x-1)^2(x-2)^2 = 0$ when $x = \frac{3}{2}$; it is easier to find the minimum of $(x-1)(x-2)$, without necessarily differentiating (see Chapter 15). In the notation of Chapter 5, Exercise E, the shape of the function is $0^+DD0^+$; there are no zeros, and it is symmetrical about $x = \frac{3}{2}$.

## 3. PRODUCTS OF FUNCTIONS— THE PRODUCT RULE

The approach here is based upon the rather striking fact that *fractional* (or *percentage*) errors can simply be added, if the two quantities are multiplied together. Numerical examples are easy to construct and profitable to consider.

When $\log_e$ is available, it will be useful to reconsider the rule in the light of this working:

$$y = uvw \Rightarrow \frac{d}{dx}(\log y) = \frac{d}{dx}(\log u + \log v + \log w)$$

$$\Rightarrow \frac{1}{y}\frac{dy}{dx} = \frac{1}{u}\frac{du}{dx} + \frac{1}{v}\frac{dv}{dx} + \frac{1}{w}\frac{dw}{dx}$$

$$\Rightarrow \frac{\delta y}{y} \simeq \frac{\delta u}{u} + \frac{\delta v}{v} + \frac{\delta w}{w}.$$

### Exercise C (p. 476)

1. $(14·14 \times 15·45) - (14 \times 15) \simeq 8·5$, so the error, $\frac{85}{2100}$, is about 4 %.

2. $14·5 \times 15·5 = 225$ m, $13·5 \times 14·5 = 196$ m.

3. Figure 4 of Chapter 17, of the pupils' text, with $t$ substituted for $v$, should suffice.

   The greatest possible fractional error would be

$$\frac{\delta u}{u} \times \frac{\delta t}{t} + \frac{\delta u}{u} \times \frac{\delta t}{t}.$$

If $\delta u$ or $\delta t$ could be negative, $|\delta u|$, $|\delta t|$ would replace $\delta u$, $\delta t$ here.

4. $y.\delta z+z.\delta y+\delta y.\delta z$, leading to the product rule.

5. Much of the misuse of the chain and product rules arises from a hazy idea of the circumstances in which they should be applied, and some weak pupils find it helpful to see the difference of structure through the medium of the now familiar flow diagram. Until it becomes automatic, therefore, this analysis is to be commended.

6. (a) $2x+3$;      (b) $3x^2$;      (c) $\sin x+x\cos x$;
 (d) $1/(1+x)^2$; differentiate $1-1/(1+x)$;
 (e) $(-x^2+2)/(x+1)^2(x+2)^2$; this involves a good deal of manipulation;
 (f) $1+\sin^2 x/\cos^2 x = \sec^2 x$.

7. No; exp, log, $x^x$, and so on are disallowed by the form of the question, and for 'functions' like $x \to \sqrt{(-x^2)}$, or $x \to \sqrt{x}+\sqrt{(-x)}$, whose domains consist simply of $\{0\}$, derived functions do not exist.

### Exercise D (p. 480)

There are many more examples here than will be needed on first reading. Pupils seem to pick this up best by recalling the formula in the $u, v$ form from Figure 4. Encourage them to use the results in the tables.

1. (a) $(3x^2+1)$;      (b) $(2x-1)(18x+5)$;
 (c) $(x-2)^2(x+2)^3(7x-2)$;      (d) $2x\cos x-x^2\sin x$;
 (e) $\sin^2 x+2x\cos x\sin x$;      (f) $(a^2-2x^2)/\sqrt{(a^2-x^2)}$;
 (g) $(\cos x)/x-(\sin x)/x^2$;      (h) $1/(1+x)^2$;
 (i) $(c^2-x^2)/(x^2+c^2)^2$.

2. (a) $6x^5$;      (b) $x^4(a-x)^6(5a-12x)$;
 (c) $5s^4c^8-7s^6c^6$;      (d) $\sin 3x+3x\cos 3x$;
 (e) $x^2\cos x$;      (f) $(5x^2+6x)/\sqrt{(2x+3)}$;
 (g) $(\sin x-x\cos x)/\sin^2 x$;      (h) $b^2(x^2+b^2)^{-\frac{3}{2}}$;
 (i) $4x^3-18x^2+22x-6$.

3.   (a) $\sec^2 x$;

    (b) $(2x(1-\sin^2 x)-2(1-x^2)\sin x \cos x)/(1-x^2)^2$;

    (c) $(1-5x^2)/(1+x^2)^4$;         (d) $(1+2x^2)/(1-x^2)^{\frac{5}{2}}$;

    (e) $-b/(b-x)^{\frac{1}{2}}(b+x)^{\frac{3}{2}}$;     (f) $-2\sin 2x$;

    (g) $(p(a-x)-qx)x^{p-1}(a-x)^{q-1}$;

    (h) $(p\cos^2 x-q\sin^2 x)\sin^{p-1}x\cos^{p-1}x$.

4.   (a), (b). It is easier to find maxima and minima of the reciprocals $x\pm 1/x$. Then $1\mp 1/x^2 = 0$, so that (a) has max/min at $\pm 1$, (b) has none.

    (c) $(-2x^2+5x-4)/x^3(x-2)^2 \neq 0$ for any $x$.

The shapes of the graphs are: (a) $0^-Z0^+$; (b) $0^-DZD0^+$; (c) $0^+D^2ZD0^+$;

5.   $(d/dx)(x\cos 2x) = \cos 2x-2x\sin 2x$, so, for max/min,
$$\cot 2x = 2x.$$

    $f(x) = \cot 2x-2x$;    $f(0\cdot 5) = -0\cdot 357$ $\Big\}$ correction, $-0\cdot 074$

    $f'(x) = -2\csc^2 2x-2$    $f'(0\cdot 5) = -4\cdot 83$ $\Big\}$ to give $0\cdot 426$.

    $f'(0\cdot 426) = -0\cdot 023$ $\Big\}$ correction, $+0\cdot 0049$, to give $0\cdot 4309$.

    $f'(0\cdot 426) = -5\cdot 54$

6.   $\dfrac{d}{dx}(u.v^{-n}) = v^{-n}\dfrac{du}{dx}-nuv^{-n-1}\dfrac{dv}{dx} = \left(v\dfrac{du}{dx}-nu\dfrac{dv}{dx}\right)\Big/v^{n+1}$.

    In 2(h), $v = x^2+b^2$, $n = \frac{1}{2}$; in 3(c), $n = 3$; in 3(d), $n = \frac{3}{2}$; in 3(e), $n = \frac{1}{2}$. This form is particularly useful for fractional indices.

7.   $\displaystyle\lim_{b\to a}\frac{f(b).g(b)-f(a).g(a)}{b-a} = \lim_{b\to a}\left(f(b)\frac{g(b)-g(a)}{b-a}+g(a)\frac{f(b)-f(a)}{b-a}\right)$

$$= f(a).g'(a)+f'(a).g(a);$$

$\displaystyle\lim_{b\to a}\frac{f(b)/g(b)-f(a)/g(a)}{b-a}$

$$= \lim_{b\to a}\left\{\frac{1}{g(a).g(b)}\left(g(a)\frac{f(b)-f(a)}{b-a}-f(a)\frac{g(b)-g(a)}{b-a}\right)\right\}$$

$$= \frac{g(a)f'(a)-f(a)g'(a)}{\{g(a)\}^2}.$$

## 4. FUNCTIONS DEFINED INDIRECTLY
### *Exercise E (p. 484)*

**1.** Local scale factor $= 1/3a^2$ (see Figure C)
$$= \tfrac{1}{3}b^{-\frac{2}{3}}.$$

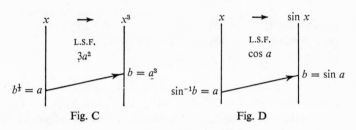

Fig. C        Fig. D

**2.** Local scale factor $= \dfrac{1}{\cos a}$ (see Figure D)

$$= \dfrac{1}{\sqrt{(1-b^2)}}, \quad \text{for acute } a.$$

**3.** $g: x \to \sqrt[3]{(2x-5)}; \quad f': x \to \tfrac{3}{2}x^2; \quad g': x \to \tfrac{2}{3}(2x-5)^{-\frac{2}{3}}.$
If $f(a) = b, g(b) = a;$ so $f'(a) = \tfrac{3}{2}a^2, g'(b) = 2/3a^2.$

**4.** $g: x \to \tfrac{1}{2}q - p/2x; \quad f': x \to 2p/(q-2x)^2; \quad g': x \to p/2x^2.$
If $f(a) = b, g(b) = a;$ so $f'(a) = 2b^2/a, g'(b) = a/2b^2.$

**5.** (a) $-1/\sqrt{(1-x^2)}$, since $\sin^{-1} x + \cos^{-1} x = \tfrac{1}{2}\pi;$
(b) $-1/(1+x^2)$, using the chain rule;
(c) $-1/(1+x^2)$, since $\tan^{-1} x + \cot^{-1} x = \tfrac{1}{2}\pi$ (or $-\tfrac{1}{2}\pi$, if $x < 0$);
(d) $1/x\sqrt{(x^2-1)}$, using the chain rule to differentiate $\cos^{-1}(1/x)$ or using the method of Example 8.

The inverse trigonometrical functions are needed primarily for integration, but this is the logical place to introduce them; the results should be just sufficiently familiar for them to be recalled when they are needed.

**6.** (a) $1/t; \tfrac{1}{2}$, putting $t = 2;$
(b) $-2 \cos t/(3 \sin t); -\tfrac{1}{3}$, putting $t = \sin^{-1}(0\cdot8);$
(c) $-1/t^2; -1$, putting $t = 1.$

(d) $\sec^2 t/(2 \sec t \tan t) = \frac{1}{2} \csc t$; $\frac{13}{24}$, putting $t = \tan^{-1}(2\cdot4)$;

(e) $3t/2$; 3, putting $t = 2$;

(f) $1/qt^{q-1}$; $1/q$, putting $t = 1$.

The parametric form, again, is often useful, and the gradients obtained in Question 6 should be compared with careful drawings (one per pupil) of the curves described in Question 7.

**7.** (a) Parabola;      (b) ellipse;      (c) hyperbola;

(d) hyperbola;      (e) semi-cubical parabola;

(f) image in $y = x$ of $y = x^q$.

**8.** Local scale factor = $1/\mathscr{E}(a) = 1/b$. This introduction to differentiating $\log_e x$ could reasonably be linked with the exponential law of growth, and a sketch could be made of the outlines of $y = \mathscr{E}(x)$ and of $y = \mathscr{L}(x)$.

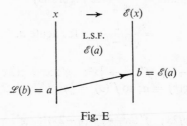

Fig. E

## Miscellaneous Exercise (p. 487)

**1.** Neglect the thickness of the wood, wastage in cutting, overlap at the corners, etc. Taking dimensions (in cm) $3x \times 5x \times 30/x^2$, area used is $15x^2 + 480/x$; so that $x = 2\sqrt[3]{2} = 2\cdot52$, approx., giving $7\cdot6 \times 12\cdot6 \times 4\cdot7$.

**2.** If $x$ is the radius in cm, the height is $160 \times (15 - x)$. The volume is $160 \pi x^2 (15 - x)$, which is a maximum for $x = 10$ (notice that if the maximum had appeared to be at, say, $x = 8$, further consideration would have been necessary). The volume is then very nearly $0\cdot25$ m$^3$.

**3.** The volume, for any top radius $x$, is $61/48$ of the volume of Question 2, so that the answer is about $0\cdot32$ m$^3$. The dimensions can be found by recognizing that, whatever the exact formula may be, $V \propto x^2h$, so that the value of $x$ that gives the maximum will be the same.

**4.** If $\theta$ is the semi-vertical angle, the curved surface area is $\sec^2\theta \cdot \csc\theta$. To minimize this, it is easier to maximize
$$\cos^2\theta \cdot \sin\theta,$$
or, better still, $s(1-s^2)$, where $s = \sin\theta$. This leads to $s = 1/\sqrt{3}$, and so to $\theta = 35\cdot3°$, and vertical angle $70\cdot5°$.

**5.** $k = \sqrt{(900-h^2)}$. It is best to maximize $k^2h^6$, that is, $900h^6 - h^8$. This leads to $h^2 = 675$, $k^2 = 225$, so that the beam is $26 \times 15$ cm.

**6.** The total cost is $\pounds A(V+V^2/100+1250/V)$; for a minimum, $V^3+50V^2-62,500 = 0$. This can be solved without fuss by the Newton–Raphson method; a first approximation 30 leads to 28, and then to $28\cdot2$ knots. The cost is then $\pounds80\cdot5A$, as compared with $\pounds100A$ at 50 km/h, and $\pounds108A$ at 55 km/h. A quick estimate is that it costs $\pounds1\cdot6A$ per km/h extra, in the region of 50 km/h; differentiation gives $\pounds1\cdot5A$.

**7.** $3600\,v(8+v+v^2/18)$ vehicles per hour. Minimize
$$(8v/v+1+v/18),$$
so that $v = 12$ gives a maximum of about 1540 vehicles per hour, with a spacing of 28 m.

**8.** The area is $(1+\cot\theta)(1+\tan\theta) = 2+\cot\theta+\tan\theta$
$$= 2+1/t+t.$$
This is minimized at $t = 1$, the symmetrical position.

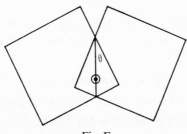

Fig. F

9. If $\theta$ is half the acute angle of the rhombus, $40(\cot \theta + \tan \theta)$ ft is needed. As in Question 8, this is minimized when $\tan \theta = 1$, and the length is 80 m. The area is, of course, simply 5 m multiplied by the perimeter, so that area and perimeter reach a minimum together.

10. The marginal cost is the cost of producing an *extra* unit, approximately (which we may think of as $f(a+1) - f(a)$, the average scale factor for an interval of length 1). Consider the extra cost of teaching one more pupil at a school, and of feeding him; and consider the cost of an extra copy of a cyclostyled sheet of which you are already producing 100 copies.

$$\frac{d}{dQ}\left(\frac{C}{Q}\right) = \left(Q\frac{dC}{dQ} - C\right)\Big/ Q^2, \text{ so that } \frac{C}{Q} \text{ is a minimum when } \frac{C}{Q} = \frac{dC}{dQ}.$$

Figure G shows that the gradient of $OP$ is a minimum when it is equal to the gradient at $T$. In non-mathematical terms, if the next item costs less than the average, it will reduce the average, and if it costs more than the average, it will increase the average.

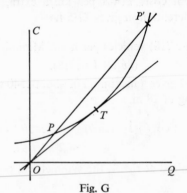

Fig. G

To make the average as small as possible, therefore, we go on adding more items until the average has been reduced to the cost of an extra item.

11. $f'(x) = -na \sin nx + nb \cos nx = nR \cos (nx + \theta)$,

$f''(x) = -n^2a \cos nx - n^2b \sin nx = -n^2R \sin (nx + \theta) = -n^2f(x)$,

where $R^2 = a^2 + b^2$ and $\theta = \tan^{-1}(a/b)$. This leads to simple harmonic motion, whose characteristic is that $\ddot{x} = -n^2x$.

**12.** If $\theta$ is the angle with the wall of the 1·5 m corridor, the shortest line from wall to wall across the angle occurs when $\tan^3 \theta = 0\cdot75$, so that $\theta = 42\cdot2°$. The length is 4·9 m horizontally, and 5·5 m if the height of the passage is used.

**13.** $2 \cos^2 x - 2 \sin^2 x = 2 \cos 2x$.

**14.** $f'(x) = -2 \cos x \sin x - 2 \sin x \cos x$,

$g'(x) = -2 \cos x \sin x + 2 \sin x \cos x$;

again, $d/dx (\cos 2x) = -2 \sin 2x$, and $d/dx (1) = 0$.

We can also consider $g(x) \pm f(x)$, giving $2 \sin^2 x$ and $2 \cos^2 x$.

**15.** ($a$) $\cos x \cos \theta - \sin x \sin \theta = \cos (x+\theta)$;

($b$) $-\sin x \cos \theta - \cos x \sin \theta = -\sin (x+\theta)$.

**16.** ($a$) $2 \sec^2 x \tan x$;

($b$) $2 \sec^2 x \tan x$, $\sec^2 x = 1 + \tan^2 x$.

**17.** $\sec^2 x - \csc^2 x = (\sin^2 x - \cos^2 x)/\sin^2 x \cos^2 x$

$$= -4 \cos 2x/\sin^2 2x = -4 \csc 2x \cot 2x.$$

$\tan x + \cot x = (\sin^2 x + \cot^2 x)/\sin x \cos x = 2 \csc 2x$.

**18.** ($a$) $-(a-b)^2 (\sin ax \cos bx - \cos ax \sin bx)$

$$= -(a-b)^2 \sin (a-b)x;$$

($b$) $-4 \cos 2(\pi - x) = -4 \cos 2x$;

($c$) $-(\cos x + \cos (x + \tfrac{2}{3}\pi) + \cos (x + \tfrac{4}{3}\pi)) = 0$, since

$$\cos x + \cos (x + \tfrac{4}{3}\pi) = 2 \cos (x + \tfrac{2}{3}\pi) . \cos (\tfrac{2}{3}\pi).$$

**19.** Any equilateral triangle, one of whose sides makes an angle $x$ with the axis; the sum of the projections of the three sides on the axis is zero.

(Compare $(1 + \omega + \omega^2)a = 0$, where $\omega = \cos (\tfrac{2}{3}\pi) + j \sin (\tfrac{2}{3}\pi)$.)

**20.** $\dfrac{d}{dx} \tan (\tan^{-1} x) = \sec^2 (\tan^{-1} x) \dfrac{d}{dx} (\tan^{-1} x)$

$$= (1 + x^2) \dfrac{d}{dx} (\tan^{-1} x) = 1.$$

**21.** Maximum and minimum at $(1, 1)$ and $(-1, -1)$. Graphs, see p. 94 of this volume.

$x = 2n\pi - 0\cdot305$ *or* $(2n+1)\pi + 0\cdot305$; $t = -0\cdot154$ *or* $-6\cdot506$; $\sin x = 2t/(1 + t^2)$ is satisfied.

**22.** Near $x = 0$; $\sec x > 1$ and $\cos x < 1$, but at $x = 0$ each is equal to 1. $\sec x/x > \csc x > 1/x > \cot x > \cos x/x$ shows how $\csc x$, $\cot x$ compare with $1/x$.

$x \sec x > \tan x > x > \sin x > x \cos x$ shows how $\tan x$, $\sin x$ compare with $x$. The relationships for other values of $n$ follow by symmetry (see p. 94, Question 4).

**23.** See p. 95, Question 5 and pupils' text Book 2, p. 390.

**24.** The graphs are the same as those of Question 23; if $x = \tan \frac{1}{2}\theta$, $f(x) = \csc \theta$, $g(x) = \cot \theta$, and $(f(a))^2 - (g(a))^2 = 1$.

**25.** (*a*) When $t = \pm(1+h)$, $y$ behaves like $-18/h$, and like $-12/h$, for small $h$;

(*b*) $y \to -5$, and $y$ behaves like $-5 - 6/h$ when $h$ is large;

(*c*) maximum and minimum at $(-3, -4)$, $(-\frac{1}{3}, 4)$ respectively.

**26.** Minimum value, $+4$, when $\tan x = -\frac{3}{4}$. Now, if $t = \tan \frac{1}{2}x$, $\tan x = 2t/(1 - t^2)$, so $t = -\frac{1}{3} \Rightarrow \tan x = -\frac{3}{4}$.

**27.** $f(0) = f'(0) = f''(0) = f'''(0) = 0$;

$f(\frac{1}{4}\pi) = 0 \cdot 0155$;  $f(\frac{1}{2}\pi) = 0 \cdot 2337$.

Values of $f(x)$ for $x = 0 \cdot 0(0 \cdot 1)1 \cdot 5$ are:

$0 \cdot 0000$, $0 \cdot 0000$, $0 \cdot 0001$, $0 \cdot 0003$, $0 \cdot 0011$, $0 \cdot 0026$,
$0 \cdot 0053$, $0 \cdot 0098$, $0 \cdot 0167$, $0 \cdot 0266$, $0 \cdot 0403$,
$0 \cdot 0586$, $0 \cdot 0824$, $0 \cdot 1125$, $0 \cdot 1500$, $0 \cdot 1957$.

**28.** We use the approximation $f(a+x) \simeq f(a) + xf'(a) + \frac{1}{2}x^2 f''(a)$; the first two terms give the answer, and the third the approximate error.

$1° \simeq 0 \cdot 0175$; so

$\tan 46° \simeq 1 \cdot 035$, with error about $-0 \cdot 0006$,
$\sin 29° \simeq 0 \cdot 4848$, with error about $-0 \cdot 00008$,
$\tan^{-1}(1 \cdot 75) \simeq 1 \cdot 0516$, with error about $-0 \cdot 00004$.

**29.** The increase in area is approximately equal to the circumference multiplied by the increase in the radius.

(*a*) $d/dr\left(\frac{4}{3}\pi r^2\right) = 4\pi r^2$, so that the rate of change of volume is given by the surface area.

(*b*) $V = \pi r^2 h$; if $r$ remains constant, so that $V$ is a function of $h$, $dV/dh = \pi r^2$; if $h$ remains constant, so that $V$ is a function of $r$, $dV/dr = 2\pi rh$.

(*c*) $V = \frac{1}{3}\pi r^2 h = \frac{1}{3}\pi r^3 \cot \alpha$; there is no obvious connection.

**30.** $f(x) = \sqrt{x} \Rightarrow f'(x) = 1/2\sqrt{x} \Rightarrow \frac{1}{2}f''(x) = -1/8\sqrt{(x^3)}$; so
$$\sqrt{(a^2+h)} \simeq a+h/2a-h^2/8a^3.$$
Similarly
$$\sqrt[3]{(a^3+h)} \simeq a+h/3a^2-h^2/9a^5.$$

$\sqrt{(30)} = \frac{1}{2}\sqrt{(11^2-1)} \simeq 5{\cdot}47727$,    error $0{\cdot}00004$;

$\sqrt{(10)} = \frac{1}{10}\sqrt{(32^2-24)} \simeq 3{\cdot}1625$,    error $0{\cdot}0002$;

$\sqrt{(11)} = \frac{1}{3}\sqrt{(10^2-1)} \simeq 3{\cdot}31667$,    error $0{\cdot}00004$;

$\sqrt[3]{2} = \frac{1}{4}\sqrt[3]{(5^3+3)} \simeq 1{\cdot}26000$,    error $0{\cdot}00008$;

$\sqrt[3]{(37)} = \frac{1}{3}\sqrt[3]{(10^3-1)} \simeq 3{\cdot}3322222$,    error $0{\cdot}0000004$;

$\sqrt{5} = \frac{1}{4}\sqrt{(9^2-1)} \simeq 2{\cdot}23611$,    error $0{\cdot}00004$;

$\sqrt{7} = \frac{1}{3}\sqrt{(8^2-1)} \simeq 2{\cdot}64583$,    error $0{\cdot}00008$;

$\sqrt{6} = \frac{1}{2}\sqrt{(5^2-1)} \simeq 2{\cdot}4500$,    error $0{\cdot}0005$.

**31.** $\dfrac{1}{1+x} \simeq 1-x+x^2-x^3+x^4$;    $\dfrac{1}{1+x^2} \simeq 1-x^2+x^4-x^6+x^8$;

$\tan^{-1} x \simeq x-\frac{1}{3}x^3+\frac{1}{5}x^5-\frac{1}{7}x^7+\frac{1}{9}x^9$.

**32.** $\sec x \simeq 1+\frac{1}{2}x^2+\frac{5}{24}x^4$;    $\sin^{-1} x \simeq x+\frac{1}{6}x^3$;

$\sqrt{(1-x)} \simeq 1-\frac{1}{2}x-\frac{1}{8}x^2-\frac{1}{16}x^3-\frac{5}{128}x^4$;    $x^2/\sqrt{(1-x^2)} \simeq x^2+\frac{1}{2}x^4$.
Notice that $\sec x$ can be formed as $1/\cos x$; $\sin^{-1} x$ (being odd)
as $x+ax^3$, considering what $a$ must be for $\sin(\sin^{-1} x)$ to be
equal to $x$; and $x^2/\sqrt{(1-x^2)}$ as a direct deduction from the first
two terms of $1/\sqrt{(1-x)}$.

**33.** (a) $\sin x \simeq x-\frac{1}{6}x^3$;       (b) $\cos x \simeq 1-\frac{1}{2}x^2+\frac{1}{24}x^4$;

(c) $\cos 2x \simeq 1-2x^2+\frac{2}{3}x^4$;

$\sin^2 x = \frac{1}{2}(1-\cos 2x) \simeq x^2-\frac{1}{3}x^4 \simeq (x-\frac{1}{6}x^3)^2$.

**34.** $f(x)$    $x\cos x$;    $x^2\sin x$;    $x^3\sin 2x$.

$f'(x)$    $-x\sin x+\cos x$;    $x^2\cos x+2x\sin x$;
         $2x^3\cos 2x+3x^2\sin 2x$.

$f''(x)$    $-x\cos x-2\sin x$;    $-x^2\sin x+4x\cos x+2\sin x$;
         $-4x^3\sin 2x+12x^2\cos 2x+6x\sin 2x$.

$f'''(x)$    $+x\sin x-3\cos x$;    $-x^2\cos x-6x\sin x+6\cos x$;
         $-8x^3\cos 2x-36x^2\sin 2x+36x\cos 2x+6\sin 2x$.

$f^{iv}(x)$    $+x\cos x+4\sin x$;    $+x^2\sin x-8x\cos x-12\sin x$;
         $+16x^3\sin 2x-96x^2\cos 2x-144x\sin 2x+48\cos 2x$.

271

$f^{v}(x)$  $-x \sin x + 5 \cos x$;  $+x^2 \cos x + 10x \sin x - 20 \cos x$;
$$+32x^3 \cos 2x + 240x^2 \sin 2x - 480x \cos 2x - 240 \sin 2x.$$

$$x \cos x \simeq x - \tfrac{1}{2}x^3 + \tfrac{1}{24}x^5;$$

$$x^2 \sin x \simeq x^3 - \tfrac{1}{6}x^5;$$

$$x^3 \sin 2x \simeq 2x^4; \quad \text{all these check.}$$

**35.** $(1-x^2)y^2 = 1 \Rightarrow 2(1-x^2)y\dfrac{dy}{dx} - 2xy^2 = 0$, by differentiation

$$\Rightarrow (1-x^2)\frac{dy}{dx} - xy = 0$$

$$\Rightarrow (1-x^2)\frac{d^2y}{dx^2} - 3x\frac{dy}{dx} - y = 0.$$

**36.** $y = x \Rightarrow (1-x^2)y_2 - 2xy_1 + 2y = 0$  (writing $dy/dx$ as $y_1$, and so forth);

$y = \tfrac{1}{2}(3x^2 - 1) \Rightarrow (1-x^2)y_2 - 2xy_1 + 6y = 0$;

$y = \tfrac{1}{2}(5x^3 - 3x) \Rightarrow (1-x^2)y_2 - 2xy_1 + 12y = 0$;

$y = \tfrac{1}{8}(35x^4 - 30x^2 + 3) \Rightarrow (1-x^2)y_2 - 2xy_1 + 20y = 0$.

A lot of elegant work can be done on these polynomials, but a first look at their behaviour is all that is needed here.

**37.** (a) $\pm 1{\cdot}414$;  (b) $\pm 3{\cdot}146$, $\pm 0{\cdot}318$;  (c) $\pm 2{\cdot}475$.

**38.** (a) $14°$;  (b) $34°$;  (c) $20°$ *and* $137°$.

**39.** About $0{\cdot}654$; maximum, $(\tfrac{1}{2}\pi, 1)$, minimum, $(-\tfrac{1}{2}\pi, -1)$; maximum $(\sqrt{2}, \tfrac{2}{3}\sqrt{2})$, minimum $(-\sqrt{2}, -\tfrac{2}{3}\sqrt{2})$; intercepts, $n\pi$, $(\pm \sqrt{6}, 0)$.

**40.** The point of inflexion is $(b/a, -2b^3/a^2 + 3bc/a - d)$; if this point is translated to $O$, the equation becomes $y = ax^3 + 3(c - b^2/a)x$, which is an odd function of $x$.

**41.** See Figure H.

**42.** See Figure I. Maximum at $(1, 2)$, minimum at $(2, 1)$.

(a) There are three possible continuous inverse functions (for different restrictions of the domain of $f$) over the interval $(1, 2)$.

(*b*), (*c*) There is one restriction of the domain which gives a continuous inverse function, though of course several discontinuous inverse functions can be defined.

(*d*) Of several possible restrictions of the domain, none gives a continuous inverse function.

(This question arose in an investigation of the limits in an integration by substitution.)

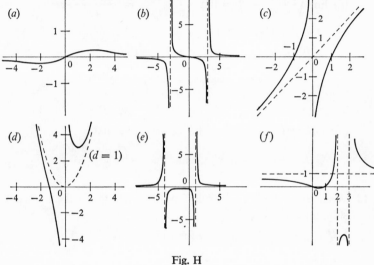

Fig. H

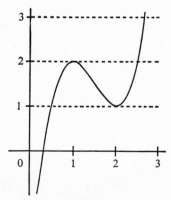

Fig. I

**43.** (a) $\lim\limits_{b \to a} \dfrac{f(b)/g(b) - f(a)/g(a)}{b-a}$

$$= \lim_{b \to a} \left( \frac{1}{g(a)\,g(b)} \left( g(a)\frac{f(b)-f(a)}{b-a} - f(a)\frac{g(b)-g(a)}{b-a} \right) \right)$$

$$= \frac{g(a)\,f'(a) - f(a)\,g'(a)}{(g(a))^2} \, ;$$

(b) $\lim\limits_{\delta x \to 0} \left( \dfrac{\dfrac{u+\delta u}{v+\delta v} - \dfrac{u}{v}}{\delta x} \right) = \lim\limits_{\delta x \to 0} \dfrac{v\,\delta u - u\,\delta v}{v(v+\delta v)\,\delta x} = \dfrac{v\dfrac{du}{dx} - u\dfrac{dv}{dx}}{v^2}.$

(c) $(d/dx)\,(f\,.\,1/g) = f'\,.\,1/g + f\,.\,(-1/g^2)\,.\,g' = (f'\,.\,g - f\,.\,g')/g^2;$

(d) $(d/dx)(k\,.\,g) = k\,.\,g' + k'\,.\,g = f'$, so that

$$k' = \frac{f' - k\,.\,g'}{g} = \frac{f'\,.\,g - f\,.\,g'}{g^2}.$$

The extension to $f/g^n$ is illustrated for case (d).

$(d/dx)(k\,.\,g^n) = k\,.\,ng^{n-1}\,.\,g' + k'\,.\,g^n = f'$, so that

$$k'\,.\,g^n = f' - nf\,.\,g'/g, \quad \text{and} \quad k' = \frac{f'\,.\,g - nf\,.\,g'}{g^{n+1}}.$$

**44.** We assume the product rule for two functions in the inductive step, and write $P_n = f_1\,.\,f_2 \ldots f_n$.

If $T$ is the set of numbers $n$ for which $P'_n = \sum\limits_1^n P_n\,.\,f'_i/f_i$,

(a) $2 \in T$ (the product rule);

(b) $k \in T \Rightarrow P'_{k+1} = P'_k\,.\,f_{k+1} + P_k\,.\,f'_{k+1}$

$$= \sum_1^k P_{k+1}\,.\,f'_i/f_i + P_{k+1}\,.\,f'_{k+1}/f_{k+1}$$

$$= \sum_1^{k+1} P_{k+1}\,.\,f'_i/f_i$$

$$\Rightarrow k+1 \in T;$$

the result follows by the principle of induction.

**45.** $\dfrac{dy}{dx} = \dfrac{dy}{dt} \div \dfrac{dx}{dt} = \dfrac{3(t^2+1)}{2t}$ ;

$$\frac{d^2y}{dx^2} = \frac{d}{dt}\left(\frac{dy}{dx}\right) \div \frac{dx}{dt} = \left(\frac{3}{2} - \frac{3}{2t^2}\right) \div 2t = \frac{3(t^2-1)}{4t^3}.$$

**46.** $\dfrac{dy}{dx} = \dfrac{3x}{2\sqrt{(x-1)}}$; $\dfrac{d^2y}{dx^2} = \dfrac{3x-6}{4\sqrt{(x-1)^3}}$.

$$t = \sqrt{(x-1)} \Rightarrow y = (x+2)\sqrt{(x-1)}.$$

**47.** $\dfrac{dy}{dx} = \dfrac{1}{t}$; $\dfrac{d^2y}{dx^2} = \dfrac{d}{dt}\left(\dfrac{dy}{dx}\right) \div \dfrac{dx}{dt} = -\dfrac{1}{t^2} \div 2at = \dfrac{-1}{2at^3}$.

$$y^2 = 4ax \Rightarrow 2y\dfrac{dy}{dx} = 4a \Rightarrow y\dfrac{d^2y}{dx^2} + \left(\dfrac{dy}{dx}\right)^2 = 0; \quad \text{so } \dfrac{d^2y}{dx^2} = \dfrac{-4a^2}{y^3}.$$

**48.** $\dfrac{dy}{dx} = \dfrac{g'(t)}{f'(t)}$; $\dfrac{d^2y}{dx^2} = \dfrac{d}{dt}\left(\dfrac{dy}{dx}\right) \div \dfrac{dx}{dt} = \dfrac{f'(t) \cdot g''(t) - f''(t) \cdot g'(t)}{\{f'(t)\}^3}$.

**49.** Since $p, q$ are integral,

$$dy/dx = pt^{p-1}/qt^{q-1} = p/q \cdot t^{p-q} = p/q \cdot x^{p/q-1} = mx^{m-1}.$$

$x^{p/q}$ has two values if $q$ is even, and we must restrict the domain, to deal with one at a time. $p/q$ need not be in its lowest terms, but whereas $t^{\frac{1}{3}}$ is unique, $t^{\frac{2}{6}}$ is not.

**50.** The extension is obvious, in cases (a), (b), (c). The extension to real numbers may be made through sequences of rational numbers (restricting all powers to positive numbers, for this purpose). For if we define the real number $\pi$ by a Dedekind section of the rational numbers, if $2^x$ is monotonic, we can define $2^\pi$ by a corresponding section, this time of the real numbers. Practically, since we can find $a < \pi < b$ so that $a, b$ are rational numbers arbitrarily close together, $2^a < 2^\pi < 2^b$ can be used to define a series of nesting sets which will suffice to define the number $2^\pi$. For another approach, see Chapter 29.

18-2

# 18

# UNITS AND DIMENSIONS

This chapter was written to show that when mathematics is applied to the physical world a new and powerful restriction is imposed—the principle of dimensional consistency. The quantities with which we are dealing—mass, length, time, charge, temperature—are not themselves numbers, though they are measured by numbers called *scalars*, which express them as multiples of certain *unit* quantities.

There are four points which the teacher should constantly bear in mind. First, we are now dealing with the real world, and not only with mathematical abstractions. The quantities we handle have dimensions, and therefore correspond to some physical reality; and however interesting the mathematics may be, we always have to check back at the end to make sure that our conclusions have some correspondence with the real life situation with which we began.

The second question is what we actually mean when we write $s/t$, or $ds/dt$, that is to say when we produce a quantity which appears as a result of dividing a distance by a time. Pupils will usually have an intuitive idea of what they mean by this, particularly if they think of a motor-car going along a road. They think they know what it means to say the car is going at 50 km/h. The physical meaning is not quite so clear when you think about it; and this excursion into dimensional analysis may give a clearer idea of what is involved.

Thirdly, the reason why dimensional analysis can be so helpful in physical problems springs from the realization that the numbers on the two sides of a physical equation must have the same dimension. Much can be deduced about physical systems from a preliminary consideration in dimensional terms—examples which spring to mind are the pendulum law, the motion of a body through a resisting medium, the prediction of results of full-scale experiments from the observation of small-scale models, and the blue of the sky—but there are two important limitations. The first is that the numerical constants cannot be deduced in this way; dimensional analysis will lead us to $k\sqrt{(a/g)}$, but cannot lead us to discover that $k = 2\pi$; and the second

276

is the formidable difficulty of being sure, say, in the case of convection, that you have written down *all* the relevant quantities. If you have not, you may be led to completely erroneous results. Another aspect of the same difficulty is that the physical quantities involved may appear in dimensionless combinations—such as the Reynolds number or the quantity $v^2/ag$—though there is a comforting theorem (the Buckingham Pi theorem) which tells us that if we start with $n$ quantities in a system involving $r$ fundamental quantities (generators of the group), only $(n-r)$ such quantities will occur.

Fourthly, the need to write down the units in which you are working, at every stage, cannot be stressed too much. This discipline not only helps to correct numerical errors, but also to keep in mind the physical realities which lie behind the mathematical formulation.

# 1. PHYSICAL MEASUREMENTS
## *Exercise A (p. 493)*

The difficulties in this exercise spring from two sources—the inaccuracy of our measuring instruments and the intrinsic variability of the quantity to be measured.

1.  It is well known that the earth's orbit about the sun is not circular, but elliptical, and that the distance is therefore by no means constant, and that the sun's size and shape add theoretical difficulties to the practical difficulty of determining its distance. However, 150,000,000 km can be taken as a fair average distance, though 1 % would be an optimistic estimate of its accuracy.

2.  A ball falling through a viscous liquid; the deformation of a squash ball due to its rotation; the change in diameter under the application of heat; the wear on a ball bearing, or the setting up of a gas bearing (in which a ball will rotate for many hours).

3.  *Any* mechanical quantities can be constructed from the three fundamental quantities.

4.  The questions of bouncing, skidding, and cost will come into this, though the details are extremely difficult.

**5.** The physical apparatus in schools is becoming rapidly more refined, but the following may be a guide. Time can be measured to a thousandth of a second, but the long period brings in the intrinsic accuracy of the machine significantly, and this may be of the order of $1/10^3$. The best clocks so far devised have an accuracy of about $1/10^{10}$.

Your weight might be measured to the nearest gram, small movements and the difficulties of exact calibration make greater accuracy unlikely.

Roughness of a surface might be measured under a microscope, racking the instrument up and down; there are refined techniques, depending on the wavelength of light, for measuring down to $10^{-5}$ cm, but $10^{-3}$ would be quite good in a school. (The Mossbauer effect should, perhaps, be mentioned here.)

The three measurements of length, for different reasons, are unlikely to be accurate to more than 1 cm. The gas flame is likely to be unsteady, and its top hard to define; and the instruments used are likely to be affected by heat, gravity, and elasticity, as indeed is the cotton itself.

The pitch of middle $C$ would be determined by a 'beats' method, and an accuracy of perhaps $\frac{1}{2}$ cycle in 256.

## 2. PHYSICAL UNITS
### Exercise B (p. 494)

**4.** (i) Movement of a glacier; (ii) number of atoms in a region of extra-galactic space; (iii) a blood count, on a calibrated microscope slide; (iv) escape velocities from the earth; (v) deviation of a ray of light (if a second of arc), or speed of sound in air—for example, for the estimation of the distance of a lightning flash; (vi) accuracy of a normal clock; (vii) the spread of rats resistant to a particular poison in Shropshire; (viii) a searching project—or perhaps 'seven maids with seven mops' may be suggested.

## 4. UNITS AND CHANGE OF UNITS
### Exercise D (p. 497)

1.  Megatonnes (explosives), kilogrammes (weights), metres and centimetres, milligrams, microseconds, nanoseconds (flight of nuclear particles), picofarads (units of capacitance).

## 5. DIMENSIONS: SUMS
### Exercise E (p. 499)

2.  The word 'cycle' is usually used in a context of some sort of wave motion, and since

$$\sin n_1 t + \sin n_2 t = 2 \sin \tfrac{1}{2}(n_1 + n_2) t \cos \tfrac{1}{2}(n_1 - n_2) t$$

the difficulties in describing such a system are formidable.

## 6. DIMENSIONS: PRODUCTS
### Exercise F (p. 500)

This idea of a group, generated by the fundamental quantities, is the most important idea of the chapter. Each element generates an infinite cyclic group, of course, and up to five different fundamental quantities may be needed in a single physical situation; mechanics, however, only needs mass (or force) to complete the system.

## 7. QUOTIENTS: DERIVATIVES

The reduction of each quantity to a scalar multiple of a basic unit is a difficult idea for a beginner, especially as the symbols 3, 2, 1 are *not* numbers in the first formulation, though they *are* numbers in the second formulation; and the method of incorporating the units used in the third formulation, though attractive, may be found rather sophisticated. It may be easier, to begin with, to concentrate upon what the numbers 3, 2, 1 physically represent; it then becomes natural to write

$$x = \frac{3x_0}{t_0^2} t^2 - \frac{2x_0}{t_0} t + 1 x_0$$

before converting it into the given form, and indeed to go further and say

$$x = 3\frac{\text{m}}{\text{s}^2}\,t^2 - 2\frac{\text{m}}{\text{s}}\,t + 1 \text{ m},$$

pointing out that

$$x = 3 \text{ m}$$

is (despite the objections raised in early model-making to the phrase 'let $x$ be bananas') a legitimate—and, indeed, a helpful—equation. See pp. 714–15 of pupils' text Book 2.

### Exercise G (p. 502)

2. $V$ in litres, $t$ in seconds. The bath contained 6000 litres, and emptied in 60 s;

$$V_0 = 1 \text{ l}, \quad t_0 = 1 \text{ s};$$

$$\frac{V}{V_0} = 6000 - 40\frac{t}{t_0} - \frac{t^2}{t_0^2};$$

if $R = dV/dt$, $\qquad \dfrac{R}{V_0} = \dfrac{-40}{t_0} - \dfrac{2t}{t_0^2},$

so the initial rate of flow is $40\,V_0/t_0 = 40 \text{ l/s}$; the final rate appears to be $16a\,V_0/t_0 = 160 \text{ l/s}$.

3. $V = \frac{4}{3}\pi r^3$, $A = 4\pi r^2$; so $dV/dA = 4\pi r^2/8\pi r = \frac{1}{4}\sqrt{(A/\pi)}$.

   The dimensions of the three equations are $\mathbf{L}^3$, $\mathbf{L}^2$, $\mathbf{L}$ respectively. The range of change is $\frac{3}{2}$ cm (i.e. $\frac{3}{2}$ cm$^3$/cm$^2$).

## 8. DERIVATIVES OF POLYNOMIALS

It is worth noticing that any results in the field of pure mathematics suggested by dimensional considerations can be established by these 'change-of-variable' methods. Thus, if we are considering the rather sluggish oscillation when a mass vibrates perpendicular to the line of the strings, being fastened to two elastic strings which in the position of equilibrium are just taut, we encounter the definite integral

$$t = \int_0^x \frac{k}{\sqrt{(a^4 - x^4)}}\,dx,$$

$k$ having dimension $\mathbf{LT}$.

Now, if the integral

$$\phi(x) = \int_0^x \frac{1}{\sqrt{(1-x^4)}} \, dx$$

is tabulated, it is possible to deduce by mere change of variable (writing $y = x/a$, say) to show that $t = (k/a).\phi(x/a)$, and, in particular, that the period varies inversely as the amplitude; but it is also possible to see this as a very plausible result on purely dimensional grounds, for $\phi$ is essentially a function that maps reals into reals.

Similarly, we may remark that equations such as $y = \sin x$, $y = e^x$, $y = \log x$ all imply that $y$ and $x$ are dimensionless quantities—to see why, consider their expansion in series. It is interesting, in the light of this, to re-interpret such equations as

$$\frac{d}{dx}(e^{ax}) = a e^{ax}; \quad \frac{d}{dx}(\sin ax) = a \cos ax;$$

$$\frac{d}{dx} \tan^{-1}\left(\frac{bx}{a}\right) = \frac{ab}{a^2 + b^2 x^2}.$$

281

# 19

# KINEMATICS

The main point of this chapter is the set of relations between the path taken by a moving particle, its velocity and its acceleration. The chapter is essentially a practical one in the sense that, though calculations have to be used, as much as possible is done by drawing to make people realize and see the above relations. (It must be added that the drawing, though adding some depth to the understanding, also adds some minutes to the time taken.) For this reason, most of the examples are in two dimensions.

This is really another vector chapter and may be considered to be a continuation of Sections 3 and 4 of the chapter called Further Vectors.

**Sections 1–4:** These sections contain the development of the ideas of differentiation of vectors. In fact, this is done by expressing the varying vectors in terms of fixed unit vectors and varying scalars. It is the scalars that undergo the techniques of differentiation. This method was chosen because it allows the discussion of fairly complicated motion and because the techniques and the notation are easy and familiar. The development of the differentiation of vectors in terms of varying unit vectors is mentioned in Sections 5.5. and 5.6.

---

## 1. AVERAGE VELOCITY
### *Exercise A (p. 506)*

**1.**  **i**, 1 unit parallel to the $x$-axis.

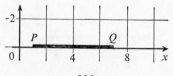

**2.** $7(\mathbf{i}+\mathbf{j})$, 9·90 at 45° to the $x$-axis.

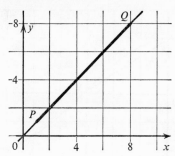

**3.** $\mathbf{j}$, 1 unit at 90° to the $x$-axis.

**4.** $\mathbf{i}-\mathbf{j}$, 1·41 units at 315° to the $x$-axis.

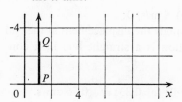

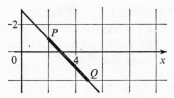

**5.** $\mathbf{i}+5\mathbf{j}$, 5·1 units at 78·7° to the $x$-axis.

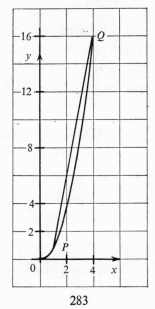

283

**6.** $\mathbf{i} - 2\mathbf{j}/\pi$, 1·19 units at 327·5° to the x-axis.

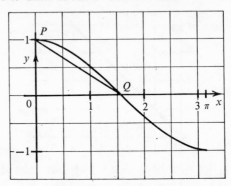

**7.** (*a*) 60 km/h; 45 km/h;     (*b*) 8 m/s, 0;
(*c*) when the distance moved equals the displacement at the end of the interval, i.e., when motion is a straight line in a constant direction.

**8.** (*a*) 3·75; (*b*) 2·3; (*c*) 1·5; (*d*) 1·0; (*e*) 0·83; (*f*) 0·76 cm/s.
These answers apparently tend to about 0·7. The calculated answer when $t = 0$ is 0·693.

**9.** The average velocity in the first:
(*a*) second = 4·24 cm/s;     (*b*) $\frac{1}{2}$ second = 4·59 cm/s;
(*c*) $\frac{1}{4}$ second = 4·68 cm/s;     (*d*) $\frac{1}{8}$ second = 4·70 cm/s.
The actual velocity at $A$ is 4·71 cm/s in the direction of the tangent.

## 2. VELOCITY: $v = dr/dt$

### *Exercise B* (*p. 512*)

**1.** $\mathbf{v} = \mathbf{i}$; $t = 0$, $\mathbf{v} = \mathbf{i}$,    1 unit parallel to x-axis;

$t = 1$, $\mathbf{v} = \mathbf{i}$,    1 unit parallel to x-axis;

$t = 3$, $\mathbf{v} = \mathbf{i}$,    1 unit parallel to x-axis.

**2.** $\mathbf{v} = \mathbf{i} - \mathbf{j}$; $t = 0$, $\mathbf{v} = \mathbf{i} - \mathbf{j}$,   1·41 units at 315°;

$t = 1$, $\mathbf{v} = \mathbf{i} - \mathbf{j}$,   1·41 units at 315°;

$t = 3$, $\mathbf{v} = \mathbf{i} - \mathbf{j}$,   1·41 units at 315°.

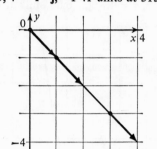

**3.** $\mathbf{v} = \frac{1}{2}\pi \cos \frac{1}{2}\pi t \mathbf{i}$; $t = 0$, $\mathbf{v} = \frac{1}{2}\mathbf{i}$,   1·57 units at 0°,

$t = 1$, $\mathbf{v} = 0$,   0;

$t = 3$, $\mathbf{v} = 0$,   0.

The points oscillate on the $x$-axis from $^-1$ to 1 as $t$ increases.

**4.** $\mathbf{v} = 3t^2(\mathbf{i} + 2\mathbf{j})$;

$t = 0$, $\mathbf{v} = 0$, 0;

$t = 1$, $\mathbf{v} = 3(\mathbf{i} + 2\mathbf{j})$,

     6·71 at 63·4°;

$t = 3$, $\mathbf{v} = 27(\mathbf{i} + 2\mathbf{j})$,

     60·4 at 63·4°.

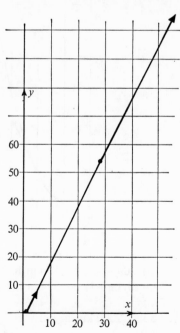

**5.**   $\mathbf{v} = \mathbf{i} + 2t\mathbf{j}$; $t = 0$, $\mathbf{v} = \mathbf{i}$,   1 unit at $0°$;

$t = 1$, $\mathbf{v} = \mathbf{i} + 2\mathbf{j}$,   2·24 units at 63·4°;

$t = 3$, $\mathbf{v} = \mathbf{i} + 6\mathbf{j}$,   6·08 units at 80·5°.

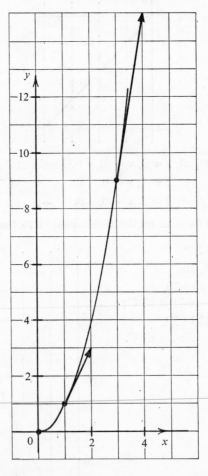

**6.**   (a) 3e, 3 units, due east;

(b) 20n + 30e, $10\sqrt{13}$ km/h, N 56·3° E;

(c) 46·0n + 19·6e, 50 km/h, N 23·1° E.

**7.**   5 km, 2000 km/h, north-east, approximately 167 km.

8. $t = 0$; together with velocities $(4\mathbf{n}+2\mathbf{e})$ and $2\mathbf{n}+1\cdot57\mathbf{e}$ units.
   $t = 4$; $8\sqrt{2}$ units, with velocities $4\mathbf{n}+2\mathbf{e}$ and $2\mathbf{n}+9\cdot57\mathbf{e}$ units.

9. Increasing. $\mathbf{v} = 1000\mathbf{e}-1732\mathbf{n}-32t\mathbf{u}$.

10. (a) $\mathbf{r} = 2t^2\mathbf{e}$, $\mathbf{v} = 4t\mathbf{e}$, (assuming that the acceleration is 4 ft/s²).
    (b) $\mathbf{r} = 920\,(\cos\tfrac{86}{920}t\,\mathbf{e}+\sin\tfrac{86}{920}t\,\mathbf{n})$;
    $\mathbf{v} = 86\,(-\sin\tfrac{86}{920}t\,\mathbf{e}+\cos\tfrac{86}{920}t\,\mathbf{n})$.

## 3. AVERAGE ACCELERATION
### Exercise C (p. 514)

1. (a) $2\mathbf{i}$, $\mathbf{i}$;  (b) 0;  (c) $6\mathbf{j}$, $2\mathbf{j}$;
   (d) $5(\mathbf{i}+2\mathbf{j})$, $5(\mathbf{i}+2\mathbf{j})$.

2. 20·6 m/s at 14·0°, 22·4 m/s at 26·6°; 28·3 m/s at 45°, 102 m/s at 78·7°.

   (Angles measured downward from the horizontal.)

3. 1·92 s.

4. $10^7$ m/s at 36·9° to the original direction.

5. 572 m/s² at 147° to the original direction; this is approximately the direction in which the ball was played.

6. 53 m/s² at 105° to the original direction. Towards the centre.

# 4. ACCELERATION: $a = dv/dt$

## *Exercise D (p. 518)*

(All angles are given anti-clockwise from positive $x$-axis)

**1.**

| | $\dot{x}$ | $\dot{y}$ | Velocity | $\ddot{x}$ | $\ddot{y}$ | Acceleration |
|---|---|---|---|---|---|---|
| $t = 1$ | 8 | 6 | 10 at 36·9° | 0 | $^{-}2$ | |
| 4 | 8 | 0 | 8 at 0° | 0 | $^{-}2$ | 2 units at 270° |
| 7 | 8 | $^{-}6$ | 10 at 323·1° | 0 | $^{-}2$ | |

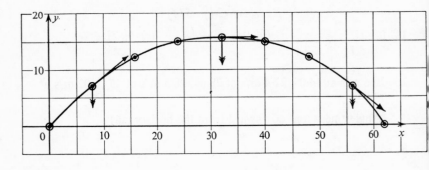

**2.**

| | $\dot{x}$ | $\dot{y}$ | Velocity | $\ddot{x}$ | $\ddot{y}$ | Acceleration |
|---|---|---|---|---|---|---|
| $t = {}^-2$ | $^-4$ | 12 | 12·6 at 108·5° | 2 | $^-12$ | 12·2 units at 279·5° |
| $^-1$ | $^-2$ | 3 | 3·61 at 123·7° | 2 | $^-6$ | 6·32 units at 288·4° |
| 0 | 0 | 0 | 0 | 2 | 0 | 2  units at  0° |
| 1 | 2 | 3 | 3·61 at  56·3° | 2 | 6 | 6·32 units at  71·6° |
| 2 | 4 | 12 | 12·6 at  71·5° | 2 | 12 | 12·2 units at  80·5° |

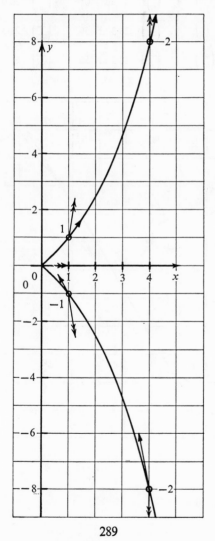

**3.**

| $t$ | $\mathbf{r}$ | $\dot{\mathbf{r}} = \begin{pmatrix} 3t^2 \\ 20t-20 \end{pmatrix}$ | | $\ddot{\mathbf{r}} = \begin{pmatrix} 6t \\ 20 \end{pmatrix}$ | |
|---|---|---|---|---|---|
| 0 | $\begin{pmatrix} 0 \\ 0 \end{pmatrix}$ | $\begin{pmatrix} 0 \\ -20 \end{pmatrix}$ | 20 at 270° | $\begin{pmatrix} 0 \\ 20 \end{pmatrix}$ | 20 at 90° |
| 1 | $\begin{pmatrix} 1 \\ -10 \end{pmatrix}$ | $\begin{pmatrix} 3 \\ 0 \end{pmatrix}$ | 3 at 0° | $\begin{pmatrix} 6 \\ 20 \end{pmatrix}$ | 20·9 at 73·3° |
| 2 | $\begin{pmatrix} 8 \\ 0 \end{pmatrix}$ | $\begin{pmatrix} 12 \\ 20 \end{pmatrix}$ | 23·3 at 59° | $\begin{pmatrix} 12 \\ 20 \end{pmatrix}$ | 23·3 at 59° |
| 3 | $\begin{pmatrix} 27 \\ 30 \end{pmatrix}$ | $\begin{pmatrix} 27 \\ 40 \end{pmatrix}$ | 48·3 at 56° | $\begin{pmatrix} 18 \\ 20 \end{pmatrix}$ | 26·9 at 48° |

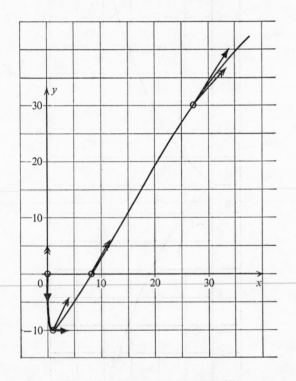

**4.**

| $t$ | $\begin{pmatrix} t^2 \\ \sin t \end{pmatrix}$ | $\begin{pmatrix} 2t \\ \cos t \end{pmatrix}$ | | $\begin{pmatrix} 2 \\ -\sin t \end{pmatrix}$ | |
|---|---|---|---|---|---|
| $0$ | $\begin{pmatrix} 0 \\ 0 \end{pmatrix}$ | $\begin{pmatrix} 0 \\ 1 \end{pmatrix}$ | 1 at 90° | $\begin{pmatrix} 2 \\ 0 \end{pmatrix}$ | 2 at 0° |
| $\tfrac{1}{2}\pi$ | $\begin{pmatrix} \tfrac{1}{4}\pi^2 \\ 1 \end{pmatrix}$ | $\begin{pmatrix} \pi \\ 0 \end{pmatrix}$ | 3·14 at 0° | $\begin{pmatrix} 2 \\ -1 \end{pmatrix}$ | 2·24 at 333·4° |
| $\pi$ | $\begin{pmatrix} \pi^2 \\ 0 \end{pmatrix}$ | $\begin{pmatrix} 2\pi \\ -1 \end{pmatrix}$ | 6·36 at 351° | $\begin{pmatrix} 2 \\ 0 \end{pmatrix}$ | 2 at 0° |
| $\tfrac{3}{2}\pi$ | $\begin{pmatrix} \tfrac{9}{4}\pi^2 \\ -1 \end{pmatrix}$ | $\begin{pmatrix} 3\pi \\ 0 \end{pmatrix}$ | 9·43 at 0° | $\begin{pmatrix} 2 \\ 1 \end{pmatrix}$ | 2·24 at 26·6° |
| $2\pi$ | $\begin{pmatrix} 4\pi^2 \\ 0 \end{pmatrix}$ | $\begin{pmatrix} 4\pi \\ 1 \end{pmatrix}$ | 12·6 at 4·5° | $\begin{pmatrix} 2 \\ 0 \end{pmatrix}$ | 2 at 0° |

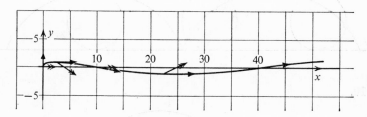

Gradient at $t = 2\pi$ is $1/4\pi = 0{\cdot}0796$.

Approximate solutions of $\tan t = -1/t$ are $n\pi$ where $n$ is a positive integer.

**5.** $y = \sin \sqrt{x}$.

**6.** 1 unit at $\tfrac{1}{2}\pi + t$, 1 unit at $\pi + t$ with the $x$-axis.

The velocity and acceleration have the same magnitude and are perpendicular to each other, with the acceleration at $+\tfrac{1}{2}\pi$ with the velocity. A circle centre $(0, 1)$ radius 1.

**7.** $\dot{x} = -\omega \sin \omega t$. The distance from the origin is 1 unit for all $t$. $\dot{y} = \omega \cos \omega t$. The magnitude of the velocity is $\omega$ which is constant.

Velocity $= \omega$ with direction $\tfrac{1}{2}\pi + \omega t$ with $x$-axis.

Acceleration is $\omega^2$ with direction $\pi + \omega t$ with $x$-axis. The acceleration is at $+\tfrac{1}{2}\pi$ with direction of velocity and is towards the centre of the circle.

**8.** The distance from the origin is constant, the direction of the velocity is at $\frac{1}{2}\pi$ to the radius vector. It moves in a circle but with increasing speed.

$$\ddot{\mathbf{r}} = \ddot{x}\mathbf{i} + \ddot{y}\mathbf{j} = (-2\sin t^2 - 4t^2\cos t^2)\mathbf{i} + (2\cos t^2 - 4t^2\sin t^2)\mathbf{j}$$
$$= 2(-\sin t^2\,\mathbf{i} + \cos t^2\,\mathbf{j}) + 4t^2(-\cos t^2\,\mathbf{i} - \sin t^2\,\mathbf{j})$$

which gives the answer.

**9.** $\dot{\mathbf{r}} = (1-\cos t)\mathbf{i} + \sin t\,\mathbf{j}$   and   $\ddot{\mathbf{r}} = \sin t\,\mathbf{i} + \cos t\,\mathbf{j}.$

The curve is called a cycloid.

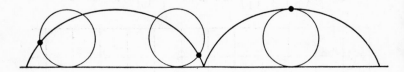

**10.**

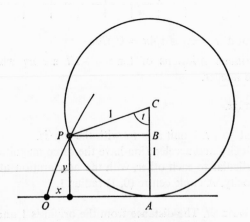

$OA = \text{arc } AP = t.$   $x = OA - PB = t - \sin t.$
$y = CA - CB = 1 - \cos t.$

**11.** $\ddot{\mathbf{r}} = -\sin t\,\mathbf{i} + (-2\sin t - t\cos t)\mathbf{j}$.

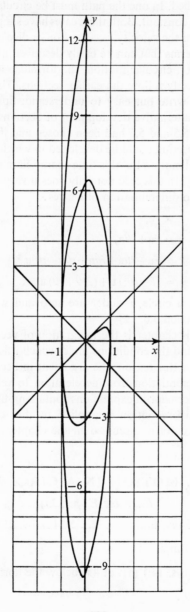

293

**Sections 5 and 6:** These sections consider two cases in which some limitation is specified. In one the path must be circular; in the other, the acceleration is constant. Both these cases have simple applications, and expressions for the velocity, acceleration or displacement need to be developed in terms that can be easily described and measured.

In the section on circular motion, the formulae are found using methods that directly follow the earlier sections. This proves to be rather clumsy to write but easy to understand. Some people may prefer to use the alternative development of Sections 5.5. and 5.6.

If the Sections 5.5 and 5.6 had been chosen and if there was time enough, another section could be developed in which there would be a return to general motion but this time expressed in terms of **u** and **n** rather than **i** and **j**. In this case not only does **u** vary but so does the magnitude of $r$, so differentiation of **r** gives:

$$\mathbf{r} = r\mathbf{u},$$
$$\dot{\mathbf{r}} = \dot{r}\mathbf{u} + r\dot{\theta}\mathbf{n},$$
$$\ddot{\mathbf{r}} = \ddot{r}\mathbf{u} + \dot{r}\dot{\theta}\mathbf{n} + \dot{r}\dot{\theta}\mathbf{n} + r\ddot{\theta}\mathbf{n} - r\dot{\theta}^2\mathbf{u}$$
$$= (\ddot{r} - r\dot{\theta}^2)\,\mathbf{u} + (2\dot{r}\dot{\theta} + r\ddot{\theta})\,\mathbf{n}.$$

For motion in a circle, $\dot{r}$ and $\ddot{r}$ are zero and we return to the expressions of Section 5.6.

Nowhere in this chapter is the integration of vectors mentioned. It is not defined and the conditions under which it is meaningful are not described. For this reason, the argument in Section 6 takes the form of anti-differentiation from acceleration to velocity and from velocity to displacement in expressions containing fixed vectors and where the anti-differentiation is applied to the scalar quantities. Integration of vectors is discussed in the chapters on Energy and Momentum.

# 5. MOTION IN A CIRCLE
## *Exercise E (p. 523)*

**1.** 10 rad/s, 95·5 rev/min.     **2.** 5·24 rad/s, 21 m/s.

**3.** 27·3 m/s, 22·7 m/s.

**4.** 20 rad/s, 20 m/s, 14·1 m/s at 45° below the horizontal.

**5.** 16·5 m/s, 36·9°.

**6.** $\omega^2 D^3$ is constant, $v^2 D$ is constant, $\omega/v^3$ is constant.

**7.** Consider lines $A'B'$ and $P'Q'$. If $\phi = \theta - \alpha + \beta$, then

$$\dot{\phi} = \frac{d}{dt}(\theta - \alpha + \beta) = \dot{\theta}.$$

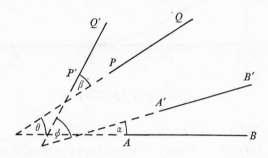

**8.**

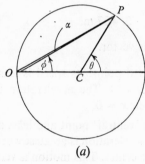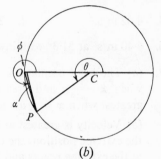

In (a): $\phi = \frac{1}{2}\theta + \alpha,$
$\dot{\phi} = \frac{1}{2}\dot{\theta} + \dot{\alpha}.$

In (b): $\phi = \pi + \frac{1}{2}\theta - \alpha,$
$\dot{\phi} = \frac{1}{2}\dot{\theta} - \dot{\alpha}.$

Where $\dot{\alpha}$ is small the angular velocity of $OP = \frac{1}{2}\dot{\theta}$.

**9.** If $\dot{y}$ is the steady upward speed of one end and $\theta$ is the angle with the horizontal, then $\dot{\theta} = \dot{y}/(l\cos\theta)$.

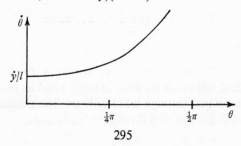

295

**10.** $v = h \sec^2 \theta . \dot{\theta}$.

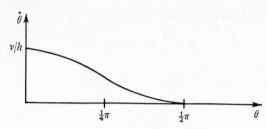

*Exercise F* (*p. 526*)

**2.**

| $t$ | Radial | Tangential | Total |
|---|---|---|---|
| 2 | 864 m/s² | 72 m/s² | 867 m/s² at 4·8° with radius vector |
| 3 | 4370 m/s² | 108 m/s² | 4370 m/s² at 1·4° with radius vector |

**3.** 4·02 m/s.²  **4.** 22·2 m/s².  **5.** 37 m.

**6.** 6·40 m/s² at 51·3° with inward radius vector.

**7.** (*a*) The bead oscillates about the fixed point: its speed is least when $x = \pm a$ and greatest when $x = 0$. The acceleration is greatest when $x = \pm a$ and least when $x = 0$.

(*b*) Velocity is greatest at the lowest 'central' point and least at the extreme position: the tangential acceleration is greatest when at the extreme points and least at the centre. This motion is very similar to that in (*a*).

**8.** 4:9.

**9.** 108 m/s², 144 m/s², 5·65 m/s in both cases.

**10.** 0·034 m/s², 0·017 m/s².

**11.** 35·5 m/s² at 17·4° with inward radius vector.

**12.** $\omega^2 L \sin \alpha$.

**13.** 13·8 m. No. The motion will be tangential to the circle on which it moved. It will reach the floor in 0·568 s and its position vector will have rotated through 0·517 radians. The position vector of the feet will have moved through 0·568 radians.

## 6. CONSTANT ACCELERATION
### Exercise G (p. 530)

**1.** $\mathbf{OM} = \begin{pmatrix} 5 \cdot 5 \\ 0 \end{pmatrix}$ and is the velocity halfway through the time interval. The displacement vector is 6**OM**. **OM** is velocity after 3 s and the acceleration is $\frac{1}{3}$**AM**. They are $\begin{pmatrix} 5 \cdot 5 \\ 0 \end{pmatrix}$ cm/s and $\begin{pmatrix} \frac{1}{2} \\ -1 \end{pmatrix}$ cm/s².

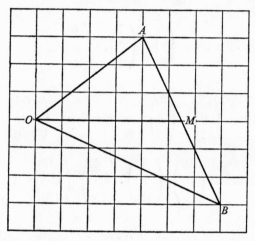

**2.** $\begin{pmatrix} 20 \\ 22 \end{pmatrix}$ m/s, $\begin{pmatrix} 33 \\ 39 \end{pmatrix}$ m.

**3.** 25 m/s, 208 m. Distance travelled can be found as area under the graph *after* the velocity units have been changed.

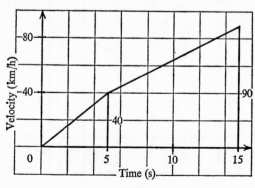

297

**4.** $\begin{pmatrix} 1 \cdot 16 \\ -7 \cdot 99 \end{pmatrix}$ m/s, 8·08 m/s at 151·7°.

**5.** $7 \cdot 81 \times 10^6$ m/s, 26·3°, 3·124 cm.

**6.** Displacements: $\begin{pmatrix} 0 \\ 6 \\ 18 \end{pmatrix}$, $\begin{pmatrix} 8 \\ 8 \\ 48 \end{pmatrix}$, $\begin{pmatrix} 48 \\ 0 \\ 144 \end{pmatrix}$.

Average velocities: $\begin{pmatrix} 0 \\ 3 \\ 9 \end{pmatrix}$, $\begin{pmatrix} 2 \\ 2 \\ 12 \end{pmatrix}$, $\begin{pmatrix} 6 \\ 0 \\ 18 \end{pmatrix}$.

**8.** Velocities: $\begin{pmatrix} 12 \\ 0 \\ 15 \end{pmatrix}$, $\begin{pmatrix} 0 \\ 6 \\ 15 \end{pmatrix}$; acceleration: $\begin{pmatrix} -0 \cdot 3 \\ 0 \cdot 15 \\ 0 \end{pmatrix}$,

displacements: $\begin{pmatrix} 105 \\ 7 \cdot 5 \\ 150 \end{pmatrix}$, $\begin{pmatrix} 75 \\ 22 \cdot 5 \\ 150 \end{pmatrix}$, $\begin{pmatrix} 45 \\ 37 \cdot 5 \\ 150 \end{pmatrix}$, $\begin{pmatrix} 15 \\ 52 \cdot 5 \\ 150 \end{pmatrix}$; total: $\begin{pmatrix} 240 \\ 120 \\ 600 \end{pmatrix}$.

**9.** (*a*) Gradient of *AB*, area of *OABC*. 16 units, 55 units.

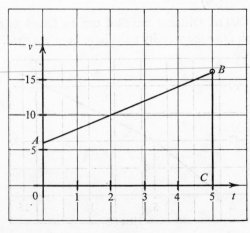

(*b*) Area of $OAC = 9$, area of $CDB = 4$. Distance travelled is the sum of these areas $= 13$ units. Displacement is the difference, 5 units.

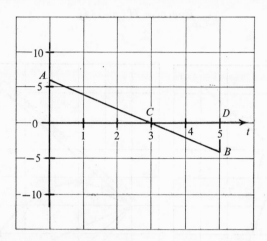

The formula gives the area of a trapezium.

In (*a*) a direct trapezium; in (*b*) a crossed-over trapezium.

10. $\frac{4}{9}$ min. Distances travelled. $\frac{1}{4}$ km $= 250$ m.

11. $-6$ cm/s; $18$ cm   $-18$ cm/s;   $-30$ cm.   4 s; 24 cm.
  4·90 cm/s; 22·4 cm/s.

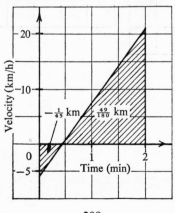

# 7. MOTION UNDER GRAVITY—
## PROJECTILES
### *Exercise H (p. 534)*

**1.**                              **2.**

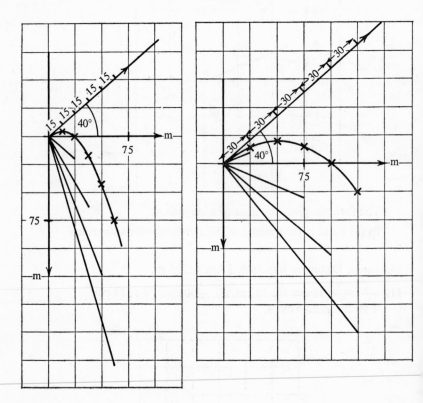

300

**3.**

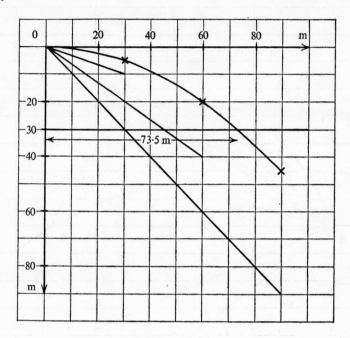

73·5 m from the base of the cliff.

**4.**

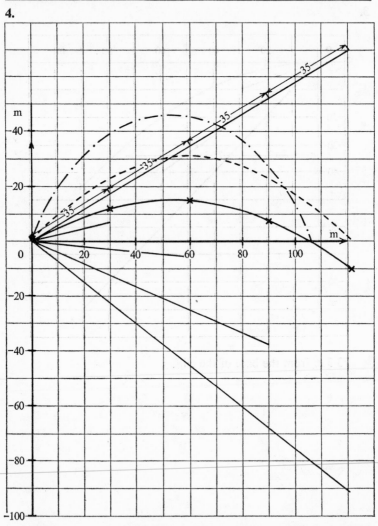

Horizontal range is 106 m when at both 30° and 60° to the horizontal; it is 122 m when at 45° to the horizontal. An elevation of 45° gives the maximum range.

**5.** 1·83 s, 16·7 m.

**6.** 8·07 m/s at 51·8° downward from the horizontal. 1·73 s, 5 m/s.

**7.** 45°.

### *Exercise I (p. 537)*

1.  2·86 s, 57 m.

    24·4 m/s at 55° to downward vertical.

    10 m above the boy.

2.  4·3 s, 90 m. 47 m/s at 63·4° to the horizontal.

3.  5·62 km.

4.  (*a*)  ±9·9 m/s;          (*b*)  7 m/s;

    (*c*)  12·1 m/s at 54·7° to the horizontal;

    9·9 m/s at 45° to the horizontal.

5.  25·9 m/s at 62·4° to the horizontal; 30·6 m.

6.  13·6 cm.          7.  104 m

8.  $y = x \tan \alpha - (gx^2/2u^2)(1 + \tan^2 \alpha)$. 45° and 63·4°.

9.  4·8 m, $\frac{2}{3}$, 14·3 m.          10. A sphere of radius $Vt$ m.

## 8. INSTANTANEOUS CENTRE OF ROTATION

This chapter has been about the motion of particles. But in the examples, we have considered the movements of objects, always assuming that they would behave like particles.

When a body moves round a point as a car does in cornering, it also moves round its own centre. This sort of movement has been mentioned only in Sections 5 and 5.2 and now in this section. We shall not develop the mathematics, but use the ideas as further opportunity for discussion and drawing in connection with angular velocity.

### *Exercise J (p. 539)*

1.  (i)  0·8 m/s down the wall;

    (ii)  0·85 m/s at 28° below the horizontal;

    1·88 m from the top.

3.  The ratio of the angular velocities of the wheels should be equal to the ratio of the radii of the circles on which the wheels are moving.

**4.**

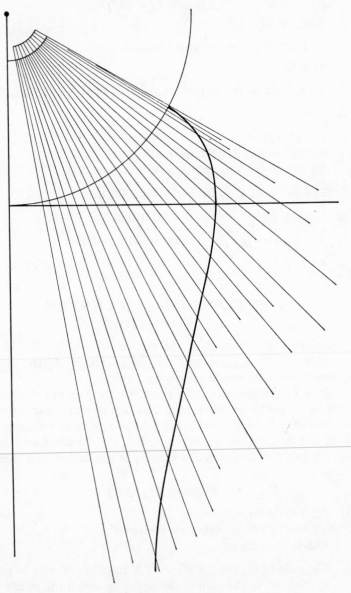

**5.** The circle $C$ remains in contact with $A$.

# REVISION EXERCISES

## 16. LOCAL APPROXIMATION (p. 541)

**1.** $\frac{1}{16} - \frac{1}{32}\alpha + \frac{3}{256}\alpha^2$.  Error $= \dfrac{16\alpha^3 + 3\alpha^4}{256(4+\alpha)^2}$.

**2.** The cosine rule applied to triangle $ABS$ gives the required equation.

When $x = 5$, $\cos\theta = \frac{3}{5}$, $\sin\theta = \frac{4}{5}$. If a small change $\alpha$ in $\theta$ then causes $x$ to increase by $h$, $4h + 15\alpha \simeq 0$, i.e.

$$4(x-5) + 15(\theta - \tan^{-1}\tfrac{4}{3}) \simeq 0 \quad \text{when} \quad x = 5.$$

$K$ moves $0.16$ in. in this position to raise $S$ by $0.1$ in.

**3.** $1.94$.

**4.** The quadratic approximation is $\pi(1 - \alpha + \alpha^2)$.

**5.** $\tan x \simeq x + \frac{1}{3}x^3 + \frac{2}{15}x^5$.

**6.** (a) $d^3y/dx^3 = -2x^2 - 2y + 8xy^2 - 6y^4$;

(b) $y = 1 + 2h - \frac{3}{2}h^2 - \frac{1}{3}h^3$.

## 17. TECHNIQUES OF DIFFERENTIATION (p. 541)

**1.** (a) $10(2x+1)^4$;     (b) $-2\cos x \sin x = -\sin 2x$;

(c) $-2\sin(2x-\pi) = 2\sin 2x$;   (d) $\frac{1}{2}(3+x)^{-\frac{1}{2}}$;

(e) $1 - \dfrac{5}{x^2}$;     (f) $x^2\cos x + 2x\sin x$.

**2.** (a) $-2$;     (b) $(8, 20)$ and $(\frac{1}{64}, \frac{17}{256})$.

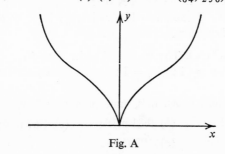

Fig. A

**3.** (a) $T^2 \propto h + (k^2/h)$. $T^2$ is a minimum when $h = k$.

(b) $W$ is a maximum when $R = 12$.

**5.** $f'(a) = \dfrac{c}{a}$ where $c = \lim\limits_{K \to 1} \left(\dfrac{\log K}{K-1}\right)$.

The method suggested gives $c = 0.424$. The correct value is $\log_{10} e = 0.4343$.

The derivative of $g$ at $\log_{10} a$ is $a/c$, so the derivative at $b$ is $10^b/c$. This means $g'(x) = 10^x/c$.

**6.** 2.

## 18. UNITS AND DIMENSIONS (p. 542)

**1.** (a) $\dfrac{h}{h_0} = 100 + 10\left(\dfrac{t}{t_0}\right) - 5\left(\dfrac{t}{t_0}\right);\quad h_0 = 1\text{ m}, t_0 = 1\text{ s}.$

(b) $4500\left(\dfrac{v}{v_0}\right) = \left(\dfrac{t}{t_0}\right)^2\left(90 - \dfrac{t}{t_0}\right).$

If $t_0 = 1$ minute, and $v_0 = 1$ km/h, this means 90 minutes elapse before the train reaches the next station, and the maximum speed is 24 km/h. This might suit a slow freight. $t_0 = 1$ second, $v_0 = 1$ m/s would make sense for a suburban train.

(c) $\dfrac{\theta}{\theta_0} = \dfrac{10\pi}{9}\left(\dfrac{t}{t_0}\right) - \dfrac{1}{18}\left(\dfrac{t}{t_0}\right);$ the turntable stops when $t = 10\pi t_0$ and $\theta = (100\pi^2/18)\,\theta_0$. $t_0$ and $\theta_0$ must be chosen to make these quantities realistic.

An angle is dimensionless, and should be thought of as a ratio; $\theta_0$ is then unnecessary. However, we are used to regarding angles as measures and using degrees or radians as units. Strictly, a statement like 1 radian = $180/\pi$ degrees is comparable with 1 whole = 4 quarters.

(d) $v/v_0 = 2\sqrt{(s/s_0)}$. The choice of units is arbitrary: $s_0 = 1$ ft, $v_0 = 1$ ft/s or $s_0 = 1$ m, $v_0 = 1$ m/s are equally sensible.

**2.** Unit of velocity $= \lambda/\tau$ m/s, unit of acceleration $= \lambda/\tau^2$ m/s$^2$.

(a) $0.0232$ m/s$^2$;    (b) $9.81$ m/s$^2$;    (c) $1.67$ m/s;

(d) $3 \times 10^8$ m/s;    (e) $1020$ m/s.

3. (a) $T^{-1}$;      (b) $MLT^{-2}$;      (c) $ML^2T^{-2}$;

    (d) $ML^2T^{-2}$;      (e) $MT^{-2}$;      (f) $ML^2T^{-2}$;

    (g) $MLT^{-1}$;      (h) $M^{-1}L^3T^{-2}$;      (i) $ML^2$;

    (j) $ML^{-1}T^{-1}$;      (k) $ML^2T^{-2}$;      (l) $T^{-1}$.

4. (a) $6\pi\eta rv = \frac{4}{3}\pi r^3\rho'g$;      (b) $v = R\sqrt{(\frac{8}{3}G\rho)}$;

    (c) this equation is already dimensionally consistent;

    (d) $t = \dfrac{1}{n}\sqrt{\left(\dfrac{Ib^2}{mr^4}\right)}$, where $m$ is a mass.

5. $p = 0$, $q = \frac{1}{2}$, $r = -\frac{1}{2}$, $s$ is indeterminate.

    $gt^2/a$ is dimensionless.

6. $\dfrac{\rho VD}{\eta}$, $\dfrac{V^2D^2\rho}{F}$, $\dfrac{VD\eta}{F}$, $\dfrac{F\rho}{\eta^2}$ are all dimensionless variables; so is any combination of these.

## 19. KINEMATICS (p. 544)

1. $t = \frac{2}{3}$.

2. $\omega = \frac{5}{6}$ radian/s. Acceleration $= 20\cdot8$ m/s$^2$.

3. (a) $\sqrt{370}$ at $\tan^{-1}(\frac{17}{9})$ to $Ox$;      (b) $\mathbf{a} = \begin{pmatrix} 12 \\ -6 \end{pmatrix}$;

    (c) $\mathbf{v}.\mathbf{a} = 6$, so the speed in increasing.

4. $v = n$. The path is a circle of unit radius, centre the origin.

5. $26\cdot6°$ or $69\cdot1°$.

6. (a) $\begin{pmatrix} 12 \\ 7\cdot5 \end{pmatrix}$ and $\begin{pmatrix} 10\cdot5 \\ -3\cdot8 \end{pmatrix}$:

    (b) The average acceleration berween

$$t = 1 \quad \text{and} \quad t = 2 \quad \text{is} \quad \begin{pmatrix} -1\cdot5 \\ -11\cdot3 \end{pmatrix};$$

    (c) $\begin{pmatrix} -1\cdot8 \\ -7\cdot5 \end{pmatrix}$;

    (d) From the theoretical equation,

$$v = \begin{pmatrix} 14 \\ 9\cdot8 \end{pmatrix} \quad \text{when} \quad t = 1 \quad \text{and} \quad \begin{pmatrix} 14 \\ 0 \end{pmatrix} \quad \text{when} \quad t = 2.$$

Average acceleration in the 2nd second $= \begin{pmatrix} 0 \\ -32 \end{pmatrix}$; this is also the acceleration at the instant when $t = 2$. There appears to be some air resistance.

**7.** (*a*) The velocity is parallel

to **i** when $t = 2n\pi + \pi$,

to **i** + **j** when $t = 2n\pi + \frac{1}{2}\pi$,

to **i** − **j** when $t = 2n\pi + \frac{3}{2}\pi$.

When $t = 2n\pi$, the velocity is zero, but for $t$ near $2n\pi$ the small velocity is nearly parallel to **j**.

(*b*) The corresponding accelerations are

$$\begin{pmatrix} 0 \\ 1 \end{pmatrix}, \quad \begin{pmatrix} 0 \\ -1 \end{pmatrix}, \quad \begin{pmatrix} 1 \\ 0 \end{pmatrix} \quad \text{and} \quad \begin{pmatrix} -1 \\ 0 \end{pmatrix}.$$

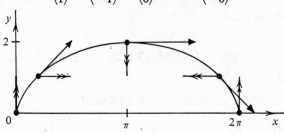

Fig. B

# 20

# PROBABILITY

## 1. BASIC IDEAS

Although pupils will have met elementary ideas of probability in the main school course, they should by this stage be ready to discuss the subject in greater depth and to consider some of the special difficulties which it poses in the matter of fundamental definitions. For this reason the chapter does not resume where the previous course left off, but begins afresh with a careful discussion from an *a priori* standpoint. One could arrive at correct answers to many of the exercises intuitively, but time spent in putting the solutions on a sound basis will be well worth while in the long run.

The pivot of the chapter is the establishment of the 'probability laws' in Sections 3.3 and 4.2. The use of the word 'law', rather than 'theorem' or 'axiom', is deliberate. Up to the point where these laws are stated the work is based firmly on an *a priori* definition of probability, and the laws summarize relationships derived from this; in this context they are in fact theorems. Once stated, however, they afford a means of discussing probabilities of events directly without reference to a space of equally likely possibilities; and they may therefore be regarded as axioms in a more general theory of probability with far broader application.

## Exercise A (p. 550)

For diagrams see Figure A.

|  | Possibility space | Equally likely? |
|---|---|---|
| **1.** | {0, 1} | Yes |
| **2.** | {0, 1, 2} | No |
| **3.** | {0, 1, 2, 3} | No |
| **4.** | {1, 2, 3, 4, 5, 6} | Yes |
| **5.** | {2, 3, 4, 5, 6, 7, 8, 9, 10, 11, 12} | No |
| **6.** | {r, g, b} | No |
| **7.** | {all cards except ◇ A} | Yes |
| **8.** | {♣, ◇, ♡, ♠} | No |
| **9.** | {2, 3, 4, ..., 10, J, Q, K} | Yes |
| **10.** | {1, 2, 3, ..., 51, 52} | Yes |
| **11.** | {1, 2, 3, ..., 48, 49} | No |
| **12.** | {1, 2, 3, ...} | No |

*Notes.* The difference between the situations in Questions 10 and 11 may be seen as follows. Suppose that the cards are drawn from the pack and placed face downwards in a line in order of drawing in the first instance; and that they are then turned face upwards, starting with the card first drawn. The effect of this is essentially the same as the experiment described. When the cards are in line the ♡ K is equally likely to be in any of the 52 places; but it is far less likely that the four kings will be in the 49th, 50th, 51st and 52nd places than that (say) the first will be in the tenth place and the rest deployed somewhere between the 11th and 52nd places. Thus in Question 10 all the possibilities are equally likely *a priori*, but in Question 11 the smaller numbers are more likely than the larger ones.

In Question 12 the possibility space is infinite, since there is no restriction on the number of tails that *may* appear in succession before the first head appears.

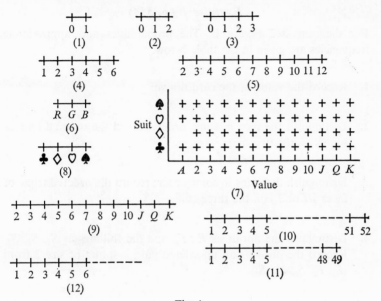

Fig. A

311

## 2. PROBABILITY OF AN EVENT
### *Exercise B* (*p. 554*)

For diagrams see Figure B. The probabilities and approximate frequencies are given in the table below.

1.  Record the value of the card drawn.

2.  Distinguish the dice in some order; record the ordered pair of scores on the two dice.

3.  Distinguish the coins in some order; record the ordered triple of faces (*H* or *T*) on the three coins.

4.  Distinguish the florins as $F_1$, $F_2$, and the shillings as $S_1$, $S_2$, $S_3$. Record the draw as an unordered pair, a subset of size 2 from $\{F_1, F_2, S_1, S_2, S_3\}$.

5.  Record an unordered pair of card-names, such as $\{\heartsuit A, \clubsuit 2\}$; there are $\frac{1}{2}.52.51$ of these, of which $\frac{1}{2}.13.12$ are pairs of clubs.

6.  Suppose that the tickets are numbered 1–100, and that I hold the five tickets 1–5. Record an unordered pair of numbers, the numbers of the two lucky tickets. If either (or both) of these is 1, 2, 3, 4 or 5, then I win a prize. There are $\frac{1}{2}.99.100$ unordered pairs, of which $99+98+97+96+95 = 5.97$ bring me in a prize.

|    | Probability | Approximate frequency |
|----|-------------|-----------------------|
| 1. | 3/13        | 230                   |
| 2. | 11/36       | 305                   |
| 3. | 3/8         | 375                   |
| 4. | 3/10        | 300                   |
| 5. | 1/17        | 60                    |
| 6. | 97/990      | 100                   |

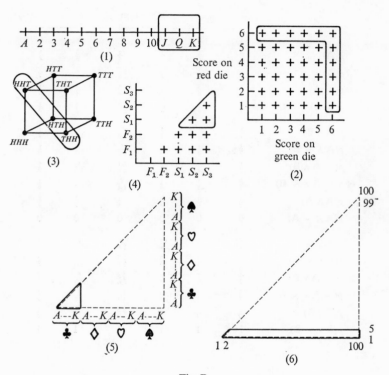

Fig. B

313

## 3. COMPOUND EVENTS

### *Exercise C (p. 556)*

For diagrams see Figure C.

| | Question 1 | 2 | 3 | 4 | 5 | 6 |
|---|---|---|---|---|---|---|
| $p(\mathbf{A})$ | $\frac{4}{7}$ | $\frac{1}{6}$ | $\frac{1}{2}$ | $\frac{1}{4}$ | $\frac{3}{5}$ | $\frac{1}{2}$ |
| $p(\mathbf{B})$ | $\frac{2}{7}$ | $\frac{1}{4}$ | $\frac{1}{2}$ | $\frac{13}{28}$ | $\frac{2}{5}$ | $\frac{2}{3}$ |
| $p(\sim \mathbf{A})$ | $\frac{3}{7}$ | $\frac{5}{6}$ | $\frac{1}{2}$ | $\frac{3}{4}$ | $\frac{2}{5}$ | $\frac{1}{2}$ |
| $p(\sim \mathbf{B})$ | $\frac{5}{7}$ | $\frac{3}{4}$ | $\frac{1}{2}$ | $\frac{15}{28}$ | $\frac{3}{5}$ | $\frac{1}{3}$ |
| $p(\mathbf{A} \wedge \mathbf{B})$ | $\frac{1}{7}$ | $\frac{1}{24}$ | $\frac{1}{4}$ | $\frac{1}{14}$ | $\frac{3}{10}$ | $\frac{1}{3}$ |
| $p(\mathbf{A} \wedge \sim \mathbf{B})$ | $\frac{3}{7}$ | $\frac{1}{8}$ | $\frac{1}{4}$ | $\frac{5}{28}$ | $\frac{3}{10}$ | $\frac{1}{6}$ |
| $p(\sim \mathbf{A} \wedge \mathbf{B})$ | $\frac{1}{7}$ | $\frac{5}{24}$ | $\frac{1}{4}$ | $\frac{11}{28}$ | $\frac{1}{10}$ | $\frac{1}{3}$ |
| $p(\sim \mathbf{A} \wedge \sim \mathbf{B})$ | $\frac{2}{7}$ | $\frac{5}{8}$ | $\frac{1}{4}$ | $\frac{5}{14}$ | $\frac{3}{10}$ | $\frac{1}{6}$ |
| $p(\mathbf{A} \wedge \mathbf{A})$ | $\frac{4}{7}$ | $\frac{1}{6}$ | $\frac{1}{2}$ | $\frac{1}{4}$ | $\frac{3}{5}$ | $\frac{1}{2}$ |
| $p(\mathbf{A} \wedge \sim \mathbf{A})$ | $0$ | $0$ | $0$ | $0$ | $0$ | $0$ |
| $p(\mathbf{A} \vee \mathbf{B})$ | $\frac{5}{7}$ | $\frac{3}{8}$ | $\frac{3}{4}$ | $\frac{9}{14}$ | $\frac{7}{10}$ | $\frac{5}{6}$ |
| $p(\mathbf{A} \vee \sim \mathbf{B})$ | $\frac{6}{7}$ | $\frac{19}{24}$ | $\frac{3}{4}$ | $\frac{17}{28}$ | $\frac{9}{10}$ | $\frac{2}{3}$ |
| $p(\sim \mathbf{A} \vee \mathbf{B})$ | $\frac{4}{7}$ | $\frac{7}{8}$ | $\frac{3}{4}$ | $\frac{23}{28}$ | $\frac{7}{10}$ | $\frac{5}{6}$ |
| $p(\sim \mathbf{A} \vee \sim \mathbf{B})$ | $\frac{6}{7}$ | $\frac{23}{24}$ | $\frac{3}{4}$ | $\frac{13}{14}$ | $\frac{7}{10}$ | $\frac{2}{3}$ |
| $p(\mathbf{B} \vee \mathbf{B})$ | $\frac{2}{7}$ | $\frac{1}{4}$ | $\frac{1}{2}$ | $\frac{13}{28}$ | $\frac{2}{5}$ | $\frac{2}{3}$ |
| $p(\mathbf{B} \vee \sim \mathbf{B})$ | $1$ | $1$ | $1$ | $1$ | $1$ | $1$ |

314

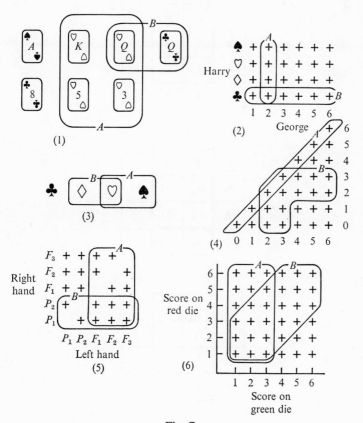

Fig. C

315

## *Exercise D* (*p. 559*)

For diagrams for Questions 1–4, see Figure D.

**1.**

|       | B              | ~B             |               |
|-------|----------------|----------------|---------------|
| **A** | $\frac{1}{6}$  | $\frac{1}{6}$  | $\frac{1}{3}$ |
| **~A**| $\frac{1}{12}$ | $\frac{7}{12}$ | $\frac{2}{3}$ |
|       | $\frac{1}{4}$  | $\frac{3}{4}$  | 1             |

**2.**

|       | B    | ~B   |      |
|-------|------|------|------|
| **A** | 0·2  | 0·3  | 0·5  |
| **~A**| 0·4  | 0·1  | 0·5  |
|       | 0·6  | 0·4  | 1    |

**3.**

|       | B               | ~B             |               |
|-------|-----------------|----------------|---------------|
| **A** | $\frac{2}{15}$  | $\frac{1}{5}$  | $\frac{1}{3}$ |
| **~A**| $\frac{4}{15}$  | $\frac{2}{5}$  | $\frac{2}{3}$ |
|       | $\frac{2}{5}$   | $\frac{3}{5}$  | 1             |

**4.**

|       | B    | ~B   |      |
|-------|------|------|------|
| **A** | 0·2  | 0·4  | 0·6  |
| **~A**| 0·3  | 0·1  | 0·4  |
|       | 0·5  | 0·5  | 1    |

316

5.  Law 1:   $p(\mathbf{B}) + p(\sim \mathbf{B}) = 1$,   so $p(\sim \mathbf{B}) = 1 - b$.

Law 2: $p(\mathbf{A} \wedge \mathbf{B}) + p(\mathbf{A} \wedge \sim \mathbf{B}) = p(\mathbf{A})$, so $p(\mathbf{A} \wedge \sim \mathbf{B}) = a - c$.

Law 2: $p(\mathbf{A} \wedge \sim \mathbf{B}) + p(\sim \mathbf{A} \wedge \sim \mathbf{B}) = p(\sim \mathbf{B})$, so
$$p(\sim \mathbf{A} \wedge \sim \mathbf{B}) = 1 - b - a + c.$$

de Morgan: $p(\sim \mathbf{A} \wedge \sim \mathbf{B}) = p(\sim (\mathbf{A} \vee \mathbf{B}))$, so
$$p(\sim (\mathbf{A} \vee \mathbf{B})) = 1 - b - a + c.$$

Law 1: $p(\mathbf{A} \vee \mathbf{B}) + p(\sim (\mathbf{A} \vee \mathbf{B})) = 1$, so
$$p(\mathbf{A} \vee \mathbf{B}) = a + b - c.$$

This proves that Law 3 is not independent of Laws 1 and 2, but can be deduced from them using the Boolean algebra of events.

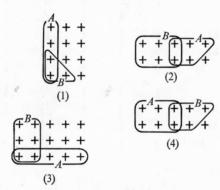

Fig. D

6.  $p(\mathbf{A} \wedge \sim \mathbf{B}) \geqslant 0$, so $a \geqslant c$. Also all probabilities are between 0 and 1, so $0 \leqslant c \leqslant a \leqslant 1$.

Similarly $p(\sim \mathbf{A} \wedge \mathbf{B}) \geqslant 0$, which gives $0 \leqslant c \leqslant b \leqslant 1$.

$p(\sim \mathbf{A} \wedge \sim \mathbf{B}) \geqslant 0$, so $a + b \leqslant 1 + c$.

The special cases are:

(a) $p(\mathbf{A} \wedge \sim \mathbf{B}) = 0$;

(b) $p(\sim \mathbf{A} \wedge \sim \mathbf{B}) = 0$,   or   $p(\mathbf{A} \vee \mathbf{B}) = 1$;

(c) $p(\mathbf{A}) = 1$.

With a *finite* possibility space, one could deduce

(a) $\mathbf{A} \Rightarrow \mathbf{B}$;

(b) either $\mathbf{A}$ or $\mathbf{B}$ must occur;

(c) $\mathbf{A}$ is certain.

317

But if there is an infinite space of equally likely possibilities, then the probability of an event can be zero without the event being impossible. For example, the probability of selecting any particular specified point on this page is zero, but it is not impossible that the point should be picked.

## 4. CONDITIONAL PROBABILITY

### *Exercise E (p. 561)*

| | Question | | | | | |
|---|---|---|---|---|---|---|
| | 1 | 2 | 3 | 4 | 5 | 6 |
| $p(\mathbf{A} \mid \mathbf{B})$ | $\frac{1}{2}$ | $\frac{1}{6}$ | $\frac{1}{2}$ | $\frac{2}{13}$ | $\frac{3}{4}$ | $\frac{1}{2}$ |
| $p(\sim \mathbf{A} \mid \mathbf{B})$ | $\frac{1}{2}$ | $\frac{5}{6}$ | $\frac{1}{2}$ | $\frac{11}{13}$ | $\frac{1}{4}$ | $\frac{1}{2}$ |
| $p(\mathbf{A} \mid \sim \mathbf{B})$ | $\frac{3}{5}$ | $\frac{1}{6}$ | $\frac{1}{2}$ | $\frac{1}{3}$ | $\frac{1}{2}$ | $\frac{1}{2}$ |
| $p(\sim \mathbf{A} \mid \sim \mathbf{B})$ | $\frac{2}{5}$ | $\frac{5}{6}$ | $\frac{1}{2}$ | $\frac{2}{3}$ | $\frac{1}{2}$ | $\frac{1}{2}$ |
| $p(\mathbf{B} \mid \mathbf{A})$ | $\frac{1}{4}$ | $\frac{1}{4}$ | $\frac{1}{2}$ | $\frac{2}{7}$ | $\frac{1}{2}$ | $\frac{2}{3}$ |
| $p(\mathbf{B} \mid \sim \mathbf{A})$ | $\frac{1}{3}$ | $\frac{1}{4}$ | $\frac{1}{2}$ | $\frac{11}{21}$ | $\frac{1}{4}$ | $\frac{2}{3}$ |
| $p(\sim \mathbf{B} \mid \mathbf{A})$ | $\frac{3}{4}$ | $\frac{3}{4}$ | $\frac{1}{2}$ | $\frac{5}{7}$ | $\frac{1}{2}$ | $\frac{1}{3}$ |
| $p(\sim \mathbf{B} \mid \sim \mathbf{A})$ | $\frac{2}{3}$ | $\frac{3}{4}$ | $\frac{1}{2}$ | $\frac{10}{21}$ | $\frac{3}{4}$ | $\frac{1}{3}$ |

The general result is

$$p(\mathbf{S}|\mathbf{T}) + p(\sim \mathbf{S}|\mathbf{T}) = 1.$$

### *Exercise F (p. 564)*

**1.** In Law 4, let the events be

**T**: There is a test.

~~**S**: The master will notice the boy's negligence.~~

Then $p(\mathbf{T}) = 0.6$, $p(\mathbf{S}|\mathbf{T}) = 0.7$, whence $p(\mathbf{S} \wedge \mathbf{T}) = 0.42$.

**2.** 0·0005.

**3.** Let the events be

**C**: I travel by car (so that $\sim \mathbf{C}$ is 'I travel by train').

**E**: I arrive early for my appointment.

Then

$$p(\mathbf{E}) = p(\mathbf{C}).p(\mathbf{E}|\mathbf{C}) + p(\sim \mathbf{C}).p(\mathbf{E}|\sim \mathbf{C}) = 0.54.$$

318

**4–8.** The probabilities are set out in the following table:

For diagrams see Figure E (p. 320).

| | Question | | | | |
|---|---|---|---|---|---|
| | 4 | 5 | 6 | 7 | 8 |
| $p(\mathbf{A} \wedge \mathbf{B})$ | 0 | $\frac{12}{25}$ | 0 | $\frac{1}{10}$ | $\frac{1}{12}$ |
| $p(\mathbf{A} \wedge \sim \mathbf{B})$ | $\frac{3}{5}$ | $\frac{8}{25}$ | $\frac{1}{6}$ | $\frac{1}{5}$ | $\frac{1}{6}$ |
| $p(\sim \mathbf{A} \wedge \mathbf{B})$ | $\frac{2}{5}$ | $\frac{1}{5}$ | $\frac{1}{3}$ | $\frac{3}{10}$ | $\frac{1}{4}$ |
| $p(\sim \mathbf{A} \wedge \sim \mathbf{B})$ | 0 | 0 | $\frac{1}{2}$ | $\frac{2}{5}$ | $\frac{1}{2}$ |
| $p(\mathbf{B})$ | $\frac{2}{5}$ | $\frac{17}{25}$ | $\frac{1}{3}$ | $\frac{2}{5}$ | $\frac{1}{3}$ |
| $p(\sim \mathbf{B})$ | $\frac{3}{5}$ | $\frac{8}{25}$ | $\frac{2}{3}$ | $\frac{3}{5}$ | $\frac{2}{3}$ |
| $p(\mathbf{A} \mid \mathbf{B})$ | 0 | $\frac{12}{17}$ | 0 | $\frac{1}{4}$ | $\frac{1}{4}$ |
| $p(\sim \mathbf{A} \mid \mathbf{B})$ | 1 | $\frac{5}{17}$ | 1 | $\frac{3}{4}$ | $\frac{3}{4}$ |
| $p(\mathbf{A} \mid \sim \mathbf{B})$ | 1 | 1 | $\frac{1}{4}$ | $\frac{1}{3}$ | $\frac{1}{4}$ |
| $p(\sim \mathbf{A} \mid \sim \mathbf{B})$ | 0 | 0 | $\frac{3}{4}$ | $\frac{2}{3}$ | $\frac{3}{4}$ |

These questions illustrate various ways in which events may be related. In Question 4 **A** and **B** are exclusive and exhaustive; in 5 they are exhaustive but not exclusive, and in 6 they are exclusive but not exhaustive. In 8 the events are independent. All these relationships are examined in detail later in the chapter.

**9.** (a) 0·008;     (b) 0·016.

$p(\mathbf{male} \mid \mathbf{colour\ blind}) = 0 \cdot 5$.

**10.** By Law 4,

$$p(\mathbf{S} \wedge \mathbf{T}) = p(\mathbf{T}) . p(\mathbf{S} \mid \mathbf{T})$$

and (replacing **S** by **R**, and **T** by **S** ∧ **T**)

$$p(\mathbf{R} \wedge (\mathbf{S} \wedge \mathbf{T})) = p(\mathbf{S} \wedge \mathbf{T}) . p(\mathbf{R} \mid \mathbf{S} \wedge \mathbf{T}),$$

from which the result follows. Take

   **T**: I get a cracker;
   **S**: the cracker contains a paper hat;
   **R**: I reach the hat before my opponent;

so that

$$p(\mathbf{T}) = \tfrac{3}{4}, \quad p(\mathbf{S} \mid \mathbf{T}) = \tfrac{1}{3}, \quad p(\mathbf{R} \mid \mathbf{S} \wedge \mathbf{T}) = \tfrac{1}{2},$$

whence        $p(\mathbf{R} \wedge \mathbf{S} \wedge \mathbf{T}) = \tfrac{1}{8}.$

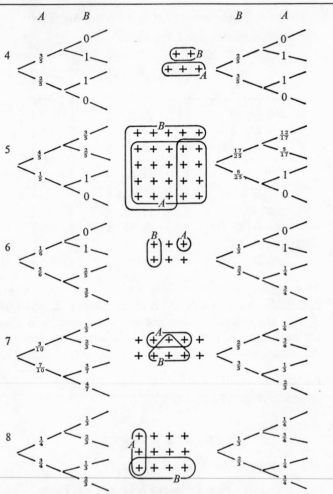

Fig. E. *Note.* In all the diagrams in Figure E the upper branches indicate the event (whether **A** or **B**), the lower branches its negation.

**11.** Since **S** ∧ **T** = **T** ∧ **S**,

$$p(\mathbf{S} \wedge \mathbf{T}) = p(\mathbf{T}) \cdot p(\mathbf{S}|\mathbf{T}) = p(\mathbf{S}) \cdot p(\mathbf{T}|\mathbf{S}).$$

**12.** Since (**R** ∧ **S**) ∧ **T** = **R** ∧ (**S** ∧ **T**),

$$p(\mathbf{R} \wedge \mathbf{S} \wedge \mathbf{T}) = p(\mathbf{T}) \cdot p(\mathbf{R} \wedge \mathbf{S}|\mathbf{T}) = p(\mathbf{S} \wedge \mathbf{T}) \cdot p(\mathbf{R}|\mathbf{S} \wedge \mathbf{T}).$$

**13.** Use the fact that (**S** ∧ **T**) ∧ **T** = **S** ∧ **T**, since $S \cap T \subset T$.

320

**14.** This formalizes the calculations of Questions 4–8. The denominator is $p(\mathbf{B})$ by the theorem of Section 4.4, and the result follows from that of Question 11.

## 6. INDEPENDENT EVENTS

### *Exercise G (p. 570)*

| | Question | | | | | |
|---|---|---|---|---|---|---|
| | 1 | 2 | 3 | 4 | 5 | 6 |
| $p(\mathbf{A} \mid \mathbf{B})$ | 0 | $\frac{1}{6}$ | $\frac{1}{6}$ | 0 | $\frac{1}{4}$ | $\frac{1}{4}$ |
| $p(\mathbf{A} \mid \sim\mathbf{B})$ | $\frac{1}{5}$ | $\frac{1}{6}$ | $\frac{1}{6}$ | $\frac{6}{31}$ | $\frac{1}{4}$ | $\frac{10}{41}$ |
| $\mathbf{A}$ indep. of $\mathbf{B}$? | No | Yes | Yes | No | Yes | No |
| $p(\mathbf{B} \mid \mathbf{A})$ | 0 | $\frac{1}{6}$ | $\frac{1}{6}$ | 0 | $\frac{3}{13}$ | $\frac{3}{13}$ |
| $p(\mathbf{B} \mid \sim\mathbf{A})$ | $\frac{1}{5}$ | $\frac{1}{6}$ | $\frac{1}{6}$ | $\frac{1}{6}$ | $\frac{3}{13}$ | $\frac{9}{40}$ |
| $\mathbf{B}$ indep. of $\mathbf{A}$? | No | Yes | Yes | No | Yes | No |
| $p(\mathbf{A})$ | $\frac{1}{6}$ | $\frac{1}{6}$ | $\frac{1}{6}$ | $\frac{1}{6}$ | $\frac{1}{4}$ | $\frac{13}{53}$ |
| $p(\mathbf{B})$ | $\frac{1}{6}$ | $\frac{1}{6}$ | $\frac{1}{6}$ | $\frac{5}{36}$ | $\frac{3}{13}$ | $\frac{12}{53}$ |
| $p(\mathbf{A} \wedge \mathbf{B})$ | 0 | $\frac{1}{36}$ | $\frac{1}{36}$ | 0 | $\frac{3}{52}$ | $\frac{3}{53}$ |

(In Question 6, the Joker is taken not to be a 'face card'.)

**7.** 16.

**8.** $p(\textbf{no chilblains}|\textbf{treated}) = \frac{7}{96} = 0\cdot073.$
$p(\textbf{no chilblains}|\textbf{not treated}) = \frac{18}{247} = 0\cdot073.$
No support for the theory.

**9.** Let $\mathbf{A}$ be '13 appears on the first spin', and $\mathbf{B}$ be '13 appears on the second spin'. $p(\mathbf{A}) = p(\mathbf{B}) = \frac{1}{37}$. $\mathbf{A}$ and $\mathbf{B}$ are independent events, as are $\sim\mathbf{A}$ and $\mathbf{B}$, $\mathbf{A}$ and $\sim\mathbf{B}$, $\sim\mathbf{A}$ and $\sim\mathbf{B}$.

(a) $p(\sim\mathbf{A} \wedge \mathbf{B}) = p(\sim\mathbf{A}).p(\mathbf{B})$      (Section 6.4)
$\qquad\qquad = (1-p(\mathbf{A})).p(\mathbf{B})$      (Law 1)
$\qquad\qquad = \frac{36}{1369};$

(b) $p(\sim\mathbf{A} \wedge \sim\mathbf{B}) = p(\sim\mathbf{A}).p(\sim\mathbf{B})$      (Section 6.4)
$\qquad\qquad\qquad = (1-p(\mathbf{A}))(1-p(\mathbf{B}))$      (Law 1)
$\qquad\qquad\qquad = \frac{1296}{1369};$

(c) $p(\mathbf{A} \vee \mathbf{B}) = p(\mathbf{A}) + p(\mathbf{B}) - p(\mathbf{A} \wedge \mathbf{B})$    (Law 3)

$\qquad\qquad = p(\mathbf{A}) + p(\mathbf{B}) - p(\mathbf{A}) \cdot p(\mathbf{B})$    (Section 6.4)

$\qquad\qquad = \frac{73}{1369};$

or   $p(\mathbf{A} \vee \mathbf{B}) = p(\sim (\sim \mathbf{A} \wedge \sim \mathbf{B}))$    (de Morgan's law)

$\qquad\qquad = 1 - p(\sim \mathbf{A} \wedge \sim \mathbf{B})$    (Law 1).

**10.** About 29 days.

**11.** The probabilities are exactly

$$\frac{300}{1000} \cdot \frac{299}{999}, \quad \frac{700}{1000} \cdot \frac{699}{999}, \quad 2 \cdot \frac{300}{1000} \cdot \frac{700}{999},$$

but to a sufficient degree of accuracy they may be taken as

$$\left(\frac{300}{1000}\right)^2, \quad \left(\frac{700}{1000}\right)^2, \quad \frac{2 \cdot 300 \cdot 700}{1000^2}.$$

**12.** (a) $\sim (\sim \mathbf{T}) = \mathbf{T}$, so that

$$p(\mathbf{S}|\mathbf{T}) = p(\mathbf{S}|\sim \mathbf{T}) \Rightarrow p(\mathbf{S}|\sim \mathbf{T}) = p(\mathbf{S}|\sim(\sim \mathbf{T})).$$

(b) Since

$$p(\mathbf{S}|\mathbf{T}) + p(\sim \mathbf{S}|\mathbf{T}) = 1 \quad \text{and} \quad p(\mathbf{S}|\sim \mathbf{T}) + p(\sim \mathbf{S}|\sim \mathbf{T}) = 1,$$

$$p(\mathbf{S}|\mathbf{T}) = p(\mathbf{S}|\sim \mathbf{T}) \Rightarrow p(\sim \mathbf{S}|\mathbf{T}) = p(\sim \mathbf{S}|\sim \mathbf{T}).$$

**13.**

|  | B | ~B |  |
|---|---|---|---|
| **A** | $ab$ | $a-ab$ | $a$ |
| **~A** | $b-ab$ | $1-a-b+ab$ | $1-a$ |
|  | $b$ | $1-b$ | $1$ |

**14.** $\dfrac{n(A)}{n(\mathscr{E})} \cdot \dfrac{n(B)}{n(\mathscr{E})} = \dfrac{n(A \cap B)}{n(\mathscr{E})}$, so that $n(A) \cdot n(B) = n(A \cap B) \cdot n(\mathscr{E})$ (see Figure F). Similarly for any other entry in the central square of the contingency table.

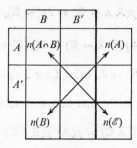

Fig. F

**15.** **A** is not independent of **A**, because

$$p(\mathbf{A}|\mathbf{A}) = 1 \quad \text{and} \quad p(\mathbf{A}|\sim\mathbf{A}) = 0.$$

To prove that independence is not in general transitive one need only note that, if **A** is independent of **B**, then **B** is independent of **A**, but we have shown that **A** is not independent of **A**.

|     | (i) | (ii) | (iii) | (iv) | (v) |
|-----|-----|------|-------|------|-----|
| **16.** | $T$ | $T$ | $F$ | $T$ | $F$ |
| **17.** | $T$ | $T$ | $F$ | $T$ | $F$ |
| **18.** | $T$ | $T$ | $T$ | $T$ | $T$ |

**19.** (a) $\frac{1}{20}$;  (b) $\frac{3}{10}$.

By 'completely independent' we mean not only that the events are independent in pairs, but also that the conditional probability of each is the same whether or not either or both of the others occurs. Thus, for example,

$$p(\mathbf{A}|\mathbf{B}\wedge\mathbf{C}), \quad p(\mathbf{A}|\sim\mathbf{B}\wedge\mathbf{C}), \quad p(\mathbf{A}|\mathbf{B}\wedge\sim\mathbf{C})$$

and

$$p(\mathbf{A}|\sim\mathbf{B}\wedge\sim\mathbf{C})$$

must all be equal. If the common value is $\lambda$, then by Law 4

$$p(\mathbf{A}\wedge\mathbf{B}\wedge\mathbf{C}) = \lambda p(\mathbf{B}\wedge\mathbf{C})$$

and

$$p(\mathbf{A}\wedge\mathbf{B}\wedge\sim\mathbf{C}) = \lambda p(\mathbf{B}\wedge\sim\mathbf{C}),$$

so that

$$p(\mathbf{A}\wedge\mathbf{B}\wedge\mathbf{C})+p(\mathbf{A}\wedge\mathbf{B}\wedge\sim\mathbf{C}) = \lambda(p(\mathbf{B}\wedge\mathbf{C})+p(\mathbf{B}\wedge\sim\mathbf{C})),$$

or

$$p(\mathbf{A}\wedge\mathbf{B}) = \lambda p(\mathbf{B}), \quad \text{by Law 2.}$$

323

Similarly $p(\mathbf{A} \wedge \sim \mathbf{B}) = \lambda p(\sim \mathbf{B})$,

so that
$$p(\mathbf{A} \wedge \mathbf{B}) + p(\mathbf{A} \wedge \sim \mathbf{B}) = \lambda(p(\mathbf{B}) + p(\sim \mathbf{B})),$$

or $\quad p(\mathbf{A}) = \lambda$, using Law 2 again.

Substituting back in the first line, therefore,

$$p(\mathbf{A} \wedge \mathbf{B} \wedge \mathbf{C}) = p(\mathbf{A}).p(\mathbf{B} \wedge \mathbf{C})$$

$$= p(\mathbf{A}).p(\mathbf{B}).p(\mathbf{C}),$$

since $\mathbf{B}, \mathbf{C}$ are independent as a pair. This justifies the method used to find the probabilities in Question 19, by multiplying together the probabilities of the three separate events.

In Questions 16–18 the conditional probabilities are:

|  | 16 | 17 | 18 |
|---|---|---|---|
| $p(\mathbf{A} \mid \mathbf{B} \wedge \mathbf{C})$ | 1 | 1 | $\frac{1}{2}$ |
| $p(\mathbf{A} \mid \mathbf{B} \wedge \sim \mathbf{C})$ | 0 | 0 | $\frac{1}{2}$ |
| $p(\mathbf{A} \mid \sim \mathbf{B} \wedge \mathbf{C})$ | 0 | 0 | $\frac{1}{2}$ |
| $p(\mathbf{A} \mid \sim \mathbf{B} \wedge \sim \mathbf{C})$ | 1 | 1 | $\frac{1}{2}$ |

Thus the events in Question 18 are completely independent, but those in Questions 16 and 17 are not, even though they are independent in pairs.

# 7. THE EVENT (S OR T)
### *Exercise H (p. 576)*

**2.** (i) Exclusive:          (ii) Exhaustive:

|  | B | ~B |  |
|---|---|---|---|
| **A** | 0 |  |  |
| **~A** |  |  |  |
|  |  |  |  |

|  | B | ~B |  |
|---|---|---|---|
| **A** |  |  |  |
| **~A** |  | 0 |  |
|  |  |  |  |

(iii) Independent: Entries are products of the partial sums: $c = ab$, etc.

|   | B | ~B |   |
|---|---|---|---|
| **A** | $c \leftarrow$ |   | $a$ |
| **~A** |   |   |   |
|   | $b$ |   |   |

(*a*) *Exhaustive and independent.* Since $p(\sim \mathbf{A}).p(\sim \mathbf{B}) = 0$, either $p(\sim \mathbf{A}) = 0$ or $p(\sim \mathbf{B}) = 0$. Now $p(\sim \mathbf{A}) = 0$ gives the contingency table:

|   | **B** | **~B** |   |
|---|---|---|---|
| **A** | $x$ | $1-x$ | $1$ |
| **~A** | $0$ | $0$ | $0$ |
|   | $x$ | $1-x$ | $1$ |

(*b*) *Exclusive and independent.* Since $p(\mathbf{A}).p(\mathbf{B}) = 0$, either $p(\mathbf{A}) = 0$ or $p(\mathbf{B}) = 0$. Now $p(\mathbf{A}) = 0$ gives the contingency table:

|   | **B** | **~B** |   |
|---|---|---|---|
| **A** | $0$ | $0$ | $0$ |
| **~A** | $x$ | $1-x$ | $1$ |
|   | $x$ | $1-x$ | $1$ |

The conditions in (*a*) are satisfied if $A = \mathscr{E}$, and those in (*b*) if $A = \varnothing$. There is, however, a difficulty in interpretation; for although one can say that **A** is independent of **B** (unless $x = 0$ or 1), it is not really meaningful to say that **B** is independent of **A**, since $p(\mathbf{B}|\sim \mathbf{A})$ is meaningless in case (*a*) and $p(\mathbf{B}|\mathbf{A})$ is meaningless in case (*b*).

(c) *Exhaustive and exclusive*. This is certainly possible, with $\mathbf{A} = \sim \mathbf{B}$. The shape of the contingency table is:

|  | B | ~B |  |
|---|---|---|---|
| **A** | 0 | $x$ | $x$ |
| **~A** | $1-x$ | 0 | $1-x$ |
|  | $1-x$ | $x$ | 1 |

3. $A \cap B = \emptyset, B \cap C = \emptyset$ and $C \cap A = \emptyset$. Then $A \cap (B \cup C) = \emptyset$, so that
$$p(\mathbf{A} \vee (\mathbf{B} \vee \mathbf{C})) = p(\mathbf{A}) + p(\mathbf{B} \vee \mathbf{C}),$$

whence the result follows.

4. Exclusive: $A_i \cap A_j = \emptyset$ for all pairs $i, j$ $(i \neq j)$.
Exhaustive: $A_1 \cup A_2 \cup ... \cup A_n = \mathcal{E}$.
If $A_1, A_2, ..., A_n$ are exclusive and exhaustive,
$$\sum_{i=1}^{n} p(\mathbf{A}_i) = 1.$$

Make the inductive assumption that the result holds for *any k* exclusive and exhaustive events. Then

$\mathbf{A}_1, \mathbf{A}_2, ..., \mathbf{A}_k, \mathbf{A}_{k+1}$ exclusive and exhaustive
$\Rightarrow \mathbf{A}_1, \mathbf{A}_2, ..., \mathbf{A}_{k-1}, (\mathbf{A}_k \vee \mathbf{A}_{k+1})$ exclusive and exhaustive
(since $A_i \cap A_k = \emptyset$ and $A_i \cap A_{k+1} = \emptyset \Rightarrow A_i \cap (A_k \cup A_{k+1}) = \emptyset$)
$$\Rightarrow \sum_{i=1}^{k-1} p(\mathbf{A}_i) + p(\mathbf{A}_k \vee \mathbf{A}_{k+1}) = 1$$

(by the inductive assumption)
$$\Rightarrow \sum_{i=1}^{k-1} p(\mathbf{A}_i) + p(\mathbf{A}_k) + p(\mathbf{A}_{k+1}) = 1$$

(since $\mathbf{A}_k, \mathbf{A}_{k+1}$ are exclusive)
$$\Rightarrow \sum_{i=1}^{k+1} p(\mathbf{A}_i) = 1.$$

The result is true for $n = 2$, and therefore for all $n \geqslant 2$.

5. If the events $\mathbf{A}_i$ are exclusive and exhaustive, and if $\mathbf{T}$ is any event,

$$\sum_{i=1}^{n} p(\mathbf{A}_i|\mathbf{T}) = 1.$$

If the events $\mathbf{A}_i$ are exclusive and exhaustive, and if $\mathbf{T}$ is any event,

$$p(\mathbf{T}) = \sum_{i=1}^{n} p(\mathbf{A}_i).p(\mathbf{T}|\mathbf{A}_i).$$

6. The condition is equivalent to $p(S \wedge T) = 0$. If the possibility space is finite, then this gives $n(S \cap T) = 0$, so that $S \cap T = \varnothing$ and the events are exclusive.

Difficulties arise, however, if the set of possibilities is infinite. For example, if the set of possibilities consisted of the real numbers between 0 and 2, and if $S$ is the event $x \leqslant 1$ and $T$ the event $x \geqslant 1$, then

$$p(S)+p(T) = p(S \wedge T)$$

but the events are not exclusive.

7. $1-p(S \vee T)$ is $p(\sim (S \vee T))$, the probability that neither $S$ nor $T$ occurs. $1-p(S)$ and $1-p(T)$ are $p(\sim S)$ and $p(\sim T)$, the probabilities that $S$ does not occur and that $T$ does not occur.

8. $p(T)\{1-p(S)\} = p(T).p(\sim S)$, so that the expression on the right is the sum of the probabilities that $S$ occurs and that $S$ does not occur but $T$ does.

9.

| Total | Probability | |
|---|---|---|
| 6 | $\frac{1}{18}(3-2K+2K^2)$ | Greatest when $K = 0$ or 1 |
| 7 | $\frac{1}{9}(1+2K-2K^2)$ | Greatest when $K = \frac{1}{2}$ |
| 8 | $\frac{1}{18}(3-2K+2K^2)$ | Greatest when $K = 0$ or 1 |
| 9 | $\frac{1}{9}$ | Independent of $K$ |
| 10 | $\frac{1}{36}(1+4K)$ | Greatest when $K = 1$ |

10. $1-\frac{40}{50}.\frac{39}{49}.\frac{38}{48}.\frac{37}{47}.\frac{36}{46} = 0\cdot69.$

11. $1-(\frac{3}{4})^3 = \frac{37}{64}.$

12. $1-\{(\frac{5}{6})^5+5\times(\frac{5}{6})^4\times\frac{1}{6}\} = 0\cdot20.$

13. (a) $5\times(\frac{1}{6})^4\times\frac{5}{6} = \frac{25}{7776}$, or $0\cdot003$;

(b) $6\times\frac{25}{7776} = \frac{25}{1296}$, or $0\cdot019$;

(c) $6\times(\frac{1}{6})^5+\frac{25}{1296} = \frac{26}{1296}$, or $0\cdot020$.

**14.** (a) $\frac{1}{4}$;      (b) $\frac{1}{4}$;      (c) $\frac{1}{16}$;      (d) $\frac{3}{16}$;

(e) $\frac{5}{16}$;      (f) $\frac{1}{16}$;      (g) $\frac{255}{256}$;      (h) 0.

Notice that it is not impossible that no decision will ever be reached, but that this event has a probability of zero (assuming that the contestants are immortal).

### Miscellaneous Exercise (p. 577)

**1.** (a) $pq(1-r)$;          (b) $q(1-p)(1-r)$;

(c) $1-(1-p)(1-q)(1-r)$;

(d) $(1-p)qr+(1-q)pr+(1-r)pq$.

**2.** The probabilities of obtaining the given sample are:

| Contents of bag | Probability |
|---|---|
| Less than 3 red | 0 |
| 3 red, 3 green | 1/5 |
| 4 red, 2 green | 8/15 |
| 5 red, 1 green | 2/3 |
| 6 red, 0 green | 0 |

The probability is highest if the bag contained five red and one green disc.

**3.** (a) $\frac{10}{49}$;      (b) $\frac{1}{7} \leqslant p \leqslant \frac{3}{14}$;      (c) $\frac{7}{312}$.

**4.** (a) 2;      (b) 2;      (c) 3;      (d) 2 or 3.

(a) £10;      (b) £10;      (c) £20;      (d) £15.

This question introduces informally the binomial probability function and the idea of expectation, both of which are dealt with in detail in later chapters.

**5.** (a) $\frac{19}{36}$;          (b) $\frac{7}{60}$;          (c) $\frac{21}{85}$.

**6.** $\frac{3}{8}$. With as few envelopes as this all the permutations can be listed and the number of derangements (that is, permutations in which every element moves to a new place) counted. If there are $n$ envelopes, the formula for the probability is

$$1-\frac{1}{1!}+\frac{1}{2!}-\frac{1}{3!}+\dots+(-1)^n\frac{1}{n!}.$$

A proof of this result will be found in C. V. Durell and A. Robson, *Advanced Algebra* (Bell).

**7.** (a) Probability $= 1-(\frac{5}{6})^4$;  (b) probability $= 1-(\frac{35}{36})^{24}$. Since $(\frac{35}{36})^6 > \frac{5}{6}$ (see Chapter 2, Exercise E, Question 12: $(1+x)^n > 1+nx$, where $x = -\frac{1}{36}$, $n = 6$), the event (a) is more likely to occur.

**8.** The events '*the point is not in the first part*', '*the point is not in the second part*', etc., are not independent, so the product rule for combining probabilities is inapplicable.

The conditional probability that the point is not in the second part given that it is not in the first is $1-[1/(n-1)]$. Therefore, by an extension of Law 4, the probability that it is not in any of the $n$ parts is

$$\left(1-\frac{1}{n}\right)\left(1-\frac{1}{n-1}\right) \quad \dots \quad \left(1-\frac{1}{1}\right) = 0.$$

**9.** $\frac{1}{3}$.  $1-(\frac{2}{3})^4 = 0\cdot8$.  $(\frac{2}{3})^n < 0\cdot05 \Rightarrow n \geqslant 8$.

**10.** Exercise G, Questions 16 and 17, afford illustrations that the triple product rule is not necessarily true. We note that, since **S, T** are independent,

$$p(\mathbf{S} \wedge \mathbf{T}) = p(\mathbf{S}).p(\mathbf{T}),$$

so that $\qquad p(\mathbf{R} \wedge \mathbf{S} \wedge \mathbf{T}) = p(\mathbf{R}).p(\mathbf{S}).p(\mathbf{T})$

$$\Rightarrow p(\mathbf{R} \wedge \mathbf{S} \wedge \mathbf{T}) = p(\mathbf{R}).p(\mathbf{S} \wedge \mathbf{T}),$$

from which we deduce that **R** and **S** $\wedge$ **T** are independent.

Also

$p(\mathbf{R} \wedge \mathbf{S} \wedge \sim \mathbf{T})+p(\mathbf{R} \wedge \mathbf{S} \wedge \mathbf{T})$

$\quad = p(\mathbf{R} \wedge \mathbf{S})$

$\quad = p(\mathbf{R}).p(\mathbf{S})$  (since **R, S** are independent)

$\quad = p(\mathbf{R}).p(\mathbf{S})\{p(\mathbf{T})+p(\sim \mathbf{T})\}$

$\quad = p(\mathbf{R}).p(\mathbf{S}).p(\mathbf{T})+p(\mathbf{R}).p(\mathbf{S}).p(\sim \mathbf{T}),$

so that $\qquad p(\mathbf{R} \wedge \mathbf{S} \wedge \sim \mathbf{T}) = p(\mathbf{R}).p(\mathbf{S}).p(\sim \mathbf{T}),$

and it follows as before that **R** is independent of **S** $\wedge \sim$ **T**; and so on.

**11.** (a)

Length of queue

| | 0 | 1 | 2 | 3 | 4 |
|---|---|---|---|---|---|
| End of minute $\begin{cases} 1 \\ 2 \\ 3 \\ 4 \end{cases}$ | | | | | |
| 1 | $\frac{2}{3}$ | $\frac{1}{3}$ | — | — | — |
| 2 | $\frac{4}{9}$ | $\frac{4}{9}$ | $\frac{1}{9}$ | — | — |
| 3 | $\frac{8}{27}$ | $\frac{12}{27}$ | $\frac{6}{27}$ | $\frac{1}{27}$ | — |
| 4 | $\frac{16}{81}$ | $\frac{32}{81}$ | $\frac{24}{81}$ | $\frac{8}{81}$ | $\frac{1}{81}$ |

(b)

Length of queue

| | 0 | 1 | 2 | 3 | 4 |
|---|---|---|---|---|---|
| 1 | $\frac{2}{3}$ | $\frac{1}{3}$ | — | — | — |
| 2 | $\frac{14}{27}$ | $\frac{11}{27}$ | $\frac{2}{27}$ | — | — |
| 3 | $\frac{106}{243}$ | $\frac{101}{243}$ | $\frac{32}{243}$ | $\frac{4}{243}$ | — |
| 4 | $\frac{838}{2187}$ | $\frac{887}{2187}$ | $\frac{370}{2187}$ | $\frac{84}{2187}$ | $\frac{8}{2187}$ |

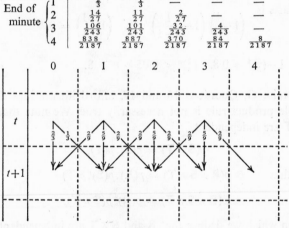

Fig. G

(c) Case (a) defines a binomial probability function with generator $(\frac{2}{3}+\frac{1}{3}x)^t$ (t being the number of minutes after the queue begins to form, and x the dummy variable). The difference equation requires initial information such as

$$q(n, 0) = \begin{cases} 1 & \text{if } n = 0, \\ 0 & \text{if } n \neq 0. \end{cases}$$

For case (b) the scheme for generating the sequence is shown in Figure G. This gives the difference equations:

$$\begin{cases} q(n, t+1) = \frac{2}{9}q(n-1, t) + \frac{5}{9}q(n, t) + \frac{2}{9}q(n+1, t) & \text{if } n \geqslant 2, \\ q(1, t+1) = \frac{1}{3}q(0, t) + \frac{5}{9}q(1, t) + \frac{2}{9}q(2, t), \\ q(0, t+1) = \frac{2}{3}q(0, t) + \frac{2}{9}q(1, t). \end{cases}$$

330

**12.** Define $\phi(n, 0) = \begin{cases} 1 & \text{if } n = 0, \\ 0 & \text{if } n \neq 0. \end{cases}$

This function is used in Chapter 38, Section 4 to illustrate the effect of taking samples of different sizes from a rectangular population. As $r$ is increased, the shape of the histogram resembles more and more the graph of the Normal probability function.

**13.** (a) $v_1 = au_0 + (1-b)v_0$;      (b) $\mathbf{A} = \begin{pmatrix} 1-a & b \\ a & 1-b \end{pmatrix}$.

(c) $\mathbf{A} = \begin{pmatrix} \frac{1}{2} & \frac{1}{4} \\ \frac{1}{2} & \frac{3}{4} \end{pmatrix}$;   $\mathbf{A}^2 = \begin{pmatrix} \frac{3}{8} & \frac{5}{16} \\ \frac{5}{8} & \frac{11}{16} \end{pmatrix}$;   $\mathbf{A}^3 = \begin{pmatrix} \frac{11}{32} & \frac{21}{64} \\ \frac{21}{32} & \frac{43}{64} \end{pmatrix}$;

$\mathbf{A}^4 = \begin{pmatrix} \frac{43}{128} & \frac{85}{256} \\ \frac{85}{128} & \frac{171}{256} \end{pmatrix}$.

$\mathbf{w}_1 = \begin{pmatrix} \frac{1}{2} \\ \frac{1}{2} \end{pmatrix}$;   $\mathbf{w}_2 = \begin{pmatrix} \frac{3}{8} \\ \frac{5}{8} \end{pmatrix}$;   $\mathbf{w}_3 = \begin{pmatrix} \frac{11}{32} \\ \frac{21}{32} \end{pmatrix}$;   $\mathbf{w}_4 = \begin{pmatrix} \frac{43}{128} \\ \frac{85}{128} \end{pmatrix}$.

(d) $\begin{pmatrix} \dfrac{b}{a+b} \\ \dfrac{a}{a+b} \end{pmatrix}$;   for the special case in (c),   $\begin{pmatrix} \frac{1}{3} \\ \frac{2}{3} \end{pmatrix}$.

**14.**

| Number of paces | Probability | |
|---|---|---|
| 0 | $6x^2 - 4x + 1$ | |
| 1 | $4x - 8x^2$ | (See Figure H) |
| 2 | $2x^2$ | |

One pace is most likely if $0 \cdot 18 < x < 0 \cdot 39$;

no paces if     $x < 0 \cdot 18$   or   $x > 0 \cdot 39$.

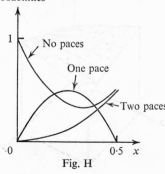

Fig. H

**15.** (*a*) $p(\mathbf{B}|\mathbf{A}) = 0$, $p(\mathbf{B}|\sim \mathbf{A}) = 1$. With a finite possibility space this implies that $\mathbf{B} = \sim \mathbf{A}$.

(*b*) $\mathbf{B}$ is independent of $\mathbf{A}$.

(*c*) With a finite possibility space, $\mathbf{B} = \mathbf{A}$.

**16.** (*a*) See Figure I. $(\frac{2}{3}, \frac{2}{3})$ is a saddle-point (see Figure J).

(*b*) $x = \frac{2}{3}$; $m(\frac{2}{3}) = \frac{13}{15}$.        (*c*) $y = \frac{2}{3}$; $M(\frac{2}{3}) = \frac{13}{15}$.

Both sides will select the town route two times in three. If they deviate from these proportions, then it is possible for their opponents to adjust their plans so as to make the probability more favourable to themselves.

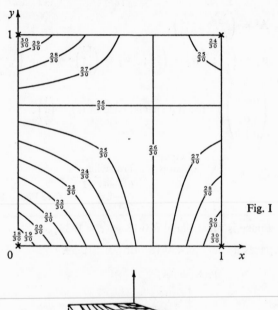

Fig. I

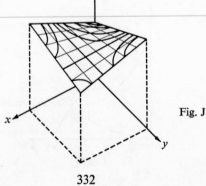

Fig. J

# 21

# LINEAR EQUATIONS

## 1. A REVIEW OF AVAILABLE METHODS OF SOLUTION

### Exercise A (p. 583)

1. (a) $7, -4$;    (b) $\frac{7}{5}, \frac{1}{15}$;    (c) no solution;

 (d) $\dfrac{dp-bq}{ad-bc}, \dfrac{aq-cp}{ad-bc}$, if $ad \neq bc$.

2. $(-1, 3), (0, -4), (5, 1)$.

3. $P = W(5 \cos \alpha + 3 \sin \alpha), Q = W(5 \sin \alpha - 3 \cos \alpha)$.

4. $(-\frac{28}{11}, \frac{75}{11})$.

5. (a) $(2, 3, 1)$;   (b) $(2, 3, 1)$.    6. $(2, -1, -2)$.

7. No solution; $5y - 11z = 17$ and $5y - 11z = 19$.

8. $5y - 11z = 17$; $x = 2 - 19t, y = -1 + 11t, z = -2 + 5t$, for any value of $t$.

## 2. THREE EQUATIONS IN $x, y,$ AND $z$

### Exercise B (p. 585)

1. No.      2. $x = 4 - 13t$;   $0z = 0$.

3. $c = -1$.

4. 16 (add the equations); 17 (subtract the first equation from twice the second). No.

5. (a) $x = 5, y = 0, z = 7$;    (b) $x = 4, y = -1, z = -3$;
 (c) $x = 5, y = 3\frac{1}{2}, z = 6\frac{1}{2}$.

The important idea in this section is that elementary row-operations are precisely equivalent to matrix premultiplication; once this is clearly grasped, Theorem C is obvious. This enables us to use matrix

333

arguments, involving the familiar ideas of associativity and inverses, instead of equivalent arguments involving row-operations which would be much more cumbrous to explain. A general treatment necessitates some knowledge of determinants. In fact, if the matrix $\mathbf{A}$ is

$$\begin{pmatrix} a & b & c \\ d & e & f \\ g & h & i \end{pmatrix},$$

we can express the matrices $\mathbf{L}$ and $\mathbf{U}$ in terms of the determinant of $\mathbf{A}$ ($\Delta$, say) and the cofactors of its elements, denoted by the corresponding capital letters. Thus, $C = dh - eg$, and so on. It will be found that

$$\mathbf{L} = \begin{pmatrix} 1 & 0 & 0 \\ -d & a & 0 \\ C & F & I \end{pmatrix}, \quad \mathbf{U} = \begin{pmatrix} a & b & c \\ 0 & I & -H \\ 0 & 0 & \Delta \end{pmatrix}$$

satisfy $\mathbf{LA} = \mathbf{U}$, but these are not unique—the rows of both $\mathbf{L}$ and $\mathbf{U}$ may be multiplied through by any constants.

### Exercise C (p. 590)

**1.** $1, 0, -2$.

**2.** From right to left, the matrices are

$$\begin{pmatrix} 1 & 0 & 0 \\ 0 & 1 & 0 \\ 0 & -5 & 1 \end{pmatrix} \begin{pmatrix} 1 & 0 & 0 \\ 0 & 1 & 0 \\ -4 & 0 & 1 \end{pmatrix} \begin{pmatrix} 1 & 0 & 0 \\ -3 & 1 & 0 \\ 0 & 0 & 1 \end{pmatrix};$$

$$\mathbf{U} = \begin{pmatrix} 1 & -1 & 1 \\ 0 & 1 & -2 \\ 0 & 0 & 3 \end{pmatrix}; \quad \mathbf{L} = \begin{pmatrix} 1 & 0 & 0 \\ -3 & 1 & 0 \\ 11 & -5 & 1 \end{pmatrix}$$

**3.** $\mathbf{Ux} = \mathbf{LAx} = \mathbf{Lp}$,

where $\mathbf{x}$ is the vector $\begin{pmatrix} x \\ y \\ z \end{pmatrix}$ and $\mathbf{p}$ is the vector $\begin{pmatrix} 3 \\ 10 \\ 20 \end{pmatrix}$,

$$\Rightarrow x - y + z = 3 \qquad \Rightarrow x = 5, \ y = 3, \ z = 1.$$
$$y - 2z = 1$$
$$3z = 3$$

In the general case,
$$x = \tfrac{1}{3}(5a - 2b + c), \quad y = \tfrac{1}{3}(13a - 7b + 2c),$$
$$z = \tfrac{1}{3}(11a - 5b + c).$$

**4.** From right to left the matrices are

$$\begin{pmatrix} 1 & 0 \\ 0 & 3 \end{pmatrix} \begin{pmatrix} 1 & -2 \\ 0 & 1 \end{pmatrix} \begin{pmatrix} 1 & 0 \\ -4 & 1 \end{pmatrix} \begin{pmatrix} \frac{1}{3} & 0 \\ 0 & 1 \end{pmatrix},$$

the product of which is

$$\begin{pmatrix} 3 & -2 \\ -4 & 3 \end{pmatrix}.$$

**5.** $E_1^{-1} = \begin{pmatrix} 3 & 0 \\ 0 & 1 \end{pmatrix}, \quad E_2^{-1} = \begin{pmatrix} 1 & 0 \\ 4 & 1 \end{pmatrix}, \quad E_3^{-1} = \begin{pmatrix} 1 & 2 \\ 0 & 1 \end{pmatrix},$

$E_4^{-1} = \begin{pmatrix} 1 & 0 \\ 0 & \frac{1}{3} \end{pmatrix}.$

**6.** See Figure A. The transformations are:

$E_1$: $x$-way stretch, factor $\frac{1}{3}$;      $E_2$: shear parallel to $y$-axis;

$E_3$: shear parallel to $x$-axis;      $E_4$: $y$-way stretch, factor 3.

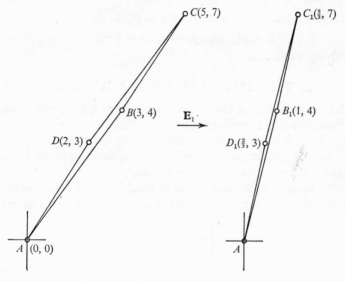

Fig. A

335

7. $\begin{pmatrix} a & b \\ c & d \end{pmatrix}$.

Shear, factor $b/a$, parallel to $x$-axis; $y$-way stretch, factor $\Delta/a$; shear, factor $c$, parallel to $y$-axis; $x$-way stretch, factor $a$.

If $\Delta = 0$, the second stretch is a projection onto the $x$-axis, and the parallelogram is reduced to four collinear points.

8. The rows are put in order 2, 3, 1.

Permutation of columns is effected by postmultiplication; for example, $\begin{pmatrix} a & b & c \\ d & e & f \\ g & h & i \end{pmatrix} \begin{pmatrix} 0 & 1 & 0 \\ 1 & 0 & 0 \\ 0 & 0 & 1 \end{pmatrix} = \begin{pmatrix} b & a & c \\ e & d & f \\ h & g & i \end{pmatrix}$.

9. $\mathbf{U} = \begin{pmatrix} 1 & 1 & 1 \\ 0 & 2 & 6 \\ 0 & 0 & 0 \end{pmatrix}$. $\mathbf{L}\begin{pmatrix} 4 \\ 7 \\ c \end{pmatrix} = \begin{pmatrix} 4 \\ 3 \\ c-8\frac{1}{2} \end{pmatrix}$.

There is a solution if and only if $c = 8\frac{1}{2}$. In this case,
$$x = 3\tfrac{1}{2}-2t, \quad y = 3t, \quad z = \tfrac{1}{2}-t,$$
for any value of $t$.

## 3. THE INVERSE OF A MATRIX

It is important to realize that, while the inverse of a $2 \times 2$ matrix can be written down by a simple rule, inverses of matrices of higher order cannot. There is a rule in terms of determinants, but the process given in this section is easier, and, in the long run, quicker—provided that adequate computing facilities are available.

It may be of interest, and of use in checking results, to give the determinantal rule here. We confine our attention to the $3 \times 3$ matrix

$$\begin{pmatrix} a & b & c \\ d & e & f \\ g & h & i \end{pmatrix}.$$

We begin by defining the cofactors, as before. These are the values of the $2 \times 2$ determinants obtained by omitting, for each element, the row and column in which it is situated. With each determinant we associate a sign, according to the following scheme:

$$\begin{pmatrix} + & - & + \\ - & + & - \\ + & - & + \end{pmatrix}.$$

336

Thus,
$$F = -\begin{vmatrix} a & b \\ g & h \end{vmatrix}, \quad G = +\begin{vmatrix} b & c \\ e & f \end{vmatrix},$$

and so on. The matrix of these cofactors

$$\begin{pmatrix} A & B & C \\ D & E & F \\ G & H & I \end{pmatrix}$$

is called the *adjoint* of the given matrix, and its *transpose*,

$$\begin{pmatrix} A & D & G \\ B & E & H \\ C & F & I \end{pmatrix},$$

is called the *adjugate* matrix. The inverse is simply the adjugate divided by the determinant of the whole matrix, $\Delta$, provided that this determinant is non-zero. Proof of this will be found in any book on determinants. (Some writers call the transposed matrix the *adjoint*.)

If $\Delta = 0$, the matrix has no inverse, and is said to be *singular*. In this case the corresponding equations have usually no solution, but if the constant vector is such that there is one solution, then there is an infinity of solutions. Compare the discussion on p. 383 of the pupils' text; the three planes represented by the equations usually form a prism, but if they have a common point, they form a sheaf and contain an infinity of common points.

### Exercise D (p. 596)

1. $\begin{pmatrix} -3 & 8 & 7 \\ -4 & 10 & 9 \\ -8 & 19 & 17 \end{pmatrix}$.  $x = 120p+1, \quad y = 150p+1, \quad z = 280p+2,$
$p = 0, 1, ..., 5.$

2. 

| Matrix | | | Identity | | | |
|---|---|---|---|---|---|---|
| 1 | 5 | 8 | 1 | 0 | 0 | |
| 1 | 7 | 12 | 0 | 1 | 0 | |
| 1 | 6 | 10 | 0 | 0 | 1 | |

| | | | | | | |
|---|---|---|---|---|---|---|
| 1 | 5 | 8 | 1 | 0 | 0 | |
| 0 | 2 | 4 | $-1$ | 1 | 0 | Row 2−row 1. |
| 0 | 1 | 2 | $-1$ | 0 | 1 | Row 3−row 1. |

| | | | | | | |
|---|---|---|---|---|---|---|
| 1 | 5 | 8 | 1 | 0 | 0 | |
| 0 | 2 | 4 | $-1$ | 1 | 0 | |
| 0 | 0 | 0 | $-\frac{1}{2}$ | $-\frac{1}{2}$ | 1 | Row 3−$\frac{1}{2}$ row 2. |

337

There is now a zero on the diagonal, and we cannot obtain a 1 in the bottom right-hand corner, or zeros elsewhere in the third column. A matrix has no inverse if its determinant (as here) is zero.

3. (a) $\begin{pmatrix} -5 & 3 \\ 2 & -1 \end{pmatrix}$; (b) $\begin{pmatrix} 4 & -3 \\ -5 & 4 \end{pmatrix}$; (c) $\begin{pmatrix} 0.28 & -0.16 \\ 0.04 & 0.12 \end{pmatrix}$;

(d) $\begin{pmatrix} d/\Delta & -b/\Delta \\ -c/\Delta & a/\Delta \end{pmatrix}$, where $\Delta = ad - bc$.

4. (a) $\begin{pmatrix} 1/k & 0 \\ 0 & 1 \end{pmatrix}$;       (b) $\begin{pmatrix} 1 & 0 \\ 3 & 1 \end{pmatrix}$;

(c) $\begin{pmatrix} 1 & 0 & 0 \\ 0 & 1/k & 0 \\ 0 & 0 & 1 \end{pmatrix}$;       (d) $\begin{pmatrix} 0 & 1 & 0 \\ 1 & 0 & 0 \\ 0 & 0 & 1 \end{pmatrix}$;

(e) $\begin{pmatrix} 1 & 0 & 0 \\ -3 & 1 & 0 \\ 0 & 0 & 1 \end{pmatrix}$;       (f) $\begin{pmatrix} 1 & 0 & 0 \\ 0 & 1 & 0 \\ -a & 0 & 1 \end{pmatrix}$.

(a) $x$-way stretch;       (b) shear parallel to $Oy'$;
(c) $y$-way stretch;       (d) reflection in plane $x = y$;
(e) shear parallel to $Oy$;       (f) shear parallel to $Oz$.

## 4. RELAXATION

This section is usually found interesting and is an important example of an iterative method of solving equations. A full account of the method will be found in Wooldridge, *Introduction to Computing* (Oxford University Press), Chapter 8. It requires a certain amount of ingenuity, and in this form is not ideally suited to the electronic computer. It is of greater value in connection with the numerical solution of differential equations.

### Exercise E (p. 600)

The exact solutions are given; those obtained by relaxation will depend on the precise steps used.

1. $5.7$, $-0.9$.      2. $34$, $53$.      4. $-1.8\dot{1}$, $0.2\dot{7}$.

5. $2.47$, $0.314$, $1.05$.      6. $0.633$, $-0.390$, $0.030$.

**7.** $-1.5$, 9, $-6$. Multiply the equations by 6, 12, 60 to clear fractions. Subtract the first from the second, and the third from 4 times the second. This gives $6x+3y+2z = 6$, $y+z = 3$, $4x+y = 3$.

**8.** $x = -110/9 = -12.22$, $\quad y = 4075/63 = 64.68$,
$$z = -3650/63 = -57.94.$$

This large and surprising difference resulting from rounding off to two decimal places illustrates the meaning of ill-conditioning most vividly. This situation arises from the very small values of the determinants of the coefficient matrices. The matrix in Question 7 has determinant $1/2160$, and that in Question 8, $6.3 \times 10^{-5}$. Geometrically, these three planes are so nearly parallel that a very small shift in their orientation makes a very large difference to the position of their point of intersection.

### Miscellaneous Exercise (p. 601)

**1.** (a) $\begin{pmatrix} 0.6 & 0.1 \\ -0.4 & 0.1 \end{pmatrix}$;    (b) $\begin{pmatrix} -\frac{7}{8} & \frac{3}{8} \\ \frac{5}{8} & -\frac{1}{8} \end{pmatrix}$;    (c) $\begin{pmatrix} -7 & 3 \\ -5 & 2 \end{pmatrix}$;

(d) $\begin{pmatrix} -0.12 & 0.32 \\ -0.08 & 0.12 \end{pmatrix}$;   (e) $\begin{pmatrix} -2.5 & -4.5 \\ -1 & -2 \end{pmatrix}$;   (f) $\begin{pmatrix} \frac{3}{28} & -\frac{1}{7} \\ \frac{1}{4} & 0 \end{pmatrix}$.

**2.** (a) $\begin{pmatrix} 1 & 0 \\ 1 & 1 \end{pmatrix}$;    (b) $\begin{pmatrix} 1 & -1 \\ 0 & 1 \end{pmatrix}$;    (c) $\begin{pmatrix} 1/k & 0 \\ 0 & 1 \end{pmatrix}$;

(d) $\begin{pmatrix} 1 & 0 \\ -p & 1 \end{pmatrix}$;    (e) $\begin{pmatrix} 1 & -q \\ 0 & 1 \end{pmatrix}$;    (f) $\begin{pmatrix} 1/k & 0 \\ 0 & 1/l \end{pmatrix}$.

**3.** $X = \begin{pmatrix} 1 & 1 \\ 1 & -1 \end{pmatrix}$.

**4.** 10. The lines are parallel.

**5.** $(2 \ 1 \ -7) = 7(1 \ 3 \ 4) - 5(1 \ 4 \ 7)$. If we call the row vectors **a, b, c**, the echelon process gives
$$\mathbf{b} - \mathbf{a} = (0 \ 1 \ 3) \quad \text{and} \quad \mathbf{c} - 2\mathbf{a} = (0 \ -5 \ -15).$$
Hence $\mathbf{c} - 2\mathbf{a} = -5(\mathbf{b} - \mathbf{a})$ and $\mathbf{c} = 7\mathbf{a} - 5\mathbf{b}$.

If the echelon process were continued there would be a zero on the main diagonal at the next stage. When this happens, as here, there is a linear relation connecting the row vectors.

For a solution, $c = 7 \times 8 - 5 \times 9 = 11$.

**6.** See Figure B. Let $x$, $y$ and $z$ be the mesh currents. By considering the EMF's in the meshes we obtain

$$5(u-x) = 20 \cdot 5$$
$$14x - 3y - 6z - 5u = 0,$$
$$6y - 3x - z = 0,$$
$$14z - 6x - y = 0,$$

from which $x = 83/18$ amp, $y = 8/3$ amp, $z = 13/6$ amp. The currents in the wires are thus as follows:

| Resistor ($\Omega$) | Current (amp) | |
|---|---|---|
| 5 | 4·1 | |
| 3 | 1·96 | |
| 6 | 2·44 | (positive from left to right) |
| 2 | 2·67 | |
| 1 | 0·5 | |
| 7 | 2·17 | |

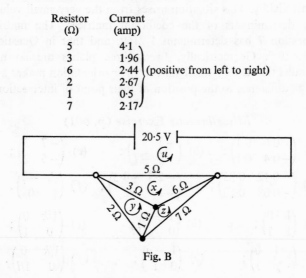

Fig. B

**7.** $(0, -\frac{1}{4}, -2\frac{3}{4})$, $(\frac{1}{2}, \frac{1}{4}, 2\frac{1}{4})$, $(2, -\frac{1}{4}, 3\frac{1}{4})$, $(1\frac{1}{2}, \frac{1}{4}, 1\frac{1}{4})$.

**8.** If I buy $x$ Totshapes, $y$ Jig-geogs and $z$ Puzzlepics, the conditions give

$$x + y + z = 24$$
$$7x + 10y + 8z < 200$$
$$5x + 6y + 9z \geqslant 144.$$

Eliminating $z$ by means of the first equation, we obtain

$$-x + 2y < 8$$
$$4x + 3y \leqslant 72,$$

340

from which $11y \leqslant 104$. To maximize $y$, I choose $y = 9$. Then $10 < x \leqslant 11\frac{1}{4}$, so that $x = 11$, and $z = 4$.

I buy 11 Totshapes, 9 Jig-geogs and 4 Puzzlepics, and have 5p change. The matron would be happier if I gave 10 Totshapes, 9 Jig-geogs and 5 Puzzlepics, but then I should have no change.

# 22

# AREA

This chapter puts the idea of integration on a rather firmer intellectual basis than usual; although it will not be long before pupils surmise that integration is 'the opposite of differentiation', it will probably be wise to lay the stress on the ideas of summation and of area consistently.

The idea of nesting sets is a very powerful one, and should be understood thoroughly; it will help considerably with later studies of limits and convergence.

## 2. THE CALCULATION OF AREA

### *Exercise A (p. 609)*

1.  If we take the side of the triangle as unit, the area of the quadrant is $\frac{1}{4}\pi$, and so is the area of the semi-circle; so that the area of the lune is equal to the area of the triangle (subtracting the area of the minor segment from each).

2.  We shear by subtracting $x^2$ from $y$, making $(1-2x)$; the area is the same as the area of the triangle, namely $\frac{1}{4}$.

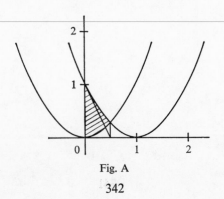

Fig. A

342

5. The area is about 12·3 cm². Counting squares, counting vertices, and refining the count of squares by counting a square in if more than half of it is in the region, and out if not.

6. The argument will work in exactly the same way, and the work of Section 3 will lead to a solid with a plane base; and the idea of 'hyper-volume' is quite straightforward, though impossible to visualize. Indeed, the determinant of an $n \times n$ matrix may be regarded as the hyper-volume of the image of the unit hyper-cube under the corresponding transformation.

7. $1(a, b, c, e)$; 2.1. The circumference of a circle is amenable to this treatment, since it contains congruent arcs.

8. Area on a sphere and (with care) on a cylinder can be defined in a similar way; but more powerful transformations than isometries are needed for ellipsoid and cone, or to deform a plane into any of these shapes. A certain amount can be done by using limiting processes (compare Section 2.3).

9. The inside area is $2m \cdot \frac{1}{2}r^2 \cos(\pi/m) \sin(\pi/m)$ and the outside area is $2m \cdot \frac{1}{2}r^2 \tan(\pi/m)$; $(m = 2^n.)$

$$m \tan(\pi/m) > \pi > m \cos(\pi/m) \sin(\pi/m);$$

$$(\sin x)/x \to 1.$$

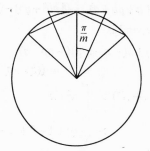

Fig. B

343

# 3. AREAS UNDER GRAPHS
## *Exercise B (p. 616)*

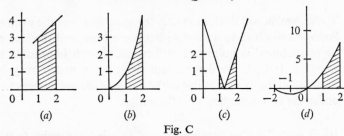

Fig. C

**1.** (a) $3\frac{1}{2}$;      (b) $2\frac{1}{3}$;      (c) $\frac{5}{6}$;      (d) $5\frac{1}{3}$.

**2.** $\frac{1}{3}(b^3-a^3)$.

**4.** See Figure D. The area is $c\sqrt{c}-\frac{1}{3}c\sqrt{c} = \frac{2}{3}c\sqrt{c}$.

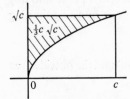 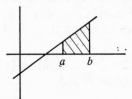 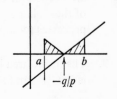

Fig. D             Fig. E

**5.** See Figure E. The area of the first is

$$\tfrac{1}{2}(b-a)(pa+q+pb+q) = (\tfrac{1}{2}pb^2+qb)-(\tfrac{1}{2}pa^2+qa);$$

the area of the second is

$$\tfrac{1}{2}(b+q/p)(pb+q)+\tfrac{1}{2}(-a-q/p)(-ap-q)$$
$$= ((bp+q)^2+(ap+q)^2)/2p.$$

**6.** $\dfrac{b^4}{N^4}(1+8+27+\ldots+N^3) > \displaystyle\int_0^b x^3\,dx$

$$> \frac{b^4}{N^4}(0+1+8+\ldots+(N-1)^3)$$

$$\Rightarrow \frac{b^4}{N^4}\tfrac{1}{4}N^2(N+1)^2 > \int_0^b x^3\,dx > \frac{b^4}{N^4}\tfrac{1}{4}(N-1)^2 N^2,$$

whence the result follows; the value of the integral is $\frac{1}{4}b^4$.

344

**7.** See Figure F. The area is $c\sqrt[3]{c} - \frac{1}{4}c\sqrt[3]{c} = \frac{3}{4}c\sqrt[3]{c} = \frac{3}{4}c^{\frac{4}{3}}$.

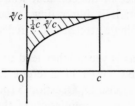

Fig. F

**8.** $\dfrac{b}{n} 2 \sin \dfrac{\frac{1}{2}b}{n} \displaystyle\sum_{r=0}^{r=n-1} \cos \dfrac{rb}{n} > 2 \left( \displaystyle\int_0^b \cos x \, dx \right) \sin \dfrac{\frac{1}{2}b}{n}$

$$> \dfrac{b}{n} 2 \sin \dfrac{\frac{1}{2}b}{n} \sum_{r=1}^{r=n} \cos \dfrac{rb}{n}$$

(note the direction of the inequalities; cos is a decreasing function in this region; the argument used in this section can of course be applied strictly only to monotonic portions of the graph, though the results can easily be combined later).

So

$\dfrac{b}{n} \displaystyle\sum_{r=0}^{r=n-1} \left( \sin \dfrac{(r+\frac{1}{2})b}{n} - \sin \dfrac{(r-\frac{1}{2})b}{n} \right) > 2 \sin \dfrac{\frac{1}{2}b}{n} \displaystyle\int_0^b \cos x \, dx$

$$> \dfrac{b}{n} \sum_{r=1}^{r=n} \left( \sin \dfrac{(r+\frac{1}{2})b}{n} - \sin \dfrac{(r-\frac{1}{2})b}{n} \right)$$

$\Rightarrow \dfrac{b}{n} \left( \sin \dfrac{(n-\frac{1}{2})b}{n} - \sin \dfrac{(-\frac{1}{2})b}{n} \right) > 2 \sin \dfrac{\frac{1}{2}b}{n} \displaystyle\int_0^b \cos x \, dx$

$$> \dfrac{b}{n} \left( \sin \dfrac{(n+\frac{1}{2})b}{n} - \sin \dfrac{\frac{1}{2}b}{n} \right)$$

$\Rightarrow \displaystyle\int_0^b \cos x \, dx = \sin b$,

since $\qquad \displaystyle\lim_{n \to \infty} \left( \dfrac{\frac{1}{2}b}{n} \Big/ \sin \dfrac{\frac{1}{2}b}{n} \right) = 1.$

**9.** This time, we use

$$2 \sin \dfrac{2br}{n} \sin \dfrac{b}{n} = \cos \dfrac{(2r-1)b}{n} - \cos \dfrac{(2r+1)b}{n},$$

345

and proceed in the same way; the result is, of course, $\frac{1}{2} - \frac{1}{2}\cos 2b$, though the presence of the constant will come as a surprise to most of the class; it is interesting to compare this with the previous result, using a stretch and a reflection.

10. See Figure G. This is yet another lead towards the logarithmic function; compare Chapter 17, Exercise E, Question 8 (p. 485), and Chapter 7, Exercise D, Question 5 (p. 211). It may be used as a corrective if the differentiation of the answer has become apparently trivial.

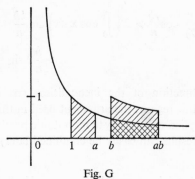

Fig. G

# 4. APPROXIMATE METHODS
## *Exercise C (p. 625)*

1. The area is $\frac{1}{3}b^3$, and the trapezium rule gives:

$$\frac{1}{2}\frac{b}{n}\left(0 + b^2 + 2\left(\frac{b^2}{n^2} + \frac{4b^2}{n^2} + \frac{9b^2}{n^2} + \ldots + \frac{(n-1)^2 b^2}{n^2}\right)\right)$$

$$= \frac{b^3}{6n^3}\left(n(n+1)(2n+1) - 3n^2\right)$$

$$= \frac{b^3}{6n^3}(2n^3 + n), \quad \text{so that the error is} \quad \frac{b^3}{6n^2}.$$

2. The formula must be divided by $nh$, the length of the interval. Not surprisingly, the mean value of the constant function is 1.

3. See Figure H for the approximating quadratic function. Simpson's Rule gives
$$\tfrac{1}{3} \cdot \tfrac{1}{2}b(0 + \tfrac{1}{2}b^3 + b^3) = \tfrac{1}{4}b^4.$$

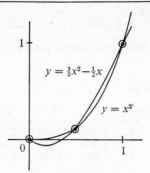

Fig. H

**4.** Simpson's Rule gives $\frac{1}{3} \cdot \frac{1}{4}\pi \cdot (1 + 2\sqrt{2})$, and the exact value is 1. So $\pi \simeq 12/(1 + 2\sqrt{2}) = \frac{12}{7}(2\sqrt{2} - 1) \simeq 3 \cdot 134$.

**5.** $\int_0^1 \dfrac{4}{1 + x^2}\, dx \simeq \frac{1}{6}(\frac{4}{1} + \frac{4}{2} + \frac{64}{5}) = 18 \cdot 8/6 \simeq 3 \cdot 133$.

**6.** Using Simpson's Rule for $\int_1^2$, $\int_2^3$, etc., we find (to four figures):

0·6944,  0·4056,  0·2876,  0·2231,  0·1823;

by this reckoning

$$\int_1^2 = 0 \cdot 6944, \qquad \int_1^3 = 1 \cdot 1000, \qquad \int_1^6 = 1 \cdot 7930.$$

**7.** The exact value is $\frac{2}{5}c^{\frac{5}{2}}$, and Simpson's Rule gives $\frac{1}{6}(1 + 2\sqrt{2})c^{\frac{5}{2}}$. The fractional error is $\frac{1}{4}(3 - 2\sqrt{2})$, about 4·4%. A parabola is bound to be a poor approximation to a curve with an infinite gradient.

**8.** $\frac{1}{12}\pi + \frac{1}{8}\sqrt{3}$ gives the area of the sector added to the area of the triangle. Simpson's Rule gives $\frac{1}{12}(1 + \sqrt{15} + \frac{1}{2}\sqrt{3})$.

Comparison of the two gives $\pi \simeq 1 + \sqrt{15} - \sqrt{3} \simeq 3 \cdot 141$. This is a surprisingly good approximation; but if it were extended to the whole quadrant, again the infinite gradient would make the quadratic trapezium unrealistic.

**9.** Simpson's Rule gives $\frac{1}{30} \times 10 \cdot 237 \simeq 0 \cdot 3412$.

**10.** This is a good question, but there is no unique way of applying Simpson's Rule to the figure as it stands; the intercepts on the grid lines of the graph paper used may be a help.

347

**11.** $\int_0^1 = 0{\cdot}0905,\quad \int_1^3 = 0{\cdot}4990,\quad \int_3^5 = 0{\cdot}3250,\quad \int_5^7 = 0{\cdot}0747,$

to four figures; the probabilities are therefore $0{\cdot}40$ and $0{\cdot}59$, approximately.

**12.** Values of $1/(1-z^\alpha)$:

| | $z = 0$ | $0{\cdot}2$ | $0{\cdot}4$ | $0{\cdot}6$ | $0{\cdot}8$ |
|---|---|---|---|---|---|
| When $\alpha = 1$ | 1 | 1·250 | 1·667 | 2·500 | 5·000 |
| $\alpha = 1\frac{1}{2}$ | 1 | 1·098 | 1·339 | 1·868 | 3·515 |
| $\alpha = 2$ | 1 | 1·041 | 1·191 | 1·563 | 2·777 |

The Simpson's Rule values are therefore $1{\cdot}62u/g$, $1{\cdot}27u/g$, $1{\cdot}17u/g$.

**13.** When $k = \sin 3°$, the values of the integrand at $0, \frac{1}{8}\pi, \frac{1}{4}\pi, \frac{3}{8}\pi, \frac{1}{2}\pi$ are
$$1{\cdot}0000 \quad 1{\cdot}0002 \quad 1{\cdot}0007 \quad 1{\cdot}0011 \quad 1{\cdot}0013;$$

and, when $k = \sin 30°$,
$$1{\cdot}0000 \quad 1{\cdot}0188 \quad 1{\cdot}0691 \quad 1{\cdot}1276 \quad 1{\cdot}1547.$$

Since the interval is $\frac{1}{8}\pi$, divide by $\frac{1}{2}\pi$ (uncorrected value) directly; so that the ratios are $\frac{1}{12} \times 12{\cdot}0079$; $\frac{1}{12} \times 12{\cdot}8785$, and the errors are $0{\cdot}07\%$ and $7{\cdot}32\%$.

# 5. EVALUATING INTEGRALS

## Exercise D (p. 631)

**1.** (a) $\frac{4}{3}\pi R^3 - \frac{4}{3}\pi r^3$;  (b) $1/b - 1/a = 1/b - 1/c$;

(c) $(2^2 - 3.2) - (1^2 - 3.1) = 0$;  (d) $\mathbf{r}_1 - \mathbf{r}_2$.

**2.** (a) $\left[\pi R^2\right]_{R_1}^{R_2}$;  (b) $\left[\dfrac{1}{x}\right]_{n+1}^1$;

(c) $\left[\theta(t)\right]_{t_1}^{t_2}$;  (d) $\left[x\right]_{x_1}^{x_2}$.

**3.** (a) $\left[\frac{1}{4}x^4\right]_1^2 = 3\frac{3}{4}$;  (b) $\left[\frac{1}{5}x^5\right]_{-1}^{+1} = \frac{2}{5}$;

(c) $\left[4x - \frac{1}{3}x^3\right]_0^2 = 5\frac{1}{3}$;  (d) $\left[-\cos x\right]_0^{\frac{1}{3}\pi} = \frac{1}{2}$;

(e) $\left[\sin 2x\right]_0^{\frac{1}{6}\pi} = \frac{1}{2}\sqrt{3}$;  (f) $\left[-1/x\right]_1^2 = \frac{1}{2}$;

348

(g) $\left[-1/2x^2\right]_1^2 = \frac{3}{8}$;  (h) $\left[\frac{3}{4}x^{\frac{4}{3}}\right]_1^2 = \frac{3}{2} \cdot \sqrt[3]{2} - \frac{3}{4}$;

(i) $\left[-\cos^4 x\right]_0^{\frac{1}{2}\pi} = 1$.

4. (a) $\left[\frac{1}{4}x^4 + \frac{3}{2}x^2\right]_{-2}^{+2} = 0$;  (b) $\left[\frac{1}{3}x^3 - \frac{3}{2}x^2 + 2x\right]_1^2 = -\frac{1}{6}$;

(c) $\left[\sin x + \cos x\right]_0^{\frac{1}{4}\pi} = \sqrt{2} - 1$;  (d) $\left[-2\cos\frac{1}{2}x\right]_0^{\pi} = 2$;

(e) $\left[-\frac{4}{3}\cos^3 x\right]_{-\frac{1}{4}\pi}^{+\frac{1}{4}\pi} = 0$;  (f) $\left[\sin x - \frac{1}{3}\sin^3 x\right]_0^{\frac{1}{2}\pi} = \frac{2}{3}$.

5. $\left[x^{m+1}/(m+1)\right]_0^a = a^{m+1}/(m+1)$. If $m$ is not positive, $x^m \to \infty$ as $x \to 0$; if $m$ is not rational, although the result is true we have as yet no means of proving it.

6. $(d/dx)(x\cos x) = \cos x - x\sin x$;

$(d/dx)(x\sin x) = \sin x + x\cos x$.

$$\left[x\sin x\right]_0^{\frac{1}{4}\pi} = \frac{\pi}{4\sqrt{2}}; \quad \left[-\cos x\right]_0^{\frac{1}{4}\pi} = 1 - \frac{1}{\sqrt{2}};$$

$$\left[x\sin x + \cos x\right]_0^{\frac{1}{4}\pi} \simeq 0 \cdot 262.$$

Similarly,

$$\int_0^{\frac{1}{4}\pi} x\sin x\, dx = \left[\sin x - x\cos x\right]_0^{\frac{1}{4}\pi} \simeq 0 \cdot 152.$$

It is very useful to sketch the graphs of these two functions, and to see how well these values agree.

7. Yes; all these are perfectly good indefinite integrals, but the relations between them are, of course:

$$\sin^2 x = 1 - \cos^2 x = \frac{1}{2} - \frac{1}{2}\cos 2x.$$

8. (a) $\sin x + k$;  (b) $x^{m+1}/(m+1) + k$;

(c) $k - 1/(x+1)$;  (d) $k + (1/a)\sin ax$;

(e) $\frac{1}{3}ax^3 + bx^2 + cx + k$;  (f) $k - x^{m-1}/(m-1)$.

9. $\frac{1}{2}x\sqrt{(1-x^2)} + \frac{1}{2}\sin^{-1} x$, by adding sector to triangle.

10. The answer may be expressed as 'Yes, to within an arbitrary constant'.

## 6. SOME GENERALIZATIONS

### *Exercise E (p. 637)*

1.   (a) $-\frac{1}{4}$;    (b) 0;    (c) $-6\frac{2}{3}$;    (d) 1;

    (e) $2\frac{1}{2}$;    (f) $-\frac{1}{6}$.

For graphs, see Figure I.

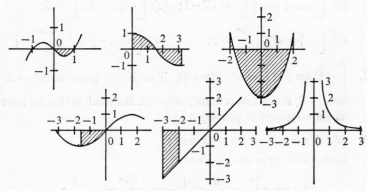

Fig. I

2.  Each is the negative of $\int_a^b (-f)$.

3.  They are equal; see Figure J.

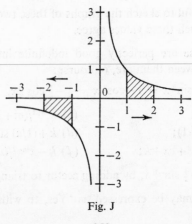

Fig. J

350

**4.** (a) $\left[1-x^{1-m}\right]_1^N$ tends to 1 as $N$ tends to $\infty$ if $m > 1$; no meaning otherwise;

(b) $\left[1-x^{1-m}\right]_k^1$ tends to 1 as $k$ tends to 0 if $m < 1$; no meaning otherwise. Again, it is profitable to examine some typical graphs.

**5.** $\left[\tan^{-1} x\right]_{-N}^{+N} = 2\tan^{-1} N$, which tends to $\pi$ as $N$ tends to $\infty$. This is therefore the total area under the 'Cauchy curve'. See Figure 32.

**6.** $\left[\sin^{-1} x\right]_{-1}^{+1} = 2\sin^{-1} 1$, which is equal to $\pi$; the problem here is that the integrand tends to infinity as $|x|$ tends to 1 from below. See the answer to Chapter 5, Exercise I, Question 3(c), for a figure (p. 97).

**7.** If $b$ is finite and $a$ tends to $\infty$,

$$\int_1^a \frac{1}{x}\,dx = \int_1^{ab} \frac{1}{x}\,dx, \quad \text{so that} \quad \int_1^b \frac{1}{x}\,dx = 0,$$

which is absurd.

### Miscellaneous Exercise (p. 638)

One of our preoccupations in this exercise is to find quick and reliable methods of estimating the values of integrals which occur in physical problems but which cannot be integrated directly. Simpson's Rule (and its refinements) and comparison methods are very useful for this purpose.

**1.** $\sin x/x$ is a decreasing function, for $0 < x < \frac{1}{2}\pi$, since the numerator is always increasing less quickly than the denominator, as we can see immediately from the two graphs. It follows that

$$0 < x < \alpha \Rightarrow 1 > \sin x/x > \sin \alpha/\alpha, \quad \text{for} \quad 0 < \alpha < \frac{1}{2}\pi.$$

It follows from the theorem that

$$\int_0^\alpha 1\,dx > \int_0^\alpha \frac{\sin x}{x}\,dx > \int_0^\alpha \frac{\sin \alpha}{\alpha}\,dx,$$

and the result follows from this.

351

2. Since $(1-x^2) \leqslant 1/(1+x^2) \leqslant 1$, for $0 \leqslant x \leqslant 1$, the integrals between 0 and 0·1 are also ordered like this; therefore

$$0·1 - \tfrac{1}{3}(0·1)^3 \leqslant \tan^{-1}(0·1) \leqslant 0·1,$$

whence the result follows.

Since $1-x \leqslant 1/(1+x) \leqslant 1$, using very similar reasoning, the integral lies between 0·095 and 0·1.

3. $g$ needs to be an integrable function, for otherwise we might have a function equal to 0 when $x$ is rational, say, and to $1/x^2$ otherwise; although the convergence is all right, the basic difficulty then remains.

Adequate limits are given by

$$(x^2)^{-\frac{2}{3}} > (1+x^2)^{-\frac{2}{3}} > (1+x^2)^{-1};$$

integrating these from 1 to $\infty$, we find that the integral lies between 3 and $\tfrac{1}{4}\pi$.

4. In each case, the constant function has the wrong average value.

5. See Question 1. Since

$$\sqrt{\left(\frac{\alpha}{\sin \alpha}\right)} \frac{1}{\sqrt{x}} > \sqrt{(\csc x)} > \frac{1}{\sqrt{x}},$$

integrating from 0 to $\alpha$, the value of the integral lies between $2\sqrt{\alpha}$ and $2\alpha\sqrt{(\csc \alpha)}$; thus, if $\alpha = \tfrac{1}{18}\pi$, the integral lies between 1 and 1·0025 times 0·8354.

The values of the integrand, for $x = \tfrac{1}{18}\pi$ $(\tfrac{1}{18}\pi)\tfrac{1}{2}\pi$, are:

$$2·3998, \quad 1·7100, \quad 1·4142, \quad 1·2478, \quad 1·1426,$$
$$1·0748, \quad 1·0317, \quad 1·0077, \quad 1·0000.$$

Simpson's Rule with eight strips gives 1·790, with four strips 1·795, and with only two strips 1·858; a good estimate of the value of the integral over the whole range is therefore 2·625.

6. Put $x_2-x_1 = x_1-x_0 = a$, and, translating $x_1$ to the right, the integrand becomes simply $f(x)$; we can therefore always reduce the problem to the integral of an appropriate quadratic, for which the result has already been established.

352

7. For functions which are 'piecewise continuous' this is easy enough, and has considerable usefulness in passing from discrete to continuous probability models, since any sum can then be presented as an integral; for example,

$$\sum_{i=0}^{i=n-1} i^2 = \int_0^n ([x])^2 \, dx,$$

in this sense, and similarly

$$\sum_{i=1}^{i=n} f(i) = \int_0^n f([x+1]) \, dx.$$

But for functions which are defined like (say) the one in Question 3 above, this demands an excursion into measure theory, which is too hard to consider seriously at this stage, except possibly to mention the idea of a set of measure zero.

# 23

# TECHNIQUES OF INTEGRATION

## 1. NOTATION

### Exercise A (p. 642)

This is intended as a leading exercise, to give pupils the idea of integration by substitution. It can be done without further introduction, and serves as a useful revision exercise on the chain rule for differentiation.

**1.** (a) $x \to 5x^4$;　　　　　　　　　(b) $x \to 6(2x-1)^2$;

　　(c) $x \to -\frac{3}{2}(3x+2)^{-\frac{3}{2}}$;　　　　(d) $x \to 6x(x^2+1)^2$;

　　(e) $x \to 60x^4(3x^5-4)^3$;　　　　(f) $x \to 2x+2\cos 2x$;

　　(g) $x \to 3\sin^2 x \cos x$;　　　　(h) $x \to \frac{1}{2}\sec^2(\frac{1}{2}x+\frac{1}{4}\pi)$.

**2.** (a) $x \to \frac{1}{6}x^6$;　　　　　　　　(b) $x \to \frac{1}{3}(2x-1)^3$;

　　(c) $x \to -\frac{2}{3}(3x+2)^{-\frac{1}{2}}$;　　　　(d) $x \to \frac{1}{4}(x^2+1)^4$;

　　(e) $x \to \frac{1}{60}(3x^5-4)^4$;　　　　(f) $x \to \frac{1}{2}x^2+\frac{1}{2}\sin 2x$;

　　(g) $x \to \frac{1}{3}\sin^3 x$;　　　　　(h) $x \to 2\tan(\frac{1}{2}x+\frac{1}{4}\pi)$.

**3.** (a) $dy/dx = \frac{2}{3}x^{-\frac{1}{3}}$;　　　　(b) $dy/dx = -\frac{1}{2}x^{-\frac{3}{2}}$;

　　(c) $dy/dx = \frac{1}{2}a(ax+b)^{-\frac{1}{2}}$;

　　(d) $dy/dx = \frac{1}{2}(2ax+b)(ax^2+bx+c)^{-\frac{1}{2}}$;

　　(e) $dy/dx = -6\cos 3x \sin 3x$;　　(f) $dy/dx = -2x/(1+x^2)^2$;

　　(g) $dy/dx = -x/\sqrt{(4-x^2)}$;

　　(h) $dy/dx = 15(x^2-1)(x^3-3x+1)^4$.

**4.**　(Arbitrary constants are omitted.)

　　(a) $\frac{2}{3}x^{\frac{3}{2}}$;　　　　　(b) $3x^{\frac{1}{3}}$;　　　　　(c) $\frac{4}{5}(x-1)^{\frac{5}{4}}$;

　　(d) $\frac{1}{3}(x^2+1)^{\frac{3}{2}}$;　　(e) $-\frac{1}{9}\cos^3 3x$;　　(f) $-1/2(1+x^2)$;

　　(g) $\frac{1}{4}(x^2+3x)^4$;　　(h) $\sin x^2$.

354

**5.** The first part is true, because when we multiply $y$ by a constant, we multiply $dy/dx$ by the same constant. In the second part, however, if we multiply $y$ by a function of $x$ other than a constant, then $dy/dx$ is not simply multiplied by that function, and the inverse process cannot be applied.

**6.** (a) 4;       (b) 0·041;       (c) $20\frac{1}{3}$;

(d) $\frac{1}{4}$;       (e) 15/16;       (f) 0;

(g) 1·65 (exactly);       (h) $\frac{1}{4}$.

Note that although in parts (b) and (d) the integral function appears to be negative, the definite integral is in fact positive.

## 2. SOME USEFUL DEVICES

The devices of Section 2 should not be thought of as techniques to be learnt, but simply as aids to integration which the pupil should at some time have seen, so that when he meets the need for them again he will be able to call upon his experience of them.

### Exercise B (p. 646)

In this exercise, constants of integration are omitted throughout.

**1.** (a) $x+3/x-1/2x^2$;       (b) $\frac{1}{30}(5x-1)(x+1)^5$;

(c) $(-x-1)(x+2)^2$;       (d) $\frac{1}{4}(x^2+4x+2)(x+2)^2$;

(e) $\frac{31}{162}$;       (f) $\frac{4}{15}$.

**2.** (a) $\frac{1}{4}\cos 2x-\frac{1}{8}\cos 4x$;       (b) $\frac{1}{2}\sin x-\frac{1}{8}\sin 4x$;

(c) $\frac{1}{4}$;       (d) $\frac{1}{8}\pi = 0·393$;

(e) $1-\frac{1}{4}\pi = 0·215$;       (f) $\frac{1}{16}\pi = 0·196$;

(g) $\frac{2}{3}$.

**3.** (a) 4 (note the use of the odd function);       (b) $\frac{2}{3}bh^3+2dh$;

(c) 0 (note the use of the odd function);       (d) 0;

(e) 0;       (f) $\frac{1}{4}\pi^2 = 2·5$;       (g) $\frac{3}{4}\pi^2-2\pi = 1·11$.

## 3. INTEGRATION BY SUBSTITUTION

### *Exercise C (p. 649)*

In Section 3, it seems wiser to set out the method in full in the first place, so that the connection with the chain rule can be clearly seen, and so that pupils can appreciate that we are trying to transform a problem into a simpler problem. Only later should they use the formalized method.

**1.** (a) $\frac{1}{5}u^5 - \frac{1}{4}u^4 = \frac{1}{20}(4x-1)(x+1)^4$;

   (b) $\frac{2}{15}(-3x-2)(1-x^2)^{\frac{3}{2}}$;    (c) $\sin^{-1} x$;

   (d) $\tan^{-1} x$;    (e) $(-1-2x)/(x+1)^2$;

   (f) $\sin^{-1} \sqrt{x} - \sqrt{(x-x^2)}$.

**2.** (a) $-2\sqrt{(1-x)}$;    (b) $-\frac{2}{3}(8+x)\sqrt{(4-x)}$;

   (c) $\sin^{-1}(\frac{1}{2}x)$;    (d) $\tan^{-1}(\frac{1}{3}x)$;

   (e) $\sec^{-1} x$;    (f) $-\sqrt{(1+x^2)}/x$.

**3.** See Section 3.2.

### *Exercise D (p. 652)*

**1.** (a) $\frac{1}{20}(4x-1)(x+1)^4$;    (b) $-\frac{2}{15}(3x+2)(1-x^2)^{\frac{3}{2}}$;

   (c) $\tan^{-1} x$;    (d) $\sin^{-1} \sqrt{x} - \sqrt{(x-x^2)}$.

**2.** (a) $-(4x-1)/8(2x-1)^2$;    (b) $\frac{2}{15}(3x+1)(x+2)^{\frac{3}{2}}$;

   (c) $\frac{1}{4}\sin^{-1} 2x + \frac{1}{2}x\sqrt{(1-4x^2)}$;    (d) $\frac{1}{16}\tan^{-1}(\frac{1}{2}x) + x/8(4+x^2)$.

**3.** (a) $\left[\frac{2}{45}u^{\frac{5}{2}} - \frac{2}{27}u^{\frac{3}{2}}\right]_4^{16} = 39\cdot9$ approx.;

   (b) $\frac{5}{24} = 0\cdot21$;    (c) $\frac{1}{4}\pi = 0\cdot785$;    (d) $\frac{1}{12}\pi = 0\cdot262$.

**4.** (a) $\left[-2u - \sin 2u\right]_{\frac{1}{4}\pi}^{\frac{1}{2}\pi} = 0\cdot658$;    (b) $\frac{1}{2}\pi = 1\cdot571$;

   (c) $\pi = 3\cdot142$;    (d) $\frac{1}{2}\pi = 1\cdot571$.

**5.** (a) $\displaystyle\int \frac{1}{\sqrt{((ac+b^2)/a - a(x-b/a)^2)}} dx$, which we can integrate if $a > 0$, $ac+b^2 > 0$;

(b) $\int \dfrac{1}{a(x+b/a)^2+(ac-b^2)/a}\,dx$, which we can integrate if $b^2 < ac$.

(In 4(c) and (d), the integrand becomes infinite, so that this question is not strictly correct at this stage.)

### Exercise E (p. 654)

1.  (a) $-\frac{1}{3}(1-x^2)^{\frac{3}{2}}$;     (b) $\frac{2}{3}\sqrt{(x^3+1)}$;       (c) $\sqrt{2}-1 = 0.414$;

    (d) $\frac{1}{2}$;           (e) $\frac{1}{10}$.

2.  (a) $\frac{1}{3}\sin^3 x$;                   (b) $\sin x\,(1-\frac{1}{3}\sin^2 x)$;

    (c) $-\frac{1}{8}(1-x^2)^4$;                 (d) $-\frac{1}{15}(3x^2+2)(1-x^2)^{\frac{3}{2}}$;

    (e) $\frac{1}{2}(a\cos x+b\sin x)^2$.

3.  (a) $\left[\frac{1}{3}u^{\frac{3}{2}}-u^{\frac{1}{2}}\right]_1^{0\cdot64} = 0.0373$;     (b) $\left[2u^{\frac{1}{2}}-\frac{2}{5}u^{\frac{5}{2}}\right]_{\frac{1}{2}}^1 = 0.257$;

    (c) $1\frac{1}{3}$;                  (d) $\frac{1}{3}\pi = 1.047$;       (e) $-\frac{1}{6}$.

4.  $-\displaystyle\int_1^{\frac{1}{2}\sqrt 3} \dfrac{u^2}{\sqrt{(1-u^2)}}\,du$; area is $\dfrac{\pi}{12}+\dfrac{\sqrt 3}{8}$, as before, considering sector and triangle.

## 4. INTEGRATION BY PARTS
### Exercise F (p. 655)

1.  $x\cos x+\sin x$;

    $\displaystyle\int x\cos x\,dx = x\sin x-\int \sin x\,dx = x\sin x+\cos x.$

2.  $-\frac{1}{2}x\cos 2x+\frac{1}{4}\sin 2x$;   $2x\sin\frac{1}{2}x+4\cos\frac{1}{2}x$.

3.  $x/\sqrt{(1-x^2)}+\sin^{-1} x$;   $\displaystyle\int \sin^{-1} x\,dx = x\sin^{-1} x+\sqrt{(1-x^2)}$.

    $2x\cos x-x^2\sin x$;

    $\displaystyle\int x^2\sin x\,dx = -x^2\cos x+2x\sin x+2\cos x.$

*Exercise G (p. 656)*

It is very profitable to sketch graphs to see what areas are represented.

**1.** (a) $\sin x - x \cos x$;    (b) $-\frac{1}{2}$;    (c) 4;

(d) $\frac{1}{2}(x^2+1)\tan^{-1} x - \frac{1}{2}x$.

**2.** (a) $-x^2 \cos x + 2x \sin x + 2 \cos x$;

(b) $x^3 \sin x + 3x^2 \cos x - 6x \sin x - 6 \cos x$.

(It is interesting to see the patterns that emerge from integrals of this type, and to learn to write them down, without further working, in the order given.)

(c) $\frac{1}{4}x^2 - \frac{1}{4}x \sin 2x - \frac{1}{8} \cos 2x$;

(d) $-\frac{1}{8}x \cos 4x - \frac{1}{4}x \cos 2x + \frac{1}{32} \sin 4x + \frac{1}{8} \sin 2x$.

**3.** (a) $\frac{2}{15}(3x-2)(x+1)^{\frac{3}{2}}$;

(b) $\frac{1}{12}\pi + \frac{1}{8}\sqrt{3}$ (cf. Exercise E, Question 4).

**4.** Either write down

$$\left[-x^n \cos x + nx^{n-1} \sin x + n(n-1)x^{n-2} \cos x - \ldots\right]_0^{\frac{1}{2}\pi}$$
$$= n(\tfrac{1}{2}\pi)^{n-1} - n(n-1)(n-2)(\tfrac{1}{2}\pi)^{n-3} + \ldots$$

or write $\displaystyle\int_0^{\frac{1}{2}\pi} x^n \sin x \, dx = I_n$;

then integrating by parts,

$$I_n = n(\tfrac{1}{2}\pi)^{n-1} - n(n-1)I_{n-2}.$$

**5.** $(d/dx)(\sin^{m-1} x \cos^{n+1} x)$

$$= (m-1)\sin^{m-2} x \cos^{n+2} x - (n+1)\sin^m x \cos^n x$$
$$= (m-1)\sin^{m-2} x \cos^n x - (m+n)\sin^m x \cos^n x,$$

because $\cos^{n+2} x = \cos^n x(1-\sin^2 x)$.

Integrating from 0 to $\frac{1}{2}\pi$,

$$\int_0^{\frac{1}{2}\pi} \sin^m x \cos^n x \, dx = \frac{m-1}{m+n}\int_0^{\frac{1}{2}\pi} \sin^{m-2} x \cos^n x \, dx.$$

All the parts of this question are special cases of this *reduction formula*.

$$\int s^3 c^4 = \frac{2}{7}\cdot\frac{1}{5} = \frac{2}{35}; \quad \int s^7 c^4 = \frac{6}{11}\cdot\frac{4}{9}\cdot\frac{2}{7}\cdot\frac{1}{5} = \frac{48}{3465};$$

$$\int s^6 c^2 = \frac{5}{8}\cdot\frac{3}{6}\cdot\frac{1}{4}\cdot\frac{1}{2}\cdot\frac{1}{2}\,\pi = \frac{5\pi}{256}.$$

**6.** If $u = \cos x$, $v = -1/x$,

$$\int (\cos x/x^2)\,dx = -\cos x/x + \int (\sin x/x)\,dx^2.$$

**7.** $\displaystyle\int_0^1 \tan^{-1} x\,dx = \left[x\tan^{-1}x\right]_0^1 - \int_0^1 \frac{x}{1+x^2}\,dx.$ Subs. $t = 1+x^2$

$$\int_0^1 \tan^{-1} x\,dx = \tfrac{1}{4}\pi - \int_1^2 \frac{1}{2t}\,dt = \tfrac{1}{4}\pi - \tfrac{1}{2}F(2).$$

# 5. SOME STANDARD INTEGRALS

## Exercise H (p. 658)

**1.** (a) $\frac{3}{4}(2x-1)^{\frac{2}{3}}$;        (b) $-2\cos(\frac{1}{2}x+\frac{1}{4}\pi)$;

   (c) $\tan^{-1}(\frac{1}{3}x)$;    (d) $\sin^{-1}(\frac{1}{5}x)$;    (e) $\frac{1}{3}\tan 3x$.

**2.** (a) $\frac{1}{2}$;          (b) 2;            (c) $3/\pi = 0{\cdot}956$;

   (d) $\frac{1}{6}\pi = 0{\cdot}524$;    (e) $\frac{1}{8}\pi = 0{\cdot}393$.

**3.** (a) $(ax+b)^{n+1}/a(n+1)$;       (b) $-\dfrac{a}{b}\cos(bx+c)$;

   (c) $(1/p)\tan(px+q)$;        (d) $-(qx+r)^{-m+1}/q(m-1)$;

   (e) $\dfrac{1}{ac}\tan^{-1}\dfrac{a}{c}(x+b)$;        (f) $\dfrac{1}{q}\sin^{-1}\left(\dfrac{qx+r}{p}\right)$.

**4.** (a) $\sin^{-1}(x-1)$;    (b) $\tan^{-1}(x+1)$;    (c) $\frac{1}{3}\tan^{-1}(x-2)$;

   (d) $\sin^{-1}(\frac{1}{10}(x+8))$;        (e) $\dfrac{1}{\sqrt{2}}\sin^{-1}\left(\dfrac{2x-3}{\sqrt{11}}\right)$.

# 6. DIMENSIONAL CONSISTENCY

There are in fact serious objections to regarding the method of dimensions as significant when it is divorced from the physical situation in which it arises naturally. Nevertheless, the point of being able to integrate most of these expressions is that they can occur in genuine physical problems, and when this is so, the symbols in them must be related in the way suggested. Thus, for example, in the solution of the simple harmonic motion equation, the integral

$$\int \frac{1}{n\sqrt{(a^2 - x^2)}} \, dx$$

arises naturally, and, in this equation $n$ is a frequency, and $x$ and $a$ are lengths. It is natural to expect that the answer will be of the form $nt = \sin^{-1}(x/a)$; the fact that these quantities must be dimensionally consistent means that when we are evaluating integrals in the abstract it is reasonable to imagine that they come from some such physical situation. This is the principle on which this section is based. It is not therefore tied in any way to the actual dimensions of length and time, but it is both interesting and useful, if not for prediction at least as a check, though the reader will find that he is soon able to write down the answers to problems of this kind at sight.

In the case of integration, the same results may always be obtained by a simple change of variable, though this is slower and more liable to error; but there are also interesting parallels, suggested by the questions of the next exercise, with the use of homogeneous coordinates in geometry, and with ideas of weight and order in algebra.

### Exercise I (p. 662)

1. (a) $m$, **1**, gradient; $c$, **L**, intercept.
   (b) $\theta$, **1**, angle; $p$, **L**, perpendicular.
   (c) $a$, $b$, **L**, intercepts.
   (d) $l$, $m$, **1**, direction cosines; $n$, **L**, perpendicular, scaled.
   (e) $p$, $r$, $t$, **L**, components of vectors; $q$, **1**, parameter.

2. $c$, **L**; $t$, **1**. $m$ is a ratio, and must depend on $t$ alone; $k$ must contain just one $c$. Thus, in fact, $m = -1/t^2$, $k = -2c/t$.
   $a$, $b$, **L**; $t$, **1**.

   Nothing to say; $m = \dfrac{b(\sin t - \cos t)}{a(\sin t + \cos t)}$, for example.

   $a$, **L**; $t$, **1**. $m = \frac{3}{2}t$; $c = -\frac{1}{2}at^3$.

3. (a) $\left(\dfrac{x}{a}\right)^2 + \left(\dfrac{y}{a}\right)^2 = 1$;  $(a\cos t,\ a\sin t)$;

   (b) $\left(\dfrac{x}{a}\right)^{\frac{2}{3}} + \left(\dfrac{y}{a}\right)^{\frac{2}{3}} = 1$;  $(a\cos^3 t,\ a\sin^3 t)$;

   (c) $\left(\dfrac{x}{a}\right)^2 - \left(\dfrac{y}{a}\right)^2 = 1$;  $(a\sec t,\ a\tan t)$;

   (d) $\left(\dfrac{x}{a}\right)^3 + \left(\dfrac{y}{a}\right)^3 = 3\left(\dfrac{x}{a}\right)\left(\dfrac{y}{a}\right)$;  $\left(\dfrac{3at}{1+t^3},\ \dfrac{3at^2}{1+t^3}\right)$;

   (e) $\left(\dfrac{x}{a}\right)^2 = \left(\dfrac{y}{a}\right)$;  $(at,\ at^2)$;

   (f) $\left(\dfrac{y}{a}\right) = 1\Big/\left(1 + \left(\dfrac{x}{a}\right)^2\right)$;  $(at,\ a/(1+t^2))$;

   (g) $\left(\dfrac{y}{a}\right)^2\left(2 - \left(\dfrac{x}{a}\right)\right) = \left(\dfrac{x}{a}\right)^3$;  $\left(\dfrac{2at^2}{1+t^2},\ \dfrac{2at^3}{1+t^2}\right)$;

   (h) $\left(\dfrac{x}{a}\right)^2 + \left(\dfrac{y}{a}\right)^2 = 2\left(\dfrac{x}{a}\right) + 2\left(\dfrac{y}{a}\right)$;

   $(a(1+\sqrt{2}\cos t),\ a(1+\sqrt{2}\sin t))$.

4. (a) $(ax+b)^{n+1}/a(n+1)$;  (b) $-(a/b)\cos(bx+c)$;
   (c) $(1/p)\tan(px+q)$;  (d) $-(qx+r)^{-m+1}/q(m-1)$;
   (e) $(1/10)\tan^{-1}(\tfrac{2}{5}x)$;  (f) $\tfrac{1}{2}\sin^{-1}(\tfrac{2}{3}x)$.

5. $3ab - 3c - a^3$ is more likely, since $a$ has dimension $\mathbf{L}$;
   $p^2+q^2+r^2$ has dimension $\mathbf{L}^2$ and cannot involve terms like $(c/a)$,
   and is $(a^2-2b)$;
   $b$; $-(b/c)$; $(3c-ab)$.

7. (a) $\dfrac{1}{b}G\left(\dfrac{bx}{a}\right) = \displaystyle\int \dfrac{1}{\sqrt{(b^2x^2-a^2)}}\,dx$;

   (b) $\dfrac{1}{b}H\left(\dfrac{bx}{a}\right) = \displaystyle\int \dfrac{1}{\sqrt{(b^2x^2+a^2)}}\,dx$;

   (c) $\dfrac{1}{ab}K\left(\dfrac{bx}{a}\right) = \displaystyle\int \dfrac{1}{a^2-b^2x^2}\,dx$;

   (d) $\dfrac{a}{b}L\left(\dfrac{bx}{a}\right) = \displaystyle\int \tan^{-1}\left(\dfrac{bx}{a}\right)\,dx$.

361

## 7. PRINCIPAL VALUES

### Exercise J (p. 667)

2.  (a) $\cot^{-1} x$ is discontinuous over $[-1, +1]$; if, however, we substitute $x = \cot u$, with $u_1 = \frac{3}{4}\pi$, $u_2 = \frac{1}{4}\pi$, the conditions of the theorem are fulfilled, and we have $\left[ -u \right]_{\frac{3}{4}\pi}^{\frac{1}{4}\pi} = +\frac{1}{2}\pi$.

(b) If $\tan u = g(u)$, $g'(u)$ is not continuous over $(0, \pi)$. If we take

$$\int_0^{\frac{1}{2}\pi} \quad \text{and} \quad \int_{\frac{1}{2}\pi}^{\pi}$$

separately, however, we have

$$\int_0^{\infty} \quad \text{and} \quad \int_{-\infty}^{0},$$

so that the correct value is

$$\left[ \frac{1}{ab} \tan^{-1} \left( \frac{ax}{b} \right) \right]_{-\infty}^{+\infty} = \frac{\pi}{ab}.$$

(c) $1/x^2$ is discontinuous at 0, and neither

$$\int_{-1}^{0} \quad \text{nor} \quad \int_0^1$$

exists.

3.  (a) $\sin^{-1} \left( \frac{2}{3} \right) - \sin^{-1} \left( \frac{1}{3} \right) = 0.39$;

(b) $\frac{1}{8}\pi = 0.393$;       (c) $2/3$;

(d) $\sqrt{3} - \frac{1}{3}\pi = 0.685$;       (e) $\frac{2}{35}$.

### Miscellaneous Exercise (p. 668)

Set Questions 14, 26, 27, 44 only in special circumstances. Constants are omitted throughout.

1.  $\frac{1}{10}(x^2+1)^5$.

2.  $\frac{-2}{105} (15x^2+12x+8)(1-x)^{\frac{3}{2}}$.

3.  $\frac{1}{5}(x-1)(2x+3)^{\frac{3}{2}}$.

4.  $x - \tan^{-1} x$.

5.  $\frac{1}{30}(5x-7)(x+1)^5$.

6.  $-(2x+1)/2(x+1)^2$.

7.  $x - 1/x$.

8.  $\frac{1}{15}(3x^2-2)(x^2+1)^{\frac{3}{2}}$.

362

**9.** $\frac{2}{3}(2x+1)^{\frac{3}{4}}$.

**10.** $\frac{2}{15}(3x^2-4x+8)(x+1)^{\frac{1}{2}}$.

**11.** $\sin^{-1} x$.

**12.** $\sin^{-1} x-\sqrt{(1-x^2)}$.

**13.** $\frac{1}{2}\tan^{-1} x+\frac{1}{2}x/(1+x^2)$.

**14.** Not yet integrable $(-\frac{1}{2}\log|4-x^2|)$.

**15.** $(x^2+4)^{\frac{1}{2}}$.

**16.** $x-2\tan^{-1}(\frac{1}{2}x)$.

**17.** $3\pi a^4/16 = 0{\cdot}589a^4$.

**18.** $\frac{3}{2}\pi$ (substitute $4\sin^2 u+\cos^2 u = x$) $= 4{\cdot}72$.

**19.** $\frac{1}{4}\pi = 0{\cdot}785$.

**20.** $\frac{2}{3}(2\sqrt{2}-1) = 1{\cdot}219$.

**21.** $\tan x-\frac{1}{3}\tan^3 x$.

**22.** $\frac{1}{2}\sec^2 x$; $\frac{1}{2}\tan^2 x$.

**23.** $\frac{1}{3}\tan^3 x+\frac{1}{5}\tan^5 x$.

**24.** $\frac{1}{5}\sec^5 x$.

**25.** $\tan x+\frac{2}{3}\tan^3 x+\frac{1}{5}\tan^5 x$.

**26.** Not yet integrable $(x\tan x-\frac{1}{2}x^2-\log|\sec x|)$.

**27.** Not yet integrable $(x\tan^{-1} x -\frac{1}{2}\log(1+x^2))$.

**28.** $\frac{1}{2}(x^2+1)\tan^{-1} x-\frac{1}{2}x$.

**29.** $\frac{1}{3}\pi = 1{\cdot}047$.

**30.** $\frac{1}{6}\pi = 0{\cdot}523$.

**31.** $\frac{1}{8}\sin 4x+\frac{1}{4}\sin 2x$.

**32.** $-\frac{1}{2}x^2\cos 2x+\frac{1}{2}x\sin 2x+\frac{1}{4}\cos 2x$.

**33.** $\frac{1}{8}\sin 2x-\frac{1}{4}x\cos 2x$.

**34.** $\frac{1}{2}x-\frac{1}{2}\sin x\cos x$.

**35.** $\frac{1}{16}x+\frac{1}{48}\sin^3 2x-\frac{1}{64}\sin 4x$.

**36.** $\frac{1}{9}\cos^9 x-\frac{1}{7}\cos^7 x$.

**37.** $\frac{1}{4}x+\frac{1}{4}\sin 2x+\frac{1}{16}\sin 4x$.

**38.** $\frac{1}{5}\sin^5 x-\frac{2}{7}\sin^7 x+\frac{1}{9}\sin^9 x$.

**39.** $0$.

**40.** $0$; $(\frac{1}{2}\pi$ if $m = n)$.

**41.** $5\pi/32 = 0{\cdot}491$.

**42.** $5\pi/32 = 0{\cdot}491$.

**43.** $\frac{1}{2}\tan^{-1}(2) = 0{\cdot}554$.

**44.** $\dfrac{1}{4\sqrt{2}}\tan^{-1}\sqrt{\dfrac{3}{2}}+\dfrac{\sqrt{3}}{20} = 0{\cdot}244$.

**45.** $\frac{4}{3}\sqrt{3} = 2{\cdot}31$.

**46.** $-x+\sqrt{2}\tan^{-1}\left(\dfrac{\tan x}{\sqrt{2}}\right)$.

**47.** $+$ve.

**48.** $0$.

**49.** $0$.

**50.** $0$.

**51.** $-$ve.

**52.** $-$ve.

### Harder Miscellaneous Exercise (p. 669)

1. (a) $\pi^2 = 9.87$;  (b) 0;
   (c) $\pi^2 = 9.87$;  (d) 0.

2. $$\int_0^1 x^m(1-x)^n \, dx = \left[ x^{m+1}(1-x)^n/(m+1) \right]_0^1$$
   $$+ n/(m+1) \int_0^1 x^{m+1}(1-x)^{n-1} \, dx,$$

   or    $B(m, n) = nB(m+1, n-1)/(m+1) \quad (m > -1, n > 0)$.

   Thus,    $B(4, 3) = \frac{3}{5}B(5, 2) = \frac{3}{5}.\frac{2}{6}.\frac{1}{7}B(7, 0) = \frac{1}{280}$.

   (Note that $x = \sin^2 u$ converts this to the type of Question 3.)

3. $(m+1) \sin^m x \cos^n x - (n-1) \sin^{m+2} x \cos^{n-2} x$
   $$= (m+n) \sin^m x \cos^n x - (n-1) \sin^m x \cos^{n-2} x.$$

   Write    $I(m, n) = \int_0^{\frac{1}{2}\pi} \sin^m x \cos^n x \, dx$;

   then $I(m, n) = (n-1)I(m, n-2)/(m+n) \quad (m > -1, n > 1)$.
   $I(2, 4) = \pi/32 = 0.098$.

4. $I(m, n) = (m-1)I(m-2, n)/(m+n)$. Both formulae work when
   the number not to be reduced is 1 or 0, though in the former case,
   for example, $I(m, 1) = 1/(m+1)$ directly. $I(0, 0) = \frac{1}{2}\pi$, which is
   useful to evaluate these quickly. Thus

   (a) $\frac{2}{35}$;  (b) $\frac{1}{60}$;  (c) $3\pi/512 = 0.0184$;  (d) $3\pi/512 = 0.0184$.

5. $$\int_0^{\frac{1}{2}\pi} \cos^n x \cos nx \, dx = \frac{1}{n} \left[ \cos^n x . \sin nx \right]_0^{\frac{1}{2}\pi}$$
   $$+ \int_0^{\frac{1}{2}\pi} \sin nx \sin x \cos^{n-1} x \, dx \quad (n > 0);$$

   using    $\cos (n-1)x = \cos nx \cos x + \sin nx \sin x$,
   $$2I(n) = I(n-1).$$

   Thus,    $I(6) = \pi/128 = 0.0245$.

6. (a) 0;  (b) $\frac{1}{2}\pi$. The same results hold for cosines, which enables
   us to express a wide range of functions as *Fourier series*,
   $$f(x) = \{a_0 + a_1 \cos x + a_2 \cos 2x \ldots\}$$
   or    $\{b_0 + b_1 \sin x + b_2 \sin 2x \ldots\}$.

The same is true for a sine and a cosine if $(m+n)$ is even; if $(m+n)$ is odd,

$$\int_0^\pi \cos mx \sin nx \, dx = 2n/(m^2-n^2).$$

7. (a) $\{n:n > -1\}$;      (b) $\{n:n < -1\}$;      (c) ø.

8. $\frac{1}{2}\tan^{-1} a - \frac{1}{2}a/(1+a^2)$. Yes; it means $\frac{1}{2}\pi$.

9. 1. The difficulty is that the integrand is infinite for $x = 0$, but it behaves like $x^{-\frac{1}{2}}$.

10. (a) No;      (b) yes: 1;      (c) yes: $\pi$;      (d) no.

11. $\displaystyle\int_0^\pi xf(\sin x)\,dx = \int_0^\pi (\pi-x)f(\sin x)\,dx$, since $\sin(\pi-x) = \sin x$;

hence $\displaystyle\int_0^\pi xf(\sin x)\,dx = \frac{1}{2}\int_0^\pi \pi f(\sin x)\,dx = \pi \int_0^{\frac{1}{2}\pi} f(\sin x)\,dx$

(a) $\frac{1}{4}\pi^2 = 2\cdot467$;      (b) $\frac{1}{4}\pi^2 = 2\cdot467$.

12. $a = \frac{14}{45}h$,   $b = \frac{64}{45}h$,   $c = \frac{24}{45}h$. (See Chapter 22, Exercise F, Question 8.) (The last term is $af(2h)$.)

Simpson's Rule gives $2\cdot0046$, this rule $1\cdot9986$, the correct answer being 2. But Simpson's Rule with eight strips gives $2\cdot0003$, better than either of them, if five figures are retained throughout.

13. In this case

$$\int_{-1}^{+1} x^3(x^2+1)^4 \, dx = 0,$$

because the integrand is odd. Its value is $987\cdot45$.

14. Put $u = 1/t$; then

$$\int_1^2 (1-1/t^2)f(t+1/t)\,dt = -\int_{\frac{1}{2}}^1 (1-1/u^2)f(u+1/u)\,du,$$

whence the result follows.

$x = t+1/t$ may be substituted over $[\frac{1}{2}, 1]$ and over $[1, 2]$; we get

$$\int_0^1 f(x)\,dx + \int_1^0 f(x)\,dx = 0.$$

The graph of $x = t+1/t$ throws considerable light on this process.

# 24

# INTRODUCTION TO MECHANICS

This chapter together with those on Momentum and Energy constitute the mechanics of the course. It deals with forces applied to particles and with statics only as a special case of dynamics. The idea of moment is not developed.

The first sections attempt to describe the development of a mathematical model. Newton's Laws are taken as hypotheses within a model that is used to describe the conditions of motion.

The later sections describe the application of Newton's Laws to particles and systems of particles and to objects that can be taken as particles under particular circumstances. Under the latter heading comes a section on friction. Finally there is a section on dimensional consistency.

## 2. NEWTON'S MODEL

The postulates of Newton's model are discussed in this section. These are Newton's First and Second Laws, the idea that forces are vectors and Newton's Third Law, the interaction principle.

The latter is mentioned in Section 2.4 and, because it is hard to visualize that one force can accelerate a body away and still be opposed by an equal and opposite force, a 'demonstrating argument' is introduced on p. 680 of the pupil's text. But this argument uses another postulate, that $m = m_1 + m_2$ (see Figure 4). So far, mass has been defined simply as a number that can be associated with a particle that in some way represents the quantity of matter in a body: in Section 3.2, it is added that the number is associated with 'the resistance to change in the state of motion'. There is nothing to suggest that mass is additive.

There is no reason why $m = m_1 + m_2$ should not be taken as a postulate and the interaction principle deduced from it but, following

Newton, the reverse process is more likely to be used. The argument would be as follows:

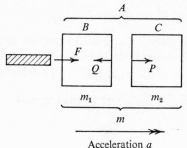

Figure 4 of the pupil's text.

Suppose that $F = ma$ and that $P = m_2 a$.
The interaction principle gives $P = Q$.

Hence $\qquad\qquad\qquad Q = m_2 a,$

and since $\qquad\qquad F - Q = m_1 a,$

therefore $\qquad\qquad F = (m_1 + m_2)a.$

But as $F = ma$, $\qquad m = m_1 + m_2$.

This argument applies to inertial mass. The fact, mentioned in Section 3.2, that it *equals* gravitational mass depends upon the units used and the fact that these masses are *proportional*. This fact is so remarkable that it might lead to the first doubts concerning Newton's model and the question might be asked, 'Is the proportionality of these masses a chance occurrence or is mass not itself fundamental but dependent upon some other quantities which in some way unify the concepts of gravity and inertia?' This question is answered in any book on relativity. Two that have been found clear and not too mathematical are *Relativity and Common Sense*, by Hermann Bondi and *The Special Theory of Relativity*, by Herbert Dingle.

### *Exercise A (p. 677)*

1. $\frac{1}{10}$ unit; 1 unit.

2. 2000 units; 20,000 units; 1 unit.

3. (*a*) 400 units retarding;
   (*b*) 300 units accelerating;      (*c*) 0.

4. (a) No;                     (b) yes;
    (c) 4 m/s is the change of velocity.
In the direction of the force.

5. (a) 575 m/s in direction at 7·05° to original direction;
        743 m/s in direction at 16·6° to original direction;
    (b) 707 units in direction at 135° with original direction.

6. 10·4 units towards the centre of the circle.

7. 142 units; 2; 4.

8. 0·265 m/s² in direction 40·9° with 1000 unit force's direction.

9. 2 units.

10. 0·47 m/s² in direction 88·4° with $AB$.

11. (a) 3·21 units;                (b) impossible;
    (c) either 8 units at 88° on the same side of the original velocity
as the first force, or $14\frac{1}{2}$ units at 89° on the opposite side.

12. 2·8 units in direction 116·6° with direction of motion.

13. 1 unit towards centre of circle. 1 unit. 4·12 units in direction 76°
with direction of motion.

14. (a) 0;     (b) 10 units parallel to $y$-axis;
    (c) 0, 42·4 and 6·66 units parallel to $y = x$;
    (d) 0, $-4·21$ and $-5$ units parallel to $y$-axis.

15. 96 units parallel to $y$-axis.
    $6\sqrt{(t^2 + 256)}$ units.

## Exercise B (p. 681)

1. 1 m/s²; 20 units.            2. 2 units; 1 unit.

3. (a) $\frac{1}{2}$ unit;     (b) 16 units;     (c) 12 units;     (d) 4 units.

4. $\frac{13}{40}$ m/s².

5. 450 units; 150 units; 150 units.

**6.** 600 units; 300 units on $B$, 150 units on $A$; $(300-150d)$ units.

**7.** 19,000 units; zero.

**8.** $\dfrac{m_1}{m_2} = \dfrac{r_2}{r_1}.$

# 3. THE APPLICATION OF NEWTON'S MODEL

When thinking of elliptical orbits, some people find it hard to believe that Kepler's Laws are true. It might help to discuss the special case where the orbit is considered to be a circle round the sun at the centre. (The earth's orbit is very nearly a circle about the sun. The minor axis is equal to the major axis multiplied by approximately $\sqrt{\frac{3599}{3600}}$.)

Notice that the Laws are derived from observations; the following in no way constitutes a proof. It is simply a connecting of geometrical to mechanical ideas to make the Laws seem reasonable.

The only force exerted upon a planet is from the sun at the centre of the circle, so $\theta$ is constant. The area of a sector is given by $\frac{1}{2}r^2\theta$, where $r$ is the radius and $\theta$ the angle measured in radians. From this, the area 'swept out' by the radius vector from the sun in *any* time interval $t$ will be $\frac{1}{2}r^2\theta t$, that is, the area will be swept out at a constant rate.

If the motion is circular and $\theta$ is constant, then the force exerted along the radius vector is $mr\theta^2$ and we also know it to be equal to $k(m/r^2)$. Equating the two,

$$k\frac{m}{r^2} = mr\theta^2, \quad k = r^3\theta^2.$$

If $T$ is the time of revolution, then $T\theta = 2\pi$. So

$$T = \frac{2\pi}{\theta},$$

$$T^2 = \left(\frac{4\pi^2}{k}\right) r^3, \quad \text{or} \quad T^2 \propto r^3.$$

In Kepler's Third Law, $r$, the mean distance of the planet from the sun, equals the semi-major axis of the planet's orbit.

### Exercise C (p. 686)

**1.** (a) 150 N;   (b) 50,000 N;   (c) 6 N;        (d) 1500 N.

**2.** (a) 10 m/s²;   (b) 0·6 m/s;   (c) $\frac{1}{50}$ m/s²,    2 cm/s².

**3.** 23$\frac{1}{3}$ N.   **4.** 35 cm.   **5.** 8 m/s.   **6.** 8·48 × 10⁻⁶ N.

**7.** 98 N.      (a) 43·6 N.      (b) 24·5 N.      (c) 0·40 N.

**8.** 0·997 : 1.   **9.** 1280 kg.   **10.** 99 N.

**11.**

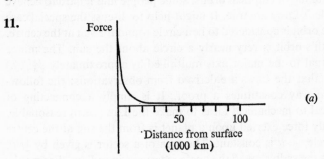

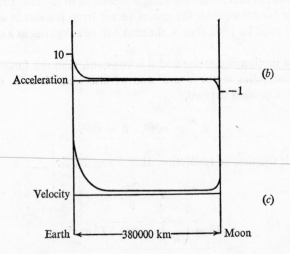

# 4. FORCE AND MASS-ACCELERATION VECTOR SYSTEMS

### Exercise D (p. 689)

**1.** 25·6 N; 13·6 N.     **2.** 8·51 m/s².

**3.** Initially and finally the contact force is 490 N.
While retarding the force increases to 640 N.

**4.** 10·2 m/s²; 5·2 m/s².     **5.** 1·2 m/s².

**6.** The reading increases; it remains constant.

**7.** 5 m/s² (neglecting the buoyancy on the cable).

**8.** 880 N; $6\frac{2}{3}$ m/s. It depends upon the effect of the loss of the parachute upon the air resistance. If this remains constant, while the total mass was lessened, he would be retarded.

**9.** 2·76 N.     **10.** 25·6 N.

**11.** 311 m/s.

**12.** The force of attraction of the earth provides the force towards the centre required for a circular orbit. So, if $g$ is the acceleration at the surface, $R$ is the earth's radius and $d$ is his height.

$$g \left(\frac{R}{R+d}\right)^2 = \frac{V^2}{R+d}.$$

**13.** 36000 km.

### Exercise F (p. 692)

**1.** 3 cm; 4 cm; $\frac{1}{2}$ cm.     **2.** 21·2 cm.

**3.** (a) 62·45 cm     (b) 10·2 m/s².

**4.** 27·7 m/s.

**5.** (a) 100 m/s²; 60 m/s².
   (b) 90·2 m/s; 69·8 m/s².

**6.** 2·39 cm.     **7.** 6 mm.

**8.**

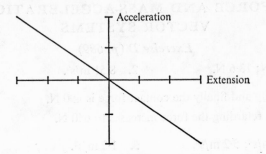

**9.** If $e$ cm is the extension, $2\theta°$ the angle between the parts of the string and $a$ the acceleration, then

$$a = 3200e \cos \theta.$$

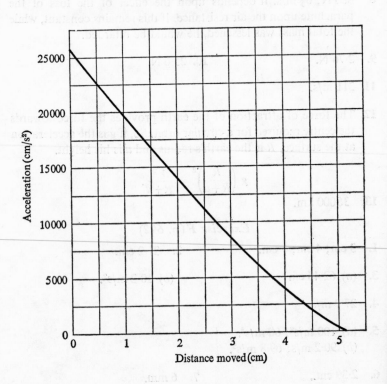

*Exercise F (p. 695)*

**1.** (a) $mg, Mg$ gravitational forces;

$P_1, P_2$ tension forces; $P_1 = P_2$.

$R_1, R_2$ resistance forces. $R_1 + R_2 > (M+m)g$.

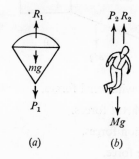

(a)          (b)

(b) $P_1, P_2$ thrust forces. $P_1 = P_2$.

(a)          (b)

(c) $m_1g, m_2g$ gravitational forces.

$R_1, R_2, P_1, P_2$ thrust forces

$R_1 = m_1g, R_2 = m_2g, P_1 = P_2$.

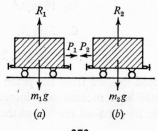

(a)          (b)

373

(d) mg, Mg   gravitational forces.

$P_1, P_2$   tension forces. $P_1 = P_2$.

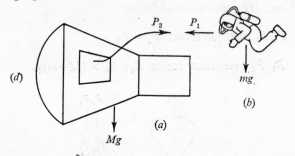

(d)

(a)

(b)

Mg

(e) mg, Mg   gravitational forces.

$R_1, R_2, F$   thrust forces.

$P_1, P_2$   tension forces.

R resistance force.

$R_1 = mg$, $R_2 = Mg$, $P_1 = P_2$, (i) $F = R$, (ii) $F > R$.

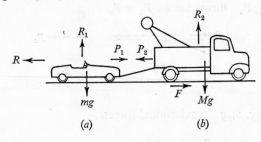

(a)

(b)

**2.** 216 N.

**3.** (a) 1000 N.;      (b) 1500 N.

**4.** (a) 18 m/s²;      (b) 18 m/s.²

**5.** 560 N; 590 N.      **6.** 31·6 N.

**7.** 6·6 N.      **8.** 300 gN; 2 m.

**9.** If the bird jumped upward from the perch before taking flight, the weight would have momentarily increased. Then it would have returned to its previous reading as the bird hovered.

**10.** $P_1 = m_1(a+g)$

$T_2 = m_2(a+g)$

$T_1 = (m_1+m_2)(a+g)$

$P_2 = m_2(a+g)$

$P_2$ becomes $m_2g$, so $T_2 = m_2g$ and $T_1 = m_1a+(m_2+m_1)g$.

Yes.

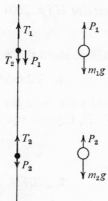

**11.** $52\cdot5$ N; $9\cdot5$ m/s upwards.

**12.** $450$ m/s; $2\cdot8$ m/s.

### Exercise G (698)

**1.** 118 N; 78 N.  **2.** $2\cdot45$ m/s²; 37 N.

**3.** $19\cdot6$ N; $6\cdot54$ N.

**4.** (a) $2\cdot45$ m/s²; 37 N.  (b) $3\cdot5$ m/s² and $0\cdot7$ m/s²; $31\cdot5$ N.

**5.** $31\cdot6$ N.

**6.** 12 N; $5\cdot2$ m/s² and $0\cdot2$ m/s² upward.

**7.** If Cat$_b$ heaves himself up over the string with an acceleration $f$ relative to the branch, and exerts a force $P$ on himself, then

$$P-mg = mf \quad \text{and} \quad P = T,$$

where $T$ is the tension in the string. Cat$_a$ will be moving up under this tension $T$ with an acceleration $f_1$ given by $T-mg = mf_1$, so $f = f_1$.

375

All now depends upon the rate that Cat$_b$ can move relative to the string (which has an acceleration past him of $2f$). If he can cope, then he will meet Cat$_a$ on top of the branch. If not, the string will slacken and both caterpillars will move upward freely under gravity, reach a maximum height and fall back with a jerk.

### Exercise H (p. 700)

**1.** $g \sin \theta$; $mg \cos \theta$.

**2.** $g \tan 10°$. It would oscillate about this position.

**3.** $g \sin 60°$.      **4.** $7 \cdot 2$ m/s² upwards; $14 \cdot 7$ N.

**5.** $0 \cdot 613$ m/s². The upward force from the 40 N force is $25 \cdot 7$ N; from the ground is 464 N, together equalling the weight of the toboggan.

**6.** 321 N; 939 N.

**7.** $\sqrt{(3rg)}$.      **8.** 207 N; 267 N.

**9.** 195 N; 365 N.      **10.** 105 N; 450 N.

**11.** $18 \cdot 4°$.      **12.** 130 m/s; 3400 N.

**13.** 515 N.      **14.** $mg \sec \alpha$.

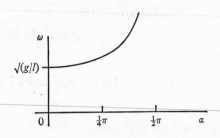

### Exercise I (p. 705)

**1.** (a) $12 \cdot 2$ N at $10 \cdot 4°$;      (b) $5 \cdot 12$ N at $15 \cdot 1°$;
     (c) $15 \cdot 3$ N at $218 \cdot 6°$.

**2.** (a) 0;      (b) $20 \cdot 0$ N; $1 \cdot 37$ m/s²;
     (c) 30 N; $1 \cdot 87$ m/s².

**3.** (*a*)  −27·2 N; 1·7 m/s² down the slope;
    (*b*)  −5·2 N; 0·32 m/s² down the slope;
    (*c*)  2·8 N; 0·17 m/s² up the slope.

**4.** 5078 N; 5083 N. None.

**5.** (*a*) 7·52 N and 5·92 N;     (*b*) 5·04 N and 8·14 N.
9·57 N at 51·8° with the horizontal. 9·07 m/s².

**6.** (*a*) 184 N, 67 N;     (*b*) $\frac{1}{4}$ m/s²;
    (*c*) 189 N;     (*d*) 18 N downwards;
                               65 N horizontally.

## 5. FRICTION
### Exercise J (p. 709)

**1.** (*a*) 39·2 N;     (*b*) 6·08 m/s²;
    (*c*) no; 1·08 m/s²;     (*d*) 100 N.

**2.** Frictional forces on the tyres. 1200 N. Yes. No, the normal reaction, and so the limiting friction, would be less.

**3.** (*a*) 3920 N;     (*b*) 784 N;
    (*c*) (i) 2740 N; (ii) 8620 N.

**3.** (*a*) (29·4 − $T$ sin 75°) N;     (*b*) 0·8 (29·4 − $T$ sin 75°) N;
    (*c*) $T$ cos 75° N. 22·8 N.

**5.** 10·3 m/s².     **6.** 1·56 m/s².

**7.** 35°; 105 $g$ N = 1030 N; 35°; 35°; $\theta < \lambda$.

**8.** $\frac{1}{2}$.

## 7. DIMENSIONS
### Exercise K (p. 716)

**1.** (*a*) 4·9 m/s²;   (*b*) 32 ft/s²;     (*c*) 416 ft/s²;
    (*d*) 0·714 ft/s²;   (*e*) 0·367 m/s².

**2.** (*a*) 12·2 kgf;   (*b*) 21 kgf;     (*c*) $\frac{1}{64}$ tonf.;
    (*d*) 6·25 lbf;   (*e*) 320 tonnals.

**3.** 0·8 tonf; 0·3 tonf.     **4.** 736 ft/s².

**5.** (a) $10^5$;     (b) $9 \cdot 8 \times 10^5$ dynes;     (c) 4116 dynes.

**6.** (a) $0 \cdot 4$ ft/s$^2$;             (b) 18,490 lbf = $8 \cdot 25$ tonf;
   (c) 1860 lbf;              (d) $0 \cdot 111$.

$$a = \frac{1}{2100} (T - 450).$$

### *Miscellaneous Exercise (p. 717)*

**1.** $P_1 + P_2 = R_1 + R_2$.
   $F_1 > F_2$.

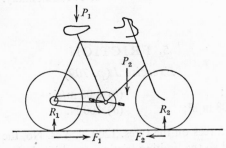

**2.** (a) $L = mg$.
     $P = R_1 + R_2 + R_3$.

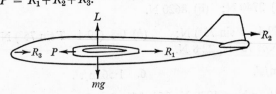

(b) $L = mg \sin \alpha$.
   $P + mg \cos \alpha - R = mf$.

If $P = 0$, $R = m(g \cos \alpha - f)$.

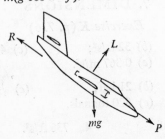

**3.** $3 \cdot 5 \text{ m/s}^2$.

**4.** $3 \cdot 48 \text{ m/s}^2$ at $28 \cdot 4°$ with the 620 N force.

**5.** $12 \cdot 6 \text{ N}$; 72 N.

**6.** 6670 N.

**7.** $500 \, g$ N.

**8.** $\dfrac{2mMg \sin \alpha}{m+M}$ units.

**9.** $17 \cdot 2$ N.

**10.** $5 \cdot 1$ N.

**11.** 7 m/s.

**13.** $\sin^{-1}(m/M)$. Both masses will oscillate about the equilibrium position. When at that position, no forces are acting along the lines of motion (the position was defined as one in which the sum of the forces was zero) and so there is no acceleration.

**14.** $g(\sin \theta - \mu \cos \theta)$; $g\{\sin \theta - \mu \cos \theta - (\mu v^2/rg)\}$ (assuming $\theta$ is to *downward* vertical).

**15.** $(mgb)/2\sqrt{(a^2 - b^2)}$; after release, the hanging ring begins to accelerate vertically downwards, and the tension in the string is reduced. Hence the horizontal acceleration of the ring on the wire is less than expected. The path of the hanging ring begins by being vertical, and symmetry is destroyed. What happens then seems only to be determinable numerically.

**16.** $(1/m)(\sqrt{\{F^2 + (mg \sin \alpha)^2\}} - \mu \, mg \cos \alpha)$ in a direction

$$\tan^{-1}(F/mg \sin \alpha)$$

with the line of greatest slope.

**17.** $\tan^{-1}(a/g)$; $\dfrac{Pg}{ml\sqrt{(g^2 + a^2)}}$; $-\dfrac{Pa}{\sqrt{(g^2 + a^2)}}$.

**18.** $\tan^{-1}\left(\dfrac{\sin \theta}{\dfrac{gd^2}{ar^2} + \cos \theta}\right)$.

**19.** $\tan^{-1}(v^2/rg)$.

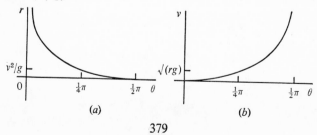

(a)

(b)

**20.** $T = ma \cos \theta;$ $(\dot{\theta} = 0 \text{ initially}).$
$\alpha = (a/l) \sin \theta.$

} Resolving along and perpendicular to $AB$ ($-l\ddot{\theta}$ and $l\dot{\theta}^2$ are accelerations relative to $B$).

$T = ma \cos \phi + m(v^2/l).$

$\alpha' = (a/l) \sin \phi.$

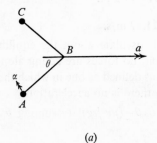

(a)  (b)

**21.** If $f_1$ is the acceleration of the wedge relative to the ground and $f_2$ is the acceleration of the mass relative to the wedge, then

$$f_1 = \frac{mg \sin \alpha \cos \alpha}{m \sin^2 \alpha + M} \quad \text{and} \quad f_2 = \frac{(M+m)g \sin \alpha}{m \sin^2 \alpha + M}.$$

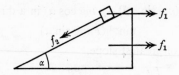

**22.** $g \cos \theta$ along the tangent away from $A$.

$$\frac{mv^2}{a} - mg(1 - \sin \theta).$$

# REVISION EXERCISES

## 20. PROBABILITY (p. 719)

1. $\frac{297}{625}$ if I wear laddered stockings; otherwise the probability is greater.

2. $\frac{13}{24}$.

3. (i) (a) $\frac{1}{3}$, (b) $\frac{2}{3}$;  (ii) (a) 0, (b) 1.

4. (a) $\frac{1}{144}$;  (b) $\frac{1}{162}$;  (c) 5.

5. The four probabilities are 0·0376, 0·0288, 0·0024, 0·9312.

   The probability that a random patient reacts positively is 0·0664.

6. (a) $\frac{2}{3}\times\frac{1}{2}+\frac{2}{3}\times\frac{1}{2}\times\frac{2}{3}\times\frac{1}{2}+\frac{2}{3}\times\frac{1}{2}\times\frac{2}{3}\times\frac{1}{2}\times\frac{2}{3}\times\frac{1}{2}=\frac{13}{27}$;

   (b) $\frac{2}{3}\times\frac{1}{2}\times\frac{2}{3}\times\frac{1}{2}\times\frac{2}{3}\times\frac{1}{2}=\frac{1}{27}$;

   (c) $\frac{1}{3}+\frac{2}{3}\times\frac{1}{2}\times\frac{1}{3}+\frac{2}{3}\times\frac{1}{2}\times\frac{2}{3}\times\frac{1}{2}\times\frac{1}{3}=\frac{13}{27}$.

   The answer to (c) tends to $\frac{1}{2}$ as the number of walks tends to infinity.

## 21. LINEAR EQUATIONS (p. 720)

1. $\begin{pmatrix} 5 & 0 & 0 \\ 0 & 5 & 0 \\ 0 & 0 & 5 \end{pmatrix}$.  $x=\frac{1}{5},\ y=-\frac{2}{5},\ z=1$.

2. (a) $x=7\cdot4,\quad y=-3\cdot8,\quad z=0\cdot4$;

   (b) $x=6,\quad y=6,\quad z=6$.

3. $\begin{pmatrix} -1 & 3 & -2 \\ -\frac{1}{2} & -3 & 2\frac{1}{2} \\ 1 & 1 & -1 \end{pmatrix}$.

4. A general point on the common line is $(-\frac{4}{5}-4t,\ t,\ 1+3t)$.

   $$35p_1-p_2-5p_3=0.$$

381

5. (a) If $K = 1$ there is no solution; the graphs of the planes form a triangular prism;

(b) if $K \neq 0$ or 1, there is one solution; the graphs are three planes in general position.

(c) if $K = 0$, there is an infinity of solutions. The graphs form a sheaf.

6. There are many solutions, of which (using the obvious notation) $t = 0$, $d = 24$, $k = 5$ gives the minimum weight, and $t = 4$, $d = 17, k = 8$ gives the greatest variety subject to the constraints.

The Simplex method can be applied (see the Teachers' Guide to Book T4) or alternatively a solution may be obtained by experiment. It soon becomes clear that $t$ must be small and that any solution will provide an excess of carbohydrates. If $t$ is taken successively as 0, 1, 2, 3, 4 all solutions can be found by the graphical method.

In retrospect, a proof that $t$ must be small can be made as follows:

$$P = 10t + 6d \geqslant 140 \text{ (the protein constraint),}$$
$$V = 2t + 5d + 9k \geqslant 160 \text{ (the vitamin constraint),}$$

$$\Rightarrow \quad \begin{aligned} 60t + 36d &\quad\quad\geqslant 840 \\ 14t + 35d + 63k &\geqslant 1120 \end{aligned}$$

$$\Rightarrow \quad 74t + 71d + 63k \geqslant 1960$$

$$\Rightarrow \quad -74t + 71d - 63k \leqslant -1960.$$

But $0 \cdot 3W = 108t + 72d + 63k \leqslant 2160$ (the weight constraint),

so $\quad\quad 34t + \quad d \quad\quad \leqslant 200,$

from which it follows that $t \leqslant 5$. It transpires that no solution can be found with $t = 5$.

Also, $\quad 10t + 6d \quad\quad \geqslant 140$
$$2t + 5d + 9k \geqslant 160$$

$$\Rightarrow 12t + 11d + 9k \geqslant 300$$

$$\Rightarrow 7t + 11d + 9k \geqslant 300 - 5t \geqslant 280 \quad \text{if} \quad t \leqslant 4.$$

Hence $C = 7t + 11d + 12k \geqslant 7t + 11d + 9k \geqslant 280$ if $t \leqslant 4$, proving that the carbohydrate constraint can be ignored if the protein and vitamin inequalities are satisfied.

## 22. AREA (p. 721)

1. $I = 1\frac{1}{4}$, $J = 2\frac{1}{3}$, $I^2 < J$.

   In general,
   $$\int_a^b fg(x)\, dx \neq f\left(\int_a^b g(x)\, dx\right).$$

2. $11,100\,\text{m} = 11 \cdot 1\,\text{km}$.

3. $\dfrac{1^3 + 2^3 + \ldots + n^3}{n^4}$ is the sum of the areas of rectangles drawn (as in Chapter 22, Figure 16(a)) above the graph of $y = x^3$ between $x = 0$ and $x = 1$. Its limit as $n$ tends to infinity is then
   $$\int_0^1 x^3\, dx = \tfrac{1}{4} = \lim_{n \to \infty} \frac{n^2(n+1)^2}{4n^4}.$$

4. Mean value $= \dfrac{1}{2} \displaystyle\int_4^6 \frac{1}{x^2+4}\, dx = 0 \cdot 0355$;

   mean of extreme values $= \frac{1}{2}(\frac{1}{20} + \frac{1}{40}) = 0 \cdot 0375$.

   The first answer is smaller because the graph is concave upwards in this interval.

5. Area enclosed $= \displaystyle\int_{a/16}^a \frac{4x^3}{a^2}\, dx + \int_a^{2a} \frac{4a^3}{x^2}\, dx - \int_{a/16}^{2a} \frac{x^2}{4a}\, dx$

   $= 2 \cdot 329a^2$.

6. (a) $0 \cdot 84$;  (b) $0 \cdot 08$.

   These answers are calculated from a naïve and literal interpretation of the question. Ambiguities arise because a probability density function is being used as an approximation in a discrete situation.

## 23. TECHNIQUES OF INTEGRATION (p. 722)

1. Simpson's Rule gives $\sqrt{73} = 15914/187 = 8 \cdot 510$; actually $\sqrt{73} = 8 \cdot 544$.

2. (a) $-\frac{1}{2}(1+x^2)^{-1} + c$;

   (b) $1\frac{1}{30}$;  (c) $\frac{1}{4}\pi$;  (d) $0$.

3. (a) Take $u$ as $\sin x$ and $v$ as $-\frac{1}{6}\cos^6 x$;

   (b) $\frac{1}{4}\pi^2 - 2$.

**4.** $0 < \sin x < x \Rightarrow 16 < (4+\sin x)^2 < (4+x)^2$

$$\Rightarrow \frac{1}{16} > \frac{1}{(4+\sin x)^2} > \frac{1}{(4+x)^2}.$$

The result follows by integration.

**5.** We require $p'(x)+q(x) = 3x-1$ and $-p(x)+q'(x) = 1-2x$. Substituting $ax+b$ for $p(x)$ and $cx+d$ for $q(x)$ we find $a = 2$, $b = 2$, $c = 3$, $d = -3$. Integration by parts gives the same answer.

**6.** It is assumed throughout that $m$ and $n$ are integers.

$\int_0^\pi \sin mx \sin nx\, dx$ equals 0 if $m \neq n$, and equals $\frac{1}{2}\pi$ if $m = n$.

$$\int_{\frac{1}{2}\pi}^\pi (\pi-x) \sin nx\, dx = -\cos n\pi \int_0^{\frac{1}{2}\pi} x \sin nx\, dx$$

$$= (-1)^{n-1} \int_0^{\frac{1}{2}\pi} x \sin nx\, dx$$

$$= (-1)^{n-1} \left( -\frac{\pi}{2n} \cos \tfrac{1}{2}n\pi + \frac{1}{n^2} \sin \tfrac{1}{2}n\pi \right),$$

$\int_0^\pi f(x) \sin nx\, dx = 0$   if $n$ is even,

and $\qquad\qquad\quad = (2/n^2) \sin \tfrac{1}{2}n\pi$   if $n$ is odd.

$$a_n = \frac{4}{\pi n^2} \sin \tfrac{1}{2}n\pi.$$

The first three non-zero terms ($g(x)$ say) give a good approximation to $f(x)$ as shown in the table.

| $x$ | 0 | $\frac{1}{6}\pi$ | $\frac{1}{4}\pi$ | $\frac{1}{3}\pi$ | $\frac{1}{2}\pi$ | $\frac{2}{3}\pi$ | $\frac{3}{4}\pi$ | $\frac{5}{6}\pi$ | $\pi$ |
|---|---|---|---|---|---|---|---|---|---|
| $f(x)$ | 0 | 0·52 | 0·79 | 1·05 | 1·57 | 1·05 | 0·79 | 0·52 | 0 |
| $g(x)$ | 0 | 0·52 | 0·76 | 1·06 | 1·47 | 1·06 | 0·76 | 0·52 | 0 |

## 24. INTRODUCTION TO MECHANICS (p. 723)

**1.** (a) $5\cdot4 \times 10^{-9}$ N.
(b) Acceleration $= 15$ cm/s². Reaction $= 520$ N.

**2.** Acceleration $= 2\cdot2$ m/s² upwards.

**3.** $20\cdot8$ m/s on a bearing of $155\cdot5°$.

**4.** 220 N.

**5.** (a) 245 N;     (b) 735 N.

**6.** 48 mm, 64 mm; 800 N.

### *Miscellaneous Problems (p. 724)*

**1.** $10 \cos \theta + 2 \sin \theta = 10\cdot2 \cos (\theta - 11\cdot3°)$.

$10 \cos \theta + 2 \sin \theta \leqslant 9$, and $10 \sin \theta + 2 \cos \theta \leqslant 8$, giving

$$39\cdot4 \leqslant \theta \leqslant 40\cdot3°.$$

**2.** (i) $6\pi$ seconds.

(ii) When $t = 2\pi$,

$$\mathbf{r} = \begin{pmatrix} -30 \\ 39 \end{pmatrix}, \quad \mathbf{v} = \begin{pmatrix} -17\cdot3 \\ -7\cdot5 \end{pmatrix}, \quad \mathbf{a} = \begin{pmatrix} 3\cdot3 \\ -4\cdot3 \end{pmatrix}.$$

(iii) The speed is greatest at $(0, 13\cdot5)$ and $(0, -13\cdot5)$.

(iv) $\mathbf{a} = -\frac{1}{9}\mathbf{r}$. The maximum acceleration $= 2 \text{ m/s}^2$, and this occurs at $(18, 0)$ and $(-18, 0)$.

(v) $\mu \geqslant 0\cdot22$.

**3.** (a) $m_1 = 54\cdot5, s_1 = 10; m_2 = 69\cdot5, s_2 = 15$.

(b) A linear function $f$ is needed with scale factor $\frac{10}{15}$ and $f(69\cdot5) = 54\cdot5$. This is $f: x \to \frac{2}{3}x + 8\frac{1}{6}$.

**4.** If $BP = x$, $x^2 + 16 = 9 + (5-x)^2$.

Hence $x = 1\cdot8$. $DQ = 1\cdot8$ by symmetry.

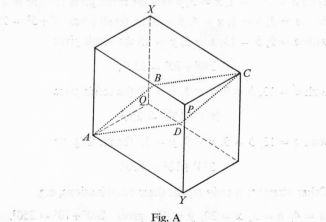

Fig. A

**5.**
$$\binom{3}{1} \rightarrow 4\binom{3}{1}. \quad \binom{-2}{1} \rightarrow -\binom{-2}{1}.$$

Lines through $P$ are drawn parallel to

$$\binom{3}{1} \quad \text{and} \quad \binom{-2}{1}.$$

Then $\mathbf{OP} = \mathbf{OQ} + \mathbf{OR}$, and $\mathbf{OP'} = 4\mathbf{OQ} - \mathbf{OR}$, so $P'$ is constructed as shown in the diagram.

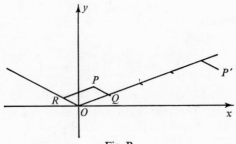

Fig. B

**6.** The probability of getting a prize $= \dfrac{481}{810,000}$.

Prizes worth $8s.\ 5d.$ each will leave the stallholder with about 99% of the takings.

**7.** With $a = 3, b = 1, x = 3, y = 4$ the result gives $13^2 + 9^2 = 250$;
with $a = 3, b = 1, x = 4, y = 3$ the result gives $15^2 + 5^2 = 250$;
with $a = 9, b = 13, x = 5, y = 15$ the result gives

$$240^2 + 70^2 = 250^2;$$

with $a = 13, b = 9, x = 5, y = 15$ the result gives

$$200^2 + 150^2 = 250^2;$$

with $a = 13, b = 9, x = 9, y = 13$ the result gives

$$234^2 + 88^2 = 250^2.$$

Other attempts merely repeat these combinations, e.g.

$a = 4,\ b = 3,\ x = 30,\ y = 40$ gives $240^2 + 70^2 = 250^2$.

8. $\tan^{-1} (1+\alpha) \simeq \frac{1}{4}\pi + \frac{1}{2}\alpha.$

$$\frac{d^2y}{dx^2} = \frac{-2x}{(1+x^2)^2}; \quad \tan^{-1}\beta \simeq \beta - \frac{1}{3}\beta^3.$$

9. $P$ is a continuous, monotonic function of $d$ with least value 0 and greatest value $A$. There is consequently a unique value of $d$ for which $P = \frac{1}{2}A$. Note that the gradient of the graph at any point is equal to the length of the segment of the corresponding $k'$ within the island.

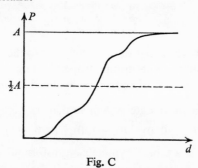

Fig. C

The diagrams for the cases where $\theta = 0°$ and $\theta = 90°$ would be identical, apart from the labelling of the axes. If $Q = f(\theta)$, $f(0°)+f(90°)$ would represent the area above the bisecting line parallel to the initial line. This is $\frac{1}{2}A$.

$$f(0°)+f(90°) = \frac{1}{2}A \Rightarrow \begin{cases} \quad f(0°) = \frac{1}{4}A = f(90°), \\ \text{or} \quad f(0°) < \frac{1}{4}A, f(90°) > \frac{1}{4}A, \\ \text{or} \quad f(0°) > \frac{1}{4}A, f(90°) < \frac{1}{4}A. \end{cases}$$

The $Q, \theta$ graph is continuous, and so must intersect the line $Q = \frac{1}{4}A$. It is not necessarily monotonic, so there may be more than one solution.

Islands with point symmetry provide good simple illustrations; the origin is then fixed.

10. It is given that $a * a = i$, $a * b = c$, $b * b = i$, $b * c = a$. Then

$$b * a = b * (b * c) = (b * b) * c = i * c = c = a * b.$$

Seven entries in the table can be made immediately since

$$i * x = x * i = x \quad \text{for all } x.$$

387

Also

$$a * c = a * (a * b) = (a * a) * b = i * b = b;$$
$$c * a = (b * a) * a = b * (a * a) = b * i = b;$$
$$c * b = (a * b) * b = a * (b * b) = a * i = a;$$
$$c * c = (a * b) * c = a * (b * c) = a * a = i.$$

|   | $i$ | $a$ | $b$ | $c$ |
|---|-----|-----|-----|-----|
| $i$ | $i$ | $a$ | $b$ | $c$ |
| $a$ | $a$ | $i$ | $c$ | $b$ |
| $b$ | $b$ | $c$ | $i$ | $a$ |
| $c$ | $c$ | $b$ | $a$ | $i$ |

The structure turns out to be isomorphic to the symmetry group of the rectangle, but group properties (e.g. the latin square property) must not, of course, be assumed in this question.

**11.** Introduce a coordinate system so that the vertices are

$$(\pm 1, 0, 0), \quad (0, \pm 1, 0), \quad (0, 0, \pm 1).$$

The matrix of a typical symmetry transformation is then

$$\begin{pmatrix} 1 & 0 & 0 \\ 0 & 0 & -1 \\ 0 & 1 & 0 \end{pmatrix}.$$

Each matrix has $+1$ or $-1$ once in each row and column, and zeros elsewhere. There are 48 such matrices, half with determinant $+1$ (corresponding to a direct isometry) and half with determinant $-1$.

There are 3 axes of symmetry joining opposite vertices, and 3 distinct rotations about each.

There are 4 axes of symmetry joining midpoints of opposite faces, and 2 distinct rotations about each.

There are 6 axes of symmetry joining midpoints of opposite edges, and 1 distinct rotation about each.

Total number of rotations $= 3 \times 3 + 4 \times 2 + 6 \times 1 = 23$.

9 indirect isometries can be obtained by reflection in a plane.

$$\begin{pmatrix} 0 & 1 & 0 \\ 0 & 0 & 1 \\ -1 & 0 & 0 \end{pmatrix} = \begin{pmatrix} 1 & 0 & 0 \\ 0 & 1 & 0 \\ 0 & 0 & -1 \end{pmatrix} \begin{pmatrix} 0 & 1 & 0 \\ 0 & 0 & 1 \\ 1 & 0 & 0 \end{pmatrix}.$$

The first matrix represents an indirect isometry which is not a reflection, the second represents reflection in $AB'A'B$, the third a rotation about the line joining the centres of faces $ABC$, $A'B'C'$. The rotation followed by the reflection maps $A$ onto $C'$, $B$ onto $A$, $C$ onto $B$, as required.

In four dimensions, there are $4! \ 4 \times 4$ matrices with $\pm 1$ occurring once in each row and column, and $2^4$ ways of allotting the signs. Hence $2^4.4!$ isometries. In $n$ dimensions, $2^n.n!$

**12.** $\begin{pmatrix} a \\ b \\ c \end{pmatrix} = \begin{pmatrix} \frac{2}{3} \\ \frac{1}{3} \\ -\frac{2}{3} \end{pmatrix}$. The matrix $\mathbf{M}$ is $\begin{pmatrix} \frac{1}{3} & \frac{2}{3} & \frac{2}{3} \\ \frac{2}{3} & -\frac{2}{3} & \frac{1}{3} \\ \frac{2}{3} & \frac{1}{3} & -\frac{2}{3} \end{pmatrix}$.

$$\mathbf{M}\begin{pmatrix} x \\ y \\ z \end{pmatrix} = \begin{pmatrix} x \\ y \\ z \end{pmatrix} \Rightarrow \left.\begin{array}{r} y+z = x \\ 2x+z = 5y \\ 2x+y = 5z \end{array}\right\} \Rightarrow \tfrac{1}{2}x = y = z.$$

Determinant $= 1 =$ enlargement factor for volumes.

**13.** (a) $\begin{array}{l} x_{n+1} = 0{\cdot}7x_n+0{\cdot}9y_n \\ y_{n+1} = 0{\cdot}3x_n+0{\cdot}1y_n \end{array} \Rightarrow \begin{pmatrix} x_{n+1} \\ y_{n+1} \end{pmatrix} = \mathbf{M}\begin{pmatrix} x_n \\ y_n \end{pmatrix}$,

where $\qquad \mathbf{M} = \begin{pmatrix} 0{\cdot}7 & 0{\cdot}9 \\ 0{\cdot}3 & 0{\cdot}1 \end{pmatrix}$.

If $x_1 = 0$, then $x_2 = 0{\cdot}9$, $x_3 = 0{\cdot}72$, $x_4 = 0{\cdot}756$.

$$\mathbf{M}\begin{pmatrix} 0{\cdot}75 \\ 0{\cdot}25 \end{pmatrix} = \begin{pmatrix} 0{\cdot}75 \\ 0{\cdot}25 \end{pmatrix}.$$

Note that $0{\cdot}75$ is the limit of the previous sequence.

(b) $K$ hours are wasted anyway and the probability of $N$ hours' detention is $\frac{3}{4}(1-K)$. So $W = K+N.\frac{3}{4}(1-K)$.

If $N = 1$, $W$ is least when $K = 0$; if $N = 2$, $W$ is least when $K = 1$.

A full hour's prep. will be done if $N > \frac{4}{3}$.

**14.** $\left(\dfrac{1}{cr}-\dfrac{1}{bq}\right)\mathbf{x}+\left(\dfrac{1}{ap}-\dfrac{1}{cr}\right)\mathbf{y}+\left(\dfrac{1}{bq}-\dfrac{1}{ap}\right)\mathbf{z} = 0.$

This is *Pappus's Theorem*.

389

# INDEX

Abelian subgroup, 178
acceleration, 288–94
accuracy of physical measurements, 277–8
addition of vectors, 150
additive inverses, 3, 45, 55
adjoint (adjugate) of a matrix, 337
affine geometry, 207
algebra, Boolean, 12, 317; of a field, 12; of residue classes, 9–11; $\Sigma$- and $E$-, linearity of, 131
algorithms, 252, 253; division, 36, 41, 43; Euclid's, 112
analysis, dimensional, 276; fundamental theorem of, 130; numerical, 222, 249
angle measure, 142, 144
angles, between lines and vectors, 210–11; dimensionless, 306; scalar product and, 207, 208; of a triangle, 233
approximations, and asymptotes, 85–91; local, 249–59, 305
area, 342–53, 383; under graphs, 344–6
arithmetic, fundamental theorem of, 37, 55
arithmetic progression, summing of, 181
associativity, 2–3, 157, 158
asymptotes, 83–91, 220
automorphism, 11
average, position and, 188–92
average scale factors, 126–9, 134
axes, in three dimensions, drawing of, 201–2
axonometric projection, 201

base vectors, 150, 201–7
binary fractions, 62
binary operations, 2–4, 12–16, 157–8; in programming, 17
binary relations, 4–6
binomial probability function, 328, 330
Boolean algebra, 12, 317
bound vectors, 150
Buckingham Pi theorem, 277

calculating machines, hand, 17, 41, 197
'cancelling', avoidance of, 49
Cayley–Hamilton theorem, 43
centroids, 153–4, 212
chain rule, 75, 128, 260, 261–2, 356
characteristic equation, 43
Chinese remainder theorem, 52
circular functions, 140–9, 176; measure, 142–3; motion, 294–6
classes, congruence, 7; equivalence, 1, 7, 8, 32, 150
codomain, of a function, 59, 60, 105–6, 125
commutativity, 9, 157, 158; and associativity, 2–3
complex numbers, 52–4, 239–40
composite functions, differentiation of, 75, 125, 260–2; inverses of, 73–8
compound events, 314–18
computers, 17–21; various uses of, 125, 138, 249
conditional probability, 318–21, 329
congruence classes, 7, 160
continuity, 68, 70, 105–7
coordinates, 201–5; homogeneous, 360; polar, 229–31
corpus or skew field, 41
$\cos^2$, graph of, 219–20
$\cos x$, derivative of, 144–5, 148–9; graph of, 220
curves, sketching of, 97–101, 220
cyclic groups, 16, 160–1, 162, 279
cycloid, 292

decimals, recurring, 160–1
decision boxes, in programming, 22–5
Dedekind section, 275
degree of freedom, 205
dependence, linear, 131, 155–6, 215
derangements, 328
derivative(s), 81, 124–39; of polynomials, 131–2; of square root, 129
determinants, 38–9, 334, 336–7, 339
deviation, mean absolute, 193, 256; standard, 185, 193–4, 245
differential equations, linear, 41, 131

integral domains, 36, 48
integrals, definite, evaluation of, 348–53
integration, 342; linearity of, 131; by
parts, 357–9; by substitution, 354,
356–7; techniques of, 354–65, 383–4
interaction principle, 366–7
interquartile range, 192
intersection of lines, 205; of planes, 215
inverse functions, composite, 73–8;
graphs of, 82, 96–7; mapping diagrams of, 125–6; trigonometrical, 265
inverse images, 67–73, 105
inverses, additive, 3, 45, 55; of
matrices, 336–8; multiplicative, 3,
36, 55
isometric projection, 201–2
isomorphism, 1, 11–12, 108, 115, 163–4
iteration, 253, 338–9

Jacobian, 124

Kepler's Laws, 369
kinematics, 282–304, 307–8
Klein group, 15, 16, 74, 94, 164
kurtosis, 199

Lagrange's interpolation formula, 45,
51
Lagrange's theorem, 44, 164, 168–73
Latin square, group table as, 158
least squares, method of, 257
length, scalar product and, 207, 208
limits, 124, 127, 144
linear approximation, 249–51, 255–7
linear dependence, 131, 155–6, 215
linear equations, 333–41, 381–2
linear mapping, 66, 67; scale factor for,
126
linearity, 131
logarithmic functions, 121, 346
loops, in computer programs, 17

manifolds, 250
mapping, see *function*
mapping diagrams, 124–6
marks, combining, 192
mass, inertial and gravitational, 366–7
matrices, determinants of, 38–9, 334;
inverse of, 336–8; as linear operators,
131; permutation, 76–7
maxima and minima, 125, 136–8
mean, 186–93, 245; theoretical, 187

mean value, 198–200
measure theory, 353
mechanics, introduction to, 366–80
median, 188–90, 198, 245
Menelaus's theorem, 155
modal class, 188–9
modulus, residues to a prime, 7, 160
moments, in statistics and in mechanics,
190
monotonic sequences, 252, 254
Mossbauer effect, 278
motion, circular, 294–6; under gravity,
300–3
multiple angles, 219–22
multiplication, not commutative in
skew field, 41; division as reverse
process to, 35–6; of integers, associative, 9, 157; of matrices, 77
multiplicative groups in finite fields,
160–1

natural numbers, 17, 18, 110–12
neighbourhood, 105
'nesting process', 41, 56
nesting sets, 275, 342
Newton–Raphson formula, 126, 254
Newton's Laws, 366–7, 369–70
Normal probability function, 174, 331
numbers, systems of, 32–58, 112–14;
theory of 7, 170; transfinite, 62
numerical analysis, 222, 249
numerical differentiation, 132–3

odd and even functions, 93–5
open set, 105, 106
orthocentres, 212

parameters, analytical, 205–7; statistical, 186, 187
Pascal's Triangle, 183
pentagon, regular, symmetry group of,
14, 172
pentatope, regular, 166
percentage errors, 262
periodic functions, 73, 93
permutation groups, 164–7
perpendicularity, 208, 210–13
planes, 205; intersection of, 215–17
polar coordinates, 229–31
polygons, regular, symmetry groups of,
173
polynomial approximations, 257

393